EXPERT EVIDENCE AND CRIMINAL JURY TRIALS

EXPERT EVIDENCE AND CRIMINAL JURY TRIALS

Ian Freckelton QC
Jane Goodman-Delahunty
Jacqueline Horan
Blake McKimmie

OXFORD
UNIVERSITY PRESS

OXFORD
UNIVERSITY PRESS

Great Clarendon Street, Oxford, OX2 6DP,
United Kingdom

Oxford University Press is a department of the University of Oxford.
It furthers the University's objective of excellence in research, scholarship,
and education by publishing worldwide. Oxford is a registered trade mark of
Oxford University Press in the UK and in certain other countries

First Edition published in 2016

Published in the United States of America by Oxford University Press
198 Madison Avenue, New York, NY 10016, United States of America

British Library Cataloguing in Publication Data
Data available

ISBN 978–0–19–874634–8

For Leo, Julia, and Lloyd, who have taught me more than I could ever teach them

Ian

For Alexander, Maisie, and Joshua, who are experts on everything

Blake

For Felix and Catherine

Jacqui

For Sorcha

Jane

PREFACE

Evidence misunderstood and misconstrued has the potential to lead to miscarriages of justice. Ideally, expert evidence should help juries resolve issues of fact. High-profile miscarriages of justice based on the flawed statistical evidence of Professor Sir Roy Meadow in the United Kingdom, the erroneous fingerprint opinions from the Scottish Criminal Record Office in the *McKie* case, the unreliable evidence of Dr Smith of the Ontario Pediatric Hospital, the scientifically unsound expert evidence by Robert Barnes in the *Eastman* case, in the Australian Capital Territory, as well as the contaminated DNA samples in the Australian trial of *Jama*, demonstrate that expert evidence does not always achieve its goal of enabling accurate fact-finding by jurors.

Compounding the problem is the fact that scientific and technological advances in the last few decades have led to exponential advances in the types of evidence available to a court. In particular, DNA technology has fundamentally changed the nature of criminal investigations and prosecutions in the twenty-first-century courtroom. Juror difficulties with new forms of forensic scientific expert evidence such as DNA profiling are well-documented anecdotally and through mock jury studies.

By its very nature, expert evidence must be unfamiliar to jurors and outside their common knowledge or the trial judge will not admit this evidence in court. Unlike lay witnesses, experts are permitted to give their opinions. In most trials the opposing experts work from the same set of facts; thus differences between conflicting expert opinions are likely to be subtle but crucial.

Whether jurors comprehend the subtleties of contemporary expert evidence has been a ongoing dilemma. Most studies of jurors' perceptions of expert evidence have been conducted in the United States. However, this research can be of limited value in jurisdictions with different exclusionary rules of evidence and different procedures governing the admission of expert evidence, such as the United Kingdom, Ireland, Canada, Australia, India, and other Commonwealth jurisdictions.

There remains a dearth of empirical information about the difficulties faced by real jurors in comprehending contemporary expert evidence in Commonwealth jurisdictions. Aside from anecdote and professional gossip, little is known about the common problems faced by experts and courtroom lawyers in presenting expert evidence in jury trials. Research directly exploring the nature of the problems, and how these problems influence the communication of expert information to jurors, is needed to provide an empirical basis for procedural reform. This volume is a response to this need.

Here, we analyse the written survey responses of 296 jurors and interview responses from a further 111 jurors who were asked about their perceptions of the expert evidence that was presented in 55 trials (one of which was a retrial). These responses are compared and contrasted with 43 interviews with judges, 115 interviews with barristers and instructing solicitors, and 80 interviews with expert witnesses.

The volume provides an empirical account of:

(1) what real jurors think about the way in which expert evidence is presented in real trials;
(2) factors that influence lawyers' presentation of expert evidence;
(3) issues that trial judges perceive are impeding effective expert evidence; and
(4) expert witnesses' experiences in giving evidence in criminal trials.

The findings of this study are translated into practical outcomes for legislative and policy reform by the courts and the legal and expert communities.

The authors have conducted a ground-breaking empirical study of expert evidence in jury trials but it has its roots in a project which commenced during the 1990s. This current study builds on prior work undertaken for the Australasian Institute of Judicial Administration by Freckelton and others, published in 1999 and 2001. Reference is made to these earlier phases of the project throughout the following pages.

The current study was funded by the Australian federal government through the Australian Research Council Linkage Grant scheme (grants LP0990833 and LP120100291), the Australasian Institute of Judicial Administration, and the Australia and New Zealand Policing Advisory Agency (National Institute of Forensic Science).

Undertaking a complex multi-jurisdictional empirical project in three Australian states would not have been possible without the co-operation of the courts, in particular the judges and jury administrators who facilitated data collection and the lawyers who assisted us to identify eligible trials. We are grateful for this preparedness to open up the courts and their processes so generously.

We would like also to acknowledge the generosity of the many judges, barristers, solicitors, jurors, and forensic experts who graciously gave their time to participate in the research.

We acknowledge the wise counsel of our co-researcher on the first part of the project, Professor Mark Israel, and are grateful for the support and guidance provided by Dr Linzi Wilson-Wilde OAM of the Australia and New Zealand Policing Advisory Agency and Professor Greg Reinhardt of the Australasian Institute of Judicial Administration.

Data collection and analysis would not have been possible without the skills and expertise of Dr Kate O'Brien and Faye Nitschke, and the team of interviewers who assisted them, especially Ruth Liston, Melissa Martin, Ida Nguyen, Mira Taitz, Paula Saunders, Thea Gumbert, Tamara Butler, and Chantelle Baguley.

We also acknowledge the generous support of the Law Research Service at the University of Melbourne and of the dedicated and professional work done on our referencing and bibliographical entries by Cate Read.

Professor Ian Freckelton QC
University of Melbourne

Professor Jane Goodman-Delahunty
Charles Sturt University

Dr Jacqueline Horan
University of Melbourne

Associate Professor Blake McKimmie
University of Queensland

June 2015

CONTENTS

TABLE OF CASES

AUSTRALIA

CANADA

INDIA

NEW ZEALAND

UNITED KINGDOM

UNITED STATES

TABLE OF LEGISLATION

AUSTRALIA

CANADA

NEW ZEALAND

SINGAPORE

UNITED KINGDOM

UNITED STATES

AUTHOR BIOGRAPHIES

Ian Freckelton QC
Professorial Fellow
University of Melbourne

Professor Freckelton QC is a practising barrister, undertaking diverse work as an advocate throughout Australia at a trial and appellate level from Crockett Chambers in Melbourne. He is a Professorial Fellow in Law and Psychiatry at the University of Melbourne, an Adjunct Professor of Law and Forensic Medicine at Monash University, an Adjunct Professor of Law at La Trobe University, and an Adjunct Professor at the Auckland University of Technology. He is a Commissioner at the Victorian Law Reform Commission, a member of the Netherlands Group on Forensic Expertise, and an elected Fellow of the Australian Academy of Law, the Academy of Social Sciences Australia, and the Australasian College of Forensic Medicine. He is a former transnational President of the Australian and New Zealand Association of Psychiatry, Psychology and Law and has held positions on ten statutory tribunals, including Victoria's Mental Health Tribunal and Medical Practitioners Board. He is a Member of the Coronial Council of Victoria and is the editor of the *Journal of Law and Medicine* and the editor-in-chief of *Psychiatry, Psychology and Law*.

Professor Freckelton was a member of the team at the Australian Law Reform Commission responsible for the research which resulted in Australia's uniform evidence law. He is the author of *The Trial of the Expert* (OUP, 1987), the co-editor of the seven-volume loose-leaf service, *Expert Evidence*, and the author of the sixth edition of *Expert Evidence: Law, Practice Procedure and Advocacy*. He led the teams for the Australian Institute of Judicial Administration in 1999 and 2001 which published surveys of judges and magistrates concerning expert evidence. He is the author of many books, including *Scholarly Misconduct: Law, Regulation, and Practice* (OUP, 2016) and of over 500 articles and chapters of books.

Jane Goodman-Delahunty
Research Professor
Charles Sturt University

Professor Goodman-Delahunty is a Research Professor at Charles Sturt University in the School of Psychology and the Australian Graduate School of Policing and Security, Manly Campus, and is also a member of the NSW Civil and Administrative Tribunal. Trained in law and experimental psychology, she practised law for 20 years in the USA before joining academe in Australia in 2001. She is a former editor of *Psychology, Public Policy, & Law* and past President of the Australian and New Zealand Association of Psychiatry, Psychology, and Law and of the American Psychology-Law Society. She served as a Commissioner at the NSW Law Reform Commission for ten years and is an elected Fellow of the American Psychological Association. She is the Australian expert on juries and author of over 170 scientific publications. She has given invited addresses in countries around the world, consults with the police and government agencies, and is a leading authority on credibility assessment. Her research is supported by the Australian Research Council, the Australian Institute of Criminology, the Royal Commission into Responses to Institutional Child Sexual Abuse, and the US Federal Bureau of Investigation. Her empirical legal studies promote evidence-based practices and policies to enhance social justice.

Jacqueline Horan
Senior Lecturer
University of Melbourne

Dr Horan is a Senior Lecturer at the Melbourne Law School (at the University of Melbourne) and a member of the Victorian Bar. She is one of the leading jury researchers in Victoria, with experience conducting field research and experimental studies. Dr Horan is the lead researcher on a current ARC project investigating juries and expert evidence. Her research interests are juries, justice systems, dispute resolution, advocacy, and professional misconduct. She is the author of *Juries in the 21st Century* (Federation Press, 2012), a book which provides a broad understanding of and critical thinking about the contemporary jury system. Current issues challenging the jury system, such as the impact that technology is having on jury trials, are discussed in her book.

Blake McKimmie
Associate Professor
University of Queensland

Associate Professor McKimmie is a social psychologist in the School of Psychology at the University of Queensland. He is a member of the Centre for Research in Social Psychology and co-leads the Applied Social Psychology Lab at the University of Queensland. He has been a member of the executive for the Society of Australasian Social Psychologists, and is the Queensland Branch President for the Australian and New Zealand Association of Psychiatry, Psychology and Law. He has published peer-reviewed research papers in the area of social cognition and group processes, with a particular focus on jury decision-making. He recently co-taught CRIME101x—a free online course about the psychology of criminal justice—to over 25,000 students. He has contributed to a number of introductory textbooks and co-authored a chapter assessing the influence of gender in the courtroom for the book *Forensic Psychology: Concepts, Debates and Practice* (2nd edn). His research is supported by the Australian Research Council.

1

INTRODUCTION

Expert evidence plays a central role in many criminal trials in helping a jury to understand often complex and unfamiliar information that may be essential to determine the guilt of the defendant. Despite the importance of expert evidence to the fact-finder's role, limited empirical information exists about how expert evidence is perceived by jurors, let alone judges and litigation lawyers. Information about how experts themselves view the task of testifying is even more difficult to find. **1.01**

The overarching aim of this volume is to facilitate a broad understanding of, and critical thinking about, the use of expert evidence in the contemporary jury trial. While the ultimate outcome of such an endeavour might be to identify any problems with expert evidence and present solutions to those problems, this volume starts with a more modest aim. We commence by exploring how jurors, experts, judges, and lawyers make sense of the current processes. We ask how these various participants in the criminal justice process think about their role within it and the roles of the other protagonists in a criminal trial. We aim to highlight avenues for further research, as well as to illustrate some initial steps where the delivery of expert testimony might be strengthened. **1.02**

A. What Does Current Research Tell us About the Expert Evidence Process?

This volume builds on the research that has been conducted to date. Most empirical research to this point has relied upon experimental studies of particular aspects of expert testimony, such as the language that an expert uses, an expert's characteristics, or different ways in which expert testimony might be presented. It has tended to use participants who have acted as mock jurors. Inevitably, such research has limitations in terms of 'ecological validity': specifically, the potential to generalize to non-laboratory settings. There **1.03** are often telling differences between a real trial and one which is simulated with mock jurors.[1]

1.04 Most of the prior research into expert evidence has been conducted in the United States of America, which has substantial differences in how a jury trial is conducted, in rules of evidence, and in procedures governing the admission of expert evidence from how these obtain in Australia, New Zealand, Canada, and the United Kingdom. Research from jurisdictions such as Australia, New Zealand, the United Kingdom, Ireland, and Canada is more relevant to other Commonwealth jurisdictions as all share an extensive legal history and legal cultures.

1.05 Apart from anecdote and professional gossip, little is known about the common problems faced by experts and jury practitioners (judges and litigation lawyers) in presenting such expert evidence in jury trials. It might be tempting to base conclusions about how expert testimony is received by jurors on well-known cases where expert testimony has, for various reasons, had a deleterious effect on the fairness of trials, such as the series of Sudden Infant Death Syndrome (SIDS) murder trials in which mothers in the United Kingdom were convicted of murdering their babies based on the flawed interpretation and presentation of statistical evidence. Those cases highlighted the difficulty in interpreting complex statistical information and the dangers of experts giving evidence outside their professional expertise. Unfortunately, such issues are not always readily identified. In Canada, an expert paediatric pathologist gave similarly flawed evidence about 'shaken baby syndrome' over a period of two decades. The legal system took fourteen years to challenge this expert's ability to give evidence. A 2008 inquiry determined that the expert failed to demonstrate objectivity and repeatedly went beyond his expertise in giving evidence.[2]

1.06 Expert evidence can also be more influential than is warranted, based on the perceived scientific underpinnings and irrefutability of that testimony. In the 2008 Australian trial of Farah Jama, DNA evidence was the sole substantive prosecution evidence available for the jury when it convicted the defendant of rape. At appeal, the DNA evidence was successfully challenged and it was revealed that the incriminating DNA sample had been contaminated at the time it was collected.[3] More recent concerns raised about other types of

---

[1] Randolph N. Jonakait, in *The American Jury System* (New Haven: Yale University Press, 2008), p. 220, observed that

> A mock trial is not a real one, and a mock juror is not a real juror. No matter what is done to induce mock jurors to take the situation seriously, the stakes are always different in a real trial. Also, mock jurors almost always know that they are being studied, and such knowledge could make them act differently from real jurors. A further concern is that jury studies by academics often rely on college students as mock jurors, and some people question whether information from this restricted pool can be generalized to the wider jury population. Mock trials are also unlike real trials because the presented evidence seldom comes from live witnesses.

However, the issue is complex. See also Roger J. R. Levesque, *The Psychology and Law of Criminal Justice Processes* (New York: Nova Publishers, 2007), p. 307; Neil Vidmar, 'Lay Decision Making in the Legal Process', in *The Oxford Handbook of Empirical Legal Research*, edited by Peter Kane and Herbert M. Kritzer (Oxford: Oxford University Press, 2010), p. 637; Emily Finch and Vanessa Munro, 'Lifting the Veil: The Use of Focus Groups and Trial Simulations in Legal Research', *Journal of Law and Society* 35, Special Issue: Law's Reality: Case Studies in Empirical Research on Law (June 2008) 30; Michael D. Wiener, Daniel A. Krauss, and Joel D. Liberman, 'Mock Jury Research: Where Do We Go From Here?', *Behavioral Sciences & the Law* 29, no. 3 (May/June 2011) 467; Dawn Watkins and Mandy Burton, *Research Methods in Law* (Oxford: Routledge, 2013), p. 64. For an exploration of this concept in the context of potential sub judice contempt arising from media publicity see *Attorney-General (NSW) v John Fairfax Publications* [1999] NSWSC 318; Ian Freckelton and Marilyn McMahon, 'Social Science Research and Experimentation in Australian Criminal Proceedings: Prejudicial Pre-trial Publicity and Psychological Research', *Journal of Law and Medicine* 9 (2002) 347.

[2] Stephen T. Goudge, *Inquiry into Pediatric Forensic Pathology in Ontario: Report* (Ontario Ministry of the Attorney General, 2008), <http://www.attorneygeneral.jus.gov.on.ca/inquiries/goudge/>.

[3] Frank H. R. Vincent, *Inquiry into the Circumstances that Led to the Conviction of Mr Farah Abdulkadir Jama: Report* (Victorian Government, 2010), <http://netk.net.au/DNA/Jama.pdf> ('The Vincent Report').

expert evidence, such as facial and body mapping, gait analysis, shoe impression evidence, and criminal profiling, have fuelled the debate.[4]

Several government-initiated inquiries have assessed and reported on the subject.[5] Law reform work has also prompted changes in expert evidence procedures. But procedural reforms implemented in the absence of a thorough understanding of the nature of how expert evidence is received and used by decision-makers run the risk of not bringing about any meaningful change, or worse, accentuating existing problems arising from the expert evidence placed before the courts or how it is expressed. In addition, by basing what we know about expert evidence on perverse, high-profile cases, anecdote, or personal experience, the focus on the routine issues that affect the vast majority of trials is ignored. Reform premised on what happens in routine trials, rather than on high-profile miscarriages of justice, is more likely to bring the greatest benefit to the criminal justice system. **1.07**

B. Why Focus on Expert Evidence?

Expert evidence is just one type of evidence commonly presented at trial, so why single out this form of evidence? Expert evidence is worth special consideration because it has unique characteristics that distinguish it from other types of evidence, and those characteristics can pose unique challenges to finders of fact. By its very nature, expert evidence deals with matters that are the subject of specialized knowledge;[6] it is unfamiliar to jurors and, in many jurisdictions, outside common knowledge, otherwise the trial judge would not permit it. Unlike lay witnesses, for the most part experts are permitted to give their evidence in the form of opinions: inferences from data. Given that in most trials the opposing experts work from the same facts, the difference between conflicting expert opinions is often subtle but can be crucial. Judge Learned Hand identified the difficulty jurors face in evaluating expert evidence when he observed: **1.08**

> The trouble with all this is that it is setting the jury to decide, where doctors disagree... But how can the jury judge between two statements each founded upon an experience confessedly foreign in kind to their own? It is just because they are incompetent for such a task that the expert is necessary at all.[7]

See also Julie Szego, *The Tainted Trial of Farah Jama* (Cheltenham, Vic: Wild Dingo Press, 2014); Kate Hagan, '15 Months' Jail a Miscarriage of Justice', *The Age*, 8 December 2009, p. 1.

[4] See further Ian Freckelton and Hugh Selby, *Expert Evidence: Law, Practice, Procedure and Advocacy*, 6th ed. (Sydney: Thomson Reuters, 2016); Gary Edmond, 'The "Science" of Miscarriages of Justice', *UNSW Law Journal* 37, no. 1 (2014) 376; Gary Edmond, Catherine Biber, Richard Kemp, and Glenn Porter, 'Law's Looking Glass: Expert Identification Evidence Derived from Photographic and Video Images', *Current Issues in Criminal Justice* 20, no. 3 (2009) 337.

[5] Law Commission of England and Wales, *Expert Evidence in Criminal Proceedings in England and Wales: Report No. 325* (London: The Stationery Office, 2011) ('Law Commission Report'), <http://www.lawcom.gov.uk/project/expert-evidence-in-criminal-proceedings/#expert-evidence-in-criminal-proceedings>; Anthony Campbell, *The Fingerprint Inquiry* (Edinburgh: 2011), <http://www.webarchive.org.uk/wayback/archive/20150428160106/> <http://www.thefingerprintinquiryscotland.org.uk/inquiry/files/TheFingerprintInquiryReport_High_res.pdf>; Expert Working Group on Human Factors in Latent Print Analysis, *Latent Print Examination and Human Factors: Improving the Practice through a Systems Approach* (US Department of Commerce, National Institute of Standards and Technology, 2012); Committee on Identifying the Needs of the Forensic Sciences Community, National Research Council, *Strengthening Forensic Science in the United States: A Path Forward* (Washington, DC: The National Academies Press, 2009).

[6] See eg *R v Turner* [1975] 1 All ER 70.

[7] Learned Hand, *Historical and Practical Considerations Regarding Expert Testimony* (1900), pp. 15–16.

Such concerns have led a number of eminent legal figures to ruminate on or even advocate for the need for complex criminal trials extensively involving expert evidence to be removed from juries' responsibilities.[8]

C. The Expert Evidence and Jury Trials Project

1.09 This volume presents the results of a Commonwealth jurisdiction project on expert evidence and jury trials, where, in 2011–12, the authors were allowed access to Australian jurors. Here, we analyse the written survey responses of 296 jurors and interview responses from a further 111 jurors who were asked about their perceptions of the expert evidence that was presented in 55 trials (one of which was a retrial). These responses are compared and contrasted with 43 interviews with judges, 115 interviews with barristers and instructing solicitors, and 80 interviews with expert witnesses. The results of this project are unique in that, for the first time, the perspective of jurors is compared with that of those who facilitate and provide the expert evidence.

1.10 Analysis of the views elicited from the various participant groups in this project provides an unparalleled opportunity to document the nature of the process and experience of the provision of expert evidence. Our approach enables us *'to capture lived experiences of the social world and the meaning people give these experiences from their own perspectives.'*[9] We have generated detailed and comprehensive analyses that offer multiple viewpoints on the issue. By comparing and contrasting the perspectives of the protagonists in numerous trials, we are able to identify common beliefs and challenges. Such a project has not been undertaken before in a Commonwealth jurisdiction. It builds upon prior work undertaken for the Australasian Institute of Judicial Administration (AIJA, a research and educational institute).[10]

(1) Methodology

1.11 In conjunction with the AIJA, a six-phase comprehensive examination of expert evidence was designed, comprised as follows:

Phase 1: Pilot study, 1997
Phase 2: Survey of judges, 1999
Phase 3: Survey of magistrates, 2001
Phase 4: Jurors' perspectives on expert evidence
Phase 5: Expert witnesses' perspectives on expert evidence
Phase 6: Lawyers' perspectives on expert evidence

1.12 Judicial officers' perceptions of expert evidence in Australian criminal jury trials were canvassed as part of the first three phases of this programme of study.[11] This volume elaborates the study by reporting the results of the research comprising the final three phases. The first three studies assisted us in developing the framework for the final three phases, and we termed the latter the 'Expert Evidence and Jury Trials Project' ('the project'). To conduct this

[8] For instance, Peter McClellan, 'The Future Role of the Judge: Umpire, Manager, Mediator or Service Provider', *New South Wales Judicial Scholarship*, no. 44 [2011]: <http://www.austlii.edu.au/au/journals/NSWJSchol/2011/44.html>.

[9] Louise Corti and Paul Thompson, 'Secondary Analysis of Archived Data', in *Qualitative Research Practice*, edited by Clive Seale and Giampietro Gobo (London: Sage, 2004), p. 297.

[10] Ian Freckelton, Prasuna Reddy, and Hugh Selby, *Australian Judicial Perspectives on Expert Evidence: An Empirical Study* (Melbourne: AIJA, 1999); Ian Freckelton, Prasuna Reddy, and Hugh Selby, *Australian Magistrates' Perspectives on Expert Evidence: A Comparative Study* (Melbourne: AIJA, 2001).

[11] Freckelton, Reddy, and Selby, *Australian Magistrates' Perspectives on Expert Evidence*.

research, we secured two Australian Research Council Linkage Project Grants. The project was also funded by the Australasian Institute of Judicial Administration, and the National Institute of Forensic Science (which is now part of the Australia and New Zealand Policing Advisory Agency (ANZPAA)).

Given that the project encompasses expert witnesses' perceptions of their experience of **1.13** giving evidence, our project partnership was extended to include the ANZPAA, which is a joint initiative of the Australian and New Zealand Police Ministers and Commissioners and incorporates the research in forensic science conducted by the National Institute of Forensic Science.

The project was conducted in the metropolitan courtrooms of the three largest Australian **1.14** jurisdictions: New South Wales (NSW), Victoria, and Queensland. The multi-jurisdictional aspect of this project enabled us to monitor different processes used in various jurisdictions as well as to identify any cultural factors that might contribute to perceptions of expert evidence.

In this volume we have collated the perceptions of the following groups of stakeholders in **1.15** criminal jury trials:

(a) jurors—their responses to expert evidence;
(b) judges—their perspectives on expert evidence;
(c) litigation lawyers—their perspectives on expert evidence; and
(d) expert witnesses—their experiences of giving evidence in criminal trials.

By comparing and contrasting the four differing viewpoints within the same trial, we were able to identify any disjunctions in the perceptions and understanding among the four groups. We then considered whether these impacted upon the way in which expert evidence should be presented. In order to preserve participant anonymity we refer to all experts and jurors as male and all judges and lawyers as female throughout the volume. Such references do not reflect the actual gender composition of the research participants.

(2) Research design

The project adopted aspects of models successfully implemented in other field studies of **1.16** real juries and real trials, such as the 1999 New Zealand Law Commission study of Juries in Criminal Trials (the New Zealand study), the 2001 Australian study on managing prejudicial publicity, the 2001 study of Victorian civil jurors, and the 1987 study of jury comprehension in complex criminal cases conducted by the American Bar Association (ABA study).[12]

Data from 55 trials were collected using three complementary methods: **1.17**

(a) surveys to obtain jurors' perceptions of the expert evidence presented to them;
(b) post-verdict interviews with jurors, trial judges, trial lawyers, and experts about the expert evidence in those trials; and
(c) wherever possible, trial observations, and reviews of the transcript of proceedings and other visual aids and documentary materials relating to the expert evidence, such as the expert's report.

[12] Warren Young, Neil Cameron, and Yvette Tinsley, *Juries in Criminal Trials Part Two: A Summary of Research Findings: Preliminary Paper 37*, vol. 2 (Wellington, New Zealand: Law Commission, 1999); Michael Chesterman, Janet Chan, and Shelley Hampton, *Managing Prejudicial Publicity: An Empirical Study of Criminal Jury Trials in New South Wales* (Sydney: Law and Justice Foundation of New South Wales, 2001); Jacqueline Horan, 'The Civil Jury System: An Empirical Study' (PhD dissertation, University of Melbourne, 2006); American Bar Association and Daniel H. Margolis, *Jury Comprehension in Complex Cases: Report of a Special Committee of the ABA Litigation Section* (Chicago: ABA, 1989).

1.18 As in the New Zealand study, the jury component of our project incorporated both quantitative and qualitative methods. In Victoria, after having delivered their verdict, jurors first completed a written survey and were then invited to elaborate on their views by participating in an in-person or telephone interview. In New South Wales jurors were first invited to participate in the interview, and were given a survey if they declined, or as a follow-up to the interview.

1.19 The juror survey and interview questions were created by a collaborative process between all project partners. Our quantitative (survey) questions and qualitative (interview) questions were formulated based on the following:

(a) what psychological research tells us about how jurors process complex information;
(b) what we know from research in the preliminary phases of this project about judicial perspectives on the issues;
(c) the pattern of mistakes evident from a series of miscarriages of justice; and
(d) issues identified in several authoritative reports that have explored this topic.

1.20 When interpreting the results of jury research, the formulation of the survey instruments should always be considered. The results of empirical research can only be as good as the questions asked. For example, leading questions are less informative than questions that allow a juror to elaborate on an issue. Wherever possible, non-leading questions were used. The jury survey contained carefully constructed questions which aimed to obtain responses that could be compared directly across the set of survey participants. The context in which each question is asked is also relevant when interpreting the results.

1.21 The jury survey provides a broad overview of jurors' perceptions of expert evidence, while the interviews gathered further details on the main areas of contention that have been identified in previous research. The interviews were semi-structured. This enabled us to explore particular issues in greater detail, for example, jurors' knowledge of DNA profiling technology and random match probabilities.

1.22 In some of the chapters we use case studies to describe the common narrative that we heard from the stakeholders in the trials. Qualitative information gives us an understanding of the contextual issues that have become the concern of expert evidence in recent years. In a legal setting, qualitative information can be used in three ways:

(a) to explain the economic, political, social, and cultural factors which influence the provision of expert evidence in criminal jury trials;
(b) to gain an understanding of how communities, such as the criminal trial community, interpret the provision of expert evidence; and
(c) to study interactions between the various stakeholders that are relevant to the provision of the expert evidence.[13]

1.23 In this project, the narrative responses of stakeholders provided in oral interviews were transcribed. This qualitative information was also useful in explaining some of the quantitative results we collected from the juror surveys. It can be difficult to know precisely what jurors mean when they score themselves or others on rating scales or select among multiple-choice items included in a written questionnaire. The qualitative interview responses enabled us to obtain a greater understanding and attribute more nuanced meaning to the juror survey responses.

---

[13] Frances Baum, 'Researching Public Health: Behind the Qualitative–Quantitative Methodological Debate', *Social Science and Medicine* 40, no. 4 (February 1995) 459: p. 464.

(3) Ethics approval

The juror survey and interview instruments (for the jurors, judges, trial lawyers, and experts) were developed by the research team during the first half of 2010, and were formally approved by the AIJA and ANZPAA. Next, we secured the consent and formal support of 14 different agencies; this was necessary before we could conduct our multi-jurisdictional jury project. We were mindful to produce documentation that emphasized the need to obtain informed consent from all participants, the need to protect the anonymity and confidentiality of participants, and the importance of de-identifying materials reported so that individual trials could not be identified.[14] **1.24**

(4) Data collection

Data collection began in Melbourne, Victoria, in March 2011. We tested the data procedures before we commenced work on trials in Sydney, New South Wales, the following month. Data collection concluded in New South Wales in June 2012 and in Victoria in September 2012. In Brisbane, Queensland, we began collection in November 2011 and concluded in November 2012. **1.25**

Whilst the majority of criminal jury trials in Australia are conducted in the metropolitan centres, expert evidence is also heard in the course of trials conducted in rural locations. Budgetary constraints did not enable us to extend this project to include expert evidence delivered in non-metropolitan trials or trials in other countries. However, we hypothesise that whilst there might be some cultural differences between metropolitan and non-metropolitan juries, the variation is unlikely to be so significant that the results of this project will not be useful in understanding similar expert evidence procedures in those jurisdictions. **1.26**

Once we had identified a trial as appropriate for the project, we wrote to the trial judge, both counsel, and the jury administrator expressing our desire to include the case. Most of the trial judges approved the inclusion of the trial in the project, subject to any unanticipated complications (such as a jury becoming increasingly stressed). In a few instances, the presiding judge responded that the trial was too sensitive to include it in the study. **1.27**

Once the trial judge's consent had been obtained, we were placed on the list of people to be contacted once a verdict was to be delivered. In the meantime, the researchers attended the trial as much as possible to observe the expert evidence. In order to promote consistency across interviews, all research interviewers were required to read an extensive procedural manual about the project and attend a training session with one of the chief investigators and the project manager before undertaking any interviews. **1.28**

Following the delivery of the verdict, many, but not all, trial judges introduced the project to the jury. Jurors were informed that when they left the courtroom, the survey would be offered to them. In order to ensure juror anonymity, the surveys were handed to the jurors by the court administrator in charge of de-briefing the jurors. All but one of the jury administrators were supportive of the project. This lack of support impacted on the response rate in that particular court. **1.29**

A total of 55 trials across the three states form the basis of the project. These are reported in Table 1.1. **1.30**

[14] The ethics approval process of this project is explained further in Jacqueline Horan and Mark Israel, 'Institutional Gate-Keeping and Jury Research', *Australian and New Zealand Journal of Criminology* (2015, forthcoming).

Table 1.1 Number and proportion of trials studied, by jurisdiction.

	NSW	Victoria	Queensland	Total
Supreme Court	9 16.4%	10 18.2%	8 14.5%	27 49.1%
District/County Court	3 5.5%	23 41.8%	2 3.6%	28 50.9%
Total	12 21.8%	33 60.0%	10 18.2%	55 100.0%

1.31 One reason why we captured only a small number of New South Wales District Court trials was the lack of availability of a private room where we could interview the jurors after they completed their surveys.

1.32 The short trial length in Queensland impacted on our ability to include many Queensland trials in the project. By the time project team members were informed that the trial contained expert evidence (and then prepared the juror questionnaire and delivered it to the court), the verdict had often already been delivered. Trials in Queensland lasted less than half the time they did in Victoria and one third of the time taken in New South Wales. A comparison of the supreme court trials in our project revealed that the average length of trial in New South Wales was 34 days, 19 days in Victoria, and 8 days in Queensland. The 55 trials ranged in length from four to 93 days.

1.33 We identified trials containing expert evidence from a variety of sources. The Offices of Public Prosecutions were the most helpful in identifying appropriate trials as they were usually the only party presenting expert evidence. Records from the relevant Offices of Public Prosecutions enabled us to identify eligible trials, and then email all trial practitioners to ask them to nominate their trial. This procedure was not always reliable because, prior to trial, practitioners tend to be busy and are unlikely to respond to a request that requires more work on their part. Other groups such as police forensic services and legal aid and defence law firms notified us if they were involved in any trials involving experts. Once again, reliance upon individual practitioners to nominate their cases containing expert evidence was a limitation.

1.34 Once we began interviewing barristers, those interviewees would sometimes inform us of another upcoming trial involving expert evidence. A few of the courts circulated an email to the trial judges asking them to contact us if they were presiding over a case involving expert evidence. Another technique we employed to identify trials containing expert evidence was to read the newspapers to uncover trials reported to include expert evidence.

1.35 Although the Offices of Public Prosecutions did provide useful assistance, the lack of basic central computerized record-keeping in the legal system in Australia presented a barrier to the implementation of the project. It can be said that it not only obstructs efficient research of justice systems in the country but is a likely impediment to the efficient management of the business of the courts and other justice system agencies such as prosecution departments and legal aid funders.

1.36 Our study sample is not comprehensive or representative for this period but was a purposeful convenience sample. The fact that most of the trials included in the project were either murder or sexual assault trials is likely to reflect the fact that these are the types of cases in which most expert evidence is used. The investigation of murder cases is likely to warrant the use of many types of scientific or medical evidence by the investigators, particularly pathology and DNA. DNA swabbing and medical evidence are also common in sexual assault trials.

The majority of District/County court trials in our study sample involved sexual assault charges, and took on average nine days to hear. These types of cases are much shorter than murder/manslaughter trials, which are held in the Supreme Courts of Australia, and took, on average, 21 days to hear. Overall, our study sample is sufficient to provide a reliable picture of the expert evidence processes in Australian metropolitan courtrooms in the period 2011–12. **1.37**

(a) Written juror surveys

The vast majority of the juror surveys were completed immediately following jury service, at the courthouse in a suitable quiet location. Given the importance to this project of obtaining a set of responses based on fresh memories and a high participation rate, we avoided mailing the questionnaires to jurors. However, questionnaires were mailed to jurors in two trials, within the first week following the jury discharge, so the evidence was still fresh in their minds when they received them. In one instance, questionnaires were sent three weeks after the trial concluded. **1.38**

(b) Juror interviews

Capitalizing on the enthusiasm of jurors to discuss their jury experience, we included an invitation to jurors to participate in a follow-up personal interview with each survey. Jurors who agreed to a personal interview were invited to stay behind on the day of the verdict or we contacted them as soon as possible by telephone and conducted either a telephone or in-person interview. Only first names were provided so that their identity could be protected. Jurors responded to a series of questions about their perceptions of the expert evidence. We conducted 111 interviews with jurors (92 of these jurors also completed a survey for the project). All juror interviews were recorded with the interviewee's consent and were subsequently transcribed. **1.39**

(c) Lawyer, judge, and expert interviews

Trial barristers (and a few trial solicitors) and judges from the 55 trials were invited to participate in an interview at the conclusion of the trial. We aimed to interview the barristers, but if they were not available we interviewed their instructing solicitors. We added to the triangulation of views by interviewing 80 of the experts who gave evidence in the selected trials. The majority of these experts also completed a survey ($n=78$). Learning from the New Zealand criminal jury project, we contacted the court stakeholders as soon after the conclusion of the trial as possible, in order to avoid difficulties for the interviewees in recalling critical information. Interviews with this group were expected to last approximately 30 minutes, but the interviewees were generally keen to keep talking and many interviews lasted 45–60 minutes. Whilst we used a structured interview to prompt the interviewees, the passion that many displayed for the topic meant that it was sometimes difficult to maintain the set structure, particularly when the subject matter was so interesting. All but a few of these interviews were recorded—with the interviewee's consent. If no consent was forthcoming, notes were taken by the researcher. **1.40**

(5) Data analysis

Quantitative data were entered into Microsoft Excel spreadsheets which were then converted into SPSS files for statistical analyses. The juror, judge, expert, and trial lawyer interviews were transcribed. Qualitative analysis tools (e.g., Nvivo and Leximancer) were used to identify the common themes in responses, based upon evaluation criteria developed by the researchers and their review of the relevant scholarly literature. **1.41**

1.42 Apart from general comparisons with previously performed studies in this field, the analysis specifically compared the present results with those from the previous phases of the expert evidence project involving judges (phase two). Traditionally, judges will manage their court (including the provision of expert evidence) based on their perceptions of what jurors need to reach a verdict. This project considers whether the judges' perceptions of what jurors need is accurate. Another aspect addressed by the analysis is the monitoring of inter-state variations in the manner in which expert evidence is presented. Inter-state comparisons allow the researchers to reflect on what is the best practice amongst the different approaches taken in three jurisdictions.

(a) Response rates

1.43 A total of 296 juror surveys were received from 55 trials, resulting in an overall participation rate of 45% for deliberating jurors. This equates to an average of 5.4 jurors per trial, and enables us to develop a reasonably representative picture of the juries' views insofar as they related to the survey questions.[15]

1.44 In all, 111 interviews were conducted with jurors—92 of these interviewees also completed a project survey (83%). An additional 204 jurors completed the survey without an interview, giving the total of 296 survey responses. This equates to two juror interviews per trial. Whilst it would have been preferable to secure a higher interview response rate per jury, in analysing the jury response we are able to cross-reference opinions expressed in the interviews with the survey responses from the same jury.

1.45 We compared the demographic profile of those jurors who volunteered to be interviewed against that of the surveyed jurors in order to see whether the self-selection induced a group of interviewees who were unrepresentative of the surveyed jurors. The interviewed jurors were adequately representative of the surveyed jurors, with one minor exception: the interviewed jurors were on average five years older than the average age of the surveyed group. When analysing interview responses from juries with a low response rate, we were mindful of this fact, and conservative in our estimation of the capacity of the views and opinions of a few jurors to represent those of that entire jury.

1.46 Forty-three interviews with 40 individual judges were conducted (some judges were interviewed more than once if they sat on more than one trial included in the project). Thirty-six judges completed at least one survey, with some judges being surveyed for more than one trial, taking the total number of surveys completed to 39. Taking into account judges who presided over a series of similar consecutive trials but were interviewed once, this produced a response rate of 76%. One hundred and fifteen interviews were conducted with 101 lawyers (with 103 survey responses by 94 respondents, and 90 completing both an interview and a survey). The majority of counsel ($n=88$) agreed to an interview. On the few occasions when counsel declined an interview, we interviewed their instructing solicitor ($n=13$ interviews). A small number of trials had multiple counsel. In those cases, the response rate exceeded 90%. Eighty experts were interviewed. Taking into account the fact that some trials had single experts and some experts gave evidence in a few different trials, the expert response rate exceeded 80%.

(b) Types of trials

1.47 The most common type of case included in the research was that of murder/manslaughter (46%), followed by cases involving sexual assault (31%). The remaining types of cases sampled for this project are reported in Table 1.2.[16]

---

[15] Young, Cameron, and Tinsley, *Juries in Criminal Trials Part Two: Preliminary Paper 37*, vol. 2, p. 2.

[16] In order to maintain anonymity, we have not specified which jurisdiction the assault, robbery, culpable driving, or fraud trials came from as the number of trials is low enough to potentially enable identification.

Table 1.2 Number and proportion of types of trial, by jurisdiction.

	NSW	Victoria	Queensland	Total
Murder/manslaughter	9 16.4%	9 16.4%	7 12.7%	25 45.5%
Sexual assault	2 3.6%	13 23.7%	2 3.6%	17 30.9%
Assault/cause injury	0 0.0%	5 9.1%	1 1.8%	6 10.9%
Culpable driving	1 1.8%	4 7.3%	0 0.0%	5 9.1%
Other	0 0.0%	2 3.6%	0 0.0%	2 3.6%

Our study sample approximates the composition of cases handled by the courts. For example, **1.48** the County Court of Victoria's annual reports for 2011 and 2012 reflected that the Court heard 378 trials to verdict, 43% of which were sexual assault trials. Difficulties in identifying eligible cases in the District Court in New South Wales and in Queensland (as noted in paragraphs 1.31–2) explain the modest number of sexual assault trials in those jurisdictions in our project.

Initially, we planned to include fraud trials in the project. Since the 1980s, the jury has **1.49** attracted criticism for being incapable of dealing with the complexity inherent in forensic accounting evidence. As Lord Roskill's *Fraud Trials Committee Report* stated, 'The ideal method of attempting to address the issue would be to question jurors on actual cases.'[17] However, unanticipated difficulties arose that deterred their inclusion in the study. Fraud trials were few and far between. All but one of the handful of fraud trials that we identified as eligible for inclusion in the project involved expert evidence which was anticipated to take only a few hours. However, these fraud trials were listed to take several months to hear. In addition, we were led to believe that the expert evidence would not feature prominently in these cases, and the substantial trial length made the cases too costly to monitor.

(c) Types of expert evidence

A broad range of expertise was included in the project. Only a third of the cases involved **1.50** contested expert evidence (i.e., opposing experts called by the prosecution and defence). In the majority of cases in the study sample, the prosecution called a few experts and the defence called none. Table 1.3 shows the type and number of expert interviews conducted in the 55 trials. DNA expert evidence was the most common type, followed by that of forensic pathology.

Given that we interviewed 23 DNA experts, making up just under a third of all the experts **1.51** who were interviewed, and that this is an area of expert evidence that features prominently in the debates surrounding problematic expert evidence, we have devoted a separate chapter to project results on this topic. Similarly, we have given over a further chapter to expert evidence by health practitioners, in particular by pathologists, psychiatrists, and psychologists.

[17] Fraud Trials Committee and Eustace W. Roskill, *Frauds Trials Committee Report* (London: HMSO, 1986), pp. 201–2 (Appendix A, para. 7).

Table 1.3 Number and proportion of types of experts interviewed.

Type of expert	Number	Percentage
DNA	23	28.7
Medical doctor	19	23.7
Forensic pathology	12	15.0
Psychiatry	11	13.8
Vehicle analysis	4	5.0
Ballistics	3	3.8
Digital evidence	3	3.8
Other: arson, fingerprints, blood spatter, handwriting	5	6.2
Total	80	100

(d) Other sources of information

1.52 Other sources of information were examined in order to complement what was learned from the qualitative and quantitative data. Legislation, court policies, and legal practices that dictate jury management and the provision of expert evidence were reviewed. Archival information was particularly necessary for this project, as we were analysing information collected from three different jurisdictions (Victoria, NSW, and Queensland). The rules and processes in these three jurisdictions differ, so it was important to understand the extent of similarities between the jurisdictions and the nature of the differences. Differences in policy, procedures, and legislation allowed us to analyse, compare, and contrast the different approaches to juries and expert evidence in the three jurisdictions. Further, analysing the outcomes in the context of the varying rules, policies, and practice enables lawyers from other jurisdictions to gauge the relevance of the project results to their jurisdiction.

1.53 Wherever possible, the researchers observed the presentation of the expert evidence that was the subject of this project. By observing the trials, the researchers were given a rich context in which to analyse the data. This approach was successfully used in the New Zealand study.

1.54 A profile of the general features of each of the trials included in the project was prepared, including details such as the trial jurisdiction, the offence, the number of experts, and the nature of the expert evidence. To provide a context within which to interpret the findings of the interviews and questionnaires, we compiled summaries of any matters raised by counsel or the judge relating to the expert evidence, including any applications made by counsel, judicial directions, or warnings.

1.55 The views of the research observers were also recorded. The observers were required to complete a written questionnaire that prompted them for their perceptions of the expert evidence. To enable a cross-comparison, many of the questions on the observer questionnaire mirrored the questions asked of the four groups of stakeholders in their surveys or interviews.

1.56 We asked each trial judge for a copy of the transcript of the expert evidence. The transcript of the expert evidence provided an accurate record of what transpired in court, avoiding reliance on the memory of those interviewed. We were able to obtain the transcript in at least two thirds of the trials in Victoria and New South Wales. The transcripts of expert evidence were not made available to us in Queensland cases. Most of the trial judges provided a copy of their summary to the jury. These provided the project with a short summary of case facts and the applicable law, and identified the issues in dispute. We also asked for and usually received copies of any exhibits or visual aids provided to the jury in relation to the expert evidence. The exhibits and visual aids provided the project with some further triangulation and corroboration for analysis.

A small number of the cases included in our project were retrials or trials within a series of related trials being heard in sequence that contained similar expert evidence. These trials offered us unique and added benefits, as we could compare the reactions of the stakeholders to the similar expert evidence across these trials. In the case of the retrials, we used the appeal judgments to further inform our analysis. **1.57**

D. Demographic Characteristics of Survey Participants

(1) Jurors' demographics

At the end of the juror survey the participants provided some basic demographic information about themselves. Two-thirds (66%) of the juror survey participants were from Victoria, 23% were from New South Wales, and 11% were from Queensland. Since we could not gather the demographic characteristics of the jurors who chose not to participate in the research, we cannot be certain that the profile of our sample was similar to that of the jurors as a whole or that the views and concerns of the participants were representative. However, a survey by the Victorian Juries Commissioners' Office[18] was undertaken during the study period in the first half of 2013—a total of 1,900 citizens who attended jury service across Victoria were surveyed. We compared the demographic profile of the Melbourne jury pool with the survey participants in this project who came from the same jury pool room in Victoria. The results of this comparison demonstrated that our Victorian sample of jurors is representative of the general Victorian jury pool. We also compared the demographic profile of the survey participants with the broader population of the 2012 Australian Bureau of Statistics census information (ABS statistics). In general, our juror participants had the same characteristics as the Australian adult population as a whole, except that they were more likely to be employed and have tertiary education. **1.58**

Jurors ranged in age from 18–83 years, with an average age of 45 years. The distribution of juror age is broadly representative of Australian citizens, taking into account predictable variation. Given that juries are a subset of the population, selected by criteria that make them jury eligible (e.g., citizens registered to vote, not engaged in a prohibited occupation, over 18 years of age, without personal connections to the case at hand, able to participate without infringing on work or care duties), it is reasonable to expect some deviation from overall population statistics. As can be seen from Table 1.4, participants had generally similar characteristics when compared to both the Victorian jury pool and the national population statistics, although they tended to be more likely to have completed a university qualification. **1.59**

(a) Past jury experience

This was the first time that 87.8% of the surveyed jurors had undertaken jury duty. There were some juries with as many as four jurors who had previously served, but three fifths of the trials (60.0%) had no jurors who had previously served. **1.60**

[18] See Victorian Law Reform Commission, *Jury Empanelment* (Melbourne: VLRC, 2014): <http://www.lawreform.vic.gov.au/sites/default/files/VLRC_Jury_Empanelment_Report.pdf>.

Table 1.4 Participant characteristics compared to jury and national characteristics.

Characteristic	Research sample (per cent)	Victorian jury pool (per cent)	ABS* population (per cent)
Age			
18–24 years	7.6		9.5
25–44 years	39.7		38.2
45–69 years	50.2		39.3
70+ years	2.4		13.0
Gender**			
Women	47.6	54.1	50.2
Men	51.0	45.9	49.8
Not disclosed	1.4		
Language			
English	91.6	93.0	76.8
Other	8.4	7.0	23.2
Country of birth			
Australia	78.4	79.0	74.0
Other	21.6	21.0	26.0
Education completed			
Secondary school	20.6	24.0	20.0
University degree***	48.3	40.0	24.7
Neither/no data	31.1	36.0	55.3
Employment			
Professionals	51.0		34.8
Labourer/Trade	9.6		24.0
Administrative/Clerical	16.2		15.0
Service worker	3.8		9.8
Sales	6.2		9.5
Machinery operator	—		6.7
Not in the workforce****	13.2		3.7

Note. *Australian Bureau of Statistics. **Gender statistics for the population level provided for those of working age (16 to 64 years), which approximates the age range of those individuals eligible for jury service. ***Percentage completing an undergraduate or postgraduate qualification. ****Includes 'home duties', 'students', 'retired', and 'unemployed'. ABS data for this category were reported by the ABS separately to the employment category data, and so do not add to 100%. Other percentages do not add to 100% due to rounding error.

(b) Science and mathematics training

1.61 Expert evidence often includes scientific and statistical content, particularly in the forensic sciences. We asked the survey participants to indicate their level of training in those areas. A substantial proportion (45.5%) of the surveyed jurors reported that they had studied science or mathematics at a tertiary level and 4.8% of the surveyed jurors were employed professionally in a scientific field. Given the emphasis on mathematics in the Australian school curriculum, it is unsurprising that nearly three quarters of all jurors studied either science or mathematics at school level (74.1%). However, the high rate of jurors who are tertiary educated in science and mathematics is striking. On some juries, half of the jurors had tertiary mathematics or science training. In 91% of trials there was at least one juror with tertiary science or mathematics training.

(2) **Experts' demographics**

1.62 On average, experts were 49 years of age, but the age of expert witnesses ranged from 28 to 76 years. Most expert witnesses were men (70.5%). For their first bachelor's degree, almost two thirds of experts reported a bachelor of science or applied science, and 39.2% had a bachelor of medicine (MBBS or MB). A quarter of the experts had two or more bachelor's degrees. A small group (7.6%) had no tertiary degree, e.g. uniformed police officers working in fingerprint and gunshot residue analysis. A relatively small proportion of the experts (12.4%) reported having a PhD. About one in every five experts (17.7%) held a master's degree, and the proportion who reported at least one postgraduate diploma was similar. On average, experts reported having 17 years' experience in their practice area, but experience ranged from less than one year to 50 years. Only one quarter of experts reported less than ten years of experience in their practice area.

Of the participating experts: **1.63**

(a) 28.2% were DNA scientists;
(b) 24.4% were medical doctors;
(c) 14.1% were psychiatrists or psychologists;
(d) 12.8% were pathologists;
(e) 5.1% were vehicle analysis experts;
(f) 3.8% were ballistics experts; and
(g) 3.8% were digital evidence experts.

The remaining 7.8% of experts are not specified in the list above as they represent small numbers of each type of expert, potentially identifying those experts who participated in the research.

Perhaps not surprisingly, nearly one third of expert witnesses were employed by the state police force (31.2%), primarily the forensic scientists. Equal proportions of experts were employed by either a government health department (22.1%) or other government organization (22.1%). This group was comprised of medical doctors, psychiatrists, and psychologists. The defence experts were employed by private organizations (7.8%) or were self-employed (16.9%), comprising one quarter of the experts who appeared in the criminal trials included in the project. **1.64**

Experts were asked to estimate the amount of time spent on work for the prosecution compared to the defence in criminal matters (out of 100%). They were also asked to estimate the proportions of their time spent on work for the plaintiff and respondent in civil cases (also out of 100%). In general, the expert participants were commissioned more frequently by the prosecution than the defence. Experts estimated on average that two-thirds of their time was devoted to work for the prosecution and a third of their time for the defence in criminal trials. Those who did civil work reported that they worked equivalent proportions of time for the plaintiff and respondent. **1.65**

Expert witnesses in general were highly experienced practitioners in their area. On average they had worked in their area of expertise for 17 years, ranging from one to 50 years. Experts were also generally highly experienced in giving evidence in court. On average, experts appeared in court 19 times per year (range: 0 to 90 times per year). Given that the courts in Australia are closed for two months of the year, that equates to experts attending court once a fortnight. The experts estimated that they prepared an average of 143 reports each year. That average, over a twelve-month period, is six reports a fortnight. These figures suggest that forensic experts are spending a considerable amount of their professional time preparing for and appearing in court. **1.66**

This frequency reveals that, for a substantial proportion of the experts in this group, the activity of 'expert witnessing' or working as a 'professional expert witness' was an apt description, whatever their foundation discipline. **1.67**

(3) Litigation lawyers' demographics

1.68 Prosecuting barristers had on average 15.9 years' experience in the legal profession (range: 1 to 36 years) and the main area of specialization for the majority of prosecutors was criminal law. Defence counsel had on average 18.1 years' experience in the legal profession (range: 1 to 45 years). Again, the vast majority of defence barristers reported predominantly practising in criminal law. Around one-fifth of barristers acting for the defence or prosecution reported that they were Queen's Counsel or equivalent. The extent of experience and high seniority of the barristers whom we interviewed confirm that the most senior members of the criminal bar in Australia are briefed for jury trials, especially in murder cases. When the barristers declined to be interviewed, we interviewed their instructing solicitors. On average, solicitors reported 6.2 years' experience in the legal profession (range: 1 to 38 years).

1.69 With the benefit of hindsight we would have liked to have asked the barristers about their level of scientific or mathematical training, to compare and contrast their scientific skill levels with those reported for jurors in the sample. One of the prosecutors whom we interviewed compared the scientific abilities of the two groups: *'Lawyers are notoriously bad at science and maths. By the looks of a lot of the jurors, they were way on top of it compared to us.'* An online search of over 2,000 members of the Victorian Bar disclosed that fewer than 100 advertise that they have a science or mathematics background.[19] Of the 30 trial judges of the Supreme Court of Victoria, one listed a qualification in mathematics or science. These figures generally indicate that fewer than 5% of trial practitioners are likely to have studied mathematics or science at a tertiary level. The vast majority of trial practitioners have either an arts or economics degree to complement their law degree and do not have tertiary degrees in science or mathematics.

1.70 The ability to undertake scientific or mathematical tasks is not a mandatory part of any law degree—it plays no role in the requirements of the United Kingdom Joint Statement issued by the Law Society and the General Council of the Bar on the academic stage of training, the Australian Threshold Learning Outcomes, the American Bar Association Standards, nor is it acknowledged in the report of the Task Force on the Canadian Common Law Degree. The Law Society of Scotland Accreditation Guidelines do, however, identify numeracy as a core skill. The only guidelines that require lawyers to be proficient in making use of numerical and statistical information derived from primary sources are the Quality Assurance Agency for Higher Education's British Subject Benchmark Statement and the Law Society of Scotland Accreditation Guidelines.[20]

1.71 Barristers are not required to understand forensic science as part of their professional development, although bar associations do provide lectures to their members on various areas of expert endeavour relevant to litigation. Some barristers are thought to be naive in their understanding of science and statistics and do not test such evidence as rigorously as other types. As Chief Judge Edwards, the chair of the United States National Academy of Science Committee on Identifying the Needs of the Forensic Science Community confessed:

> I started this project with no preconceived views about the forensic science community. Rather, I simply assumed, as I suspect many of my judicial colleagues do, that forensic science disciplines typically are well grounded in scientific methodology and that crime

---

[19] Notably, though, many barristers provide little information about themselves.

[20] See *Subject Benchmark Statement: Law: Draft for Consultation* (The Quality Assurance Agency for Higher Education, March 2015), p. 9: <http://www.qaa.ac.uk/en/Publications/Documents/SBS-consultation-Law-15.pdf>. Law Society of Scotland, *Foundation Programme (Scottish Exempting Degree) Accreditation Guidelines for Applicants*, Appendix A: Foundation Programme Learning Outcomes, p. 27.

> laboratories and forensic science practitioners follow proven practices that ensure the validity and reliability of forensic evidence offered in court. I was surprisingly mistaken in what I assumed.[21]

The scientific background of many jurors and the likely lack of training of barristers and judges in scientific disciplines is worthy of note when interpreting the results of this project.

(4) Judges' demographics

The judges in this project reported an average of nine years' experience on the bench (range: 1 to 19 years). The majority of the judges (72.1%) reported criminal cases as their main area of practice. Approximately half of the judges had practised criminal law prior to their appointment to the bench. **1.72**

E. Overview of Chapters

This chapter, the Introduction, provides the framework for the substantive chapters by summarizing the research methodology of the project. This allows the reader to understand the research design. The authors have been mindful of providing appropriate background information so that an international audience can interpret the results of the project in a meaningful way and adapt them to the context in their jurisdiction. We also provide a comprehensive demographic profile of our project sample, comparing it with the national population characteristics. **1.73**

The second chapter focuses on pre-trial matters. In particular, it examines the admissibility of expert testimony, identifying particular issues that arise in relation to the use of the concept of 'reliability' as a precondition to the expert evidence that is allowed to go before juries. **1.74**

Chapter 3 considers alternative modes of exploration of expert evidence. Some commentators contend that at least some of the problems with traditional procedures for adducing expert evidence can be addressed by adjustments to the adversary characteristics of the criminal justice trial—by using other procedures, such as pre-trial meetings/conclaves of experts, consecutive evidence by experts, concurrent evidence by experts (as in the Manchester Pilot Project), and videolinking of experts from their workplace. These matters are discussed in the criminal context with reference to our project findings. **1.75**

The fourth chapter examines some issues present in the adversary system and how they relate to expert evidence. These include the thoroughness of preparation for trial, experts who resile from their opinions, over-reaching experts who go outside the bounds of their expertise, and experts who might appear to be 'hired guns'. We take into account those aspects of the adversarial system that might tend to encourage experts to behave in particular ways which may undermine the credibility or reliability of their evidence. **1.76**

Chapter 5 explores jury comprehension of expert evidence. Many practitioners contend that contemporary evidence is too complex for the average juror to understand and evaluate. We examine the extent to which jurors' perceptions of expert testimony are shared by other criminal justice professionals such as judges, lawyers, and the experts themselves. We also explore common barriers to juror comprehension across the project case studies. **1.77**

[21] Harry Edwards, 'Solving the Problems that Plagued the Forensic Science Community', *Jurimetrics* 50, no. 1 (2009) 5: p. 7.

1.78 DNA profiling evidence is analysed in chapter 6, as such evidence is a form of expert evidence that is having a profound impact upon contemporary criminal jury trials. Although jury difficulties with DNA profiling evidence are well documented anecdotally, through field studies and in controlled experiments conducted with mock juries,[22] there remains a dearth of factual information as to how jurors evaluate and use DNA expert evidence. The chapter examines 13 of the project trials and juror responses to shed light on issues such as the level of reliance placed on DNA expert evidence, the existence of the 'CSI effect', whether jurors' perceptions of the DNA evidence differ from the views of the other stakeholders in the courtroom, and the impact of an opposing DNA expert evidence on jurors' views of the prosecution's expert. We also identify features that enhance jury understanding of DNA evidence.

1.79 Chapter 7 examines some of the issues developed in earlier chapters but with a focus on medical and mental health experts. This includes evidence by psychiatrists and psychologists, and evidence by pathologists and forensic medical officers, as such experts make up a significant proportion of expert evidence in criminal jury trials. It identifies distinctions between evidence given by assessing health practitioners and treating health practitioners.

1.80 Chapter 8 assesses how the credibility of expert evidence is influenced by various factors related to how the evidence is presented. For example, how does the expert's gender, language, demeanour, and personal style influence perceptions of the credibility of the expert and their evidence?

1.81 In the concluding chapter we summarize systemic weaknesses in the way in which expert evidence is commonly used. We identify practical ways in which the quality of the expert evidence, as presented by counsel and experts, might be improved, and how the procedural aspects of expert evidence might be improved by judges. These suggestions are made with a view to stimulating law reform discussion and further research. It is our intention to lay a foundation upon which informed debate can generate further research and law reform which has a realistic potential of enhancing the quality of criminal justice when juries are utilized.

[22] Jane Goodman-Delahunty and Lindsay Hewson, 'Enhancing Fairness in DNA Jury Trials', *Trends & Issues in Crime and Criminal Justice*, no. 392 (March 2010) 1; Jane Goodman-Delahunty and Lindsay Hewson, *Improving Jury Understanding and Use of Expert DNA Evidence: Technical and Background Paper No. 37* (Australian Institute of Criminology, 2010); Michael Briody, 'The Effects of DNA Evidence on Murder Cases in Court', *Australian and New Zealand Journal of Criminology* 37, no. 2 (August 2004) 231.

2

EXPERT EVIDENCE ADMISSIBILITY

A. Introduction

2.01 Rulings by trial judges in relation to the admissibility of expert evidence constitute a threshold issue in the criminal justice process—they determine whether expert opinions are permitted to be adduced before jurors and, if so, which opinions, and they determine the parameters within which opinions can be led in evidence. The law as to the admissibility of expert evidence differs from country to country; however, the criteria for admissibility remain internationally controversial, particularly in respect of the role of reliability as a condition precedent to expert opinions being admitted into evidence. The admissibility criteria are the product of concern about:

(a) the potential for undue weight to be given to opinion evidence from professional witnesses who are impressive and highly credentialed;[1]
(b) anxiety that expert evidence may be misunderstood or misconstrued;[2]

---

[1] See John W. Strong, 'Language and Logic in Expert Testimony: Limiting Expert Testimony by Restrictions of Function, Reliability, and Form', *Oregon Law Review* 71, no. 2 (Summer 1992) 349; Ian Binnie, 'Wrongful Convictions and the Magical Aura of Science in the Courtroom', *Judicial Review* 10, no. 2 (2011) 141. Compare 'Cornelius O'Dowd Upon Men and Women, and Other Things in General', *Blackwood's Edinburgh Magazine* 96, no. 587 (September 1864) 277: pp. 284–5: 'Armed with an hour's reading... the great man [i.e. the lawyer] comes down to court to puzzle, bewilder, and very often confute men of real ability... A pitiable specimen is that poor man of science, pilloried up in the witness-box and pelted by the flippant ignorance of his examiner! What a contrast between the different caution of true knowledge and the bold assurance, the chuckling confidence, the vainglorious self-satisfaction, and mock triumphant delight of his questioner!'

[2] See e.g. Daniel A. Krauss, John G. McCabe, and Joel D. Liberman, 'Dangerously Misunderstood: Representative Jurors' Reactions to Expert Testimony on Future Dangerousness in a Sexually Violent Predator Trial', *Psychology, Public Policy and Law* 18, no. 1 (February 2012) 18; Gary Edmond, '(Ad)Ministering Justice: Expert Evidence and the Professional Responsibilities of Prosecutors', *University of New South Wales Law Journal* 36, no. 3 (2013) 921.

(c) worry that experts may be problematically partisan in their methodology, interpretation of data, and expression of opinions;[3] and
(d) recognition that such defects may not be exposed effectively by cross-examination.[4]

2.02 In 1999, in an earlier phase of the current project, Australian judges were asked about whether 'reliability' of expert evidence should be a requirement for expert evidence to be admissible in courts. The question was posed a few years after the paradigm-shifting decision of the United States Supreme Court in *Daubert v Merrell Dow Pharmaceuticals Inc*[5] which held that reliability should be the fundamental yardstick for expert evidence admissibility and provided four indicia for identifying reliability in scientific evidence. There was a significant division of opinion amongst Australian judges on the issue—25.44% (n = 44) said that it should be a precondition; 57.46% (n = 131) said it should not; and 17.10% (n = 39) said they did not have an opinion on the subject.[6] Many judges who responded to the question indicated that they did not understand it or thought that the issue of reliability should be one for jurors. This was exemplary of a fundamental ideological division of view about the role and function of rules of evidentiary admissibility in respect of expert opinions—whether rules should constitute judges as active gatekeepers in respect of expert evidence placed before jurors, or in a more laissez-faire approach where jurors should generally be allowed to make what they can of expert evidence, assigning to it the probative value that to the jurors seems appropriate.[7] Judges were also asked whether they thought the courtroom was a forum in which the reliability of expert theories and techniques was adequately evaluated. More than half of those who responded (55.22%, n = 127) maintained that the courtroom was an adequate forum for such a purpose, although nearly a third (30.87%, n = 71) took the opposite view. Again, this question focussed upon the role and capacity of judges as decision-makers regarding the current status of theories or techniques within areas of expert endeavour.[8]

2.03 Whilst the concentration of the Expert Evidence and Jury Trials Project was not on the preliminary issue of admissibility but rather on expert evidence as it impacts upon jurors (when admitted), we did gain some insight into current perceptions of barristers and judges as to the admissibility of expert evidence, in particular the role of reliability in determining admissibility. The views are reported in this chapter a significant time after the 1999 Australian survey and after a series of high-profile cases which prompted contrasting views on the issue; controversies arising in respect of the operation of forensic science,[9]

---

[3] See Thomas G. Gutheil, *The Psychiatrist as Expert Witness*, 2nd edn. (Washington, DC: American Psychiatric Publishing, 2009); Robert I. Simon and Liza H. Gold, *Textbook of Forensic Psychiatry* (Washington, DC: American Psychiatric Publishing, 2010); Carl Meyer, *Expert Witnessing: Explaining and Understanding Science* (London: CRC Press, 1998), pp. 112ff; Douglas Walton, *Appeal to Expert Opinion: Arguments from Authority* (Pittsburgh: Pennsylvania State Press, 2010), pp. 216ff.

[4] See eg Ian Freckelton, 'Wizards in the Crucible: Making the Boffins Accountable', in *Proceedings of the First World Conference on New Trends in Criminal Investigation and Evidence*, edited by Johannes F. Nijboer and Jan M. Reijntjes (The Hague: Koninklijke Vermande, 1997).

[5] 509 US 579 (1993).

[6] Ian Freckelton, Prasuna Reddy, and Hugh Selby, *Australian Judicial Perspectives on Expert Evidence: An Empirical Study* (Sydney: AIJA, 1999), p. 78.

[7] See Deirdre Dwyer, *The Judicial Assessment of Expert Evidence* (Cambridge: Cambridge University Press, 2008).

[8] See Thomas A. Cromwell, 'The Challenges of Scientific Evidence' (MacFadyen Lecture, 2 March 2011), <http://www.scottishlawreports.org.uk/publications/macfadyen-2011.html>.

[9] Committee on Identifying the Needs of the Forensic Sciences Community, National Research Council, *Strengthening Forensic Sciences in the United States: A Path Forward* (Washington, DC: The National Academies Press, 2009). John Thomas, 'Expert Evidence: The Future of Forensic Science in Criminal Trials' (2014 Criminal Bar Association Kalisher Lecture, 14 October 2014), <https://www.judiciary.gov.uk/wp-content/uploads/2014/10/kalisher-lecture-expert-evidence-oct-14.pdf>.

medico-legal reporting systems,[10] forensic pathology,[11] and fingerprinting[12] in the United States, England, Scotland, and Canada; and a report in 2011 by the Law Commission of England and Wales[13] which recommended fundamental law reform to incorporate reliability as a criterion for expert evidence admissibility, as well as critical discussions that followed the Report.[14]

B. Expert Evidence Admissibility

Admissibility decisions are important because, amongst other things, the presence or absence of expert evidence has been found in jury studies to impact significantly upon conviction rates.[15] In addition, there is an extensive literature on the potential for impressive, confident, and articulate experts to be regarded as credible and thereby to impact upon juror decision-making.[16] As the Supreme Court of Canada put it in *R v Mohan*:[17] 'Dressed up in scientific language which the jury does not easily understand and submitted through a witness of impressive antecedents, [expert] evidence is apt to be accepted by the jury as being virtually infallible and having more weight than it deserves.' There are also studies which address the impact of experts' evidence on jurors' capacity to discriminate between accurate and inaccurate evidence given by lay witnesses.[18] In short, then, the stakes are high in relation to whether expert evidence is permitted to go before jurors. **2.04**

In the United Kingdom, and in Australia in Queensland, Western Australia, and South Australia, it is the common law of evidence that governs the admissibility of expert **2.05**

---

10 Committee for the Workshop on the Medicolegal Death Investigation System, *Medicolegal Death Investigation System: Workshop Summary* (Washington, DC: The National Academies Press, 2003).

11 Stephen T. Goudge, *Inquiry into Pediatric Forensic Pathology in Ontario: Report*, vol. 1 (Ontario Ministry of the Attorney General, 2008), p. 16, <http://www.attorneygeneral.jus.gov.on.ca/inquiries/goudge/report/v1_en_pdf/Vol_1_Eng_vi.pdf>.

12 Anthony Campbell, *The Fingerprint Inquiry* (Edinburgh: APS Group, 2011), <http://www.webarchive.org.uk/wayback/archive/20150428160103/> <http://www.thefingerprintinquiryscotland.org.uk/inquiry/files/TheFingerprintInquiryReport_Low_res.pdf>.

13 Law Commission of England and Wales, *Expert Evidence in Criminal Proceedings in England and Wales: Report No. 325* (London: The Stationery Office, 2011), <http://www.lawcom.gov.uk/project/expert-evidence-in-criminal-proceedings/#expert-evidence-in-criminal-proceedings> ('Law Commission Report'). See too, albeit principally in the civil context, Erik Arnold and Errol Soriano, *The Recent Evolution of Expert Evidence in Selected Common Law Jurisdictions Around the World: A Commissioned Study for the Canadian Institute of Chartered Business Valuators* (Campbell Valuation Partners Ltd, 23 January 2013).

14 See e.g. Gary Edmond, 'Is Reliability Sufficient? The Law Commission and Expert Evidence in International and Interdisciplinary Perspective (Part 1)', *The International Journal of Evidence and Proof* 16, no. 1 (2012) 30; Ministry of Justice, *The Government's Response to the Law Commission's Report: Expert Evidence in Criminal Proceedings in England and Wales* (Law Com No. 325, 21 November 2013), <https://www.gov.uk/government/uploads/system/uploads/attachment_data/file/260369/govt-resp-experts-evidence.pdf>.

15 See e.g. Michael J. Crowley, M. Gemma O'Callaghan, and Peter J. Ball, 'The Juridical Impact of Psychological Expert Testimony in a Simulated Child Sexual Abuse Trial', *Law and Human Behavior* 18, no. 1 (February 1994) 89; Margaret Bull Kovera, Eugene Borgida, April W. Grehsam, Ellen Gray, and Pamela C. Regan, 'Does Expert Psychological Testimony Inform or Influence Juror Decision Making?' *Journal of Applied Psychology* 82, no. 1 (February 1997) 178.

16 See eg Robert J. Cramer, Stanley L. Brodsky, and Jamie DeCoster, 'Expert Witness Confidence and Juror Personality: Their Impact on Credibility and Persuasion in the Courtroom', *Journal of the American Academy of Psychiatry and the Law* 37, no. 1 (March 2009) 63.

17 [1994] 2 SCR 9, 21. See also *United States v Addison*, 498 F 2d 741, 744 (1974): 'scientific proof may in some instances assume a posture of mystic infallibility in the eyes of a jury of laymen'.

18 See e.g. Kristy A. Martire and Richard I. Kemp, 'Can Experts Help Jurors to Evaluate Eyewitness Evidence? A Review of Eyewitness Expert Effects', *Legal and Criminological Psychology* 16, no. 1 (February 2011) 24.

opinions in criminal trials. That common law has significant features which are shared. Fundamental aspects to the criteria for admissibility decision-making have been contended to include:

a rule requiring expertise in the witness ('the expertise rule');
a rule requiring that the area about which the expert testifies be one of expertise ('the area of expertise rule');
a preclusion upon experts testifying on matters of common knowledge ('the common knowledge rule');
a requirement that the bases of an expert's opinions be proven ('the basis rule'); and
a prohibition upon experts testifying on the issue to be determined by a jury ('the ultimate issue rule').[19]

In addition, in *Dasreef Pty Ltd v Hawchar*,[20] Heydon J of the Australian High Court postulated the existence also of an 'assumption identification rule', a 'statement of reasoning rule', and a 'proof of assumption rule' as preconditions for expert evidence admissibility. Each of these rules requires of experts that they expose their reasoning processes so as to enable evaluation of the weight to be given to their opinions.

2.06 However, the orthodox determinants of expert evidence admissibility were summarized by the South Australian decision of *R v Bonython*:[21]

(1) whether the subject matter of the opinion is such that a person without instruction or experience in the area of knowledge or human experience would be able to form a sound judgment on the matter without the assistance of a witness possessing special knowledge or experience in the area;
(2) whether the subject matter of the opinion forms part of a body of knowledge of experience which is sufficiently organized or recognized to be accepted as a reliable body of knowledge or experience, a special acquaintance with which by the witness would render his opinion of assistance to the court; and
(3) whether the witness has acquired by study or experience sufficient knowledge of the subject to render his opinion of value in resolving the issues before the court.

2.07 The reasoning in *Bonython* has been applied on many occasions in the United Kingdom.[22]

2.08 In Canada it is also the common law that determines the issue, but it has evolved somewhat differently. The most authoritative decision of the Supreme Court, *R v Mohan*,[23] held that 'novel science' falls into a 'special category' of expert evidence and straightforwardly required that expert evidence be:

- relevant;
- necessary in the sense of assisting the trier of fact;

---

[19] See Tristram Hodgkinson and Mark James, *Expert Evidence: Law and Practice*, 4th edn. (London: Sweet & Maxwell, 2014); Hodge M. Malek, *Phipson on Evidence*, 18th edn. (London: Sweet & Maxwell, 2013); Alan Gold, *Expert Evidence in Criminal Law: The Scientific Approach*, 2nd edn. (Toronto: Irwin Law, 2009); Ian Freckelton and Hugh Selby, *Expert Evidence, Law, Practice, Procedure and Advocacy*, 6th edn. (Sydney: Thomson Reuters, 2016).

[20] [2011] HCA 21, (2011) 243 CLR 588. See Miiko Kumar, 'Admissibility of Expert Evidence: Proving the Basis for an Expert's Opinion', *Sydney Law Review* 33, no. 3 (September 2011) 427.

[21] (1984) 38 SASR 45, 46–47.

[22] See eg *R v Hodges* [2003] EWCA Crim 290, [2003] 2 Cr App R 15; *R v Dallagher* [2002] EWCA Crim 1903, [2003] 1 Cr App R 12; *R v G* [2004] EWCA Crim 1240, [2004] 2 Cr App R 38 [15]; *R v Luttrell* [2004] EWCA Crim 1344, [2004] 2 Cr App R 31 [32]; *R v Dudley* [2004] EWCA Crim 3336 [30]; *R v Harris* [2005] EWCA Crim 1980, [2006] 1 Cr App R 5 [270]; *R v Reed* [2009] EWCA Crim 2698, [2010] 1 Cr App R 23 [111]; *R v Henderson* [2010] EWCA Crim 1269, [2010] 2 Cr App R 24 [206]; *R v Ahmed* [2011] EWCA Crim 184, [2011] Crim LR 734 [57].

[23] [1994] 2 SCR 9.

- not excluded by any other exclusionary rule of evidence; and
- given by a witness shown to have acquired special or peculiar knowledge through study or experience in respect of the matters on which he or she undertakes to testify.[24]

As Binnie J later put it in *R v J-LJ*[25]:

> Mohan kept the door open to novel science, rejecting the 'general acceptance' test formulated in the United States in *Frye v United States*, 293 F 1013 (DC Cir 1923), and moving in parallel with its replacement, the 'reliable foundation' test more recently laid down by the US Supreme Court in *Daubert v Merrell Dow Pharmaceuticals, Inc.*, 509 US 579 (1993).

In the United States the Federal Rules of Evidence, particularly Rules 702,[26] 703,[27] 704,[28] and 705,[29] are the principal determinants of admissibility for expert evidence. They focus upon whether expert opinions will provide assistance to the trier of fact; Rule 702 requires not only that evidence be based on 'sufficient facts or data' but also explicitly invokes notions of reliability, requiring that evidence be 'the product of reliable principles and methods' and that 'the expert has reliably applied the principles and methods to the facts of the case'. In addition, Rule 403 permits exclusion of expert (and other) evidence if its probative value is substantially outweighed by a danger of 'unfair prejudice, confusing the issues, misleading the jury, undue delay, wasting time, or needlessly presenting cumulative evidence.'[30] This has generated controversial debate and caselaw about the forms of presentation of expert evidence (such as resemblance thinking and problematic forms of portrayal of likelihood by statistical evidence) with a tendency to be inapt for effective evaluation by jurors—to be unacceptably misleading or confusing.[31] **2.09**

In New Zealand s. 25 of the Evidence Act 2006 (NZ) is the yardstick for admissibility.[32] **2.10**
Again, the principal test is whether 'substantial help' is likely to be provided by the proposed

24 See also *R v J-LJ* [2000] 2 SCR 600 [28]–[47]; *R v DD* [2000] 2 SCR 275 [11]–[41]; *R v Trochym* [2007] 1 SCR 239 [34].

25 [2000] 2 SCR 600 [33].

26 'A witness who is qualified as an expert by knowledge, skill, experience, training, or education may testify in the form of an opinion or otherwise if: (a) the expert's scientific, technical, or other specialized knowledge will help the trier of fact to understand the evidence or to determine a fact in issue; (b) the testimony is based on sufficient facts or data; (c) the testimony is the product of reliable principles and methods; and (d) the expert has reliably applied the principles and methods to the facts of the case.'

27 'An expert may base an opinion on facts or data in the case that the expert has been made aware of or personally observed. If experts in the particular field would reasonably rely on those kinds of facts or data in forming an opinion on the subject, they need not be admissible for the opinion to be admitted. But if the facts or data would otherwise be inadmissible, the proponent of the opinion may disclose them to the jury only if their probative value in helping the jury evaluate the opinion substantially outweighs their prejudicial effect.'

28 '(a) In General—Not Automatically Objectionable. An opinion is not objectionable just because it embraces an ultimate issue. (b) Exception. In a criminal case, an expert witness must not state an opinion about whether the defendant did or did not have a mental state or condition that constitutes an element of the crime charged or of a defense. Those matters are for the trier of fact alone.'

29 'Unless the court orders otherwise, an expert may state an opinion—and give the reasons for it—without first testifying to the underlying facts or data. But the expert may be required to disclose those facts or data on cross-examination.'

30 See Mary Mivka, 'An Indelicate Balance: Rule 403 of the Federal Rules of Evidence', *Evidence* 30, no.1 (2003) 36.

31 See e.g. Kenneth R. Foster and Peter W. Huber, *Judging Science: Scientific Knowledge and the Federal Courts* (Cambridge, Mass: MIT Press, 1999), pp. 207ff.

32 Section 25 reads as follows:

> (1) An opinion by an expert that is part of expert evidence offered in a proceeding is admissible if the fact-finder is likely to obtain substantial help from the opinion in understanding other evidence in the proceeding or in ascertaining any fact that is of consequence to the determination of the proceeding.

expert evidence.[33] It has been held that: 'Evidence will be substantially helpful where it helps the Court as fact finder to understand other evidence in the proceeding.'[34] In this regard, the yardstick is stated to be helpfulness, but clear criteria to assist evaluation of helpfulness are not provided by statute.

2.11 The law in the jurisdictions in Australia which are governed by statutory law on the subject (the federal jurisdictions, New South Wales, Victoria, Tasmania, the Australian Capital Territory, the Northern Territory, and Norfolk Island) requires the possession by a person of a particular form of knowledge before they are permitted to express opinions:

> If a person has specialised knowledge based on the person's training, study or experience, the opinion rule does not apply to evidence of an opinion of that person that is wholly or substantially based on that knowledge.[35]

2.12 In addition, the statutory provisions state that opinion evidence is not inadmissible only because it is about a fact in issue or an ultimate issue or a matter of common knowledge.[36] Both provisions have been subject to extensive and at times diverse interpretation. However, a clear requirement has been that expert evidence derive from specialized knowledge which in turn must derive from training, study, or experience. This has been held to preclude 'speculation, inference, personal and second-hand views' masquerading as expert evidence—such as theories by a psychologist about the propensity of children to transpose the identity of persons who have sexually assaulted them.[37]

C. Diverse Perspectives on Reliability

2.13 It was apparent from comments and observations made by those who participated in this project that the notion of 'reliability' is often invoked in relation to admissibility of expert evidence but also in the context of the evaluation of the quality of experts and expert evidence. It can be used loosely, sometimes in terms of a witness's reliability, credibility, or honesty (or an amalgam of these), sometimes in terms of the reliability of theories or techniques within what might be called an 'area of expertise' or 'specialized knowledge'. One expert witness in the project noted that a broad issue in terms of his expertise on memory had been in issue, which in turn impacted upon the inferences that could be drawn about the reliability not so much of him but of the complainant in a sex offence trial. A defence lawyer expressed a strong view that controls need to be exercised upon the entitlement of witnesses to commentate upon the credibility of lay witnesses—in general, the orthodox position is that it is the

(2) An opinion by an expert is not inadmissible simply because it is about—(a) an ultimate issue to be determined in a proceeding; or (b) a matter of common knowledge.
(3) If an opinion by an expert is based on a fact that is outside the general body of knowledge that makes up the expertise of the expert, the opinion may be relied on by the fact-finder only if that fact is or will be proved or judicially noticed in the proceeding.
(4) If expert evidence about the sanity of a person is based in whole or in part on a statement that the person made to the expert about the person's state of mind, then—(a) the statement of the person is admissible to establish the facts on which the expert's opinion is based; and (b) neither the hearsay rule nor the previous consistent statements rule applies to evidence of the statement made by the person.
(5) Subsection (3) is subject to subsection (4).

[33] See e.g. *Aryan v The Queen* [2010] NZCA 57, [2010] BCL 271 in relation to counter-intuitive evidence.

[34] *R v Douglas* [2012] NZHC 844 [21]; Suzanne Blackwell and Fred Seymour, 'Expert Evidence and Jurors' Views', *Psychiatry, Psychology and Law* 22, no. 5 (2015) 673.

[35] See e.g. *Evidence Act 1995* (Cth) s. 79(1).

[36] See e.g. *Evidence Act 1995* (Cth) s. 80.

[37] *HG v The Queen* (1999) 197 CLR 414 [41].

preserve of jurors to evaluate witnesses' honesty, credibility, and even their cognitive capacity unless they are mentally unwell or intellectually disabled.

The law has long been reasonably clear about the role of an expert witness in a criminal trial to assist the capacity of jurors for informed and discerning finding of facts. As long ago as the sixteenth century in *Buckley v Rice Thomas*,[38] Justice Saunders made what has since become a famous statement: 2.14

> [I]n matters arising in our law which concerned other sciences or faculties, we commonly applied to the aid of that science or faculty which it concerns, which is an honourable and commendable thing in our law. For thereby it appears that we do not despise all other sciences but our own, but we do approve of them and encourage them as things worthy of commendation.

More recently, in the Scottish decision of *Davie v Magistrates of Edinburgh*[39] Lord President Cooper observed that the duty of experts is 'to furnish the judge or jury with the necessary scientific criteria for testing the accuracy of their conclusions, so as to enable the judge or jury to form their own independent judgment by the application of these criteria to the facts proved in evidence.'[40] In 1987, McIntyre J in the Supreme Court of Canada decision of *R v Beland*[41] developed the analysis further: 'The function of the expert witness is to provide the jury or other trier of fact an expert's opinions as to the significance of, or the inference which may be drawn from, proved facts in a field in which the expert witness possesses special knowledge and experience going beyond that of the trier of fact.'[42]

In addition, in principle, expert witnesses are 'merely' witnesses. As pointed out in the joint judgment of the Australian High Court in *Ramsay v Watson*:[43] 'A qualified medical practitioner may, as an expert, express his opinion as to the nature and cause, or probable cause, of an ailment. But it is for the jury to weigh and determine the probabilities. In doing so they may be assisted by the medical evidence. But they are not simply to transfer their task to the witnesses.' To a similar effect the Singapore Court of Appeal observed in 2010 that: 2.15

> Where there is conflicting evidence between experts it will not be the sheer number of experts articulating a particular opinion or view that matters, but rather the consistency and logic of the preferred evidence that is paramount. Generally speaking, the court should also scrutinise the credentials and relevant experience of the experts in their professed and acknowledged areas of expertise. Not all experts are of equal authority and/or reliability. In so far as medical evidence is concerned, an expert with greater relevant clinical experience may often prove to be more credible and reliable on 'hands-on' issues although this is not an inevitable rule of thumb. Having said that, there is no precise pecking order or hierarchy relating to expert evidence. Experts may sometimes be abundantly eminent while lacking credibility in a particular matter.[44]

---

[38] (1554) 1 Plowden 118, 125; 75 ER 182, 192.

[39] [1953] SC 34, 40.

[40] Similarly in *Singh v State of Uttaranchal* [2012] INSC 425 [32]–[34] the Supreme Court of India held that: 'The purpose of expert testimony is to provide the trier of fact with useful, relevant information…the skill and experience of an expert is the ethos of his opinions, which itself should be reasoned and convincing.…the purpose of an expert opinion is to assist the Court in arriving at a final conclusion.'

[41] [1987] 2 SCR 398 [16]; see too *R v Abbey* [1982] 2 SCR 24, 42.

[42] In 2012 s. 47 of the *Evidence Act* (Cap 97, 1997 Rev Ed) (Sing) was amended to allow a court to admit expert evidence: '…when the court is likely to derive assistance from an opinion upon a point of scientific, technical or other specialised knowledge, the opinions of experts upon that point are relevant facts'.

[43] (1961) 108 CLR 642, 645.

[44] *Ong Pang Siew v Public Prosecutor* [2010] SGCA 37 [75]. See also Michael Hor, 'When Experts Disagree', *Singapore Journal of Legal Studies*, no. 1 (2000) 241.

2.16 The Victorian Court of Appeal made a similar point in *R v Juric*,[45] which in turn applied the reasoning of Gummow and Callinan JJ of the Australian High Court in *R v Velevski*:[46]

> Juries are frequently called upon to resolve conflicts between experts. They have done so from the inception of jury trials. Expert evidence does not, as a matter of law, fall into two categories: difficult and sophisticated expert evidence giving rise to conflicts which a jury may not and should not be allowed to resolve; and simple and unsophisticated expert evidence which they can. Nor is it the law, that simply because there is a conflict in respect of difficult and sophisticated expert evidence, even with respect to an important, indeed critical matter, its resolution should for that reason alone be regarded by an appellate court as having been beyond the capacity of the jury to resolve.

2.17 However, whether this role delineation and the fact that there should not be unwarranted deference to the evidence of experts by assuming them or their evidence to be reliable are effectively communicated to jurors is another matter. A juror in the current project gave the following somewhat confused account of what they considered to be the role of an expert in a criminal trial:

> They're there to present the—how would you say it—a collection of evidence of a sort and give not their opinion the known facts of that evidence, rather than what might be general knowledge of that evidence. Also not to just present it, too, but to present the—not applicability—reliability of it; of that evidence.

2.18 Another juror explicitly linked their view of the reliability of an expert witness to their lack of bias, described by reference to the witness's independence, while a further perspective was given by a judge who commented that an expert called by the prosecution was not 'too impressive, but, you know, he knows what his function is.' A prosecutor in the same trial viewed the issue of reliability in terms of how the witness was likely to have been viewed at the end of both examination-in-chief and cross-examination: 'He did remain poised throughout by objectively sitting listening to it. I thought there were some solid inroads made into his evidence that affected the reliability of his ultimate conclusion.'

2.19 The potential for a reliable and carefully constructed agreed statement of facts by two experts in relation to DNA evidence arose in an interview with a prosecutor. She indicated that she thought that because of the influence of television programmes like CSI,

> juries like to have the DNA expert in the box, and they like to see the slides. They feel like they're part of a process that they might regularly see on TV, so I think in terms of juror appeal, an agreed statement of facts just doesn't... appeal to juries so much. The other way is better, but of course the other way has the risk of somebody... causing problems or questions for the reliability of the DNA evidence.

Thus, the prosecutor was indicating that because of what she perceived as the expectations generated by portrayals of court proceedings, her practice was to call experts, even when that was not strictly necessary. Put another way, forensic theatre was prioritized over reliable presentation of evidence in written form.

2.20 A matter that is increasingly contested internationally, especially where there are jury trials, is whether the reliability of expert opinion evidence should play a role in determining whether it should be admitted in criminal trials, and, if so, how reliability should be determined.

2.21 The notion of reliability, however, has a particular technical meaning. It should be distinguished from validity. Within science reliability is the capacity of a test to achieve consistent

---

[45] [2002] VSCA 77 [18], (2002) VR 411, 426 [18].
[46] [2002] HCA 4, (2002) 76 ALJR 402 [182].

results,[47] including across raters[48] and on test and retest (test stability) under stated conditions and within a specific period of time. In psychology it is often determined by using the correlation coefficient,[49] including by Cronbach's coefficient alpha—the most commonly used measure of internal consistency.[50] The need to achieve safety by virtue of consistency of results has even given rise to fields of study which address materials degradation and device failure which are the subject of 'reliability physics' and 'reliability engineering'.[51] A number of measures are employed to evaluate reliability in scientific experimentation, including: simplicity, redundancy (providing duplicate or backup systems), margins of safety, modularity (in terms of dividing the complicated into simple components), and conservatism of employment of technology.[52] Many prophylactic measures in respect of reliability relate to reducing, so far as possible, the potential for human error.

Validity, however, is determined by reference to the context, such as the purpose for which a test is applied. It can be subcategorized into face validity (the acceptability of a test to the user and the subject for the operation being carried out), content validity (or criterion-related or domain-referenced validity), predictive validity (a major form of statistical validity, correlated between test score and an assessment of success), and concurrent validity (correlating a test with other tests purporting to measure the same construct, sometimes said to utilize the notions of convergent and discriminant validity).[53] The larger a sample, the more stable are estimates of both reliability and validity.[54] When reliability is absent, so too is validity; reliability is a criterion in respect of validity. As reliability decreases, generally validity will also do so. **2.22**

It has been asserted that the exclusionary rules of expert evidence are not adequately invoked by advocates in criminal trials and are not sufficiently applied by trial judges.[55] Edmond has gone further and argued that: **2.23**

> Many lawyers and judges are not in a position to respond credibly to the assessment of validity and reliability or appreciate the subtle methodological and statistical issues associated with forensic science and forensic medicine and the way derivative opinions are presented. Moreover, empirical evidence suggests that judges are reluctant to exclude incriminating expert evidence (if it might have some probative value). They maintain considerable, and perhaps unsustainable, confidence in trial safeguards (especially cross-examination and cautionary warnings), the jury and appellate courts, and tend to remain favourably disposed to the incriminating opinions of investigators and other 'experts'.[56]

---

47 See Geoffrey W. A. Dummer, Robert C. Winton, and Michael H. Tooley, *An Elementary Guide to Reliability*, 5th edn. (Oxford: Butterworth-Heinemann, 1997), ch. 2.

48 See e.g. Kilem Li Gwet, *Handbook of Inter-Rater Reliability*, 3rd edn. (Gaithersburg, Maryland: Advanced Analytics Press, 2012).

49 See Glynis M. Breakwell, Jonathan A. Smith, and Daniel B. Wright, *Research Methods in Psychology* (New York: Sage, 2012), ch. 7.8.

50 See, though, Bruce Thompson, *Reliability: Contemporary Thinking on Reliability Issues* (New York: Sage, 2002). See too Michael Karson and Lavita Nadkarni, *Principles of Forensic Report Writing* (Washington, DC: American Psychological Association, 2013), p. 113.

51 See Joe W. McPherson, *Reliability Physics and Engineering: Time-To-Failure Modelling* (New York: Springer, 2010); see also Dongsu Ryu, *Improving Reliability and Quality for Product Success* (Boca Raton, Florida: CRC Press, 2012).

52 See I. R. Walker, *Reliability in Scientific Research: Improving the Dependability of Measurements, Calculations, Equipment, and Software* (Cambridge: Cambridge University Press, 2011).

53 Walker, *Reliability in Scientific Research*, para. 7.9.

54 See Frederick T. L. Leong and James T. Austin, *Psychology Research Handbook* (New York: Sage, 2005), p. 135.

55 See e.g. Andrew Roberts, 'Expert Evidence and Unreliability in the High Court: *Honeysett v The Queen*', 'Opinions on High' blog, 3 September 2014, <http://blogs.unimelb.edu.au/opinionsonhigh/2014/09/03/roberts-honeysett>.

56 Gary Edmond, 'The Admissibility of Incriminating Expert Evidence in the United States, England and Canada', *Judicial Officers' Bulletin* 23, no.8 (2011) 67: p.70.

2.24 An outcome of such deficits, it is contended, is that too much expert evidence that lacks the hallmarks of scientific reliability is adduced in criminal trials with the concomitant potential for misunderstanding by jurors and for it to be accorded excessive weight:

> A great deal of evidence has been misleadingly presented in investigation, plea negotiations, trial and appeal as reliable forensic science or expressed in terms that do not reflect the actual limitations of the evidence. Many trials will have been rendered substantially unfair on that basis, and in some proportion of trials, the defendant will have lost the benefit of reasonable doubt raised by mistakes, techniques not being reliable, technical limitations not being identified (or explained), exaggeration and misrepresentation, and inattention to cognitive contamination. In some trials, the incriminating forensic science and medical evidence—derived from techniques that are yet to be evaluated, using processes that were inattentive to cognitive risks—will have simply been wrong.[57]

2.25 A risk thereby created is miscarriages of criminal justice. This has emerged as a fraught issue in the contemporary environment as a result of a series of appellate decisions in various parts of the common law world, many of them overturning the admitting at trial of unreliable scientific and medical evidence. Part of the issue is that scientific knowledge evolves—as Toulson LJ put it: 'today's orthodoxy may be tomorrow's outdated learning'.[58] Another issue is the threshold question of whether expert evidence that does not meet the criteria for reliability should be admitted so that it is evidence which goes before juries in criminal matters.[59]

D. The Impetus toward Reform

(1) England

2.26 In England, since 2000 there have been many cases which have raised the issue of whether what the Law Commission in its inquiry into the admissibility of expert evidence in criminal trials has called England's 'laissez-faire' approach to admissibility[60] has served the interests of justice adequately.

2.27 A 2005 case that became controversial was *R v Dallagher*[61] in which the Court of Appeal found that the accused man had been wrongly convicted of murder based upon expert opinion evidence about an area of expert endeavour 'in its infancy'—ear-print analysis. Comparison had been undertaken of an ear-print made by the accused man with a latent ear-print found on a window. Ultimately, after fresh evidence about the reliability of the ear-print analysis was adduced on appeal, the conviction of the accused was found to be unsafe.

2.28 In addition, until the decision of the Court of Appeal in *R v Harris*,[62] the prosecution had been permitted to rely on the proposition that non-accidental head injury to a child could be inferred from the presence of a triad of intra-cranial injuries. This was shown to be a flawed theory which was dependent upon a small and poor-quality database.

---

57 Gary Edmond, 'What Lawyers Should Know About the Forensic Sciences', *Adelaide Law Review* (2015, forthcoming).

58 *R v Holdsworth* [2008] EWCA Crim 971 [57].

59 See Gary Edmond, 'The Admissibility of Forensic Science and Medicine Evidence under the Uniform Evidence Law', *Criminal Law Journal* 38, no. 3 (2014) 136.

60 Law Commission, *The Admissibility of Expert Evidence in Criminal Proceedings in England and Wales: A New Approach to the Determination of Evidentiary Admissibility—Consultation Paper No. 190* (London: The Stationery Office, 2009), p. 22.

61 [2002] EWCA Crim 1903, [2003] 1 Cr App R 12.

62 [2005] EWCA Crim 1980, [2006] 1 Cr App R 5.

In a further sequence of decisions major questions arose in relation to the legitimacy of the reasoning process engaged in by experts, in particular certain pathologists and physicians, where multiple deaths of young children within the same family unit without a clearly identifiable aetiology had taken place. The questions that prompted consternation about the interpretative approach of investigating doctors included: what the starting point should be when such statistically unlikely deaths were identified; how jurors could be enabled to factor such unlikelihood into their evaluation of the guilt of mothers charged with homicides in respect of their children; and how the potential for further medical research developments, such as into genetic vulnerabilities, might be incorporated via expert evidence into jurors' reasoning.[63] **2.29**

In the first in this sequence of cases, *R v Clark*,[64] the Court of Appeal found Professor Sir Roy Meadow's exuberant evidence for the prosecution about the statistical likelihood of there being two non-accidental deaths in the one household of the London solicitor, Sally Clark, to be flawed, although it did not reverse the jury decision (in the first appeal) because of the existence of other evidence.[65] As Lord Thorpe was later to put it: 'He knew... that simple squaring was not a reliable basis for the calculation of the probability of recurrence given that two infant deaths within the same family are not independent events.'[66] The Court of Appeal observed that although Professor Meadow did not misuse the figures in his evidence, 'he did not help to explain their limited significance'.[67] Thereby there was the risk that a wrong impression was given to the jury of their significance, although this did not constitute the basis for the later successful appeal against Ms Clark's conviction.[68] **2.30**

However, shortly afterwards, the General Medical Council struck off Professor Meadow for the deficiencies in his forensic report and his expert evidence in the Clark trial. He appealed successfully but subsequently his matter came before the Court of Appeal. The Master of the Rolls, Sir Anthony Clarke, accepted that there had been 'serious shortcomings' in the way in which Professor Meadow wrote his reports and expressed himself at trial.[69] He affirmed that Professor Meadow was guilty of serious professional misconduct, although he concluded that his actions had not been undertaken in bad faith. Lord Justice Auld concurred, finding that: **2.31**

> In his preparation for, and presentation of evidence at, the trial of Mrs Clark he fell below the standards required of him by his profession. Although not an expert in the use of statistics or calculation of probability, he put forward a theory of improbability of recurrence of unexplained and seemingly natural infant deaths, applicable only where recurrence occurred in familial, environmental and economic circumstances wholly independent of those of a first such death. In doing so, he relied initially on statistical figures of uncertain source and scientific validity..., which had nothing to do with the probabilities of recurrence in any individual case, and which, in any event, he misunderstood and, by implication and the use

63 See e.g. *R v Cannings* [2004] EWCA Crim 1, [2004] 1 WLR 2607; *R v Kai-Whitewind* [2005] EWCA Crim 1092, [2005] 2 Cr App R 31; *R v Henderson* [2010] EWCA Crim 1269, [2010] 2 Cr App R 24; *R v Folbigg* [2003] NSWCCA 17; *R v Matthey* [2007] VSC 398, (2007) 17 VR 222. See also Emma Cunliffe, *Murder, Medicine and Motherhood* (London: Bloomsbury, 2011); Jim Fisher, *Forensics Under Fire: Are Bad Science and Duelling Experts Corrupting Criminal Justice?* (New Brunswick, NJ: Rutgers University Press, 2008); Jonathan Gornall, 'Was Message of Sudden Infant Death Study Misleading?', *BMJ* 333, no. 7579 (December 2006) 1165; Sharmila Betts and Jane Goodman-Delahunty, 'The Case of Kathleen Folbigg: How Did Justice and Medicine Fare?', *Australian Journal of Forensic Sciences* 39, no. 1 (2007) 11.

64 [2000] EWCA Crim 54.

65 See Ian Freckelton, *Scholarly Misconduct: Law, Regulation, and Practice* (Oxford: Oxford University Press, 2016).

66 *General Medical Council v Meadow* [2006] EWCA Civ 1390, [2007] QB 462 [251].

67 *R v Clark* [2000] EWCA Crim 54 [163].

68 *R v Clark* [2003] EWCA Crim 1020, [2003] 2 FCR 447.

69 *General Medical Council v Meadow* [2006] EWCA Civ 1390, [2007] QB 462 [84].

> of an inappropriate analogy, misapplied. In addition, and importantly, he did not expressly draw the court's attention to the fact that he had no expertise in the field of statistics or calculations of probability in this or any other field.[70]

2.32 The essence of the Court of Appeal's decision was that Professor Meadow's evidence had been seriously unreliable.

2.33 In *R v Luttrell*[71] the Court of Appeal was called upon to grapple with evidence from a lip-reading expert whose reliability came into serious question by reason of demonstration of a high level of fallibility in her capacity to lip-read with accuracy.[72] The Court rejected the proposition that reliability of expert evidence should constitute a criterion for admissibility but accepted that in some instances the reliability of evidence may be relevant to admissibility decision-making.

2.34 In the controversial decision of *R v T*,[73] the Court of Appeal was called upon to rule on the admissibility of Bayesian evidence in the context of likelihood ratios in respect of footwear evidence. It determined that an expert should not be permitted to use Bayes' Theorem and likelihood ratios should not be employed outside the area of DNA profiling and possibly other areas where there is a firm statistical base. Redmayne et al. have lambasted the Court of Appeal's restriction of experts to 'vague and potentially misleading conclusions' but conceded that its

> emphatic directives that expert report writing must be transparent, that experts' conclusions should be properly supported by adequate data, and that juries must not be bamboozled by statistical evidence, are valuable reminders of basic principles to which all forensic scientists and criminal justice professionals should pay heed.[74]

2.35 The controversies persisted into 2013 when the Court of Appeal, dealing with low template DNA evidence in *R v Dlugosz*,[75] upheld the reception of expert evidence but sounded a warning and articulated a clear test: 'It is essential to recall the principle which is applicable, namely in determining the issue of admissibility, the court must be satisfied that there is a sufficiently reliable scientific basis for the evidence to be admitted. If there is then the court leaves the opposing views to be tested before the jury.'

(2) Scotland

2.36 In 1997 Marion Ross was found murdered at her home. Shirley McKie was a police officer who was a member of the murder investigation team. A fingerprint found on the bathroom of the deceased woman's home was found by the Scottish Criminal Records Service to be that of Ms McKie, in spite of the fact that the team had been instructed not to enter the premises. At the subsequent murder trial of a suspect, David Ashbury, Ms McKie gave evidence that the fingerprint was not hers. The suspect was convicted and Ms McKie was prosecuted for perjury. However, she was acquitted after she adduced evidence from two independent fingerprint examiners that the fingerprint was not that of Ms McKie. This prompted an inspection of the Scottish Criminal Records Service by Her Majesty's Inspectorate of Constabulary for Scotland.[76] Mr Ashbury successfully appealed against his conviction. A parliamentary

---

70 *General Medical Council v Meadow* [2006] EWCA Civ 1390, [2007] QB 462 [210].

71 [2004] EWCA Crim 1344, [2004] 2 Cr App R 31.

72 See Jonathan Doak and Claire McGourlay, *Criminal Evidence in Context* (London: Routledge, 2009).

73 [2010] EWCA Crim 2439, [2011] 1 Cr App R 9.

74 Mike Redmayne, Paul Roberts, Colin Aitken, and Graham Jackson, 'Forensic Science in Question', *Criminal Law Review*, no. 5 [2011] 347.

75 [2013] EWCA Crim 2, [2013] 1 Cr App R 32 [13].

76 Her Majesty's Inspectorate of Constabulary, *Scottish Criminal Record Office: The Fingerprint Bureau: Primary Inspection 2000* (2000).

inquiry into the Records Service and the Scottish Fingerprint Service ensued by the Justice Committee of the Scottish Parliament.

(3) Canada

In Canada too the Goudge Inquiry found the evidence of the forensic pathologist Dr Charles Smith, which was admitted in multiple criminal cases, was so flawed and unreliable that it had led to a series of miscarriages of justice. It concluded that he was 'sloppy and inconsistent' in documenting information and indiscriminate in accepting and relying on evidence given to him, resulting in the performance of autopsies without necessary information, and an absence of independence and objectivity. The outcome was seriously unreliable evidence—'misdiagnoses with significant consequences'.[77] **2.37**

(4) Australia

Australia has also had a number of cases involving expert evidence which, with the wisdom of hindsight, was unreliable and should not have been admitted. It ultimately took Royal Commissions in 1984 to establish the flaws in the glass and paint spicule evidence adduced against Edward Charles Splatt[78] and then in 1987 to show the errors in the foetal blood analysis that played a role in convicting Lindy and Michael Chamberlain of the murder of their daughter, Azaria.[79] **2.38**

However, the problems are not entirely historical by any means. In 2010 Frank Vincent QC, a former Court of Appeal judge in Victoria, reported on the circumstances that lay behind a miscarriage of justice involving a young Somali man, Farah Jama, who was wrongfully convicted of the rape of a 48-year-old woman, known as M.[80] She had gone to a singles nightclub in a Melbourne suburb where the effects of earlier prescription medicine and later drinking in her sister-in-law's car resulted in her collapse in the club's toilet cubicle. She could not at first account for being found unconscious, but she later expressed concern that she had been drugged and raped. She was not able to identify any assailant, least of all the 19-year-old Somali student who fell under police suspicion. This suspicion was raised because of a DNA sample that matched that of the student. The sample had been extracted a week earlier in the identical room of a Melbourne hospital where M had been taken by police. No one at the nightclub could recall, or identify, a black youth attending the nightclub catering for mature-aged clientele where such a person would have certainly stood out but these problems were overcome by DNA evidence which linked Jama to M. Jama was arrested, charged, tried and convicted of rape. **2.39**

The Vincent inquiry established that the DNA results were contaminated by a failure to undertake simple cleaning processes in the location where the swab and slide were collected—the same unit where forensic samples were secured from another woman who **2.40**

---

77 Goudge, *Inquiry into Pediatric Forensic Pathology in Ontario: Report*, vol. 1, p. 16, <http://www.attorneygeneral.jus.gov.on.ca/inquiries/goudge/report/v1_en_pdf/Vol_1_Eng_vi.pdf>.

78 Carl Shannon, *Royal Commission Report Concerning the Conviction of Edward Charles Splatt* (Adelaide: Government Printer of South Australia, 1984).

79 Trevor Morling, *Report of the Royal Commission of Inquiry into the Chamberlain Convictions* (Canberra, Commonwealth Government Printer, 1987).

80 Frank H.R. Vincent, *Inquiry into the Circumstances that Led to the Conviction of Mr Farah Abdulkadir Jama: Report* (Victorian Government, 2010), p. 11, <http://netk.net.au/DNA/Jama.pdf>. Compare the Morin controversy: Fred Kaufman, *Report of the Kaufman Commission on Proceedings Involving Guy Paul Morin* (Toronto: Ministry of the Attorney General, 1998); Bibi Sangha, Kent Roach, and Robert Moles, *Forensic Investigations and Miscarriages of Justice: The Rhetoric Meets the Reality* (Toronto: Irwin Law, 2010).

had had sexual contact with Jama. Vincent concluded that the evidence in the circumstances was completely unreliable:

> The DNA evidence appears to have been viewed as possessing an almost mystical infallibility that enabled its surroundings to be disregarded. . . . It became clear that the DNA evidence was perceived as so powerful by all involved in the case that none of the filters upon which our system of criminal justice depends to minimize the risk of a miscarriage of justice operated effectively at any stage until a matter of weeks before Mr Jama's appeal was expected to be heard.

2.41 The report highlighted the many factors, including human error, which can lead to unreliability of scientific evidence and against which both systemic and forensic efforts must guard.

2.42 In 2014 the Full Court of the Supreme Court of the Australian Capital Territory quashed the 1995 conviction of David Eastman for the murder of Assistant Commissioner Winchester of the Australian Federal Police in 1989. It accepted a report from a Commission of Inquiry that concluded that the expert evidence by a gunshot residue expert, Robert Barnes, linking material found in the suspect's car to material found at the crime scene was 'deeply flawed'. The Full Court concluded that:

> Mr Eastman's trial very substantively departed from a trial in accordance with law. The jury were presented . . . with an apparently convincing and largely unchallenged forensic case. The reality was that that case was without any scientific basis, given by a biased and disingenuous witness and inadmissible. It connected Mr Eastman's car directly to the murder scene because of Mr Barnes' false and baseless assertion of the identity of the PMC gunshot residues in both. While, as Martin AJ found . . . , some of the gunshot residues may have been able to provide evidence of a link between the murder scene and Mr Eastman's car, it was a much more tenuous link than the near certainty of a connection that Mr Barnes had asserted. That unchallenged, supposedly 'scientific', evidence by an apparently unbiased expert, also apparently supported by overseas experts, is highly likely to have been very persuasive.

2.43 The Full Court found that the reception of Mr Barnes' evidence, and the evidence of other experts used to support it, created a substantial miscarriage of justice. It ordered a retrial.[81]

E. Facial and Body Mapping Evidence

2.44 An area of science that has particularly challenged the admissibility rules in both the United Kingdom and Australia, and raised the question of whether reliability should expressly be incorporated into them, has been body mapping/gait evidence and facial mapping evidence.[82] Usually such issues have arisen as a result of evidence from CCTV footage[83] which is regarded as inculpatory by criminal investigators and which the prosecution wishes to lead against the accused.

2.45 In *R v Gray*,[84] for instance, the Court of Appeal concluded that in the absence of any database 'any estimate of probabilities and any expression of the degree of support provided by particular facial characteristics or combinations of facial characteristics' constituted subjective opinion without any capacity to determine with objectivity whether it

[81] *Eastman v Director of Public Prosecutions (No 2)* [2014] ACTSCFC 2, (2014) 9 ACTLR 178 [246], [249].

[82] See Tim Valentine and Josh P. Davis, *Forensic Facial Identification: Theory and Practice of Identification from Eyewitnesses, Composites and CCTV* (London: Wiley, 2015).

[83] See generally Thomas Murphy, 'The Admissibility of CCTV Evidence in Criminal Proceedings', *International Journal of Law Computers & Technology* 13, no. 3 (1999) 383–404.

[84] [2003] EWCA 1001. See also *Shepherd v The Queen* [2011] NZCA 666.

was justified.[85] In another controversial decision, though, the Court of Appeal expressed reservations about walking gait analysis evidence from a podiatrist who specialized in pathomechanics and biomechanics but did not overturn the admission of the evidence.[86]

In Australia, in *R v Tang*,[87] the Chief Justice of New South Wales, Spigelman CJ, concluded that the view of a photo-anthropometrist who used morphological analysis failed to go beyond a 'bare *ipse dixit*' (a mere assertion) and that the evidence given by her had not been established to constitute 'specialized knowledge'. Within months the Northern Territory Court of Appeal in *Murdoch v The Queen*[88] overturned a trial decision and concluded that 'face and body mapping' was not a technique which had a 'sufficiently scientific basis to render results arrived at by that means a proper subject of expert evidence'. Four years later, in *Morgan v The Queen*,[89] the New South Wales Court of Criminal Appeal was called upon again to deal with body mapping evidence and concluded that a trial decision to admit such evidence had erred: 'It tended to cloak evidence of similarity in a mantle of expertise, described by Mr Stratton as a "white coat effect",[90] which it did not deserve' by reason of the absence of any data about the proportion of the population which would fit the anatomical description provided by the expert, and ultimately an absence of specialized knowledge in respect of the expert's opinions. **2.46**

In 2014 the Australian High Court provided Australia's most authoritative decision on the subject in *Honeysett v The Queen*.[91] It concluded that the same anatomist whose evidence was the subject of successful challenge in *Morgan* should not have been permitted to express opinions at trial as they were not based on his specialized knowledge of anatomy. It found that his 'evidence gave the unwarranted appearance of science to the prosecution case that the appellant and Offender One share a number of physical characteristics.' Thus his opinion was found not to be based wholly or substantially on his specialized knowledge, as required under the uniform evidence legislation, and the High Court concluded that admitting the evidence was an error of law. **2.47**

F. A Reliability Precondition to Admissibility in Australia

However, the propriety of importation of a reliability yardstick has not yet been finally resolved in Australia.[92] In a battered woman syndrome case, *Osland v The Queen*,[93] Kirby J noted that critics of the syndrome had described it as failing to meet the 'established criteria for "scientific reliability".' In doing so he referred to an author who canvassed the *Daubert* indicia for reliability. However, the decision does not constitute any form of precedent on the subject. **2.48**

An option for Australia is for reliability to be incorporated into the concept of 'specialized knowledge'. Another is that it be enlivened by the operation of the discretion that exists at common law and under s. 137 of the *Evidence Act 1995* (Cth) which enables a trial judge to **2.49**

---

[85] *R v Gray* [2003] EWCA Crim 1001 [16]. Compare *Attorney-General's Reference (No 2 of 2002)* [2002] EWCA Crim 2373, [2003] 1 Cr App R 21; *R v Gardner* [2004] EWCA Crim 1639; *R v Atkins* [2009] EWCA Crim 1876, [2010] 1 Cr App R 8.

[86] *R v Otway* [2011] EWCA Crim 3.

[87] [2006] NSWCCA 167, (2006) 65 NSWLR 681.

[88] [2007] NTCCA 1, (2007) 167 A Crim R 329 [297].

[89] [2011] NSWCCA 257, (2011) 215 A Crim R 33.

[90] *Morgan v The Queen* [2011] NSWCCA 257, (2011) 215 A Crim R 33 [145].

[91] [2014] HCA 29, (2014) 253 CLR 122.

[92] See Gary Edmond, 'Specialised Knowledge, the Exclusionary Discretions and Reliability: Reassessing Incriminating Expert Opinion Evidence', *University of New South Wales Law Journal* 31, no. 1 (2008) 1.

[93] [1998] HCA 75, (1998) 197 CLR 316 [164].

exclude evidence adduced by the prosecution in a criminal proceeding 'if its probative value is outweighed by the danger of unfair prejudice to the defendant.' These have been described as 'incommensurable considerations'.[94]

(1) Specialized knowledge

2.50 In *R v Tang*,[95] as noted above, a case dealing with the admissibility of body mapping evidence, Spigelman CJ held that in the context of 'specialised knowledge', as used in s. 79 of the *Evidence Act 1995* (NSW), 'knowledge' has a connotation that is different to that which it might have in the context of 'common knowledge'.[96] He found that for s. 79 the meaning of 'knowledge' is the same as found by the majority in *Daubert v Merrell Dow Pharmaceuticals*[97]: '[T]he word 'knowledge' connotes more than subjective belief or unsupported speculation. The term applies to any body of known facts or any body of ideas inferred from such facts or accepted as truths on good grounds.' This was in contrast to the view of Gaudron J in *HG v The Queen*,[98] a decision in relation to the admissibility of evidence by a psychologist about the potential for transposition of the identity of a sex offender by a child, and then in *Velevski v The Queen*,[99] a decision in relation to the admissibility of pathology evidence about the likelihood of a death being homicide, where her Honour, citing *R v Bonython*,[100] stated that it imports matters which are outside the knowledge or experience of ordinary persons and 'sufficiently organised or recognised to be accepted as a reliable body of knowledge or experience'.

2.51 In *Tang*[101] the court held that: 'The focus of attention must be on the words "specialised knowledge", not on the introduction of an extraneous idea such as "reliability"'. In *Honeysett v The Queen*[102] this issue was revisited. It was argued on behalf of the appellant that, in order to constitute an area of 'specialised knowledge', 'there must be an independent means of gauging the reliability and validity of an opinion based on that knowledge'. The Court applied the *Daubert* formulation of 'knowledge'[103] but determined (on the basis of concessions) that 'the appeal does not provide the occasion to consider the appellant's larger challenge respecting the requirement of an independent means of validation before an opinion may be found to be based on "specialised knowledge"'.[104]

2.52 In the DNA case of *Tuite v The Queen*[105] the Victorian Court of Appeal affirmed the absence of warrant to read into s. 79(1) a test of evidentiary admissibility. It concluded that the focus of inquiry by a court (usually at *voir dire*) should be upon the expert's 'acquaintance with facts, truths or principles, as from study or investigation', with the witness needing to be shown to have knowledge 'which is outside that of persons who have not by training, study or experience acquired an understanding of the subject matter.'[106] The Victorian court distinguished the *Daubert* analysis on the basis of the terms of Rule 702 of the United States

---

94 *R v Shamouil* [2006] NSWCCA 112, (2006) 66 NSWLR 228 [60].

95 [2006] NSWCCA 167, (2006) 65 NSWLR 681 [137].

96 *R v Tang* [2006] NSWCCA 167, (2006) 65 NSWLR 681 [138].

97 509 US 579, 590 (1993).

98 (1999) 197 CLR 414 [58].

99 (2002) 76 ALJR 402 [82].

100 (1984) 38 SASR 45, 46–7.

101 [2006] NSWCCA 167, (2006) 65 NSWLR 681 [137].

102 [2014] HCA 29, (2014) 253 CLR 122 [38]. See too Gary Edmond and Mehera San Roque, '*Honeysett v The Queen*: Forensic Science, "Specialist Knowledge" and the Uniform Evidence Act', *Sydney Law Review* 36, no. 2 (June 2014) 323.

103 *Honeysett v The Queen* [2014] HCA 29, (2014) 253 CLR 122 [23].

104 [2014] HCA 29, (2014) 253 CLR 122 [42].

105 [2015] VSCA 148 [70].

106 *Tuite v The Queen* [2015] VSCA 148 at [72]–[73].

Federal Rules of Evidence and concluded that s. 79(1) 'does not itself establish "a standard of evidentiary admissibility"'.[107] However, the Victorian Court of Appeal was at pains to emphasise the need for 'rigorous assessment of evidentiary reliability when expert opinion evidence is proposed to be called.... we view this as a matter of the first importance to the integrity and fairness of the criminal justice system.'[108]

Thus the potential for reliability to play a role in determining whether a person possesses 'specialized knowledge' remains, but the balance of authority is now against such an option and the outcome of the decisions in *Honeysett* and *Tuite* is likely to be that on the basis of statutory construction the inquiry as to admissibility of expert opinions under s. 79 will not incorporate considerations of reliability. **2.53**

(2) Prejudice–probative discretion

A number of Australian decisions have leaned against importing *Daubert* reliability considerations into the meaning of either 'probative value' or 'prejudice'. For instance, in *R v Shamouil*[109] Spigelman CJ observed that: 'The preponderant body of authority in this Court is in favour of a restrictive approach to the circumstances in which issues of reliability and credibility are to be taken into account in determining the probative value of evidence for purposes of determining questions of admissibility.' In *Dupas v The Queen*,[110] by contrast, the Victorian Court of Appeal held that the common law required a trial judge in assessing probative value to evaluate the weight that a jury *could* rationally attach to the evidence. **2.54**

In *R v XY*,[111] Basten JA sought a rapprochement between the two lines of authority. He concluded that it was consistent with the decision in *Shamouil*[112] that '... in carrying out the "weighing" exercise, it would be necessary for the trial judge to consider where the prosecution evidence fell on a scale of probative value ranging from strong to weak. Secondly, the unreliability of the evidence was a factor to be weighed on the other side of the scale, together with the likely effectiveness of warnings about the nature of such unreliability.' In the same decision, though, Simpson JA was concerned to emphasize that determination of the weight to be given to any item of evidence will depend not only on where the evidence fits in the overall mosaic of the evidence at the trial 'but, in many cases, upon an assessment of a witness after cross-examination. It may also depend upon an assessment of the evidence of one witness against the evidence of another (or others). That is not something that can readily be undertaken at a pre-trial or interlocutory stage.'[113] This led her to disagree with the proposition that assessment of the weight that could be given to evidence could play a role in determining its probative value: 'To embark upon a partial assessment of weight could, in my opinion, be potentially productive of real injustice. No boundaries with respect to the extent to which the weight of the evidence is to be explored are discernible in any of the provisions that call for evaluation of probative value.'[114] **2.55**

The Victorian Court of Appeal in *Tuite* applied the *Dupas* approach and expressed the view that 'the touchstone of reliability for scientific evidence must be trustworthiness, and trustworthiness depends on validation'.[115] In the DNA testing context, it concluded that the focus **2.56**

107 *Tuite v The Queen* [2015] VSCA 148 [75].
108 *Tuite v The Queen* [2015] VSCA 148 [82].
109 [2006] NSWCCA 112, (2006) 66 NSWLR 228 [60].
110 (2012) 40 VR 182, [2012] VSCA 328.
111 [2013] NSWCCA 121, (2013) 84 NSWLR 363 [48].
112 [2006] NSWCCA 112, (2006) 66 NSWLR 228 [71] (Spigelman CJ).
113 *R v XY* [2013] NSWCCA 121, (2013) 84 NSWLR 363 [170].
114 *R v XY* [2013] NSWCCA 121, (2013) 84 NSWLR 363 [171].
115 [2015] VSCA 148 [101]. See also *Meade v The Queen* [2015] VSCA 171.

of attention for the purposes of assessing the reliability of scientific evidence should be on proof of validation: 'ideally, there should be proof of both in-house validation and independent external validation.'[116] It concluded that special care should be taken where proposed expert evidence is based on 'new science'. It applied the Supreme Court of Canada approach in *Trochym* and concluded that in such a case the party proposing to rely on the expert evidence will need to establish that 'the underlying science is "sufficiently reliable to be admitted in a court of law".'[117] The Court of Appeal called for the establishment of an entity equivalent to the United Kingdom's Forensic Science Regulator and Forensic Science Advisory Council to 'provide independent, expert assessments of the reliability of particular scientific theories and techniques, which would in turn greatly assist the Court in determining the reliability of evidence to be given by a particular expert.'[118] The Court observed that guidance could be gained from the draft bill promulgated by the Law Commission of England and Wales and the Practice Direction subsequently formulated. The Court observed that: 'Consideration could be given to the development of a further practice note [in Victoria] to assist trial judges in assessing evidentiary admissibility'.[119]

2.57 Thus it can be seen that in a series of Australian decisions the issue of the reliability of evidence has arisen in ways which have impacted upon whether expert opinions have been found on appeal to have been admitted in criminal trials correctly. At present there is the potential for reliability considerations to be incorporated into the notion of specialized knowledge, although the *Honeysett*, *Tuite* and *Meade* decisions have suggested otherwise. The potential for reliability to be a consideration which is incorporated within assessment of 'probative value' remains, although there is a difference of approach on the issue between the New South Wales and Victorian Courts of Appeal, which will need to be resolved authoritatively by the High Court.

G. International Perspectives on Reliability as an Admissibility Criterion

2.58 Many measures can be postulated to determine whether expert opinion evidence is admissible. The issue has been internationally controversial for at least two decades, with a momentum building for incorporation of reliability considerations to determine when and how expert evidence should be admissible.

(1) The United States

2.59 The best-known reform in this regard is the 1993 United States Supreme Court decision of *Daubert v Merrell Dow Pharmaceuticals Inc*,[120] where the Court overturned previous authority that focussed upon whether a theory or technique had gained general acceptance within the relevant scientific community[121] and ruled that the principal consideration for admissibility of scientific evidence (under the Federal Rules of Evidence) is reliability. The Court identified four indicia of reliability:

(1) whether it can be or has been tested—the Court cited Popper, 'The criterion of the scientific status of a theory is its falsifiability, or refutability, or testability';

---

116 *Tuite v The Queen* [2015] VSCA 148 [102].
117 *Tuite v The Queen* [2015] VSCA 148 [106].
118 *Tuite v The Queen* [2015] VSCA 148 [109].
119 *Tuite v The Queen* [2015] VSCA 148 [114].
120 509 US 579 (1993).
121 *Frye v United States*, 293 F 1013 (DC Cir, 1923) in respect of a precursor to the polygraph.

(2) whether the theory or technique has been subjected to peer review and publication as a means of increasing the likelihood that substantive flaws in methodology will be detected;
(3) the known or potential rate of error and the existence and maintenance of standards controlling the technique's operation; and
(4) whether a technique has gained general acceptance within the scientific community.

The first and third of these indicia relate to whether the methodology and attributes of the technique are accurate, while the second and fourth address how the relevant communities have received the processes.[122] In subsequent decisions, the Supreme Court consolidated this approach.[123] However, the impact of the reformist position of the Supreme Court is far from clear. It has spawned an extensive literature[124] which has canvassed the relative importance of each of the indicia, the extent to which judges understand and apply the indicia, the potential application of the indicia to different forms of expert evidence, and the implications for the admissibility and perceptions of legitimacy of such forms of expert endeavour.[125] There has been some empirical analysis of the impact of *Daubert*, although much of it has focussed upon appellate decisions. **2.60**

On the basis of a review of the first 15 years of application of the *Daubert* indicia Dwyer[126] has argued that civil expert evidence has tended in the aftermath of *Daubert* to be more heavily scrutinized by the courts in admissibility rulings than by criminal courts but that criminal prosecutors (and civil defendants) seeking to adduce expert opinion evidence have been treated more favourably than criminal defendants (and civil plaintiffs).[127] **2.61**

However, in an important survey of 400 state trial judges 48% (n = 191) respondents were found to believe that their education had left them inadequately prepared to make *Daubert* admissibility decisions.[128] About a third (32%, n = 126) stated that they believed that the intent of *Daubert* was to raise the threshold for admissibility of evidence, whereas 23% (n = 90) had the opposite view. A little over a third (36%, n = 142) believed the intent of the Supreme Court was neither to raise nor lower the threshold but to articulate a framework for admissibility and to give judges a discretion to apply the guidelines as appropriate. Just over a half of the judges answering (55%, n = 220) reported that *Daubert* had a 'great deal' of value. Overwhelmingly (91%, n = 364), they stated that they thought the role of gatekeeper in respect of such matters was appropriate for judges, and almost two thirds (62%, n = 249) reported taking an 'active role' in the admissibility process. Just over a half of the judges **2.62**

[122] Deidre Dwyer, '(Why) are Civil and Criminal Expert Evidence Different?', *Tulsa Law Review* 43, no. 2 (Winter 2007) 381.

[123] *General Electric Co v Joiner*, 522 US 136 (1997); *Kumho Tire Company v Carmichael*, 526 US 137 (1999).

[124] For a useful early analysis see Edward J. Imwinkelried, 'The Next Step After *Daubert*: Developing a Similarly Epistemological Approach to Ensuring the Reliability of Nonscientific Expert Testimony', *Cardozo Law Review* 15, no. 6 (April 1994) 2271.

[125] See e.g. Stephen Odgers and James T. Richardson, 'Keeping Bad Science Out of the Courtroom: Changes in Australian and American Expert Evidence Law', *University of New South Wales Law Review* 18, no. 1 (1995) 108; Michael J. Saks, 'The Aftermath of *Daubert*: An Evolving Jurisprudence of Expert Evidence', *Jurimetrics* 40, no. 2 (Winter 2000) 229; Christopher Slobogin, 'The Admissibility of Behavioral Science Information in Criminal Trials: From Primitivism to *Daubert* to Voice', *Psychology, Public Policy and Law* 5, no. 1 (1999) 100; Liz Heffernan, 'Gauging the Reliability of Scientific Evidence in Tort', *Judicial Studies Institute Journal* 6, no. 1 (2006) 140.

[126] Deidre Dwyer, '(Why) are Civil and Criminal Expert Evidence Different?', 381.

[127] See also D. Michael Risinger, 'Navigating Expert Reliability: Are Criminal Standards of Certainty Being Left in the Dock?', *Alberta Law Review* 64, no. 1 (2000) 99.

[128] Sophia I. Gatowski, Shirley A. Dobbin, James T. Richardson, Gerald P. Ginsburg, Mara L. Merlino, and Veronica Dahir, 'Asking the Gatekeepers: A National Survey of Judges on Judging Expert Evidence in a Post-*Daubert* World', *Law and Human Behavior* 25, no. 5 (2001) 433.

responding from *Daubert* states (52%, n = 206) indicated that they thought that their judicial role had changed as a result of *Daubert*, most of them saying that their role had become more active.

2.63 A very strong majority of judges surveyed (88%, n = 352) believed that falsifiability was a useful guideline for determining the merits of proffered scientific evidence. A similar percentage thought that consideration of error rate was useful (91%, n = 364), that peer review was useful (92%, n = 368), and that general acceptance was useful (93%, n = 371), with 64% of the latter group (n = 254) regarding it to be 'very useful'. Amongst the *Daubert* indicia, general acceptance tended to be given the greatest weight. There was significant disagreement amongst judges responding to the survey about the distinction between 'science' and technical areas. An example in this regard was that 64% of judges (n = 156) designated psychological evidence derived from laboratory studies to be 'science', whereas 31% (n = 75) regarded it as 'technical or otherwise specialized knowledge'.[129]

2.64 The authors noted that: 'When judges were asked to what extent, if any, and under what circumstances they would weight and combine the four guidelines, there was little consensus. Although most judges agreed that a distinction could be made between "scientific" and "technical or otherwise specialized" knowledge, their ability to apply the *Daubert* guidelines seemed to have little bearing on whether specific types of expert evidence were designated as "science" or "nonscience."'[130] What emerges from this analysis is that the *Daubert* introduction of criteria to enable judges to act as gatekeepers in respect of unreliable evidence has posed complex challenges for United States trial judges—it cannot readily be said that the fundamental reform to the law made in *Daubert* has necessarily achieved the objective of facilitating informed exclusion of unreliable evidence, especially in criminal trials where it is the prosecution that seeks to adduce the evidence; the *Daubert* reform is not a panacea.

(2) Canada

2.65 In Canada, the Supreme Court, by increments, has taken a similar approach to that of the United States Supreme Court. In *R v Mohan*[131] Sopinka J emphasized in respect of expert evidence that there is a risk that it may be accorded unjustified deference. He held that in the exercising of discretion to exclude evidence, reliability is important: 'The reliability versus effect factor has special significance in assessing the admissibility of expert evidence.' This led him to the conclusion that:

> In summary, therefore, it appears from the foregoing that expert evidence which advances a novel scientific theory or technique is subjected to special scrutiny to determine whether it meets a basic threshold of reliability and whether it is essential in the sense that the trier of fact will be unable to come to a satisfactory conclusion without the assistance of the expert.[132]

2.66 Building on this concern, in 2000 the Court embraced a reliability test for the reception of expert evidence in a case relating to the use of the penile plethysmograph, *R v J-LJ*,[133] observing that in *Daubert* the United States had listed 'a number of factors that could be helpful in evaluating the soundness of novel science'[134] and holding that the criteria for reception of

[129] See Jane Goodman-Delahunty, 'Forensic Psychological Expertise in the Wake of Daubert', *Law and Human Behavior* 21, no. 2 (1997) 121.
[130] Goodman-Delahunty, 'Forensic Psychological Expertise in the Wake of Daubert', 453.
[131] [1994] 2 SCR 9, 21.
[132] *R v Mohan* [1994] 2 SCR 9, 25.
[133] [2000] 2 SCR 600.
[134] [2000] 2 SCR 600 [33].

such evidence are 'relevance, reliability and necessity measured against the counterweights of consumption of time, prejudice and confusion.'[135]

In *R v Trochym*,[136] a case dealing with the status of post-hypnosis evidence, the majority was clearer in relation to the role of reliability. Deschamps J (McLachlin CJ, and Binnie, LeBel, and Fish JJ concurring) explicitly utilized the *Daubert* indicia and emphasized that 'a judge should, in exercising his or her role as "gatekeeper", carefully scrutinize the admissibility of novel scientific evidence'.[137] **2.67**

(3) India

There are significant indications that the essence of the *Daubert* approach will be applied to the reception of expert evidence in India. For instance, in *Chaudhary v CBI*,[138] a case dealing with the admissibility of expert evidence about the recreation of documentation after an explosion, Nandrajog J on appeal observed 'expert evidence can be both powerful and at the same time quite misleading because of the difficulty in evaluating it.'[139] He found that, although in many countries rules have been enacted concerning the admissibility of expert evidence, 'the basic principles laid down' in the Frye test (general acceptance within the relevant scientific community) 'continue to apply because of the inherent strength of logic' in its principles.[140] Having reviewed the indicia of *Daubert*, he concluded that: 'It is apparent to every logical mind that the key to determine whether a theory or technique is scientific knowledge which will assist the trier of fact is whether the theory or technique can be and has been tested.'[141] **2.68**

(4) New Zealand

In New Zealand there have been a number of indications of preparedness to follow the approach of the United States in *Daubert*.[142] The foundation for this was laid in 1999. In its report that formed the basis for the 2006 Act, the New Zealand Law Commission observed that the *Daubert* factors would '... continue to be important in the inquiry about reliability that is inherent in the substantial helpfulness test. As the Court in *Daubert* emphasized, "The focus... must be solely on principles and methodology, not on the conclusions that they generate"'.[143] The Court of Appeal has suggested that s. 25 of the Evidence Act 2006 (NZ) is an amalgam of three filters: relevance, reliability, and probative value.[144] **2.69**

In 2014, in *R v Lundy*,[145] Los J went further and proffered the following 'tentative list of general principles regarding the receipt of scientific opinion evidence': **2.70**

(a) Relevance, relative probativeness versus unfair prejudice, and substantial helpfulness under s 25, are distinct filters that should each be applied to any scientific opinion evidence, as is the case for all expert opinion evidence.

---

135 [2000] 2 SCR 600 [47].
136 [2007] 1 SCR 239.
137 *R v Trochym* [2007] 1 SCR 239 [54].
138 (High Court of Delhi, 15 May 2009).
139 (High Court of Delhi, 15 May 2009) [125].
140 *Chaudhary v CBI* (High Court of Delhi, 15 May 2009) [126].
141 *Chaudhary v CBI* (High Court of Delhi, 15 May 2009) [131].
142 See *R v Calder* (High Court of New Zealand, 12 April 1995) (Tipping J); *R v Brown* (High Court of New Zealand, 19 September 1997).
143 New Zealand Law Commission, *Evidence: Report No. 55*, vol. 2 (Wellington, NZ: Law Commission, 1999), C100.
144 *Mahomed v The Queen* [2010] NZCA 419 [35], not varied on appeal: [2011] NZSC 52, [2011] 3 NZLR 145. See Richard Mahoney, Elisabeth McDonald, Scott Optican, and Yvette Tinsley, *The Evidence Act 2006: Act & Analysis*, 3rd edn. (Wellington, NZ: Brookers, 2014).
145 [2014] NZHC 2527 [55].

(b) It follows that scientific opinion evidence may be excluded where the scientific technique: (1) cannot yet be said to be reliable (that is to say, its reliability has not been demonstrated to the Court's satisfaction so as to be of substantial help to the jury); (2) is reliable, but the witness is not expert in its application; (3) is reliable, but the evidence is not relevant, because it does not tend to prove or disprove any fact in issue; (4) is reliable, and the evidence is relevant, but it does not provide the fact finder with substantial help (perhaps because of flaws in performance of the technique, or in the inferences and conclusions drawn from it); and (5) is reliable, and the evidence is relevant, but its admission would be unfairly prejudicial to the defendant.

(c) The novelty of a scientific technique is not a per se basis for exclusion. Novel scientific evidence can be received by the Courts in both criminal and civil trials (and often is)...

(d) Rather, where a scientific technique appears novel, the Court must take particular care to be satisfied that that evidence, if relevant and not unduly prejudicial, has a 'sufficient claim to reliability' to be put to the jury.

(e) In considering whether scientific evidence has a 'sufficient claim to reliability', the 'Daubert factors' are relevant, particularly in the evaluation of novel scientific techniques. They include: (1) whether the theory or technique can be or has been tested and, if false, disproved; (2) whether the technique has been subjected to peer review and/or publication; (3) the known or potential error rate, or the existence of standards; and (4) whether the technique has been generally accepted. The Daubert factors are not, however, a closed list. Nor are they a test, where failure to meet one of the factors identified is fatal to admission.

(f) In deciding whether particular scientific evidence has a 'sufficient claim to reliability' to be put to the jury, it is important to bear in mind the role of the jury.... it is not there to arbitrate scientific disputes, but it is there to decide whether the Crown has proved each essential element of a charge beyond reasonable doubt. Where a particular fact alleged is crucial to establish the charge, that fact (perhaps expressed as a scientific proposition) may have to be proved beyond reasonable doubt. Otherwise it does not.

(g) 'Substantial helpfulness', for the purposes of s 25, may entail wider considerations than simply whether the scientific technique has a 'sufficient claim to reliability'. The ability of a jury to process information which is both uncertain and highly complex, in the whole context of the case, will need to be borne in mind. The nature of the evidential contest will be important.

2.71 Although New Zealand's Court of Appeal and Supreme Court are yet to rule authoritatively on the issue, impetus appears to be growing for resort to reliability as a criterion for admissibility of expert evidence and for incorporation of *Daubert* considerations to enable such decision-making by trial judges.

(5) England and Wales

2.72 In 2011 in England and Wales a proposal for fundamental reform to the criteria for admissibility of expert evidence was advanced by the Law Commission.[146] The Commission was responding to the recommendation of the House of Commons' Science and Technology Committee report on *Forensic Science on Trial*[147] that a new test should be developed for determining the admissibility of expert evidence in criminal proceedings. The Committee's

[146] Law Commission of England and Wales, *Expert Evidence in Criminal Proceedings in England and Wales: Report No. 325* (London: The Stationery Office, 2011), <http://www.lawcom.gov.uk/project/expert-evidence-in-criminal-proceedings/#expert-evidence-in-criminal-proceedings>.

[147] House of Commons Science and Technology Committee, *Forensic Science on Trial: Seventh Report of Session 2004–05* (London: The Stationery Office, 2005), p.76, <http://www.publications.parliament.uk/pa/cm200405/cmselect/cmsctech/96/96i.pdf>.

report also observed that: 'Jury research is vital to understand how juries cope with highly complex forensic evidence. Jury research would also be instructive for understanding differences in the way that jurors respond to oral and written reports by experts, and how easy they find interpretation of these reports.'[148]

2.73 The Law Commission recommended a statutory admissibility test which would provide that an expert's opinion is admissible in criminal proceedings only if it is sufficiently reliable to be admitted ('the reliability test'); namely if the opinion is soundly based and the strength of the opinion is warranted, having regard to the grounds on which it is based. The Commission proposed that there should be the following reasons why an expert's opinion is not sufficiently reliable to be admitted:

(a) the opinion is based on a hypothesis which has not been subjected to sufficient scrutiny (including, where appropriate, experimental or other testing), or which has failed to stand up to scrutiny;
(b) the opinion is based on an unjustifiable assumption;
(c) the opinion is based on flawed data;
(d) the opinion relies on an examination, technique, method, or process which was not properly carried out or applied or was not appropriate for use in the particular case;
(e) the opinion relies on an inference or conclusion which has not been properly reached.

2.74 However, in November 2013, for purportedly pragmatic reasons, the government declined to support the Law Commission's recommendations:

> The Government shares the Law Commission's concern about problems caused by the use of inappropriate or unreliable expert evidence, and is persuaded of the benefits of taking action on this. It recognises the potential value of the proposed reliability test in reducing the risk of unsafe convictions arising from unreliable expert evidence. However, there is no robust estimate of the size of the problem to be tackled—either in terms of the number of cases where unreliable expert evidence is adduced, nor in the impact this has in terms of subsequently quashed convictions. The impact assessment published with the Law Commission's recommendations indicates that application of the new test would involve additional pre-trial hearings, with the concomitant additional costs, but without sufficient reliably predictable savings to compensate for those costs. Without certainty as to the offsetting savings which might be achieved, when set against current resource constraints it is not feasible to implement the proposals in full at this time.[149]

2.75 Rather than creating a statutory reliability test, taking into account the fact that guidance for expert witnesses was available from a variety of sources,[150] the government invited the Criminal Procedure Rule Committee to consider amending the Criminal Procedure Rules to ensure that judges were provided, at the initial stage, with more information

[148] Law Commission of England and Wales, *Expert Evidence in Criminal Proceedings in England and Wales: Report No. 325*, p. 88, <http://www.lawcom.gov.uk/project/expert-evidence-in-criminal-proceedings/#expert-evidence-in-criminal-proceedings>.

[149] Ministry of Justice. *The Government's Response to the Law Commission's Report: Expert Evidence in Criminal Proceedings in England and Wales*, (Law Com No. 325, 21 November 2013), p. 4, <https://www.gov.uk/government/uploads/system/uploads/attachment_data/file/260369/govt-resp-experts-evidence.pdf>.

[150] See Crown Prosecution Service, *Guidance Booklet for Experts* (May 2010), <http://www.cps.gov.uk/legal/assets/uploads/files/Guidance_for_Experts_-_2010_edition.pdf>; Forensic Science Regulator, *Codes of Practice and Conduct: For Forensic Science Providers and Practitioners in the Criminal Justice System* (2014), <https://www.gov.uk/government/uploads/system/uploads/attachment_data/file/351197/The_FSR_Codes_of_Practice_and_Conduct_-_v2_August_2014.pdf>; General Medical Council, *Acting as a Witness in Legal Proceedings* (2013), <http://www.gmc-uk.org/guidance/ethical_guidance/21188.asp>; and Health and Safety Executive, 'Expert Evidence', in *HSE Enforcement Guide (England & Wales)* (2003), <http://www.hse.gov.uk/enforce/enforcementguide/investigation/expert-intro.htm>.

about proposed expert evidence. Thus, statutory evidence law reform to introduce reliability as a criterion or determinant for expert evidence admissibility appears unlikely in the short term. However, an important change was incorporated into Part 33 of the Criminal Procedure Rules, which came into force on 14 October 2014. Rule 33.4(h) now provides that an expert's report must 'include such information as the court may need to decide whether the expert's opinion is sufficiently reliable to be admissible as evidence.' Practice Direction 33A.4 referred to the Court of Appeal's reasoning in *R v Dlugosz*[151] and commented that: 'Nothing at common law precludes assessment by the court of the reliability of an expert opinion by reference to substantially similar factors to those the Law Commission recommended as conditions of admissibility, and courts are encouraged actively to enquire into such factors.'

2.76 Practice Direction 33A.5 provides that the factors which a court dealing with a criminal matter may take into account in determining the reliability of expert opinion, and especially of expert scientific opinion, include:

(a) the extent and quality of the data on which the expert's opinion is based, and the validity of the methods by which they were obtained;
(b) if the expert's opinion relies on an inference from any findings, whether the opinion properly explains how safe or unsafe the inference is (whether by reference to statistical significance or in other appropriate terms);
(c) if the expert's opinion relies on the results of the use of any method (for instance, a test, measurement, or survey), whether the opinion takes proper account of matters, such as the degree of precision or margin of uncertainty, affecting the accuracy or reliability of those results;
(d) the extent to which any material upon which the expert's opinion is based has been reviewed by others with relevant expertise (for instance, in peer-reviewed publications), and the views of those others on that material;
(e) the extent to which the expert's opinion is based on material falling outside the expert's own field of expertise;
(f) the completeness of the information which was available to the expert, and whether the expert took account of all relevant information in arriving at the opinion (including information as to the context of any facts to which the opinion relates);
(g) whether there is a range of expert opinion on the matter in question, where in the range the expert's opinion lies and whether the expert's preference has been properly explained; and
(h) whether the expert's methods followed established practice in the field, and, if they did not, whether the reason for the divergence has been properly explained.

2.77 In addition, Direction 33A.6 provides that in considering reliability, and especially the reliability of expert opinion:

the court should be astute to identify potential flaws in such opinion which detract from its reliability, such as:
(a) being based on a hypothesis which has not been subjected to sufficient scrutiny (including, where appropriate, experimental or other testing), or which has failed to stand up to scrutiny;
(b) being based on an unjustifiable assumption;
(c) being based on flawed data;
(d) relying on an examination, technique, method, or process which was not properly carried out or applied, or was not appropriate for use in the particular case; or
(e) relying on an inference or conclusion which has not been properly reached.

[151] [2013] EWCA Crim 2, [2013] 1 Cr App R 32 [13].

Thus, although the Criminal Procedure Rules and the Criminal Practice Directions are not wholly statutory, they incorporate the essence of the Law Commission's recommendations and mean that England and Wales have as part of their criminal law a significant and broad-based focus on reliability as a precondition to the admissibility of expert evidence. **2.78**

H. Admissibility Challenges

In Australian criminal trials the admissibility of expert evidence is generally determined during a preliminary hearing at trial—the voir dire.[152] This occurs in the absence of the jury. During the project we explored whether the voir dire process was being used effectively in decisions about whether to admit expert evidence. Thirteen judges (35.1%, n = 37) said they had used a voir dire to determine the admissibility in the trial about which they were asked, 23 said that they had not done so (62.2%, n = 38), and one judge said they could not recall. **2.79**

It was apparent that there were two potential focuses of a voir dire: to determine (1) whether the witness was the possessor of specialized knowledge—whether he or she possessed the requisite expertise; and (2) whether the area in respect of which the witness proposed to give evidence was a suitable subject for expert evidence—whether it constituted a form of specialized knowledge. **2.80**

The trial judges in three trials reported they did not hold a voir dire to test whether the particular expert had sufficient expertise in the area about which their opinion evidence was proffered. In one of the three trials, the trial judge prompted opposing counsel as to whether the evidence was going to be challenged as inadmissible, but the barrister opted not to challenge the admissibility of the evidence. One judge commented that it was her practice always to remind experts if they gave evidence after a voir dire, this time in front of the jury, not to say 'as I told you before'. **2.81**

In Australian jurisdictions, defence counsel are generally given clear notice of the expert evidence to be called by the prosecution prior to the committal hearing, if one takes place. However, if for some reason this does not occur, for instance because an expert report is obtained shortly before the trial, a '*Basha* hearing'[153] can be conducted; this essentially enables the deficit of a witness not having been called at committal to be redressed by a comparable cross-examination to be undertaken prior to the criminal trial proper, before a jury has been empanelled. The determination of an application to grant a *Basha* hearing has been held to 'depend on the interests of justice and whether a fair trial to both parties may be achieved. Relevant to that is whether an application was made to cross-examine at the committal and if there was, an examination of the Magistrate's reasons and whether the reasons were adequate or appropriate in the circumstances.'[154] **2.82**

In one trial in the study, the prosecution proposed to call an expert who had not been called at the committal. The trial judge explained that because the expert 'hadn't given evidence at the committal hearing and therefore the barristers wanted to hear what the expert was saying, even though they knew what the expert was going to say because they had a report, they still wanted to be able to do a test run'. In another trial a form of *Basha* hearing was held on the **2.83**

[152] See Judicial College of Victoria, *Victorian Criminal Proceedings Manual* (Melbourne: Judicial College of Victoria, 2014), ch. 17.1, <http://www.judicialcollege.vic.edu.au/eManuals/VCPM/index.htm#27318.htm>; Kerry Stephens, *Voir Dire Law: Determining the Admissibility of Disputed Evidence* (Melbourne: Criminal Law Publications, 1997).

[153] *R v Basha* (1989) 39 A Crim R 337.

[154] *R v Stacey* [2014] QDC 299 [17].

basis that the report of an expert to be called by the prosecution which had been provided to the defence lacked material upon which the prosecution proposed to rely. In a further trial, a similar approach was taken, as a number of important matters relating to the operation of repressed memory had not been addressed adequately at committal, so a *Basha* hearing was convened to enable that evidence to be scrutinized. The trial judge commented that this was useful because it emerged that the evidence was shown not to be strictly 'repressed memory' evidence as the complainant's memories had never left: 'she was referring to something that she had always remembered, that she had simply pushed to the back of her life as she went about her life, but she had never forgotten it.' By clarifying this, a point of significant and potentially confusing disputation was avoided.

2.84 The energy invested in the voir dire varied, depending on the exigencies of the trial and the forensic tactics employed—generally by the defence. In one case the trial judge observed that although attacks were made on an expert witness's expertise throughout the trial, the opinion evidence was permitted to be adduced almost without object at the voir dire. This is likely to have been for strategic reasons. The decision itself whether to convene a voir dire is discretionary. A trial judge commented that in a case before him it came to his attention that the prosecution was not proposing to lead evidence in respect of a diagnosis. Rather than have a voir dire, the judge 'weighed in' on the issue after submissions, and concluded that the best approach was to extend some leeway and leave the issues to be ventilated before the jury.

2.85 In another case, a voir dire was convened because of complaints on behalf of the accused that the report of the prosecution expert was not sufficiently detailed to enable the defence to commission their own expert to meet the prosecution case.

2.86 In a case where the expert seemed to be changing their evidence from what they had said at committal, a trial judge convened a voir dire not to determine the admissibility of the evidence, but so that the defence was enabled to know what it was that the prosecution expert was going to say before the jury. Thus, what took place was a form of *Basha* hearing.

2.87 However, in another case, which involved proposed evidence by a forensic anthropologist and anatomist, the evidence was excluded after an energetically contested voir dire on the basis that it was not the product of specialized knowledge—the expert was providing the jury with information that they could garner themselves from a photograph.

2.88 In a trial where the prosecution depended heavily on scientific evidence, defence counsel challenged the DNA expert called for the prosecution on voir dire on the basis that the expert was not sufficiently qualified, and that the tests conducted by the expert were not sufficiently reliable. Despite this, the evidence was ruled by the trial judge to be admissible. Whilst the expert opinion evidence was permitted, the trial judge (in a subsequent interview as part of the study) did express concern over the convoluted nature of the evidence that the DNA expert gave during the voir dire:

> The DNA evidence...I found that very difficult to follow. The witness—we'd had him on a voir dire just before the jury was empanelled—and I found it pretty hard to follow the technical nature of it then. And then, when he presented it to the jury, quite a bit of it was—he was reading it, and reading it fairly fast, and I had to tell him to slow down...I said: 'Hold on, we're all trying to absorb this', and then the prosecutor said: 'Look, I'm having trouble understanding what you're saying, I don't quite understand this.' And I was having trouble—and I know a little bit about DNA, I've had cases before with it—so I thought 'Well if I'm having those problems, what about the jury?'.

The voir dire procedure was utilized creatively by defence counsel in another trial in order to clarify an ambiguous aspect of the prosecution expert's report. The trial judge said that while there was a voir dire: 2.89

> It was in part to explore whether there was going to be a challenge to the admissibility of all or any of the prosecution expert's evidence, but ultimately, after the voir dire, defence counsel said that they'd made a forensic decision and they didn't have a basis for challenging the admissibility. They were entitled to have that voir dire because their expert's report had raised some issues that needed to be explored, and if they'd got a particular set of answers it may well have led to a proper challenge to the admissibility of some of the evidence.

Defence counsel cross-examined the prosecution expert using information from their own expert. Based on the responses to this cross-examination during voir dire, those representing the defendant were able to satisfy themselves that they did not need to call their own expert at the trial as the information that they needed could be provided by the prosecution expert. 2.90

In a trial in which DNA evidence figured prominently, it was contended at voir dire on behalf of the defendant that the tests conducted were not sufficiently reliable. However, the trial judge stayed away from the controversies in respect of the prejudice–probative discretion and the meaning of 'specialized knowledge', ruling the evidence to be admissible: 'I ruled that it was a matter for the jury to determine. Because normally if it's reliability, unless it's...very unreliable, it's really a matter for the jury; it's not for me.' 2.91

I. Conclusions

The terminology of 'reliability' is diversely used to include reference to the credibility of expert witnesses, the probative value of their opinions, and increasingly often the admissibility of their evidence. Reliability has become significant for the admissibility of expert evidence in criminal trials in many common law countries. In Australia the situation is unclear; some resolution has been achieved in that, if reliability is to play any role in the application of the prejudice–probative exclusionary discretion, it is very limited. However, it may well be held to have a significant part to play in the threshold determination of whether knowledge is 'specialized' in the sense of that word as prescribed by the United States Supreme Court in *Daubert v Merrell Dow Pharmaceuticals*. The *Daubert* decision has been utilized in Australia in respect of the meaning of 'knowledge' and applied in Canada and New Zealand on multiple occasions, apparently exercising increasing sway in admissibility determinations. The notion of reliability, heavily influenced by the *Daubert* decision, has been incorporated into the Criminal Procedure Rules and the Criminal Practice Directions in England and Wales, with the consequence that as of 2014 there has been a multi-faceted inquiry into the status of expert opinion evidence by reference to reliability. 2.92

What can be said internationally is that the notion of the reliability of expert evidence is increasingly being regarded as fundamental to whether expert evidence should be permitted to go before jurors. This arises from a concern that jurors may be confused, misled, or deceived by evidence which is unreliable if cross-examination processes do not effectively expose the deficiencies in such evidence. As will be seen in chapter 8, jurors generally expect to trust opinion evidence that is given by experts from many disciplines. These expectations also lead to more positive credibility assessments about specific experts from whom they hear. Taking these factors into account, the possibility that jurors may be misled by expert evidence with a scientifically untested basis is very real and there needs to be more focus on evidence reliability, either at the stage when decisions are made about admissibility or in educating jurors about how they should evaluate expert evidence. 2.93

2.94 Pressures have built to incorporate aspects of the concept of reliability into the threshold decision-making about expert evidence. Australia is now unusual in the common law world in not utilizing indicia of reliability as a threshold to admissibility. The United States, Canada, England and Wales, New Zealand, and even India have embarked on the 'reliability road'. However, there remains a need to reflect on the suitability/capacity of trial criminal courts to discriminate between reliable and unreliable expert evidence and whether the *Daubert* indicia are the best way to achieve such an objective. Australia is well positioned to evaluate the outcome of the Criminal Practice Rules and Criminal Practice Directions of England and Wales in terms of assessing whether they are achieving their stated objectives, and can thus decide whether to emulate such reforms or take a different course, either by similar means, or by statute or common law.

2.95 In most criminal cases fundamental issues about the reliability of expert evidence do not arise. The evidence from our project suggested that orthodox *Basha* hearings and voir dire hearings play a constructive and effective role in identifying cases where unfairness may be wrought by inadequately disclosed, unclear, or ambiguous expert evidence, or where questions arise as to the expertise of a person offered as an expert, especially by the prosecution. The question in terms of principle is whether the problems demonstrated by the two decades of case law in reception of expert opinions of dubious scientific legitimacy (such as lip-reading evidence, body and facial mapping evidence from CCTV images, and non-statistically based analysis of likelihood of match between crime scenes and suspects' samples) need to be addressed by incorporation of a reliability prerequisite, and if so how such a prerequisite can best be formulated and then implemented.

3

ALTERNATIVE MODES OF PRESENTATION OF EXPERT EVIDENCE

A. Introduction

In the 1999 judicial survey undertaken as part of an earlier phase of this project, Australian judges expressed significant levels of concern about what they identified as the problematic consequences of the adversary system upon the reliability of expert evidence adduced in their courts. Their concerns embraced criminal, civil, and family law litigation.[1] They were asked about the utility of a number of procedures to adduce expert evidence outside the orthodox, adversarial mode. These included the use of court-appointed experts, assessors, and referees. Since that survey, other modes of presenting expert evidence, particularly in the civil and family courts, have been emerging. These include the use of pre-trial conclaves/ joint conferences, concurrent evidence, consecutive evidence, and the provision of expert evidence by videolink. Whilst these alternative modes of presenting expert evidence are yet to be common features of criminal jury trials in Australia, videolink in particular is gaining in frequency of use. **3.01**

In this chapter we review the various alternative modes of presenting expert evidence in criminal jury trials. We draw upon the examples of the use of such alternative modes in the 55 trials we analysed and we present the views of the stakeholders as to the suitability of such alternative processes to the criminal context. **3.02**

This chapter reviews the interview responses received within the current project about innovative options for adducing expert evidence in Australian criminal trials and considers the advantages and disadvantages of, and potential for, such modes of expert evidence being utilized before jurors in criminal trials. **3.03**

[1] Ian Freckelton, Prasuna Reddy, and Hugh Selby, *Australian Judicial Perspectives on Expert Evidence: An Empirical Study* (Melbourne: AIJA, 1999).

B. Comprehension Difficulties and Opposing Expert Evidence

3.04 A difficulty for jurors in understanding and evaluating evidence arises through its fragmented nature when the usual order for witnesses is adhered to—namely, that lay witnesses for the prosecution give evidence, followed by its police witnesses, and then expert witnesses for the prosecution. After them, the usual procedure is for lay witnesses and expert witnesses for the defence to be called. The lapse of time between the evidence by the two sets of expert witnesses can be significant in a complex trial, which may consume weeks or months. In our study, eleven of the trials lasted a month or longer, with the longest trial lasting 19 weeks. Nine of those trials featured multiple experts and four of those trials included competing expert evidence.

3.05 The temporal and informational gaps in long trials with competing expert evidence can make comparison of the views of the experts challenging for jurors and can render recall of the subtleties of the prosecution expert evidence difficult, inhibiting comparison with the evidence from experts for the defence. This is particularly so where there are multiple differential points in matters as fundamental as the language utilized, the assumptions upon which opinions are based, the views ultimately expressed, and the reasons for these views. The adverse side of such a sequence of evidence from the perspective of the quality of decision-making is that in a complex trial there can be a considerable passage of time between the two sets of expert evidence, meaning that issues of uncertainty and of difference of opinion are not well crystallized to assist a logical and orderly evaluative process.

3.06 It might be thought that the party more likely to be assisted by such a gap in time is the defence because its expert witnesses will give evidence late in the trial, and such evidence is likely to be more prominent in jurors' minds when they retire to consider their verdict. This is not necessarily in the interests of justice, as it potentially undermines informed and focussed decision-making by jurors. On the other hand, one might see an advantage for the prosecution in the traditional order of calling witnesses, as its expert witnesses give evidence first, thereby shaping the mindset and expectations of the tribunal of fact. In the field of psychology, the former possibility is referred to as a 'recency effect', and the latter is called a 'primacy effect'. A review of primacy and recency effects in jury decision-making has suggested that it is the most recent information that is most influential in jurors' decisions.[2] Consistent with this, the decisions of judges acting as triers of fact were influenced in one study by the order of the evidence—the most recent evidence was most influential—but the judges themselves did not consciously weigh that recent evidence as being more probative.[3] Others argue that it is not as simple as primacy or recency.[4] The earlier information appears to shape the interpretation of the later information, in line with what the cognitive story model of jury decision-making suggests.[5] According to the story model, jurors construct narrative stories during the trial to organize and interpret the evidence. Jurors then evaluate and interpret all subsequent evidence as it is presented, in line with the story. We discuss the story model in more detail in chapter 5. Finally, it is worth noting that such effects might be modest in practice, as some

[2] Adrian Furnham, 'The Robustness of the Recency Effect: Studies Using Legal Evidence', *The Journal of General Psychology* 113, no. 4 (October 1986) 351.

[3] Raluca Enescu and André Kuhn, 'Serial Effects of Evidence on Legal Decision-Making', *The European Journal of Psychology Applied to Legal Context* 4, no. 2 (2012) 99.

[4] Galen V. Bodenhausen, 'Stereotypic Biases in Social Decision Making and Memory: Testing Process Models of Stereotype Use', *Journal of Personality and Social Psychology* 55, no. 5 (November 1988) 726.

[5] Nancy Pennington and Reid Hastie, 'Explaining the Evidence: Tests of the Story Model for Juror Decision Making', *Journal of Personality and Social Psychology* 62, no. 2 (1992) 189.

research suggests that neither early nor late evidence is particularly influential, but rather it is first commitment to a verdict that predicts final verdicts.[6]

The more pressing issue may well be that the elapse of a significant period of time between the giving of expert evidence by witnesses for the prosecution and for the defence makes it difficult for jurors to compare that evidence. This could mean that issues of uncertainty and of difference of opinion are unsatisfactorily difficult for jurors to resolve; the sequencing may mean that the differences in the evidence are crystallized in such a way as to assist a logical and orderly evaluative process. **3.07**

C. Consecutive Evidence

An option to address this difficulty is for the defence expert evidence to follow immediately after the prosecution expert evidence, namely before the conclusion of the prosecution case, thereby enabling a more ready process of comparison and evaluation. A further option is for the defence to call its own experts as its first witnesses. Either option means that a specific component of the criminal trial is allocated to expert evidence issues and allows for identification of those matters which are actually in dispute within the litigation. It also has the potential to facilitate the posing (and answering) of juror questions to clarify issues of uncertainty and confusion. **3.08**

Consecutive expert evidence has been used on a number of occasions in Australian criminal cases, including in prominent trials. An example was the lengthy *Pong Su* litigation in Victoria which involved four men convicted of importing heroin on board the so named North Korean ocean freighter.[7] However, as of 2016 hearing evidence consecutively is still rare in Australia's criminal courts. **3.09**

The option of consecutive expert evidence is one for the trial judge and the parties. The onus of proof beyond reasonable doubt lies on the prosecution in criminal trials and the opportunity exists for the defence at the end of the prosecution case to argue that no case has been made that the accused person is required to answer.[8] If at the close of the evidence adduced by the prosecution there is insufficient evidence upon which a reasonable jury could be satisfied of the guilt of the accused person, there is binding High Court authority in Australia that the case should at that time be removed from the jury.[9] Thus the defence might be opposed both in principle and in many specific instances to interposing its own expert evidence within what traditionally would be perceived to be the prosecution case. A corollary of this is that there is no power at common law for trial judges to order the defence to adduce its evidence before the conclusion of the prosecution case. **3.10**

In addition, while it is open to the defence to determine its order of witnesses, and thus to call its own expert(s) first, thereby creating consecutive expert evidence, it is under no obligation to do so. **3.11**

---

6 Vernon A. Stone, 'A Primacy Effect in Decision-Making by Jurors', *The Journal of Communication* 19, no. 3 (September 1969) 239.

7 See on appeal *R v Teng* [2009] VSCA 148, (2009) 22 VR 706.

8 In the United Kingdom, see the test in *R v Galbraith* [1981] 1 WLR 1039 (Lord Lane CJ); see also *Haw Tua Tua v Public Prosecutor* [1982] AC 236; *R v Courtney* [2007] NICA 6.

9 *May v O'Sullivan* (1955) 92 CLR 654; *Antoun v The Queen* [2006] HCA 2, (2006) 80 ALJR 497. See too *R v Antoun* [2004] NSWCCA 268; *R v Bilick* (1984) 36 SASR 321; *Questions of Law Reserved on Acquittal (No 2 of 1993)* (1993) 61 SASR 1; *Morison v Kiwi Electrix Pty Ltd* (1998) 19 WAR 482; *State of Western Australia v Burke* [2011] WASCA 190, (2011) 42 WAR 124.

3.12 As outlined above, there can be strategic reasons why the defence might prefer to retain the traditional order of witnesses so as to optimize their influence on jurors. If the tactic of the defence is obfuscatory, namely to create as much confusion and uncertainty as possible about the status of the prosecution expert evidence, then the defence may perceive it to be unhelpful to have defence expert evidence immediately juxtaposed beside prosecution expert evidence; such a sequence might clarify the issues actually in dispute in a way which may be inconsistent with the chosen strategy of the defence.

3.13 The tactical use of obfuscation in respect of expert evidence is a live issue, and is controversial. A former Commonwealth Director of Public Prosecutions and later a Chief Judge of the County Court of Victoria has expressed concern about the kinds of tactics adopted on occasion by the defence.[10] Justice Ipp in an extra-curial article also commented on the 'perversion' of the adversarial system of justice arising from an obfuscatory strategy, especially in cases of serious commercial fraud, where some defence lawyers resort to what he called the 'filibuster defence' in an effort to secure the acquittal of their client 'through exhausting and confusing witnesses and the jury by causing as much delay and obfuscation as possible'.[11]

3.14 In a 1994 decision, Hunt CJ at CL also criticized this style of defence advocacy, contrasting the advocate who restricts their fight to the real issues with the vexatious advocate 'familiar to those with experience of the criminal courts' who fights every issue, in the apparent hope that by doing so an important prosecution witness might be hit by a bus on the way to court and the prosecution will fail.[12] Thus, a conflict can readily be identified between a preference in the interests of justice to simplify the decision-making function of jurors by enabling them to hear cognate evidence by experts in juxtaposition, and the employment of obfuscatory tactics on behalf of defendants, as permitted and, perhaps, enabled by adherence to the traditional characteristics of the adversary system. It is also increasingly accepted that trial judges have a responsibility to manage forms of advocacy that may interfere with the capacity of jurors to make considered decisions based upon effective evaluation of the evidence.[13]

3.15 What can be said is that recalibration of witness order so that expert evidence is presented consecutively is currently an option that generally arises by agreement between the parties, usually at the initiative of the trial judge, or is embraced for strategic reasons by the defence (out of a perception that juxtaposition of evidence by expert witnesses from the prosecution and defence will create a tactical advantage) rather than by a requirement that can be imposed by the trial judge.

3.16 In two of the trials included in this project, experts gave evidence consecutively. In sexual assault trial 18, the expert medical evidence addressed an unfamiliar and complex topic. This

[10] Michael Rozenes, 'The Role of the DPP in the Investigation and Prosecution of Complex Fraud' (lecture, ASC Law Enforcement Conference, Perth, 16 September 1994), <http://www.cdpp.gov.au/news/the-role-of-the-dpp-in-the-investigation-and-prosecution-of-complex-fraud/>. See also David Plater and Lucy Line, 'Has the "Silver Thread" of the Criminal Law Lost its Lustre? The Modern Prosecutor as a Minister of Justice', *University of Tasmania Law Review* 31, no. 2 (2012) 55; John H. Phillips, 'Practical Advocacy: The Duty of Counsel', *Australian Law Journal* 68, no. 11 (1994) 834, <http://www.austlii.edu.au/cgi-bin/LawCite?cit=%281994%29%2068%20Australian%20Law%20Journal%20834>.

[11] See David Ipp, 'Lawyers' Duties to the Court', *Law Quarterly Review* 114 (January 1998) 63: 96–7, 98–102; John H. Phillips, 'Practical Advocacy: The Duty of Counsel'.

[12] *R v Sandford* (1994) 33 NSWLR 172, 188–9.

[13] See e.g. New South Wales Law Reform Commission, *Jury Directions: Report No. 136* (Sydney: New South Wales Law Reform Commission, 2012).

evidence was crucial to the defence. The prosecutor commented that presenting the expert evidence was 'essential', maintaining that:

> the jury will have a better command of the factual material that the opinions are being expressed upon and will have an opportunity, whilst statements are fresh in their mind, of both comparing the various opinions expressed, and asking questions at the time when witnesses are available to be recalled or answer them on the spot.
>
> Q: In the past five years have you used that approach in many trials?
>
> A. I prefer experts to follow each other wherever possible. That is my preferred approach.

A number of persons interviewed in the study raised the option of the order of expert evidence being reformed. One prosecutor asserted that, in circumstances where the defence bore the burden of proof on the particular issue that the expert evidence related to, the order of expert evidence should be varied. She suggested that in those circumstances the defence expert should precede the prosecution expert. Her view was that the expert evidence should be called consecutively at the end of all of the other evidence in the whole case—in other words, at the end of the defence case. This would have the effect of placing before the jury the prosecution expert evidence close to the time the jurors retired to consider their verdict. **3.17**

A judge extolled the advantages of consecutive expert evidence, observing that while it 'would rely very much on co-operation between the parties', 'if the jury are able to hear one [expert witness] very shortly, if not immediately, following the other, or others, it would very much aid in comprehension of their evidence to see where there is common ground, and where there's not.' **3.18**

However, not all interviewees were enthusiastic about the option of consecutive evidence. One judge was firmly opposed to it: **3.19**

> It means that a party will be calling their expert out of turn. It interrupts the traditional flow of an adversarial case. I do think that people have a capacity to retain this complex evidence for longer than the fifteen minutes between experts and perhaps that should happen in [some] cases but I think that's better than calling the witnesses out of order.

In trial 1, the expert psychiatric evidence was presented to the jury consecutively—the defence expert gave evidence immediately after the prosecution experts. Eight of the jurors from that trial were surveyed and three of those jurors were interviewed and they displayed a solid comprehension of the expert psychiatric evidence, which was complex and inconsistent amongst the experts. **3.20**

In Victoria, Australia, in 2014, the Supreme and County Courts issued Practice Note No 2, *Expert Evidence in Criminal Trials*. It provides that, where one or more parties in a criminal trial have served expert evidence relating to the same issue or to two or more 'closely related issues', and the commissioning parties agree, and the court so orders, evidence may be given by experts consecutively, with the procedure to be within the discretion of the court.[14] **3.21**

Acknowledging the adjustment that the consecutive expert evidence initiative would make to the traditional contours of the adversary trial, it would be constructive for there to be further discussion about permitting trial judges the option, in the interests of justice, of requiring expert evidence to be given consecutively so as to enhance juror decision-making in respect of technical issues. **3.22**

[14] County Court of Victoria, *Practice Note: Expert Evidence in Criminal Trials* (last updated: 24 June 2014); Supreme Court of Victoria, *Practice Note No 2, Expert Evidence in Criminal Trials.*

D. Conclaves/Joint Conferences of Experts

3.23 Conclaves of experts or joint conferences are meetings of expert witnesses prior to a trial. They are generally court-ordered and take place after expert reports have been filed with the court. The purpose of conclaves is to crystallize issues, identifying what experts agree upon and what they disagree about. The 2010 amendments to the Ontario *Rules of Civil Procedure* introduced a power for the Ontario courts (including Rule 20.05(2)(k)) to order opposing experts to meet and confer in order to clarify different interpretations and specific issues of disagreement. The report of Justice Osborne's *Civil Justice Reform Project: Summary of Findings & Recommendations*, provided as a rationale for this amended power: 'Expert bias can... best be reduced or somewhat controlled by a "meet and confer" requirement.'[15] To similar effect, in South Africa Meintjes-Van Der Walt has put it that: 'Pre-trial meetings between experts could contribute to consensus-delineation, leaving only disputed issues for trial.' She has argued for greater preparedness on the part of judicial officers to order such forms of communication between experts.[16]

3.24 On occasions, conclaves are ordered by trial judges with respect to particular topics that are to be the subject of dispute within the litigation.[17] It is common for an order that the outcome of a conclave be the subject of a joint report by the experts. Justice Garling has observed that:

> The aim of any such conference is to:
> (a) minimise the areas of disagreement between the experts about their opinions, and maximise the areas of agreement;
> (b) enable the production of a joint expert report which records the areas of agreement and of disagreement, together with a short statement from each expert as to their respective opinions on the issues which are not agreed; and
> (c) enable the concurrent evidence of the experts to proceed in an orderly and efficient manner.[18]

3.25 A variety of powers enables courts in civil matters to order conclaves of experts or conferences of experts. An example is Rule 31.24 of the Uniform Civil Procedure Rules 2005 (NSW):

> (1) The court may direct expert witnesses:
> (a) to confer, either generally or in relation to specified matters, and
> (b) to endeavour to reach agreement on any matters in issue, and
> (c) to prepare a joint report, specifying matters agreed and matters not agreed and reasons for any disagreement, and
> (d) to base any joint report on specified facts or assumptions of fact,
> and may do so at any time, whether before or after the expert witnesses have furnished their experts' reports.
> (2) The court may direct that a conference be held:
> (a) with or without the attendance of the parties affected or their legal representatives, or
> (b) with or without the attendance of the parties affected or their legal representatives, at the option of the parties, or

---

[15] Coulter A. Osborne, *Civil Justice Reform Project: Summary of Findings and Recommendations* (November 2007), p. 77, <http://www.attorneygeneral.jus.gov.on.ca/english/about/pubs/cjrp/CJRP-Report_EN.pdf>.

[16] Lirieka Meintjes-Van de Walt, 'Expert Odyssey: Thoughts on the Presentation and Evaluation of Scientific Evidence', *South African Law Journal* 120 (2003) 352: p. 361.

[17] See e.g. *Matthews v SPI Electricity Pty Ltd (Ruling No 10)* [2012] VSC 379 (Forrest J); *Avery v Flood* [2013] NSWSC 996; *Porter v Le; Porter v Western Sydney Local Health District* [2014] NSWSC 883 [1].

[18] *Hudson v Howes* [2010] NSWSC 1503 [2]. See too Garling J in *John v Henderson (No 1)* [2013] NSWSC 1435 [11]–[12] in respect of medical negligence cases.

(c) with or without the attendance of a facilitator (that is, a person who is independent of the parties and who may or may not be an expert in relation to the matters in issue).

(3) An expert witness so directed may apply to the court for further directions to assist the expert witness in the performance of his or her functions in any respect.

(4) Any such application must be made by sending a written request for directions to the court, specifying the matter in relation to which directions are sought.

(5) An expert witness who makes such an application must send a copy of the request to the other expert witnesses and to the parties affected.

Unless the parties affected agree otherwise, the content of such discussions is generally precluded from being the subject of reference by witnesses in court when they give evidence. **3.26**

Enthusiasm was expressed by a number of interviewees in our study for the pre-trial assembly of experts to discuss their findings and to identify what is agreed upon and what is not. An expert called by the prosecution stated that on one occasion when such a gathering took place involving the subject of forensic pathology it was very constructive: *'as it turned out, everybody agreed, so end of story.'* **3.27**

Some experts, particularly in the fields of pathology and psychiatry, stated that such practices already took place informally. One psychiatrist expert observed that: **3.28**

> Sometimes we'll get together and say, 'Hang on, did you think of this?' and sometimes a consensus is achieved, and I think sometimes at the direction of the court, a meaningful and honest consensus can be achieved because there is room for variation of opinion drawing on precisely the same facts, and that a legitimate difference of opinion sometimes [exists].

Another psychiatrist recounted a situation in which experts were: **3.29**

> sent off to give a consensus statement. We did that. Came up with an almost unanimous consensus statement and so they decided that they wanted to look at it and then they wanted to question us individually again anyway.

Another pathologist identified the pressure to arrive at compromise agreements as one of the dynamics affecting experts asked to enter conclaves. He commented that senior colleagues could be experienced to some degree as oppressive in the environment of a conclave. **3.30**

A judge recounted persuading the parties in a criminal trial to have a joint conference of experts to identify what was in dispute: **3.31**

> Ultimately, after the joint conference, the parties decided none of the expert evidence was successful in the sense that, instead of having it turn out to be of no use in front of the jury, by the joint conference and the participation of counsel in that and hearing what the experts had to say when they faced each other, both barristers took the view that the evidence was of no assistance—that what the defence had tried to put up was going to be knocked down by the prosecution and that it ultimately wouldn't have any probative value.

There has been debate whether powers such as exist in respect of expert evidence in civil matters should be extended to the domain of criminal trials. As previously noted, such a practice exists to some degree informally. It is probably within trial judges' common law powers to order such conferences. **3.32**

In Victoria, Australia, in 2014 the Supreme and County Courts formalized the situation by issuing Practice Note No 2, *Expert Evidence in Criminal Trials*, Part 10 of which enables a trial judge to direct experts to discuss the expert issues in the proceedings and prepare a statement for the court of the matters on which they agree and disagree, giving their reasons. **3.33**

Aside from the latter statement of agreement and disagreement, such a discussion cannot be referred to during the trial without permission from the court.[19] This approach has initiated the important process of enabling trial judges to manage expert evidence in such a way as to enhance jurors' capacity to focus on those issues which are authentically in dispute, rather than being distracted by collateral matters which ought not to consume time or distract from their decision-making. However, the option of consecutive evidence has been the subject of some judicial consternation.[20]

E. Concurrent Evidence

(1) The procedure

3.34 Concurrent evidence, or 'hot-tubbing' of experts, is a

> procedure where evidence is given by all of the experts together at the same time. It resembles a discussion in which a co-operative endeavour is engaged [in] to identify the relevant issues and where possible, arrive at an agreed resolution of them. To the extent appropriate, the joint evidence is subject to judicial control, much like the control by a chair of a meeting, although all necessary formality is observed.[21]

3.35 Justice McClellan who pioneered the procedure in the New South Wales Land and Environment Court, has described the procedure in his court:

> All experts in relation to a particular topic are sworn to give evidence at the same time. What follows is a discussion, which is managed by the judge or commissioner, so that the topics requiring oral examination are ventilated. The process enables experts to answer questions from the court, the advocates and, most importantly, from their professional colleagues. It allows the experts to express in their own words the view they have on a particular subject. There have been cases where as many as six experts have been sworn to give evidence at the same time.
>
> For hearings in my court, the procedure commonly followed involves the experts being sworn and their written reports tendered together with the document which reflects their pre-trial discussion—matters upon which they agree or disagree. I then identify, with the help of the advocates and in the presence of the witnesses, the topics which require discussion, in order to resolve outstanding issues. Having identified those matters, I invite each witness to briefly speak to their position on the first issue followed by a general discussion of the issue during which they can ask each other questions. I invite the advocates to join in the discussion by asking questions of their own of any other witness. Having completed the discussion on one issue we move on until the discussion of all the issues has been completed.
>
> Experience shows that, provided everyone understands the process at the outset, in particular that it is to be a structured discussion to inform the judge and not an argument between the experts and the advocates, there is no difficulty in managing the hearing. Although I do not encourage it, very often the experts, who will be sitting next to each other, normally in the jury box in the courtroom, end up referring to each other on first-name terms. Within a short time of the discussion commencing, you can feel the release of the tension which

---

[19] Supreme Court of Victoria, *Practice Note: Expert Evidence in Criminal Trials* (last updated: 24 June 2014), <http://assets.justice.vic.gov.au//supreme/resources/49532674-51d5-478a-a5a7-a93a746de768/practice+note+2+of+2014+expert+evidence+in+criminal+trials+25+june+2014.pdf>.

[20] See *Ta-Vuong v The Queen* [2015] VSCA 238 at [109]–[110].

[21] *John v Henderson (No 1)* [2013] NSWSC 1435 [11] (Garling J). See too Patricia Bergin, 'The Expert's Lament' (lecture, Land and Environment Court of New South Wales Annual Conference, Sydney, 5 May 2011), <http://www.austlii.edu.au/cgi-bin/sinodisp/au/journals/NSWJSchol/2011/14.html?stem=0&synonyms=0&query=%22concurrent%20evidence%20%22>.

normally infects the evidence-gathering process. Those who might normally be shy or diffident are able to relax and contribute fully to the discussion.[22]

Justice Pepper, also of the Land and Environment Court in New South Wales, has identified seven separate aspects of concurrent evidence: **3.36**

(1) Identification of the issues upon which expert evidence is needed.
(2) The preparation of individual expert reports.
(3) A conference between the experts, without lawyers, in order to prepare a joint report that sets out the matters upon which there is agreement and the matters upon which there is disagreement, including, where possible, short reasons as to why they disagree.
(4) The preparation of the joint report.
(5) The experts are called to give evidence together, at a convenient time in the proceedings, usually following the tendering of the lay evidence.
(6) The experts are given the opportunity to explain the issues in dispute in their own words. Each expert is then allowed to comment on or question the other expert.
(7) Cross-examination of the expert is permitted. During this process, each party is permitted to rely on their own expert for clarification of an answer.[23]

Thus, inherent in the concurrent evidence procedure is a degree of encroachment upon the extent of control exercised by parties over their own experts. In this regard, important issues arise in respect of the amenability of translation of the procedure from civil procedure to criminal trials before juries. **3.37**

(2) International uptake of the procedure

Concurrent evidence is an initiative that originally came from Australia but was trialled in the United Kingdom in the Manchester Technology and Construction Court and the Mercantile Court, and then the Manchester Chancery Court, during 2012. Professor Dame Hazel Genn identified from the trial a range of benefits from concurrent evidence and no significant disadvantages from the point of view of the judiciary, counsel, solicitors, or experts.[24] **3.38**

The taking of expert evidence in the form of concurrent evidence in the United Kingdom can be traced back to the *Final Report on Civil Litigation Costs* by Lord Justice Jackson,[25] in which he raised concerns about the length of expert reports and their cost in civil litigation. This resulted in Part 35 of the Civil Procedure Rules which allows civil courts a discretion to order that concurrent expert evidence from some or all experts from like disciplines be the preferred method of taking evidence in civil litigation.[26] **3.39**

---

22 Peter McClellan, 'Expert Witnesses: The Experience of the Land & Environment Court of NSW' (lecture, XIX Biennial LawAsia Conference, Gold Coast, 20–24 March 2005). See too Vance Hughston and Tina Jowett, 'In the Native Title "Hot Tub": Expert Conferences and Concurrent Expert Evidence in Native Title', *Land, Rights, Laws: Issues of Native Title* 6, no. 1 (2014) 1, <http://www.aiatsis.gov.au/_files/ntru/ip_hughstonjowett_web.pdf>.

23 Rachel Pepper, *Expert Evidence in the Land and Environment Court* (21 January 2013), para. 68, <http://www.lec.justice.nsw.gov.au/Documents/expert%20evidence%20in%20the%20land%20and%20environment%20court%20v2.pdf>; Neil J. Young, 'Expert Witnesses: On the Stand or in the Hot Tub: How, When and Why' (lecture, Commercial Court CPD Seminar, 27 October 2010).

24 Hazel Genn, *Manchester Concurrent Evidence Pilot: Interim Report* (January 2012), <http://www.judiciary.gov.uk/wp-content/uploads/JCO/Documents/Reports/concurrent-evidence-interim-report.pdf>.

25 Rupert Jackson, *Review of Civil Litigation Costs: Final Report* (December 2009), <https://www.judiciary.gov.uk/wp-content/uploads/JCO/Documents/Reports/jackson-final-report-140110.pdf>.

26 See *Bluewater Energy Services BV v Mercon Steel Structures* BV [2014] EWHC 2132. See also *Homebase Ltd v Rengasamy* [2015] EWHC 68 where consideration was given to using the procedure but

3.40 In Canada, too, the Federal Courts Rules relating to expert witnesses were amended in 2010 to enable judges to ensure that expert evidence is adduced in the most efficient, least costly, and most fair manner. The rules allow judges to order that some or all expert witnesses in a case testify as 'a panel', and in the course of the trial they can comment on the views of other panel members and may ask each other questions. In Ontario, the Rules of Civil Procedure include provisions that permit judges to order pre-trial hot-tub meetings to identify areas of agreement and disagreement and to prepare a joint statement. The procedure has also been used for some time in administrative agencies such as the Ontario Workplace Safety and Insurance Appeals Tribunal.

3.41 Enthusiasm about concurrent expert evidence has also been expressed in the United States, by commentators who have drawn attention to the difficulties generated by expert partisanship.[27] For instance, Mnookin[28] has proclaimed that: 'The future…may belong to Australia. Hot tubbing…is much more interesting than neutral experts.'

(3) Advantages of the procedure

3.42 Many Australian commentators have extolled the virtues and attributes of concurrent evidence. It has been argued that it enables diffident experts to contribute to a structured discussion in a court environment in a way that otherwise they could not, and that it enables a better form of evaluation of experts and their views because of the kind of discourse that takes place amongst them in the hot tub.[29] Cheeseman has argued that concurrent evidence *can* have a number of virtues over the traditional process:

(a) The evidence on one topic is all given at the same time.
(b) The process refines the issues to those that are essential.
(c) Because the experts are confronting one another, they are much less likely to act adversarially.
(d) A narrowing and refining of areas of agreement and disagreement is achieved before cross-examination.
(e) Cross-examination takes place in the presence of all the experts so that they can immediately be asked to comment on the answers of colleagues.[30]

3.43 In Australia, in evaluating the advantages of concurrent evidence, the New South Wales Law Reform Commission observed that:

> The process moves somewhat away from lawyers interrogating experts towards a structured professional discussion between peers in the relevant field. The experience in the Land and Environment Court indicates that the nature of the evidence is affected by this feature, and that experts typically make more concessions, and state matters more frankly and reasonably,

---

Knowles J ultimately determined not to proceed on the basis that all of the issues had not been 'fully explored' before him.

[27] See David Sonnenstein and Charles Fitzpatrick, 'The Problem of Partisan Experts and the Potential for Reform Through Concurrent Evidence', *The Review of Litigation* 32, no. 1 (Winter 2013) 1; Megan A. Yarnall, 'Dueling Scientific Experts: Is Australia's Hot Tub Method a Viable Solution for the American Judiciary?', *Oregon Law Review* 88 (2009) 311.

[28] Jennifer Mnookin, 'Expert Evidence, Partisanship and Epistemic Competence', *Brooklyn Law Review* 73, no. 3 (Spring 2008) 1009; Adam Liptak, 'Experts Hired to Shed Light Can Leave US Courts in Dark', *The New York Times*, 11 August 2008, <http://www.nytimes.com/2008/08/12/us/12experts.html?pagewanted=all&_r=0>.

[29] See Mia Louise Livingstone, 'Have We Fired the "Hired Gun"? A Critique of Expert Evidence Reform in Australia and the United Kingdom', *Journal of Judicial Administration* 18, no. 1 (2008) 39: p. 51.

[30] Elizabeth Cheesman, 'Hot Tubbing: Concurrent Expert Evidence', *Bar News* [Summer 2006/2007] 54: p. 57.

> than they might have done under the traditional type of cross-examination. Similarly, it seems that the questions may tend to be more constructive and helpful than the sort of questions sometimes encountered in traditional cross-examination.[31]

However, it emphasized that it was difficult to predict whether the widespread implementation of concurrent evidence procedures would generate tangible benefits and concluded that their utility would depend on 'the skills, preparedness and cooperation of lawyers and experts involved', as well as the skill of individual judges in 'structuring and [maintaining] control of the discussion.'[32] Three years later, the Victorian Law Reform Commission concluded that: **3.44**

> Hot tubbing, as evidenced by experience in NSW, has the potential not only to reduce the hearing time devoted to expert evidence (and therefore costs) but also to improve the integrity of opinion evidence and the usefulness of that evidence for decision makers.[33]

Within the area of civil litigation there are many proponents of concurrent evidence, particularly within the judiciary.[34] McDougall JA in *Caruana v Darouti*, an occupier's liability case, commented: **3.45**

> [T]his court has had occasion in the past to comment on the unsatisfactory practice of tendering reports of experts, whose views are sharply in conflict, without any attempt to resolve the conflict through processes such as conclave and joint report, concurrent evidence sessions, or old fashioned cross-examination...[35]

Similar points were made by McClellan CJ at CL observing that: **3.46**

> This process [of concurrent evidence] proved both highly productive and efficient and has been of great benefit to me in resolving this case. The discussion was sustained at a high level of objectivity by all participants, each of whom displayed a genuine endeavour to assist the court to resolve the problems. The fact that ultimately they disagreed on critical issues was not due to anything other than a genuine difference of opinion about the appropriate conclusion to be drawn from the known facts.[36]

---

31 New South Wales Law Reform Commission, *Expert Witnesses: Report No. 109* (Sydney: New South Wales Law Reform Commission, 2005), s. 6.51.

32 New South Wales Law Reform Commission, *Expert Witnesses: Report No. 109*, s. 6.56.

33 Victorian Law Reform Commission, *Civil Justice Review: Report* (Melbourne: Victorian Law Reform Commission, 2008), p. 512.

34 See e.g. Peter McClellan, 'Expert Witnesses: The Recent Experience of the Land and Environment Court', *Judicial Officers Bulletin* 17 (2005) 83; Peter McClellan, 'Expert Evidence: Aces Up Your Sleeve?' (lecture, Industrial Relations Commission of New South Wales, 20 October 2006); Peter McClellan, 'Concurrent Expert Evidence' (lecture, Medicine and Law Conference, Law Institute of Victoria, 29 November 2007), <http://www.austlii.edu.au/au/journals/NSWJSchol/2007/15.pdf>; Peter McClellan, 'New Method with Experts: Concurrent Evidence', *Journal of Court Innovation* 3, no. 1 (Winter 2010) 259; Gary Downes, 'Concurrent Expert Evidence in the Administrative Appeals Tribunal: The New South Wales Experience' (lecture, Australasian Conference of Planning and Environment Courts and Tribunals, Hobart, 27 February 2004); Peter Heerey, 'Expert Evidence: The Australian Experience', *Bar Review* 7 (January–February 2002) 166; Peter Heerey, 'Recent Australian Developments', *Civil Justice Quarterly* 23 (October 2004) 386: p. 389; Stephen Rares, 'Using the "Hot Tub": How Concurrent Expert Evidence Aids Understanding Issues', *Federal Judicial Scholarship* [2010] 20; Peter Garling, 'Concurrent Expert Evidence: Reflections and Developments', *Law Society Journal* 49, no. 10 (2011) 5; Peter Garling, 'Concurrent Expert Evidence, Reflections and Developments' (lecture, Australian Insurance Law Association Twilight Seminar Series, 17 August 2011); Rachel Pepper, *Expert Evidence in the Land and Environment Court*, para. 68, <http://www.lec.justice.nsw.gov.au/Documents/expert%20evidence%20in%20the%20land%20and%20environment%20court%20v2.pdf>.

35 *Caruana v Darouti* [2014] NSWCA 85 [123].

36 *Halverson v Dobler* [2006] NSWSC 1307 [101]. For judicial comment as to the benefits of concurrent evidence in assisting with the efficient conduct of proceedings and enabling the courts to better understand complex issues which arose in the course of commercial litigation see: *Visy Packaging Pty Ltd v Siegwerk*

(4) Reservations about the procedure

3.47 However, enthusiasm about concurrent evidence is not unalloyed; some have expressed reservations. For instance, Rackeman J has emphasized that it is not a panacea to the challenges of expert evidence, merely a tool.[37] Justice Davies has gone further, contending that it tends to exacerbate the adversarial character of proceedings, turning expert witnesses into advocates, and generating the risk of the two following undesirable consequences:

> The first is that the judge will be left with two opposed but apparently convincing opinions by equally well-qualified experts, neither of them has been shaken in the process. The second, and unfortunately more likely, consequence is that the judge will be unwittingly convinced by the more articulate and apparently authoritative personality. The likelihood of this latter consequence increases as the complexity of the question in issue increases.[38]

3.48 Concern has also been expressed that the effectiveness of concurrent expert evidence is substantially dependent upon the involvement of the trial judge, including his or her capacity to direct the experts' discussion, ensure that all viewpoints are aired, and avoid the evidence becoming an argument amongst experts; it also depends on the skills of forensic experts and the constructive involvement of well-briefed counsel.[39] Such involvement, of necessity, is circumscribed by the distinctive requirements of the criminal trial process.

3.49 In Canada, reservations about hot-tubbing have been expressed by a significant number of trial lawyers.[40] When Grant Thornton[41] asked 108 lawyers across Canada about alternative approaches of adducing expert evidence, concurrent evidence was reported in 2015 as the least favoured, with concerns being expressed that:

- lawyers from each side are required to agree on how the process will run;
- counsel needs to consider not only the expertise of the expert, but the expert's debating skills and ability to react quickly in a concurrent evidence process;
- presenting concurrent evidence may unintentionally give the perception that the two experts are equal in credentials, reputation, and experience, when in fact it is not the case;
- some experts may become advocates in a concurrent evidence setting;
- the personality of the experts can impact the case, such as bullying tactics;
- matters involving opinion evidence are not usually black or white, so it is still up to the judge to assess the credibility of each expert and make a decision;
- it is possible that the two experts will not agree on anything, thus defeating the purpose of finding commonality within the expert evidence.

Australia Pty Ltd [2013] FCA 231, (2013) 301 ALR 560 [53] (Gray J); *Rabaxy Laboratories Limited v AstraZeneca AB* [2013] FCA 368, (2013) 101 IPR 11 [39] (Middleton J).

[37] Michael E. Rackemann, 'The Management of Experts', *Journal of Judicial Administration* 21, no. 3 (February 2012) 168: p. 176.

[38] Geoffrey L. Davies, 'Recent Australian Developments: A Response to Peter Heerey', *Civil Justice Quarterly* 23 (October 2004) 396.

[39] See e.g. Lisa C. Wood, 'Experts Only: Out of the Hot Tub and into the Joint Conference', *Anti-Trust* 22, no. 1 (Fall 2007) 89; Freckelton, Reddy, and Selby, *Australian Judicial Perspectives on Expert Evidence: An Empirical Study*, p. 407.

[40] See Yoram Beck and Suzanne Loomer, 'Reforming Expert Evidence', *National Magazine* (Spring 2015), <http://nationalmagazine.ca/Articles/March-2015-Web/Reforming-expert-evidence.aspx>.

[41] Grant Thornton LLP, *National Litigation Survey Report* (2015), <http://insights.grantthornton.ca/i/453877-national-litigation-survey-report/2>.

(5) The utilization of the procedure in criminal trials

To date, the overwhelming majority of the uptake of concurrent evidence as a style of providing expert evidence to the courts has been in civil litigation.[42] However, in a modest number of cases in Australian criminal courts the procedure has been used with consent of the parties before a judge sitting alone, in voir dire examinations, and before magistrates in summary criminal proceedings in New South Wales. In addition, it is regularly used in Queensland's Mental Health Court. **3.50**

An example of its usage was in the New South Wales District Court in a judge-alone trial which dealt with charges of dangerous driving occasioning bodily harm.[43] The issue in dispute related to whether the driving of the accused was dangerous to other persons at the time of the impact of the one vehicle on the other. Both the prosecution and the accused called an expert on how fast the vehicle was travelling and whether it had become airborne as it travelled over the crest of a dune immediately after the victims suffered their injuries. Judge Berman described the process adopted for the trial in his reasons. He noted that the experts had prepared a joint report that identified where one expert's opinion had changed, where they had reached agreement, and where they continued to disagree. **3.51**

Similarly, concurrent evidence was given in the Western Australian Supreme Court trial of barrister Lloyd Rayney for the murder of his wife. Commonwealth Scientific and Industrial Research Organisation (CSIRO) scientists gave concurrent evidence in relation to comparability of brick dust found on the deceased woman's bra and bricks that paved the Rayney home. Ultimately, Mr Rayney was found not guilty. However, the situation was unusual in that the two scientists who gave concurrent evidence were joint authors of the same report.[44] **3.52**

Another high-profile criminal case in which concurrent evidence was used was the murder trial of Jeffrey Gilham, who was charged with killing both of his parents at the family home. Three forensic pathologists gave evidence in a concurrent format.[45] **3.53**

In Canada, reflections on the repercussions of problematic evidence which has led to miscarriages of justice led the Public Prosecution Service to observe: **3.54**

> At present, the concept of 'hot-tubbing' is not a staple in criminal trials. As noted by Jackson LJ in his Final Report, it remains to be seen which types of cases respond well to the concurrent evidence approach, what costs are saved, and whether the parties involved perceive the process as enabling each side's case to be properly considered. There is little doubt, however, that successfully soliciting the viewpoints of multiple expert witnesses at the same time by allowing them to discuss complex, difficult issues together can be very useful for any trier of fact.[46]

[42] See particularly in the medical negligence context Bill Madden, Bill Cockburn, and Tina Cockburn, 'Adapting to Concurrent Expert Evidence in Medical Litigation', *Journal of Law and Medicine* 22, no. 3 (2015) 610; and generally Ian Freckelton and Hugh Selby, *Expert Evidence: Law, Practice, Procedure and Advocacy*, 6th edn. (Sydney: Thomson Reuters, 2016). See also in respect of coronial proceedings, Coroners Court of Queensland, *Practice Direction for the Use of Concurrent Evidence in the Queensland Coronial Jurisdiction* (2012).

[43] *R v Stanyard* [2012] NSWDC 78 [30].

[44] See 'Scientists "Hot Tubbing" in Rayney Trial Evidence', *ABC News*, 14 August 2012, <http://www.abc.net.au/news/2012-08-14/research-scientists-give-evidence-at-rayney-trial/4197874>.

[45] See *Gilham v The Queen* [2012] NSWCCA 131, (2012) 224 A Crim R 22. Compare the Norwegian practice of court appointment of two or more psychiatrists to give expert evidence: see Asne Seierstad, *One of Us* (London: Virago, 2013) in respect of the trial of Anders Breivik.

[46] Public Prosecution Service, *The Path to Justice: Preventing Wrongful Convictions* (autumn 2011), Ch. 9: <http://www.ppsc-sppc.gc.ca/eng/pub/ptj-spj/ch9.html>.

(6) A Victorian criminal trials initiative

3.55 In 2014, Victoria Practice Note No 2 for the County and Supreme Courts, *Expert Evidence in Criminal Trials*, explicitly contemplate concurrent evidence in criminal trials, and provided that, where two or more parties have served expert evidence relating to the same issue or relating to two or more closely related issues, the commissioning parties agree, and the Court so orders:

> evidence may be given concurrently (i.e. with all of the experts present in court, sworn or affirmed at the same time).

(7) Project feedback

3.56 Participants in the interviews undertaken as part of the present project were asked whether they had been involved in criminal trials in which the procedure of concurrent evidence had been used, and, regardless of their answer, were asked whether they thought concurrent evidence should be used as a means of adducing expert evidence. The tendency was for both judges and prosecutors to be enthusiastic or at least interested in the procedure, but for defence lawyers to express reservations about whether it would be advantageous to their clients, although some expressed guarded support for it in appropriate cases. In a number of instances defence lawyers in particular differentiated between the role of the prosecution and the responsibility of the defence to optimize the prospects of their client being found not guilty. This was a relevant distinction, it was said, because experts called by the prosecution tend to be mainstream, while those called by the defence can be fringe, iconoclastic, or alternative; they may not bear comfortable comparison with the credentials, experience, and reliability of experts called by the prosecution. It was perceived that the comparison may be more apparent, and damaging for the defence, if experts either gave evidence one after the other or, more particularly, if they gave evidence at the same time via concurrent evidence.

3.57 Judges were asked if they had had concurrent evidence adduced in trials over which they had presided, and, if not, what had been the reasons. The view from a number of trial lawyers and judges was that it may not be possible to use concurrent evidence without specific authorization, unless the parties agree or it is in the course of a voir dire. It was also noted that concurrent evidence had been used occasionally in judge-alone criminal trials, including where the experts were in agreement. However, a number of counsel, in particular defence counsel, were not sufficiently familiar with how the option would function in criminal trials, and entertained misapprehensions about how concurrent evidence works, for instance confusing it with pre-trial expert meetings.

3.58 When judges were asked why they had not availed themselves of the concurrent evidence option, a number said that the parties had not asked for it. This was a similar answer to that given by a high proportion of judges who were asked in the 1999 survey why they had not used court-appointed experts or assessors.[47]

3.59 Some members of counsel had encountered concurrent evidence in other domains and had been impressed by it. For instance, a defence barrister commented of its use in a coronial inquest:

> I thought it was an interesting process.... it gave experts an opportunity to express their view. I actually thought it was a better way of assessing the reliability, honesty, and credibility of the expert because they were immediately confronted by their colleagues, who

[47] Freckelton, Reddy and Selby. *Australian Judicial Perspectives on Expert Evidence*, Pt. 11, pp. 95ff.

> were able to comment specifically on an answer that one of them had given, and I felt there was a greater capacity to expose an answer as being unreliable in that forum. So I thought the experts bouncing off each other... really exposed some of the flaws of one of the experts' evidence.

A defence barrister had experienced concurrent evidence and was enthusiastic about it: **3.60**

> I think it's a good idea. The experts... should have a go at each other and see whether they can get some common ground and then we can work out what the differences are and I just think it makes it a lot simpler, and I think it's good; beneficial for juries too.

Another defence barrister who had experienced concurrent evidence also gave it endorsement, albeit with qualifications: **3.61**

> It works well where the area of expertise is well defined. When you have experts in a field who both understand their material and agree with their field of expertise, it works well, particularly with juries, so that they can understand what that expertise is. When you have bickering between experts, often juries seem to be more interested in who's right rather than the actual material.

As indicated above, there was a spectrum of opinion among defence lawyers in relation to concurrent evidence, although the balance of opinion tended toward mistrust. One identified an advantage in hearing experts at the one time: 'It benefits both sides, and it makes it easier for the jury to understand, particularly in a long trial.... it helps clarify any differences or any doubts or questions that they might have; they can be answered a lot quicker or they can see if there are any... competing areas; they can see those quite quickly.' Another was positive on the basis that 'you're likely to get to the kernel of the issue when [the experts] can argue it out for themselves rather than have the lawyers become the Chinese whisperers in the interchange. But you'll find a lot of resistance to that from those that are fond of the adversarial system in the criminal law because we like to control our own witnesses.' **3.62**

By contrast, though, another defence lawyer expressed opposition to concurrent evidence: 'Hot tubbing might work in theory but I doubt whether it would work to a defendant's interest because it's usually the mainstream expert that's giving evidence for the Crown and you need a renegade, maverick for the defence.' Another was uncomfortable with the option on the basis of the lack of control that could be exercised over the evidence: 'I'd rather know what my expert's going to say in advance.' **3.63**

In one trial, a member of counsel for the defence explained that while the trial judge and she were keen on using concurrent evidence in a criminal trial, it was counsel for the prosecution who had intervened to stop its taking place. However, in another case a defence lawyer expressed qualified reservations about concurrent evidence, in part on ideological grounds and in part on pragmatic grounds: **3.64**

> As an advocate in the adversarial system my initial reaction to it is one of resistance but I can see that there would be some cases where it would be appropriate, depending upon... being confident that your expert's opinion is not going to be overborne by the Crown's expert opinion. So where you have experts who have the same level of experience I don't think there'd be a problem, again depending upon the issue.

Another defence barrister described concurrent evidence as 'fraught with danger' because of the risk that experts could be intimidated by the presence of other witnesses, such as those who are more experienced or senior in the profession. A prosecutor expressed similar ambivalence, stressing the adversarial nature of trials but conceding that in a 'given case' 'there's no reason, in theory, it's something that could not work.' **3.65**

3.66 Another prosecutor related her experience of the concurrent evidence format being used in a voir dire. She related that: 'It was more effective, and more efficient in dealing with the issue'. She described the procedure utilized as very similar to that employed in civil trials:

> The circumstances were two experts in the area of DNA, one for the Crown, and one for the defence, and they were examined in the absence of the jury.... One of them sat where the foreman would sit, on the jury, and the other witness sat in the witness box, as ordinary. The judge was told by me, appearing for the Crown, and by defence counsel, what the disagreement was, what the issue was. She then proceeded to ask both of them a series of questions. She then gave all of the barristers the opportunity to ask any questions, just of the facts of the case.

3.67 The prosecutor described the concurrent evidence format allowing the evidence to emerge and highlighted that when it became apparent that the experts agreed, the evidence was excluded. This led her to argue that concurrent evidence should be used more frequently, although she emphasized logistical impediments to this in terms of co-ordinating expert witnesses who have multiple commitments and some of whom need to travel long distances to attend court. It may be that increasing resort to video technology will alleviate this difficulty.

3.68 The views of participants in the current study were diverse, and it is apparent that any proposal to allow trial judges to mandate concurrent expert evidence would prompt expression of concern from a number of quarters, not only from defence lawyers. A prosecutor anticipated that there would be opposition too from some witnesses: 'One witness will not wish to engage in a panel discussion without knowing, in advance, what the other has said, and being prepared to answer it; because their professional credibility is subject to potential attack.'

3.69 A prosecutor who had not used the hot tub procedure himself, but had spoken to colleagues who had, said:

> I know the concept and the approach that's taken and it seems like a very effective way to deal with experts. In theory I think it's great and in practice when you could get it to occur I think it would assist the jury, but the practical difficulty is it is very hard to get a defence, to find a defence who would be happy for that to occur. Often the defence don't disclose things in advance.

3.70 An option that the same prosecutor raised was the calling of all of the evidence in the case and then the expert evidence. She saw merit in the use of concurrent evidence in judge-alone trials and voir dire but otherwise was emphatic that the prosecution should be able to call its own evidence.

3.71 In another trial a defence barrister commented:

> I think there is merit in the hot-tubbing kind of situation and that is because in civil trials I think experts are people and they have their own...feel their own allegiance, sometimes to those who engage them. I know that they...start out giving evidence consistent with their code of conduct and such things but that is so far but it doesn't necessarily...it's not inconsistent with their code of conduct that they not be forthcoming about weaknesses in their testimony or in their opinion, for example, not inconsistent that they don't proffer that. And I think that we're more likely to get to the bottom of the expertise when the experts get to ask each other some of those questions, because I think they're more... I think you're likely to get to the kernel of the issue when they can argue it out for themselves rather than have the lawyers become the Chinese whisperers in the interchange. But you'll meet a lot of resistance to that from those that are fond of the adversarial system in the criminal law because we like to control our own witnesses, but be that as it may in a case

such as this where the jury ultimately reject the experts there was little utility in all of us being concerned about trying to control them because they [the jury] didn't believe any of them [the experts], though. I think there's certainly a place for it and it—I know in Western Australia they sort of have a two-tiered system where pre-trial proceedings are videotaped and then replayed in front of a jury. So I could imagine if there is a real issue about expertise that why couldn't you sort of hot-tub the experts, video it, and then edit it as may be fit for the jury—something like that. But it's met a lot of resistance because lawyers like to confine and control.

A different perspective was provided by another defence barrister who pronounced himself unequivocally opposed to hot-tubbing: 'I think it can create a sanitized, limited view of a matter, that it is the view of what the two experts think is relevant, which may not correspond to what is actually the legal issue. I think it's very dangerous.' **3.72**

A judge with experience of concurrent evidence in civil cases proclaimed herself 'a great supporter of it', although another recalled with mirth concurrent evidence over which she had presided which had become a 'shambles'; 'I said I'd never do it again.' Another recalled using it in a civil trial where the experts 'started out with daggers drawn. And by the end, they were bending over to agree with each other wherever they could, which I thought was a very interesting psychological effect of the process.... It enabled the two experts to assert their superiority over the collection of lawyers around the courtroom. They sort of formed a common bond against the enemy.' **3.73**

Another judge commented: 'It does work in civil trials, there is no question.' A further one expressed the opinion that 'it works brilliantly in the civil jurisdiction. It makes it so much easier when you get a discussion going between the experts, and prior to their giving their evidence, you have them conferring with each other, and discussing their differences, and producing a joint report in which they identify what is common ground and where the differences are.' She lamented that: 'we'd need legislative change to permit it occurring. The only way it can occur at the moment is with the agreement of the parties.' She argued: 'I think it needs more of a push from judges to pose the questions suggested to the parties, and get them thinking about it, and talking amongst themselves about whether they'll agree to it occurring.' **3.74**

A judge who had not used concurrent evidence emphasized the adversarial nature of the criminal trial and also raised the issue of the procedure being somewhat novel: 'I really need to know more about how it would work.' A further judge raised a threshold issue for the use of concurrent evidence in criminal cases arising from the way in which this evidence is adduced in civil trials: 'The way it's done in civil cases is that the judge is usually the one who asks the questions, and that doesn't fit in well with the role of a judge in a criminal trial. I think it becomes too much [a case of the judge] entering the fray.' **3.75**

One judge, who perceived that expert partisanship was a major problem in criminal trials, commented that 'professional witnesses who are very glib at presentation, very smooth' might function as hired guns but that 'hot tubbing keeps people honest', involves greater accountability, generates evidence that is easier for the jury to understand, and usefully narrows issues in dispute. **3.76**

By contrast, another judge was troubled at the dynamics she thought likely to be generated by concurrent evidence: **3.77**

I don't like the idea of hot-tubbing.... particularly in front of juries, it's just an opportunity for people's personality and egos to come through. That's what I found, and they were trying to big-note themselves and show how much smarter they were than the other.

3.78 Some experts confused the idea of concurrent evidence (and also expert conclaves) with the idea of experts being asked to reach consensus with other experts with whom in fact they disagreed.

3.79 However, there was significant enthusiasm for the procedure from most of the experts interviewed. A number were positive about the experience of giving concurrent evidence. The most effusive proclaimed: 'It's a fantastic way to give evidence. It's great for the court.'

3.80 A forensic pathologist acknowledged the potential for the seniority of a particular practitioner to be a factor in the dynamics within the hot tub but said:

> Ultimately you rely, whether they're in court or not, and on people being rational and being prepared to concede things, so I can't see why that's any different to really relying on people to be professional.

3.81 Another said that:

> I think it's good because it gets the issues down to one or two court issues—we all agree on this, there are the two issues, this is why I say this, this is my evidence for it—and you can just have two people. The negative would be that there are people who are very good in the witness box; who are just good performers, more aggressive.

3.82 The concern about presentation style led the expert to suggest that only two people should be in the witness box at the same time.

3.83 Another advantage identified by an expert who was interviewed was that:

> One can fill in gaps for each other, because the border of one's knowledge is always a vague area and it depends very much on a person's professional experience as to how clear that border is or how vague or grey the border area is with anybody's expert evidence.

3.84 To similar effect, a psychiatrist expert expressed concern that a 'danger of having hot-tubbing with two psychiatrists together is that you could easily mount arguments for and against each other's reports. And then you could... end up moulding each other's report and you could come back to the same position or something a bit closer to each other.'

3.85 Another expert commented that:

> One of the interesting things that comes out in the hot-tubbing process is that there is often very broad agreement about the facts which might be there and what actually happened and what symptoms the person experienced.... So one of the advantages that I see of hot-tubbing is that you get everyone to agree.... Hot tubbing at least gets you down to the base line where you agree on certain basic facts and so you then clarify what the differences are... that saves a lot of time.

3.86 However, it was observed that:

> You can ask the same question to another expert and hear his answer and try and resolve why there is a difference. Yes, I think that would be very useful for a jury, although, in the more complicated cases, I wonder how much a jury actually understands.

3.87 In a similar vein an expert recounted an experience in which the experts were sent away by a trial judge to produce a 'consensus statement', but

> the barristers got all flustered and it seemed to me generally... that what was holding up concurrent evidence was that the barristers don't want to do it. They either are a bit anxious around how it will be done or they just don't want to give up their chance of their ability to cross-examine an individual witness in court.

3.88 Another expert emphasized that he would need to be provided with the proposed evidence for the defence in advance so that he could consider it before constituting the expert hot tub.

F. Videolink Evidence

Another mechanism that is used increasingly often, and which is likely to be availed of more often with the development of better technology to enable expert evidence to be given remotely, is the videolink.[48] **3.89**

It has clear logistical difficulties, all of which are capable of being overcome by suitable preparation. These involve suitable arrangements being made in advance by examining and cross-examining counsel to ensure that relevant documents are available for witnesses. **3.90**

In the study, experts appeared by videolink in seven trials. The experience of giving evidence in this way was described by one of the prosecution's medical experts in a sexual assault trial as engendering a feeling of some degree of alienation and artificiality: 'I felt cocooned from the court process to some degree.' However, the expert who reported this did not suggest that this feeling in any material way inhibited his capacity to give his evidence or adversely affected his capacity to express opinions in relation to the questions asked. **3.91**

A psychiatric expert who gave evidence in the biological sciences field said that about half of his evidence now tended to be given by videolink and that this was very convenient. However, he felt that videolink evidence was impersonal and limited the flexibility of communication, such as the ability to point to photographs while explaining their significance. **3.92**

A judge related having declined to allow further videolink evidence beyond a certain point because she felt that it 'tended to discourage the precision which was required' in the witness's evidence. **3.93**

A car crash investigation expert commented that he thought it was a little more difficult to gain rapport with a jury when giving evidence by videolink, while a medical expert said that he disliked giving evidence in this way because of the problems with being heard and the risk of audio glitches generally. However, this was not a common report from the experts interviewed. **3.94**

One medical expert, who had rarely given evidence in court before, suggested indirectly that his giving evidence via videolink may have affected his evidence by virtue of the limited pre-trial preparation done with him by the prosecutor. The prosecution lawyers had spoken to this expert on the telephone for only a few minutes before the trial and the contents of that discussion was mainly about the logistics of the video link-up. The same expert also reflected upon the impact of giving evidence via videolink and observed that a benefit to him was that the experience was: **3.95**

> probably a bit less intimidating than being in the courtroom. Technically, there were no difficulties. I could see everyone that I was supposed to see. It was a little bit disconcerting that I didn't actually see the jury, so I didn't know... at some point they left, they were asked to leave the room and then come back, and I didn't actually realize that they had gone until they were asked to come back.

This trial was identified as including problematic expert evidence and is discussed further in chapter 4.

---

[48] See also Anne Wallace, 'Using Video Link to Take Forensic Evidence—Lessons from an Australian Case Study', *The International Journal of Evidence & Proof* 17, no. 3 (July 2013) 221.

G. Conclusions

3.96 This chapter has identified a number of contemporary options in relation to the adducing of expert evidence. It has not canvassed the use of court-appointed experts, assessors, or referees, as these mechanisms are the province of civil trials. Nor has it dealt explicitly with the option for a single-expert system, such as has become prevalent in the civil jurisdiction.

3.97 It is likely that the pre-trial procedure of having experts confer and identify issues upon which they agree and disagree will be consolidated to become an orthodox part of criminal trial procedure. The provision of expert evidence remotely via videolink is similarly on its way toward procedural orthodoxy. With improvements in technology, this is likely to become a mainstay of criminal trials and the artificiality which attends it at present will become less pronounced with the passage of time and the refinement of the procedure.

3.98 The use of consecutive expert evidence and concurrent expert evidence have their origins in civil litigation, particularly in Australia. This study suggests that to translate the use of consecutive and concurrent expert evidence into the criminal law trial process before juries has much to commend it in principle as each has the potential to enhance decision-making by jurors. However, each involves important encroachments upon the adversarial process. If they are to be able to be mandated by trial judges, further consideration needs to be given as to whether they can be implemented in a way consistent with the interests of justice and also that preserves fundamental aspects of the criminal trial balance. The fact that the procedures have come from a non-criminal origin and that they cannot be wholly replicated from civil litigation is not a reason to refrain from exploring the feasibility of translating them into criminal trials, but it is a sound reason for the adoption of significant care to ensure that the balance of the criminal trial is not unfairly tilted.

3.99 The Victorian initiative of clarifying judges' powers to order expert conferencing has much to commend it as it is likely to enhance the crystallization of matters actually in dispute, and thereby to lead to greater efficiencies, reduced costs, and enhanced juror decision-making.

3.100 Although concurrent evidence has been utilized for well over a decade in Australia in land and environment cases, civil litigation generally, administrative cases, and coronial inquests, the option of concurrent expert evidence in criminal trials was novel to a significant number of participants in the project, especially to lawyers who tended to undertake defence work exclusively. Some found the concept amusing and were derisive of it. Both judges and prosecution and defence lawyers identified impediments arising from the adversary system in relation to any attempts by judges to order evidence to be given in such a way.

3.101 Concerns were expressed about the suitability of concurrent evidence for criminal trials on multiple bases. Some related to the requirement that concurrent evidence would impose upon the defence to go 'out of order' and, in effect, adduce their evidence during the prosecution case. Other concerns related to the appropriateness of such a procedure for a criminal trial and also the logistical difficulties of cross-examination, especially for the defence, and thus the potential for disadvantaging defendants. However, what was apparent from the reflexive opposition to concurrent expert evidence from many defence lawyers was that their position arose not so much from principle as from a perception that a mechanism (such as concurrent evidence, or even consecutive evidence) that enabled readier comparison between the content and quality of expert opinion evidence adduced by the prosecution and the defence may be tactically disadvantageous to defendants.

3.102 While concurrent evidence has the potential to crystallize issues in dispute and enable readier evaluation of the differences between expert opinions from witnesses called for the prosecution as against the defence, it is no panacea for the challenges posed by expert evidence. It may provide a platform for some experts to be intimidating and domineering in a way which does not contribute to sound evaluation. This is more problematic in the forum of a criminal trial where a trial judge would be likely to feel greater constraints on exercising the kind of active control over the concurrent evidence procedure that has made it successful in many forms of civil disputation. This role of the trial judge in respect of concurrent evidence in criminal trials before jurors requires further consideration; the mere fact of its success in other legal domains does not mean per se that it is suitable for criminal jury trials.

A related issue arising from the concurrent evidence procedure is that its use in criminal trials **3.103** would require the development of clear and fair protocols to address the limitations upon the trial judge's role, including clarification of who will adduce the evidence from the witnesses, and how cross-examination will function, as well as the acquisition of skills by counsel so as to ensure that witnesses are made properly accountable.[49] The issue in this regard is of real consequence because the concurrent evidence dynamic is significantly different from that of orthodox adducing of expert evidence—as is the facility for experts to commentate upon each other's opinions and ask each other questions within the witness box. The advocacy involved in dealing with these often unpredictable aspects of the expression of opinions is different from that which is customarily practised in adversarial criminal trials. This is not a reason not to utilize more concurrent evidence in criminal trials before jurors, but it emphasizes that its introduction involves a significant adjustment to traditional adversarial contests, requiring clear articulation of rights and obligations so as to preserve a proper balance within the criminal trial between the state and the accused person, as well as the need for development of advocates' skill-sets to ensure that the questions that should be asked are posed in ways which are consistent with an effective representation of the interests of both the prosecution and the defence.

The extent of enthusiasm for concurrent expert evidence in all areas of contested litigation **3.104** outside the criminal domain[50] means that the pressures will continue to build for the further introduction of the procedure into criminal trials. The results of this study confirm the existence of such pressures. As yet, there are relatively few examples of concurrent evidence in contested criminal matters. The Victorian County and Supreme Court reforms, though, underline that the broad interests of efficiency and clarification of issues in dispute amongst expert witnesses are highly likely to result in court reforms which enable trial judges to order expert evidence to be adduced in a concurrent format. The question is ceasing to be whether this will occur and is transitioning to the question of when, and under what circumstances, and with what protections it will occur. The challenge ahead is to adapt the procedures pioneered by McClellan J in the land and environment context to the criminal jury environment. Just as there remain procedural issues yet to be resolved about how many experts at a time should be permitted to give concurrent evidence and how such evidence should take place in the civil trial context, further consideration needs to be devoted to the ways in which the concurrent evidence procedure can be harnessed to the exigencies of the criminal trial.

---

[49] See Antonia Croke and Louise Mallon, 'Hot-Tub: Lessons from Australia', *Ashurst: Commercial Litigation Newsletter* (October 2013), <https://www.ashurst.com/publication-item.aspx?id_Content=9604>.

[50] See e.g. Gary Downes, 'Concurrent Expert Evidence in the Administrative Appeals Tribunal: The New South Wales Experience'; Gary Downes, 'Ten Years as President' (lecture, 2012 AAT National Conference, Lorne, 20 March 2012), <http://www.aat.gov.au/about-the-aat/engagement/speeches-and-papers/the-honourable-justice-garry-downes-am-former-pre/ten-years-as-president>; Freya Kristjanson, '"Hot Tubs" and Concurrent Evidence: Improving Administrative Proceedings', *Canadian Journal of Administrative Law and Practice* 25, no. 1 (March 2012) 79; Peter Garling, 'Reflections on Concurrent Expert Evidence', *Bar News* (Summer 2011–22) 12.

3.105 Logistics, expense, and considerations of efficiency all suggest that, in the years to come, expert evidence is likely to be given more regularly via videolink from the expert's workplace. Considerations of optimizing communication effectiveness suggest that often it will be considered tactically preferable by advocates to secure the physical presence of expert witnesses within the courtroom.

3.106 However, given the ubiquity of available 'on-screen information', there is no reason why expert evidence should not more often be given via videolink, with a direction from trial judges to jurors that they should view in court and out-of-court expert evidence equally. In addition, the physical presence of expert witnesses, and thereby the ability to draw inferences from their demeanour, is arguably not as important as it is with respect to lay witnesses.

3.107 Some of those experts who gave their evidence via videolink did note that they felt restricted in their ability to communicate effectively with the jury. In trials where the expert evidence is central to the decision to be made by the jury and the evidence is opposed by an opposing expert, these experts would prefer to be in the courtroom in order to maximize their ability to communicate their opinion effectively to jurors. However, it may be that in turn this consideration requires a reframing of skills and attitudes as part of the different expectations and experiences that are part of the Internet era.

3.108 It is apparent therefore that processes of adducing expert evidence, and testing it, will continue to evolve in the years ahead, with a number of the benefits identified from the more flexible procedures that have been utilized in the civil justice context being imported (with necessary adjustments) into criminal trials.

4

INFLUENCES ON EXPERT EVIDENCE ATTRIBUTABLE TO THE ADVERSARY PROCESS

A. Introduction

Many infamous trials have created a perception that errant, biased experts are primarily responsible for miscarriages of justice. The court in the disciplinary hearing relating to Sir Roy Meadow's provision of expert evidence on Sudden Infant Death Syndrome in the murder trial against London solicitor, Sally Clark, said Professor Meadow gave his evidence 'in a colourful way which might well have been attractive to a jury without expressly disclaiming any expertise in the field on an issue the only possible relevance of which can have been…to support the prosecution's case that the children had both died from unnatural causes.'[1] The evidence of eminent Canadian paediatrican Dr Charles Smith, in a series of Sudden Infant Death murder trials spanning almost 20 years, was found to be woefully lacking in independence. Dr Smith 'admitted his own arrogance and the dogmatic manner in which he often presented his opinions…As well, his deeply held belief in the evil of child abuse caused him to become too invested in many of these cases. As a result, the objectivity and self-discipline that must be the foundation of the expert's role proved to be beyond him.'[2] The professional ties between Dr Smith and his supervisor left the latter increasingly incapable of evaluating Dr Smith's work with objectivity.[3] **4.01**

[1] *General Medical Council v Sir Roy Meadow* [2006] EWCA Civ 1390, [2007] QB 462 [83] Clark MR (dissent).

[2] Stephen T. Goudge, *Inquiry into Pediatric Forensic Pathology in Ontario: Report* (Ontario Ministry of the Attorney General, 2008) ('Goudge Report'), p. 203, <http://www.attorneygeneral.jus.gov.on.ca/inquiries/goudge/>.

[3] Goudge, *Inquiry into Pediatric Forensic Pathology in Ontario*, p. 334

4.02 Infamous miscarriages of justice have prompted a number of government inquiries, in which bias has featured as a prominent concern.[4] The report by the Law Commission of England and Wales 2011, *Expert Evidence in Criminal Proceedings*, considered whether expert evidence was being admitted in criminal proceedings with insufficient scrutiny.[5] The Commission's recommendations focussed on the expert's duty to be impartial. They recommended that expert evidence be subject to a new impartiality test whereby evidence is inadmissible 'if there is a significant risk that the expert has not complied with, or will not comply with, his or her duty to provide objective and unbiased evidence, unless the court is nevertheless satisfied that it is in the interests of justice to admit the evidence'.[6] A further recommendation was also made to amend the *Criminal Procedure Rules 2010* (UK) to include that: 'before giving oral evidence, an expert witness should be referred to his or her overriding duty to give expert evidence that is...objective and unbiased....'[7] That has since been implemented in the Criminal Procedure Rules 2014 (UK).

4.03 Recent Australian law reform has focussed on promoting impartiality by requiring legal and professional guidelines for experts that emphasize these principles.[8] The New South Wales Law Reform Commission's 2005 report on expert witnesses, too, acknowledged that it is difficult to quantify the extent of conscious bias but assumed it exists. The report's focus for redressing the problem of conscious bias was to amend the behaviour of the experts. It recommended measures 'specifying the duty of expert witnesses to assist the court honestly and objectively (such as codes of conduct) and sanctions for experts found to have deliberately breached their duties.'[9]

4.04 Professional associations have been motivated to produce guidelines that address the issue of bias. For example, the United Kingdom General Medical Council has issued a guidance note, *Acting as a Witness in Legal Proceedings*, which provides, among other things, that: 'You must not allow your views about a person to affect the evidence or advice you give.' In a footnote accompanying this duty, the guide states that:

> This includes your views about a patient's lifestyle, culture or their social or economic status, as well as the characteristics protected by legislation: age, disability, gender reassignment,

---

[4] See eg Anthony Campbell, *The Fingerprint Inquiry* (Edinburgh, 2011), <http://www.forensicdna.co.za/index.html/downloads/fingerprint_inquiry_report.pdf>; Law Commission of England and Wales, *Expert Evidence in Criminal Proceedings in England and Wales: Report No. 325* (London: The Stationery Office, 2011) ('Law Commission Report'), <http://www.lawcom.gov.uk/project/expert-evidence-in-criminal-proceedings/#expert-evidence-in-criminal-proceedings>; Goudge, *Inquiry into Pediatric Forensic Pathology in Ontario: Report*; Committee on Identifying the Needs of the Forensic Sciences Community, National Research Council, *Strengthening Forensic Science in the United States: A Path Forward* (Washington, DC: The National Academies Press, 2009); Expert Working Group on Human Factors in Latent Print Analysis, *Latent Print Examination and Human Factors: Improving the Practice through a Systems Approach* (US Department of Commerce, National Institute of Standards and Technology, 2012).

[5] Law Commission of England and Wales, *Expert Evidence in Criminal Proceedings in England and Wales: Report No. 325*, para. 1.2, <http://www.lawcom.gov.uk/project/expert-evidence-in-criminal-proceedings/#expert-evidence-in-criminal-proceedings>.

[6] Law Commission of England and Wales, *Expert Evidence in Criminal Proceedings in England and Wales: Report No. 325*, para. 4.9.

[7] Law Commission of England and Wales, *Expert Evidence in Criminal Proceedings in England and Wales: Report No. 325*, para. 4.46.

[8] See Ian Freckelton, 'Forensic Codes of Ethics and Practice', in *Expert Evidence: Law, Practice, Procedure and Advocacy*, edited by Ian Freckelton and Hugh Selby, 6th edn. (Sydney: Thomson Reuters, 2016). See for example *Supreme Court (General Civil Procedure) Rules 2005* (Vic) r. 44.03: A key requirement for a court expert is that they are independent and impartial and are 'not an advocate for a party'.

[9] New South Wales Law Reform Commission, *Expert Witnesses: Report No. 109* (Sydney: New South Wales Law Reform Commission, 2005), para. 5.19 and recommendation 9.3.

race, marriage and civil partnership, pregnancy and maternity, religion or belief, sex and sexual orientation.[10]

Similar guidelines have been promulgated by Medical Boards in other jurisdictions.[11] The primary focus of recent Canadian policies, such as autopsy guidelines for criminally suspicious cases, has been on promoting an open-minded, objective approach for forensic pathologists that is based upon evidence.[12] However, such guidelines have not been generated from rigorous research that confirms that having an expert make a declaration will ameliorate the perceived problem of expert bias. **4.05**

Whilst governments and other authorities have focussed attention on the problem of bias and the expert, what is apparent is the dearth of factual understanding of the issues at hand to guide law reformers on how to address the subject. As Edens and others noted: 'Despite considerable interest in the topic of expert objectivity, relatively little systematic investigation has been undertaken to ascertain the scope of this issue.'[13] In 1999, in an earlier phase of the current project, Australian judges were surveyed about their perceptions of expert evidence in civil and criminal trials. The judges perceived that bias was a significant problem with expert evidence. Two thirds of judges said that they encountered bias 'occasionally', while a quarter encountered it 'often'. Seventy per cent of judges estimated that the same expert witnesses appeared regularly before them for the same side. Eighty-five per cent said that they encountered partisanship in expert witnesses. Of those, 47% (40% of all respondents) said that this was a significant problem for the quality of fact-finding in their court.[14] **4.06**

Whilst biased expert evidence has been the focus of law reform initiatives in the United Kingdom, Australia, and Canada this century, this ignores the empirical research that has identified the absence of robust scientific underpinnings in the expert opinions as a significant cause.[15] The fact that the unreliable evidence of expert witnesses such as Meadow, Smith, the United States blood spatter expert Duane Deaver, and the Australian gunshot residue expert Robert Barnes was repeatedly admitted in multiple jurisdictions implies systemic problems in the way in which expert evidence is managed in the adversarial system that extend beyond any particular errant expert.[16] **4.07**

In this chapter, systemic influences on expert evidence attributable to the adversary process are reviewed. These are factors associated with aspects of the impact of the adversarial system **4.08**

[10] General Medical Council, *Acting as a Witness in Legal Proceedings* (2013), p. 2, <http://www.gmc-uk.org/guidance/ethical_guidance/21188.asp>. In an earlier guidance note, withdrawn on 22 April 2013, the issue of bias was dealt with in General Medical Council, *Acting as an Expert Witness: Supplementary Guidance* (July 2008), para. 14, <http://www.gmc-uk.org/guidance/archive.asp>.

[11] See for example, Medical Board of Australia, *Good Medical Practice: A Code of Conduct for Doctors in Australia* (March 2014), ch. 8.8, <http://www.medicalboard.gov.au/Codes-Guidelines-Policies/Code-of-conduct.aspx>.

[12] Goudge, *Inquiry into Pediatric Forensic Pathology in Ontario: Report*, p. 349.

[13] John F. Edens and others, '"Hired guns," "Charlatans," and Their "Voodoo Psychobabble": Case Law References to Various Forms of Perceived Bias Among Mental Health Expert Witnesses', *Psychological Services* 9, no. 3 (August 2012) 259: p. 261. See also Steve D. Charman, 'The Forensic Confirmation Bias: A Problem of Evidence Integration, Not Just Evidence Evaluation', *Journal of Applied Research in Memory and Cognition* 2, no. 1 (March 2013) 56: p. 57.

[14] See Ian Freckelton, Prasuna Reddy, and Hugh Selby, *Australian Judicial Perspectives on Expert Evidence: An Empirical Study* (Melbourne: AIJA, 1999).

[15] See further Gary Edmond, 'Constructing Miscarriages of Justice: Misunderstanding Scientific Evidence in High Profile Criminal Appeals', *Oxford Journal of Legal Studies* 22, no. 1 (2002) 53.

[16] See further Ian Freckelton, *Scholarly Misconduct: Law, Regulation, and Practice* (Oxford: Oxford University Press, 2016).

on expert witness roles and performance at trial, emerging from our analysis of the views expressed about 55 Australian criminal trials including:

(a) expert familiarity or unfamiliarity with the courtroom;
(b) the extent of preparation in advance of trial by the lawyers and the experts;
(c) the extent of consultation between lawyers and experts prior to trial;
(d) disparities between pre-trial expert opinions and evidence presented in court;
(e) the role and use of expert reports at trial;
(f) the match between an expert's scope of expertise and opinions expressed in court; and
(g) partisanship of expert witnesses.

4.09 In some instances, these influences emerged in the facts of the case; in others they were mentioned by interview participants. For example, in one trial, both the trial judge and the defence barrister perceived that an expert went beyond his expertise. This perception was confirmed by a successful 'no case' submission, which was based solely on the inadequacies of the expert's evidence.

B. Expert Familiarity with Trial Procedures

4.10 One factor that may influence the effectiveness of an expert witness in interacting with the criminal justice system is the extent of that expert's familiarity with trial procedures and prior experience as an expert. The nature and extent of prior experience in court among the experts who participated in this project was very diverse, ranging from novices who were inexperienced in giving expert testimony[17] to expert expert witnesses who had mastered the demands of the courtroom setting over many years.[18]

4.11 On average, the experts who participated in this project appeared in court 15 times a year and prepared 145 reports annually, averaging approximately twelve reports per month. At one extreme are the highly experienced experts who make repeated and frequent appearances in court. At the other extreme are inexperienced tyros unfamiliar with the demands and procedures of criminal jury trials. We asked the experts how often they attended court and have reported the results in Table 4.1.

4.12 More than half (53.8%) of the experts estimated that they appeared in court once a month or less. Just under a third (31.1%) said that they attended court at least once a week. There were no obvious correlations between the type of expert evidence and the frequency of court attendance.

4.13 Many cases in which experts are commissioned for reports may settle, or fail to proceed to trial for other reasons. Thus, the extent of engagement of expert witnesses with the criminal justice system is not reflected solely by the number of court appearances per expert. One defence Queen's Counsel explained her preference to use consulting experts to prepare for trial, even if she did not intend to call any expert evidence in rebuttal. In many cases, experts are briefed to prepare a report on a particular topic, and after reports are reviewed, the case may settle, or the issues in dispute may change, and the expert evidence may not be required at trial. Thus, many experts prepare more reports for cases than are used at trial. We asked the

[17] Stanley Brodsky and Tess Neal, 'Preparing and Giving Expert Testimony', in *Psychologist's Desk Reference*, edited by Gerald Koocher, John Norcross, and Beverly Greene, 3rd edn. (New York: Oxford University Press, 2013), pp. 604–8.

[18] Stanley Brodsky, *The Expert Expert Witness: More Maxims and Guidelines for Testifying in Court* (Washington, DC: American Psychological Association, 1999).

Table 4.1 Annual frequency of court appearances by expert witnesses.

Number of court appearances	Frequency description	Number of experts	Percentage
1–12	One appearance per month or less	43	53.8
13–50	Between two and four appearances per month	21	26.2
50+	One or more appearances per week	4	5.0
Did not answer question	N/A	12	15.0
Total		80	100.0

Table 4.2 Annual frequency of court reports submitted by experts.

Number of reports	Frequency description	Number of experts	Percentage
1–12	One report per month or less	5	6.3
13–52	One report per week or less	20	25.0
53–104	Two reports per week or less	17	21.3
105–156	Three reports per week or less	3	3.8
157–208	Four reports per week or less	10	12.5
209–260	Five reports per week or less	3	3.8
261–312	Six reports per week or less	3	3.8
313–364	Seven reports per week or less	2	2.5
365+	Eight or more reports per week	4	5.0
Did not respond to question	N/A	13	16.3
Total		80	100.3

Note. Percentages do not add to exactly 100.0% due to rounding error.

participating experts to estimate how often they submitted expert reports. As we anticipated, the frequency of report preparation by the experts far exceeded that of their in-court appearances. The average frequency with which the experts submitted reports for cases in litigation is shown in Table 4.2.

Results indicated that a relatively small proportion of the experts, 6.3% ($n = 5$) wrote between one and 12 court reports per year. At the other extreme were the 11.3% ($n = 9$) of the experts who estimated that they submitted in excess of 260 court reports a year, which equates to at least one report every workday. These findings revealed that one in ten of the experts in our study sample devoted all of their professional time to forensic report-writing and giving expert evidence. **4.14**

(1) Repeat player effects and professional experts

Individual experts with more forensic experience, who devoted a substantially higher proportion of their work time to the preparation of expert reports and to giving expert evidence, were professional experts. The vast majority of the professional experts, who were well-acquainted with trial procedures and were established repeat players in the criminal justice system attending court on a weekly basis, were perceived by the judge, the lawyers, and the jurors to have provided adequate evidence in court. **4.15**

However, seven of the nine highly experienced experts who appeared in seven different project trials were identified by the interview participants as providing evidence in court that **4.16** was problematic in some respect. Three of these experts appeared for the prosecution and four for the defence. These seven experts each attended court three to four times per month, on average 40 times annually. Each authored in excess of 200 expert reports each annually, averaging four per week.

4.17 Most commonly, the judge and lawyers had been previously acquainted with these professional experts or their reputation, before the expert appeared in court and gave evidence at trial. During their interviews, the judges and lawyers compared their adverse expectations with the expert's actual performance in the project trial. Five of the experts lived up to their adverse reputations. One defence expert defied his reputation when he gave his evidence 'in a fairly straightforward fashion, and reasonable fashion' which 'pleasantly surprised' the judge (Trial 18). Another expert, who was called by the prosecutor, had a solid reputation but appeared to be over-used because of his 'courtroom success': 'He's become this sort of fall-back expert for everything' (defence counsel, trial 16). This professional expert straying beyond the limits of his expertise was the root of the perceived problems with the expert evidence in that trial. Trial 16 is discussed further in paragraphs 4.73–7 of this chapter.

4.18 Trial 50 provided a typical example of how the expert evidence of a seasoned professional expert was received. The stakeholders who were interviewed in that trial were uniformly underwhelmed by the performance of the highly experienced prosecution expert. Defence counsel curtailed the cross-examination as: 'I suspect he's a bit of a star, and he was behaving like that, and I thought "hmm, the more I ask you questions, the more I'm giving you oxygen to your star fire", so I just decided to wrap it up.' The jury was not wholly impressed by this expert's seniority. One of the jurors was quite negative about this witness: 'There is no doubt that the expert impressed most of the jury, but he was not consistent, and was defensive...'

4.19 One of the reasons why parties continue to rely on experts despite their negative reputations emerged in trial 22, which was a case of historical sexual assault. In that trial, the judge identified what we designated the repeat player effect, arising from that expert's extensive familiarity with the courtroom. This expert called on behalf of the accused: 'didn't react as neutrally to questions or challenges in cross-examination as [the prosecution expert] did, so he was a little more an advocate for his own cause, a little more sort of prepared to argue he was right...a bit sort of dismissive about anybody who would dare challenge his conclusions.' The prosecutor viewed this defence expert as evasive: '[He] likes to talk a lot and he doesn't necessarily answer the question.' The prosecutor sympathized with the unsatisfactory predicament of the defence in having to rely on this repeat player, providing some insight as to why parties continue to call experts with negative reputations:

> ... really he's the only expert that the defence—and this is Australia wide—he's pretty much the only person that they have to call to dispute this kind of evidence. So, he's been in a lot of trials, and we have transcripts of his evidence from other trials. So I can review that and get some idea of the kind of points he makes.... What you find is what he's critical of in one case, he's not critical of in another case. So you start finding that there are a lot of things that he says that don't add up.

4.20 When interviewed, the defence expert explained that he had approached the trial with a desire to help out the defence as far as was scientifically possible. As a scientist, he could not support the case theory proposed to him by counsel for the defence. Consequently, he strayed from the questions asked in an effort to find some positive point that the defence could make against the prosecution's expert evidence. The defence counsel found this annoying because the expert was evading the questions asked rather than providing the evidence which counsel was attempting to elicit. Skirting the question in examination-in-chief and cross-examination was the way that this expert dealt with this uncomfortable position.

(2) The impact of novice experts

At the other end of the spectrum were experts unfamiliar with the courtroom. Eight of our eighty experts (10%) were identified as novice experts who provided problematic evidence. These eight experts appeared in eight trials (14.5%). All but one of these experts was called by the prosecution. One of the novice experts appeared in two project trials. The inexperienced experts attended court infrequently, up to four times a year, with half of them attending no more than twice a year. On average, they wrote fewer than ten forensic reports annually. The inexperienced experts were usually proficient practitioners, who were highly knowledgeable on the topic in issue in the trial or had intimate knowledge of the person discussed in court, but had rarely been examined and cross-examined in court. As judge 14 explained: **4.21**

> From time to time, there's an expert witness who doesn't perform particularly well. Usually it's because they're not accustomed to it and often it will be young doctors who maybe spent a year or whatever period it might've been doing their internship in a hospital and so they come across this case and they have to come to court. They are the ones who are often the least equipped to deal with the context of the trial and being cross-examined. Yeah, so the younger, less experienced ones, for whom it would be a once-in-five-years experience, maybe.

The judge in trial 2 perceived a problem with the clinician who gave expert evidence in that trial: **4.22**

> He'd actually seen him and seen his family, and engaged in the testing of him, and he was a doctor. So, in that sense it perhaps is not that surprising— but I didn't think he was particularly objective... He wasn't a particularly polished witness. There was a massive chasm, I thought, between he and [the highly experienced opposing expert] who was very familiar with court and what he could and couldn't say.

No findings indicated that the poor performance of the inexperienced experts impacted significantly upon the jury verdicts in seven of the eight trials included in the project. Many of the lawyers were of the opinion that with a few more years of experience, these experts would provide competent performances in court. For example, in murder trial 26, where psychiatric evidence was central to the mental impairment defence, the prosecution psychiatrist lacked confidence, and was unfamiliar with the materials as he had not reviewed them before the trial, and gave oral evidence which was inconsistent with the opinion in his report. The judge noted: **4.23**

> He didn't come across as a person who was comfortable with the topic of mental impairment, but again, he hasn't been practising for a long period of time... I don't want to be hard about it because I think it's a difficult concept, and that with time and experience he'll be very good at it, but he didn't come across very confidently at this trial.

In sexual assault trial 13, the expert witness's inexperience, combined with a lack of preparation by the expert, contributed to poor evidence that probably was at least partially responsible for the acquittal by the jury. In that trial, the complainant reported a violent assault but there were few injuries, which the defence contended made the complainant's version of events unreliable. Furthermore the complainant declined an internal examination when she reported the assault, a matter that troubled the jury. The expert called by the prosecution was the doctor who examined the complainant for injuries and asked her to undergo an internal examination within a few hours of the alleged assault. **4.24**

4.25 All the lawyers noted that the expert needed further training on how to conduct the forensic examination of an alleged victim of sexual assault. The expert made little attempt to ask the complainant about her version of events, and then relate this information to the injuries that the expert observed on the complainant's body. The defence barrister explained that this would 'take a lot of the heat out of aspects of cross-examination of the complainant, but [this expert] seemed not to do that.'

4.26 The prosecutor acknowledged that the expert's evidence in relation to the complainant's refusal to consent to an internal examination was unhelpful. The expert failed to address:

> the reasons why a complainant did not consent and why consent is important in the particular circumstances of people who have been raped just to assist the jury to understand the reasons why a person may not consent and what the role of consent is in medical treatment. I think that he took that a little bit for granted and he just said 'oh well, she didn't consent and patient consent is important' but didn't...I couldn't extract it out of him as to why.

4.27 The expert did not attempt to dispel the common misperception that you would expect to find a bloodied and torn vagina after a violent assault. As the judge summarized, the expert was inexperienced, and tended to brush over important aspects of the injuries and 'the defence got a bit of mileage out of him actually'.

4.28 The expert reported to the court that the complainant refused to be examined internally but the expert failed to explain to the court whether he discussed the importance of an internal examination with the complainant. This was a significant issue for the jury.

4.29 The jurors confirmed that they found this expert's evidence in relation to the patient consent damaging to the prosecution case and that this expert's evidence was unsatisfactory on this particular issue. The jurors noted the inexperience of this witness. When asked how the witness handled cross examination, juror 4 said:

> Not terribly well. He was clearly under a bit of pressure and...I think his records were a little inadequate. He referred to his records a lot as if he hadn't possibly done the homework on the case before he was interviewed. I think probably the witnesses if they know they are going to be cross-examined, they need to review the case a bit in their own minds and with their notes.

4.30 The prosecutor reported extremely limited time to confer with the expert. She said she 'had two minutes with the expert prior to his evidence being given.' The expert also admitted that 'I wasn't prepared...I suppose...[My evidence] went on for over an hour, which I wasn't really prepared for.' This suggested that this expert did not appreciate the role of his evidence in the trial. Time preparing this inexperienced expert for his courtroom performance, well in advance of the trial, could have ameliorated the juror's perception that the expert had not prepared himself adequately for trial. Lack of adequate trial preparation was a recurring theme in many trials, and we look at this in more detail now.

C. Inefficiencies of Expert Evidence at Court

4.31 We monitored the 55 trials in this project to identify instances of inefficiencies related to expert evidence that had a detrimental impact on expert evidence at court. Difficulties with expert evidence were reported in 22 of the 55 trials. Whilst there were examples of the expert evidence that failed to address the disputed facts and the use of hypothetical scenarios put to the experts that caused confusion amongst the lawyers and jurors and consequent courtroom inefficiencies, these were isolated instances.

The dominant cause of courtroom inefficiency was the lack of preparation for trial by both the experts and the lawyers calling the experts. Other significant inefficiencies were linked to experts who strayed beyond their expertise and problems which arose when the expert opinions expressed in pre-trial reports differed from those provided in oral evidence in court. **4.32**

(1) Lack of preparation by the lawyers and experts

Adequate and timely pre-trial preparation is key to ensuring that the expert evidence in criminal trials is of maximum assistance to the jury. A last-minute, brief chat between expert and counsel at the door of the courtroom is not going to provide the expert with sufficient context of the facts to ensure that they present their evidence in the most appropriate way. Nor will it provide counsel with detail that might assist them in formulating the best case theory. Experts also have the potential to offer sound advice to counsel when they are preparing to cross-examine the opposing expert. In this project, we explored the extent that counsel used experts as a resource in preparing for trial, and the nature of the contact between counsel and the experts in advance of trial. **4.33**

In their interviews, expert witnesses were asked two questions about their experiences with the lawyers in preparing the case for trial. Only two-thirds (66.2%) of the expert witnesses who were interviewed reported that they had conferred (whether in person or by phone) with the barrister who was calling them prior to giving evidence in court. The remaining 29.7% of the expert witnesses either did not confer with the barrister who commissioned their evidence (29.7%) or could not recall whether they had done so or not (4.1%). **4.34**

Experts were asked whether the lawyers had adequately prepared them to give evidence. Of the expert witnesses who responded to this question, half (50.0%) agreed that the lawyers had prepared them sufficiently, one quarter (25.8%) stated that the lawyers had not prepared them sufficiently, and 22.7% stated that it was not the lawyer's job to prepare them to present testimony. A small proportion, the remaining 1.5%, were unsure whether the extent of pre-trial preparations was adequate. **4.35**

Some experts who held the view that it was not the job of the commissioning lawyer to prepare them nonetheless assumed that a discussion between an expert and barrister was part of the expected preparation for giving evidence. These experts acknowledged that the discussion enabled both the expert and barrister to be better prepared for court. One pathologist with extensive experience as an expert witness described the consultation in advance of murder trial 17 in somewhat uncertain terms: **4.36**

Q Do you feel that the lawyers adequately prepared you to give evidence in this case?

A Well, I think I wouldn't say that it's a lawyer's function to prepare me. I think the point of having a conversation beforehand is to ensure that the lawyer understands what I'm going to say and/or what I can say and what I can't say, and that I perhaps get to hear some more of the circumstances, and what the real issues are, so that I get a bit more time to prepare for that.

The forensic medical expert in the same trial explained the importance to him of the opportunity to talk to the barrister before he gave evidence, particularly to reduce the risk of there being a gap between what the expert can offer and what the lawyer asks: **4.37**

Q Did the lawyers adequately prepare you to give evidence in this case?

A No.

Q Why not?
A There was just like I said no interaction, and I guess perhaps from their perspective, we are considered expert evidence providers. And perhaps we are aware of the role we are playing. But every case I feel is different, and the angle that they may be taking could be different, and we can only present the information in the way we have structured it in our statement...
Q If you ever do meet them how does that improve your experience in court?
A Well there's only been one occasion in the three years that someone has met me. It gives you a little bit more confidence in the direction of the case and how your information is to be used... the other thing, we feel limited on the stand when there's questions that could be asked of us that aren't asked. Whether it's a lack of understanding on the behalf of the individual, it's quite frustrating that perhaps there's something missed that you could point out.

4.38 Overall, more than three quarters (77.3%, $n = 17$) of the 22 trials in which difficulties with the expert evidence were reported featured a lack of trial preparation in the form of failure to conduct timely and adequate pre-trial discussions between the experts and the barrister leading this evidence.

(a) Inadequate preparation by legal counsel for in-court expert examinations

4.39 A common problem that became evident in the interviews with the experts and lawyers was that counsel failed to prepare themselves properly for the examination-in-chief with experts. The successful 'no case' submission in the dangerous driving case (trial 16) in which a professional expert, familiar with court procedures, gave opinions beyond the scope of his expertise, occurred because the prosecutor failed to ask her expert necessary questions in re-examination to ensure that the evidence was adequate to support the allegations. The defence counsel in that trial observed that the highly experienced expert did not fully understand the circumstances of the accident.

4.40 This expert did not spend any time with the prosecutor in preparation for this trial. He strayed beyond his expertise because he was caught off guard. He had not been provided with all the relevant documents in advance of the trial, and was cross-examined on information that he had not previously seen. He also noted that helpful elements within his expertise could have been provided during examination-in-chief, but were omitted as the prosecutor did not know of them to ask about them: '... in retrospect it would have been interesting to have been asked other questions by the prosecution that I didn't get a chance to come out with during my cross-examination.'

4.41 When asked whether there was anything else she would like to raise, the judge in that trial explained:

> I think the real issue is preparation by counsel. The real issue is counsel thinking how they are going to present the evidence to the jury. That's the real fundamental issue, and that's where the failure is. None of the evidence is ever that complicated. It's a question of how do they present it. And in that case it was quite clear the defence barrister knew her stuff... she knew the technicalities of the expert evidence and was able to home in on the so-called expert evidence as to what were the deficiencies.

4.42 In sexual assault trial 2, where the expert evidence was central to the defence, the prosecutor had no conference with her inexperienced expert and defence counsel had two short conversations with her inexperienced expert: 'When I say "short", ten minutes or so, so that's not long, and maybe I should have had longer, but I just expected him to give evidence in the same way that he did last time.'

In his interview, the novice treating doctor from trial 55 explained that he had only given evidence once before in a court. He admitted to feeling uncomfortable in court. He believed that he was a perceptive witness, testifying about his personal experience in treating the complainant. He commented that the questions asked by the barristers were undermining what he said. As a treating clinician, he was unaware that he was attending court as an expert witness: **4.43**

> Do you think that the court, or somebody, had a responsibility to me to explain to me, first off that I was an expert witness, and what was expected, not of me in the case, but what is expected of me as an expert witness?... They asked me all these open-ended questions about the disorder, so they obviously considered me an expert, but I wasn't considering myself an expert. It was confusing.

This expert did not understand or appreciate his role in the trial.

In sexual assault trial 13, where the complainant's behaviour was integral to the defence's contention that the contact was consensual, the prosecutor called an expert to explain the sometimes counter-intuitive behaviour of victims of sexual assault. The prosecutor reported that she spent almost no time with the expert prior to presentation of this evidence in court 'because he was overseas. He arrived on the morning to give evidence... I think I would have had three minutes with him in total, which is not ideal.' **4.44**

In another sexual assault trial, where the expert evidence was central to the defence (trial 18), the prosecutor said: **4.45**

> I did not have the opportunity of conferring with him... I would have liked the opportunity to confer with him, but one of the reasons the Crown put 'experienced' people in is on the basis that they should be able to qualify a witness and lay a proper basis. But, no, I was not given that luxury.

By comparison, two senior counsel emphasized the importance of spending time with their expert pre-trial. One prosecuting Queen's Counsel explained the importance of conferencing with their own expert before the trial: **4.46**

> You cannot present a case that is involving expert evidence without having spoken to your expert... I can't imagine anybody not conferencing their expert... you've got to understand what your expert's saying. How can you lead the evidence, and how can you then, if there's another expert, how can you understand that yourself?... So the trick is to have the conferences with the expert so that you as a prosecutor know what it is, and then you can stop the expert when he's saying things that you think the jury can't understand. If you don't have that ability, you don't understand it yourself, then how are you going to get the jury to understand it? So I don't follow why anyone would not have a conference unless it's laziness. When I say conference—sometimes many conferences, not just one, depending on the importance of the evidence.

(b) The influence of lack of preparation of inexperienced expert witnesses

Preparing the expert pre-trial is likely to be particularly important for inexperienced expert witnesses. In analysing the 22 trials, we observed that the reported lack of adequate preparation contributed to the perceived problems associated with less experienced expert witnesses. The need for more extensive preparation of inexperienced witnesses was mentioned by several stakeholders. For example, the judge in trial 55, a sexual assault trial, suggested that the expert was uninformed about available conventions to provide additional information to supplement an answer given on the witness stand: **4.47**

> I think he's just a bit inexperienced and not used to cross-examination. It was my conclusion that he might have done better if someone had prepared him by explaining to him the nature of cross-examination and his rights to explain if he wanted to.

(c) Lack of access to experts for consultation

4.48 Some counsel explained that the lack of pre-trial consultation with the experts was because they had difficulty in accessing the experts. One defence counsel was extremely frustrated by her inability to arrange a meeting with the prosecution expert in advance of the trial. She explained that to do so, you first have to request legal aid funding and then have to get the medical expert to agree to legal aid rates. Furthermore, '[t]he prosecution expert positively sort of resisted the idea... They're not obliged to meet with us... I think it makes it really unworkable and they turn up to court at five to ten'.

4.49 The defence counsel encountered the same preparation barriers with her own experts:

> One of my experts turned up at [the time court starts] so I couldn't even run the issues past my own expert... So, in this case, it was impossible for me to meet with them earlier and say, look, this case raises all of these problems. Let's identify together how best to communicate this idea. And I think that was part of the problem...

4.50 Problems reported by counsel in accessing experts before trial were more common with medical experts, particularly those whose mainstream area of work was not forensic.

4.51 In trial 26, a murder trial, where the psychiatric evidence was central to the defence, the prosecutor reported a total of two or three phone conversations with her expert: 'probably because of my own struggle to understand exactly what he was saying.' Counsel for the defence acknowledged that the time she spent with her expert before trial was minimal: 'It wasn't much. He's a hard man to get hold of. I think half an hour. I mean I had his reports.'

(2) **Disparities between opinions in expert reports and oral evidence in court**

4.52 An expert who backs down from his or her written opinion when giving oral evidence can be problematic for the criminal justice system. If the jury has a copy of the expert report, the expert's credibility is likely to come into question because of the changed opinion. Furthermore, counsel rely upon what is said in expert reports on the basis that this accurately reflects what the expert will say in court. In reliance on the expert report, counsel analyse the strength of the case and advise their client on the basis of that analysis. Before trial, counsel also formulate a case theory consistent with the expert opinion as expressed in the report. When the expert evidence changes between the time of the submission of the report and the presentation of oral evidence in court, the case theory is likely to need modification. Thus, when an expert in court significantly qualifies the opinions expressed in the pre-trial forensic report, this leaves that party with a weakened case. The inconsistency should be picked up during pre-trial conferencing or by a supplementary report but this is not always the case. This issue is addressed further in the discussion about the lack of pre-trial preparation of expert witnesses in paragraphs 4.33–46.

4.53 When testifying in court, four experts in four trials (7.3%) moved away from the opinions that they had offered in their pre-trial written reports. Three of these experts had extensive experience with the court process. This change of opinion created uncertainty for the lawyers who relied upon the written reports when preparing for trial. The outcome was confusing expert evidence.

4.54 In trial 18, a sexual assault trial, the judge noted the defence expert had changed his opinion between the time of writing the report and the giving of evidence at trial. This seasoned expert indirectly acknowledged that his written opinion went further than he was prepared to go in his oral evidence, and that the defence counsel struggled with the change in opinion:

> Well, obviously I wasn't saying—although the Crown were trying to say that I was, and I think even our barrister was, to a certain extent... our barrister got the gist of that, and

> that's as far as I was prepared to go, anyway. I wasn't going to say, even if he wanted me to say something [more]. I was only prepared to say that she could have [had this reaction to the drug].

Despite his extensive experience, the expert justified the softening of the opinion he expressed in court by suggesting that the report was prepared only for the defence counsel, and that he had not expected it to be presented in court: 'I had a copy of my general report which, was really written for the solicitors, not for the court, but it went to the court.' As the general report was clearly a forensic report, such an assertion was either disingenuous, or this expert had laboured under a misunderstanding about the purpose and uses of written forensic reports. **4.55**

In this trial, the jurors were not provided with a copy of the expert report, so they were unaware of the process, and consequently did not comment on the disparities between the two opinions. However, it is becoming more common to provide expert reports to the jury, and our juror survey responses indicated that more jurors would like to receive copies of the expert reports, so this issue is likely to become more significant in the future. The defence barrister in trial 18 declined to be interviewed, so we cannot gauge the impact that this change of opinion had upon her case theory. **4.56**

In trial 10, also a sexual assault trial, the highly experienced expert provided a report which was strident in its support of the defence case. The judge's reaction to the report was as follows: **4.57**

> It made me angry, I must say. Having seen a number of sex cases and what forensic experts are prepared to say on the issue of consent, you can't be assisted one way or the other by the lack of genital injury. For him to weigh in and say more than that [in his report] caused me great concern about his level of integrity, actually... But in the end, I really think that that was probably not as contentious as the report of [the defence expert] was perhaps indicating. He seemed to water down what he was prepared to say in that regard.

The judge further noted that this is not an uncommon problem: **4.58**

> ... if the report says one thing and then the experts, as they sometimes do, get in the witness box and 'water down' what they want to say; I've seen a lot of prosecution experts do that, too, because they are faced with a bit of a dilemma sometimes as to having said some things that are rather strong in their reports, and then, when they're cross-examined, I don't know if it's vanity, or fear, or whatever it is that takes over, but they often back off.

In trial 44,[19] a murder trial, opposing experts gave evidence on the issue of mental impairment which was the key question for the jury. The defence counsel described the prosecution expert's opinion as one that *'blows in the wind'*. The judge observed that the prosecution evidence 'seemed quite confused, partly due to the fact he changed his mind.' In the judge's view, the expert **4.59**

> hadn't done his homework... gave a report prior to his final report... which did not accurately reflect his final views... and he had to explain away his error, and the result was completely confusing... He made a mess of his evidence in this case.

The prosecutor confirmed that the expert 'provided differing views at differing times. He provided three reports which all came up with different views.' Each report explained a different scenario. The defence lawyer regarded the reports as 'unintelligible' and suggested that the cause of the poor performance was a lack of adequate preparation: **4.60**

> They then write a report, then they don't look at again until—it could be 12 or 18 months later when they're called to give evidence in the trial, and often that can happen very

[19] This trial is discussed further in the case study featured in chapter 7, paragraphs 7.14–7.36.

> quickly, and all they do is they just go back to their report, and they will just rehash the contents of that report. So in his case, I think the reports with which I was served were unintelligible, and that meant that things had to be resolved on the hop. In some respects, they were resolved in the witness box, and that doesn't assist anyone. So I think that they need to be a little bit more alive to... preparing reports with clarity, as though their audience was the jury.

4.61 Despite the consensus among all the lawyers in the room that they were unimpressed by the prosecution expert, three of the four jurors interviewed were impressed with this expert. They did not complain of confusion in the evidence and they particularly liked the alternative scenarios the expert provided. However, the fourth juror interviewed suggested that the jury was divided in its impressions of this expert's evidence. He explained that whilst the majority responded well to this expert, he and two other jurors found the alternative scenarios confusing:

> Me and two other jury members thought that the scenarios actually made the whole thing a lot more confusing. And I think the judge even said that in the court later on. I found that... confusing because it was all 'if something happened' and 'if this happened' and 'if you believe that'. It was a lot of 'ifs' and I thought that confused us a lot more.

4.62 The verdict, however, suggested that the jury either did not understand the evidence or rejected the expert evidence altogether.

4.63 The cumbersome examination of the major expert witness could have been avoided by more preparation by counsel for the task. The prosecutor confirmed this, and admitted that he 'only spoke to him [the expert] about an hour all up in preparation before his evidence.' When asked whether the prosecutor had taken any steps to assist jurors to understand this expert's evidence, the prosecutor said he had not. The prosecutor did not speak with the two opposing experts called by the defence either, despite their availability, since there is no constraint on contacting a witness before trial: there is no property in an expert witness.[20] The judge observed that this expert's performance was not true to past form, indicating that the lack of pre-trial preparation was a significant factor contributing to the presentation of confusing expert evidence to the jury.

4.64 Trial 26, a murder trial, was another case in which opposing experts gave evidence on the issue of mental impairment (insanity) of the accused, which comprised the key question for the jury. The defence highlighted during cross-examination that the prosecution expert inserted additional elements of analysis of the defendant from the witness box which had not been mentioned in his pre-trial reports. Furthermore, midway through his evidence, this inexperienced expert explained to the court that his report and evidence up to that point were inaccurate. Over a recess, he had read the notes in relation to the defendant that were taken at the time of the offence, and the content of those notes contradicted the opinion and evidence he had provided. This inconsistency was discussed in the absence of the jury.

4.65 The prosecution witness changed his evidence from the opinions expressed in his reports. As the defence expert explained: 'It was from his second report that he delivered spontaneously I think, much to everyone's surprise I think, including the prosecution, but they were pretty much heading down the road of mental impairment by agreement at that point, procedurally

[20] See *Harmony Shipping Co v Saudi Europe Line* [1979] 1 WLR 1380, 1384 (Lord Denning LJ); *In Re L* [1997] AC 16, 34 (Lord Nicholls of Birkenhead); *State of New South Wales v Jackson* [2007] NSWCA 279 [33]; *Ward v The Queen* (1981) 3 A Crim R 171.

at least and then it went off the rails.' The prosecutor was disappointed by her ill-prepared expert: 'I'm not so sure he clarified things for the jury.' With the benefit of hindsight, the prosecutor said she would have prepared the case differently.

There was a consensus in the interviews with the lawyers and judge that the prosecution expert lacked confidence due to his lack of previous courtroom experience and a failure to prepare adequately. By comparison, the defence expert was perceived as a confident courtroom performer who was well prepared. The 12 juror surveys revealed no differences in the assessments of the prosecution and defence experts, with half the jurors preferring the prosecution expert. The jury deliberated for three days following this ten-day trial. The extensive jury deliberation time and the fact that none of the jurors volunteered to be interviewed for this project suggested that deliberations were fraught. Without the benefit of post-trial interviews with the jurors we could not achieve more in-depth understanding of the impact of this witness on jury deliberations. **4.66**

(3) Lack of provision of expert reports to the jury

In the 55 trials surveyed, 57.8% of the jurors who responded said that they received a copy of the expert report(s) and 42.2% said that they did not.[21] Of those who did not receive a copy of the expert reports, 46.3% would have liked to have received them. Only 2.8% asked the court for copies but were refused. Of those that did receive a copy, 15.4% of jurors reported that their jury had requested the copies. Of the 158 individual jurors who reported that they were given a copy of the expert's report, 54.5% of them said that they received the full report and 45.5% said they received only part of the report. **4.67**

When jurors had access to the expert reports, they reported that they referred to them 'reasonably frequently.' These jurors also generally agreed that the report was helpful, saved time in deliberation, and was not distracting, as shown in Table 4.3. **4.68**

Experts were also asked whether the jury received a copy of their written report. Most expert witnesses did not know (74.6%), with most of the remaining experts stating that the jury had not been provided a copy of the report (18.4%). Only a small proportion of experts confirmed that the jury had received a copy of their report (7.0%). The common theme from the experts was that they would be content if their report went to the jury. In contrast, the legal professionals thought it was inappropriate for the jurors to be provided with a copy of **4.69**

Table 4.3 Jurors' evaluations of expert reports.

Evaluation of report	Mean score
Report was helpful	3.88 (1.14)
Report saved time	3.40 (1.17)
Report was distracting	1.82 (1.09)

Note. Higher mean scores indicate more agreement with the statement. Standard deviations are provided in parentheses. Ratings were made on a five-point scale from (1) *Strongly disagree* to (5) *Strongly agree.*

[21] 275 responses were received to this question: 158 jurors said that they received the expert report(s) and 117 did not.

the expert report on grounds that the reports contained irrelevant material or material that would only serve to confuse the jurors and complicate the trial.

(4) Experts who strayed beyond the scope of their expertise

4.70 In the 1999 survey of Australian judges, they were asked what was the single most serious problem that they had encountered with expert evidence. Bias was identified as the most serious problem, but 14 judges (5.74%) identified a failure by the expert to stay within the parameters of their expertise.[22] In 2001, when magistrates were asked the same question, 18 (9.18%) gave the same answer in respect of a failure to adhere to parameters of expertise.[23]

4.71 Two experts in the current project, who were highly experienced, professional experts in the criminal justice system, strayed beyond the bounds of their expertise. While the frequency of this problem was rare among the 80 experts whose evidence was examined in this project, the impact of this behaviour on the criminal justice system warranted some examination of aspects of the system that enabled such inappropriate evidence.

4.72 One expert who strayed beyond the scope of his expertise appeared in court on average once a week, and said that he wrote hundreds of reports each year. His evidence was rated as problematic in one of the four project trials in which he appeared, a dangerous driving case.

4.73 In trial 16, this medical expert provided evidence about ergonomics in accident reconstruction. This topic was unrelated to his training and field of practice. Whilst the defence counsel didn't think 'he was the right expert for that job', before trial, she did not challenge his evidence with a view to having it excluded. The judge may well have been sympathetic to an application of that nature:

> In my view, he didn't have the relevant expertise and if it had been challenged I might well have said 'Look, I don't think he's got the expertise'. He had a degree in electrical engineering, [but] he'd never actually practised as an engineer. He said he had given evidence four or five times before on movement of passengers in a major impact type collision, [but] he couldn't remember the last time he had, and he agreed that a mechanical engineer would be far more competent to give the type of expert opinion he was expressing...

4.74 Under cross-examination, the expert rightly conceded that his opinion as to the causes of the car accident offered only one hypothesis and that alternative hypotheses might exist. Later in cross-examination, the expert conceded again that there were other reasonable possibilities open to the decision-maker as to the cause of the car accident. Again, the expert 'did not suggest that the other possibilities were far-fetched or fanciful' or that it was not a 'reasonable possibility'. Upon re-examination, the prosecutor did not elicit the necessary qualification to the expert's opinion. Both the prosecution expert and the prosecutor failed in their respective roles. The defence counsel was aware of this failing and capitalized on the error.

4.75 After two weeks of the trial, the defence barrister successfully submitted there was 'no case to answer' on the basis that the prosecution's expert evidence did not support the case put by the prosecution. By accepting that the alternative explanation was possible without clarifying that these alternatives were either unlikely, highly unlikely, or even fanciful, the matter was left open for the judge to conclude 'that the jury could not rationally conclude that the

---

[22] Freckelton, Reddy, and Selby, *Australian Judicial Perspectives on Expert Evidence*, p. 144.

[23] Ian Freckelton, Prasuna Reddy and Hugh Selby, *Australian Magistrates' Perspectives on Expert Evidence: A Comparative Study* (Melbourne: AIJA, 2001), p. 97.

expert's opinion is the only reasonable inference available on the evidence and that therefore the accused has no case to answer.'[24]

When asked about their impression of this expert,[25] the judge and defence expert both identified that the inadequate performance of this seasoned expert was probably the result of poor preparation by the prosecution's legal team. In providing evidence on a topic beyond the bounds of his expertise and about which he had little experience, he was unaware of the information he needed before formulating his opinion. As the defence counsel explained: **4.76**

> But I think his main problem in cross-examination was he didn't understand the accident, and he would sort of be quite unmoving on something, and then I'd point out 'Well, that's what the other prosecution witness said', and then he'd go 'Oh well if that what the other prosecution expert says it, it must be right'. You undermine your credibility when you do that, because it's like 'Oh what? So, if the prosecution expert says it, they must be right, and if another defence expert says it, they can't be.' I thought he was all right, but he just didn't understand what he was talking about.

In his interview, this expert provided no indication that he understood that he should have declined to give evidence on the ergonomic issues in the case. The expert suggested that he was inadequately prepared for his court appearance as not all relevant information was provided to him before trial and he was caught off guard when this was raised in cross-examination. The major failing was that the competence of the expert to address the ergonomic issues was not ascertained prior to trial and screened during the pre-trial process to ensure the reliability of the proffered evidence. Poor preparation contributed to the problematic expert evidence in this case, as has been discussed in paragraphs 4.33–46 of this chapter. **4.77**

In trial 18, opposing experts gave evidence about the effects of a specific drug in relation to a claim of sexual assault. The prosecution expert was appropriately qualified to speak about the effects of the drug, but the defence expert, whilst a highly experienced expert, familiar with trial procedures, lacked the requisite qualifications on the effects of drugs. As the judge explained, this highly experienced defence expert strayed beyond the scope of his expertise: **4.78**

> What he was doing was repeating what he'd read on the internet... I didn't think he was qualified as an expert to speak about the effects of the drug, even though he was a highly qualified expert... I queried the prosecutor about this... It seemed to me that he was essentially saying what he'd read on the internet about different studies, but he wasn't really expressing an opinion about those studies by reference to his particular expertise.

The prosecutor chose not to challenge the expert even though she acknowledged the expert lacked sufficient expertise on the topic to qualify: 'I did not think his qualifications were as well-based as the prosecution witness. I did not think that his research was particularly credible. I thought he had trawled the internet desperately to look for some material to assist the defence.' The prosecutor was of the opinion that this was a case in which no expert evidence was necessary to educate the jury about disputed issues of fact. The sole reason the prosecution called an expert was to rebut the defence expert. The prosecutor gave the impression that she did not challenge the defence expert out of due regard to the defendant's right to a fair trial and the right to introduce evidence to defend himself. **4.79**

---

24 This quotation was taken from the unreported 'no case' ruling in that trial.

25 As was common with truncated trials where the jury did not reach the deliberation phase, we have no juror interviews to refer to and only three juror surveys were completed. The juror surveys gave us no further insight into this issue as those jurors chose not to elaborate.

4.80 The expert conceded that his qualifications were less than ideal when asked how he found testifying in court in that trial:

> I suppose the negatives were perhaps that this is not my mainstream area of expertise. It's on—getting towards—the periphery, although I'm obviously entitled to give the evidence. So, I had to do a bit more research work in it, and in fact, I did quite a lot more research, because, as I was saying, we were looking at this particular family of drugs... and there's been no papers written on this particular drug causing a problem...

4.81 This expert justified his decision to provide evidence on a topic strictly beyond his usual area of work, but conceded that this pushed the boundaries of his mainstream area of expertise.

4.82 In this case, two jurors participated in an interview. One juror identified the weakness in the defence expert's evidence:

> I think that he was put in a position where professionally, the fact that he presented evidence on drugs that weren't exactly the one in question, immediately put him on the back foot. Now I don't know whose decision it was to accept that... whether he provided that information to the defence, and the defence realised that at the time? I don't know. He came across as though he Googled that information... I don't think he did it any favours... The thing that crossed my mind is... well that wasn't money well spent.

4.83 These observations suggest that this juror astutely observed that this expert had strayed beyond the boundaries of his expertise. This juror realized that this expert did nothing more than Google and regurgitate what he had read in the online product leaflet. Had the jury been provided with the leaflet, this task was within their capacity, as this required no special expertise. The defence expert could have been challenged successfully for lacking the requisite expertise, as he gave evidence that was straightforward for the jury, and arguably not 'specialized' and problematically time-consuming. This unnecessary expert evidence took up at least a day of trial time, and prompted the prosecution to call a rebuttal expert witness, further adding time and costs to the trial.

D. Expert Partisanship and Perceived Lack of Neutrality

4.84 As noted, it was expert partisanship that prompted the most stringent concern amongst judges in the 1999 survey of Australian judges. In this project, we explored that theme further. Five of the professional experts identified in this project were described by the majority of stakeholders interviewed in their trial as displaying 'dismissive, biased behaviour'. These were the only experts in the entire project who were described as biased by the majority of stakeholders interviewed in their trial. Most commonly, the judges and opposing lawyers described these experts as partisan, biased, or 'guns for hire'. The defence counsel in trial 50 elaborated on the unconscious bias of the prosecution expert as follows:

> Quite frankly I think he was partisan. I wouldn't go so far as to say it was conscious. He's a pathologist, he deals with cops, he deals with the crown, and this is the danger with expert witnesses. They take on the cause of the side that calls them, and I think that that's done largely unconsciously. But to me, he'd gone into that courtroom to secure a conviction for the cops, and I don't think he was of assistance to the court, and I don't think he was of assistance to the jury. Put it this way, if it was my expert with that attitude, I'd really think long and hard before I called him, because any time I call an expert witness, I want them to be seen to be, and to be, assisting the court.

4.85 The lawyers who called the biased expert acknowledged that the expert was not ideal, but their criticism was muted. For example, the expert was described by the barrister that called him as 'Fairly robust, such that he can appear to be condescending towards counsel, which

I don't think always plays well to the jury... So his court manner was not ideal, in my view, for that.' Another biased expert was described by the counsel that called him as 'a little bit emotional' (trial 4). In other words, the bias was alluded to by reference to the attitude or demeanour displayed by the expert.

The jurors did not typically label a biased expert as such. It was more common for the jurors to describe the biased expert's inappropriate personality, attitude, or behaviour. For instance, jurors described biased experts as egotistical, rude, arrogant, and evasive. Regarding the expert in trial 50, one juror commented 'He was too confident... and made fun of the prosecution.' (juror A, trial 50). Other examples that appeared indicative of a perceived lack of neutrality included: 'he wouldn't give a straight answer... and he was a little bit of a smart ass' (juror B, trial 1) and 'a little too self-assured, a bit of a "show-pony"' (juror B, trial 22). **4.86**

The jurors' responses to the biased expert in trial 22, a sexual assault trial, provided some insights into how jurors react to biased expert evidence. At least five of the jurors in that trial perceived the defence expert as biased. As juror B from that trial explained during the interview: 'I had an impression that, let's say [the defence expert] had a stake in the outcome, in terms of this is a blow to his ego....' **4.87**

Despite misgivings about the motives of this expert, two jurors did not dismiss his evidence outright, but appreciated the assistance he gave to the jury. **4.88**

As juror J explained: **4.89**

> It was ironic that it was the defence expert witness who helped us to understand the science better, but we ultimately chose to believe in the integrity of [the prosecution expert's] data, for reasons that he had made clear. [The defence expert] could not rule out the possibility that [the prosecution expert's] results were accurate. The defence was not able to convince the jury that contamination was a reasonable possibility, given all the other circumstantial evidence.

These jurors demonstrated a nuanced understanding of the role of the expert for the defence within an adversarial system. Whilst they identified arrogance in the defence expert, this did not prevent them from appreciating and acknowledging the value of his evidence and the assistance that it offered them. **4.90**

What is noteworthy is that the prosecution expert in trial 22 had worked for many years for the prosecution only. However, the prosecution expert was not criticized by a single respondent for his 'one-sided' background. On the other hand, the defence expert was criticized by many respondents because he appeared only on behalf of the defence. As one juror explained 'it turned me off a little bit as well, realizing that this guy seems to make a good part of his living by hopping up in the witness box for the defence.' **4.91**

Aside from the five trials where one of the experts was perceived to lack neutrality, interview participants frequently discussed the expert evidence in terms of whether it was 'biased'. Participants commented on the commendable objectivity of some expert witnesses, for instance, when an expert was willing to make concessions, defer to another expert, or admit to the limitations of their expertise. These actions were interpreted as indicators of impartiality. For example, juror C in trial 18, a sexual assault trial, said: 'I didn't walk away thinking that the prosecution expert hadn't honestly answered questions from either the prosecution or defence. I didn't get any indication in his answers of bias. It was just straight down the line.' The opposing defence expert in trial 18 explained his view of the prosecution expert: **4.92**

> Where he [the prosecution expert] had to concede, he did, and he agreed with some of the propositions that I'd put forward. There are some experts that will be entirely partisan, and will not even agree to a reasonable proposition from the other side, let alone whether the proposition's right or wrong. But no, this guy I thought was quite reasonable.

4.93 When we asked juror C in trial 18 about his understanding of an expert's role in the trial, the default position was the assumption that the expert for the defence was a 'gun for hire':

> So initially I guess the starting point is: are they a defence expert witness or are they an expert witness for the prosecution? So you have to filter that out. I think also one of the things with the expert witnesses that goes to their role is that I think there is a general perception that an expert witness called by the defence is a paid-for opinion, and that opinion may be tainted by those limitations... I think you do as a juror, have an opinion of anyone who has been called by the defence—they're not there out of the goodness of their heart; they're a paid opinion... So I think that's the starting point for anyone's perception of an expert witness called by the defence.

4.94 These and other comments from jurors suggest that it was common for jurors to scrutinize expert evidence for signs of bias.

E. Conclusions

4.95 Overall, our review of the influences on expert evidence attributable to the adversary process suggested that the current system is working reasonably well. The majority of the expert evidence provided in the 55 project trials was perceived by the judges, lawyers, experts, and jurors as appropriate and adequate. Evidence was perceived as less than optimal in 40% of the trials analysed. In ascertaining the source of the difficulties with the expert evidence in these trials, no single prominent cause emerged. Experts who provided evidence that evoked dissatisfaction from the stakeholders fell predominantly into two groups: the first group was comprised of highly experienced professional experts, and at the other extreme was the group of novice experts who had little prior exposure to adversarial procedures and the demands of the courtroom.

(1) Systemic issues with highly experienced professional experts

4.96 It is somewhat counter-intuitive that the evidence provided by highly experienced professional experts was just as problematic as that provided by experts who rarely appeared in court. Two of the highly experienced professional experts gave evidence which was beyond the scope of their expertise. Counsel chose not to challenge their evidence even though both judges suggested that the evidence should not have been admitted at trial. More systematic screening of the reliability of the proffered evidence may assist in avoiding these issues at trial.

(2) Systemic issues with novice experts

4.97 Several novice experts were perceived to provide inadequate evidence that lacked clarity. The overwhelming response to this evidence was that it wasted precious court time, rather than undermined the ability of the criminal justice system to deliver a fair trial.[26] The consensus from stakeholders was that more courtroom experience for these novice experts and greater assistance from the lawyers that called them would fill the breach of their inexperience and improve performance.

---

[26] Interestingly, Rule 403 of the United States Federal Rules of Evidence permits expert evidence to be excluded in this scenario: 'The court may exclude relevant evidence if its probative value is substantially outweighed by a danger of one or more of the following: unfair prejudice, confusing the issues, misleading the jury, undue delay, wasting time, or needlessly presenting cumulative evidence.' In Australia in the uniform evidence jurisdictions 'The court may refuse to admit evidence if its probative value is substantially outweighed by the danger that the evidence might... (c) cause or result in undue waste of time.' However, it is comparatively rarely utilized in respect of expert evidence.

Litigation lawyers need to spend time explaining the role of the expert to novice experts. Small but important practical steps can eliminate many of the observed inefficiencies. Whilst the initial letter of instruction to experts should canvass any applicable expert's code of conduct and ethical obligations, inexperienced experts will benefit from a reminder email before they appear in court, explaining to them what their role is in a criminal trial. The email could include a link to all relevant expert guidelines and codes of conduct. **4.98**

It is also important to remind novice experts to re-read their notes and reports well in advance of the day they give evidence. When novice experts were unfamiliar with what they had previously said about the individual in question, jurors perceived them to be unreliable or lacking in authority on the topic. This undermined their credibility in the eyes of the jurors. Another small but important process that can readily be incorporated into trial preparation is to meet with the novice expert and ask if they have any questions about their role, the procedures to be followed in court, etc. Any misconceptions about the trial process and their role in court can be explained. These small practical steps will contribute to building familiarity with the trial process and the confidence in the expert, and have the potential to impact positively on the credibility of the novice expert in court. **4.99**

(3) Need for more and better pre-trial preparation needed

Improvements to pre-trial preparation of both experienced and inexperienced experts are one way to reduce the impact of problematic expert evidence at trial. When expert evidence was identified as problematic by the stakeholders, it was usually evident that the barristers had spent little time with the expert who provided inadequate evidence. This was equally apparent for both the highly experienced professional experts and the novice experts. When barristers reported that they spent significant time in preparation with their expert, the evidence was perceived by the majority of the trial stakeholders to have run smoothly. **4.100**

Even when diligent defence counsel invested the time to meet with the trial experts, some encountered practical barriers to this access. The time and effort required to access further legal aid funding was identified as one impediment to adequate pre-trial preparation of expert evidence. A second problem was the failure of the prosecution experts to make themselves available for such consultations with counsel for the defence. Prosecutors and expert groups, particularly medical professionals, can encourage this process by ensuring that experts to be called by the prosecution understand that making themselves available to defence counsel prior to the trial for questioning is an intrinsic aspect of their role as an expert witness. The Supreme Court and the County Court in Victoria have implicitly encouraged greater access to opposing experts by setting out a process by which such access can be sought. The 2014 practice note provides: **4.101**

> **Availability of expert to other parties**
>
> 8.1 A party who serves an expert report on another party must—
> (a) promptly inform the expert of that fact; and
> (b) if so requested by a recipient party, arrange for the expert to be available for interview by that party and/or his/her representatives.[27]

Disparities between opinions in pre-trial reports and oral evidence in court can be ameliorated by more and better pre-trial preparation by both experts and lawyers; we turn to this now. **4.102**

[27] Supreme Court of Victoria, *Practice Note No. 2: Expert Evidence in Criminal Trials* (25 June 2014).

(4) Disparities between opinions in pre-trial reports and oral evidence in court

4.103 Findings of instances of experienced experts softening the initial opinion expressed in their report when they give oral evidence in court were sufficiently prevalent to warrant consideration as to how this behaviour can be avoided. Barristers should be able to proceed with a case theory that relies upon what the expert says in the written report exchanged prior to the trial. An expert who changes his mind and will not swear up to the opinions provided in his report has the potential to undermine a case completely. For example, the defendant loses his chance of putting forward the best defence available if a defence barrister who prepares a defence based on the expert's pre-trial opinion discovers for the first time in the course of the trial that the expert will no longer state that opinion in the same terms as were expressed in the report. Early trial preparation is one practical way in which a barrister can protect him from that predicament. A practical step to avoid this problem is to explain to the expert in the letter of instruction that the lawyers will be relying upon the expert's written report when preparing the case for trial. The need for consistency between the opinions expressed in a report prior to the trial and oral evidence given in court is important to ensure both fairness and that the best possible case on behalf of that party is presented to the jury.

4.104 Clearly there are occasions when thinking or knowledge within an area of expertise may have evolved between the time of the writing of a report and the time of trial, or when the views of other experts may cause a reassessment of an expert's position. However, such situations should not occur often. A telephone call to the expert to ensure that they still subscribe to the point of view expressed in his written report may alert the barrister to any likely change in the expert opinion (or important shades of grey in the opinion) before the case theory is finalized.

4.105 Our results indicated that it was the professional experts who write voluminous numbers of reports each month who are the most susceptible to changes of opinion in the period between the time the initial report is drafted and when they give oral evidence in court. It would be helpful for such experts to be more alert to their vulnerability to submitting a report with which they may not be comfortable to adhere by the time of trial.

(5) Should the jury be provided with written expert reports?

4.106 The majority of jurors expressed a desire to be provided with copies of the written reports of expert witnesses. When written reports were provided to the jury, the jurors found them very helpful and reported that this saved time in deliberation. If the current processes were changed so that the assumption is that expert reports are provided to the jury (subject to any necessary redactions to address admissibility issues and similar), this might serve to focus both the lawyers and experts on better preparation of the expert evidence in advance of the trial. Inappropriate content for the jury could be redacted or edited by agreement between the parties or orders by the trial judge. Such a modification of the current procedures is consistent with the growing trend to make more written aids available to jurors in the deliberation room, such as the transcript of the evidence and written directions to aid in the comprehension and use of the evidence. Inclusion of expert reports among the available written aids for the jury is worthy of further consideration and research.

(6) Perceptions of partisanship

4.107 Concerns expressed by Australian judges in 1999 about the impact of biased expert evidence on the justice system were not repeated in this project. The lawyers, experts, and jurors did not commonly identify expert lack of neutrality as a major issue impeding the provision of expert evidence in criminal cases.

Whilst the perception of experts as biased did not feature prominently in the project findings, it was not because the participants did not turn their minds to the potential for expert bias to exert an influence on trial outcomes. Most participants gave due consideration to the issue and concluded that bias was not evident in all but five of the 55 trials—less than 10% of the project cases. **4.108**

The concept of biased expert evidence was spontaneously raised by each group of stakeholders during interviews. The fact that participants felt compelled to mention impartial behaviour, as if it were surprising, may imply that they believe that the majority of experts are not impartial. Taking into account the fact that comparatively few experts were identified as biased, reason for concern about the extent of biased evidence in the criminal justice system may be reducing. The comments by many jurors suggested a general preconception that experts called for the defence would be 'guns for hire'. Whilst some of those interviewed explained that they approached their task with a concern about potential expert bias, few participants concluded that the experts whom they observed offered partisan evidence. **4.109**

Conversely, jurors appreciated the benefit available in the adversarial system of justice of exposure to an opposing defence expert whose evidence tested that of the prosecution expert. Jurors who were exposed to experts whose views were in conflict were more satisfied that they had explored the issues rigorously than those who heard only from a single expert on behalf of the prosecution. **4.110**

5

JURY COMPREHENSION OF EXPERT EVIDENCE

A. Introduction

5.01 For decades it has been argued that expert evidence is too complex for the average juror to understand and evaluate, especially when they are exposed to conflicting opinions from expert witnesses.[1,2] For instance, 37% (n = 58) of judges in the 1999 AIJA survey contended that matters involving complex and conflicting expert accounting evidence should be withdrawn from juries and determined by judges alone; 24% (n = 38) had a comparable view in respect of equivalent medical evidence.[3] While research has identified a number of topics about which jurors do struggle to comprehend expert evidence, self-report data from jurors based on their subjective experience indicate that they believe they understand expert evidence. No research to date has explored what jurors actually think about expert evidence, or whether they are aware of the difficulties that expert evidence might pose, regardless of whether they perceive that they understand it.

5.02 This chapter summarizes research that has explored why jurors may struggle with expert evidence. We identify extra-legal factors that may impact upon jurors' ability to analyse expert evidence. The literature review provides a context in which the results are presented and analysed. We consider jurors' views about expert evidence and whether their perceptions are shared by other criminal justice professionals such as judges, lawyers, and the experts themselves. We also explore barriers to juror comprehension.

[1] The authors would like to acknowledge the written contribution of Faye Nitschke to this chapter.

[2] See e.g. John Thomas, 'Expert Evidence: The Future of Forensic Science in Criminal Trials' (2014 Criminal Bar Association Kalisher Lecture, 14 October 2014), <https://www.judiciary.gov.uk/wp-content/uploads/2014/10/kalisher-lecture-expert-evidence-oct-14.pdf>.

[3] Ian Freckelton, Prasuna Reddy, and Hugh Selby, *Australian Judicial Perspectives on Expert Evidence: An Empirical Study* (Melbourne: AIJA, 1999), p. 151.

B. What Does Current Research Tell us About Juror Comprehension?

(1) What do jurors think they know about expert evidence?

5.03 Interviews conducted with jurors suggest that jurors actually do have the capacity (and the motivation) to think about expert evidence carefully, and that jurors' deliberations reflect that diligence.[4] Jurors say that they thoroughly review the evidence when reaching a verdict.[5] Research also suggests that jurors appear to use systematic processing and therefore think carefully about the expert evidence.[6] Given that these findings rely on jurors' self-reports about their comprehension, caution is necessary before concluding that jurors (adequately) comprehend expert evidence. As studies of jury directions have shown, self-report methods to assess jurors' comprehension often tell a very different story from other more objective measures of comprehension.[7] Research that does not rely on self-reports indicates that there are some circumstances in which jurors do not just rely on the content of the expert evidence but use other cues to assess it, suggesting that comprehension might at times be compromised in the sense of being affected by collateral perceptions and sources of information.

(2) The challenges posed by expert evidence

5.04 When deliberating about expert evidence, jurors can be required to evaluate highly complex and technical material that is outside the realm of ordinary knowledge and discourse. When information becomes complex and difficult to evaluate systematically, there is the risk of irrelevant factors being taken into account.[8] In addition, those forming a perception of the material in question—perceivers—tend to rely on shortcuts, called heuristics, to evaluate information under such circumstances.[9] It is precisely because expert evidence can often be complex that researchers have been interested in how jurors make sense of the evidence, and whether they rely on cues or shortcuts.

5.05 In psychology, a considerable amount of research has examined how people use their life experience and common sense to make decisions. Findings show that they use a number of strategies such as relying on schemas, stereotypes, and heuristics. A stereotype is a mental representation of information about a social category, and can include information about whether we feel positively or negatively about people in that category, and also information about what people in that category are like (their attributes), the sorts of behaviours they perform, and roles they occupy.

5.06 A stereotype is a specific example of a schema. Schemas can apply to a range of other types of constructs, such as roles and events, as well. Schemas and stereotypes are based on our prior knowledge of things; they are our theories about what things are like. They are generally

---

[4] Brian H. Bornstein and Edie Greene, 'Jury Decision Making: Implications For and From Psychology', *Current Directions in Psychological Science* 20, no. 1 (2011) 63.

[5] Dennis J. Devine and others, 'Strength of Evidence, Extra-evidentiary Influence, and the Liberation Hypothesis: Data from the Field', *Law and Human Behavior* 33, no. 2 (2009) 136; Dennis J. Devine and others, 'Deliberation Quality: A Preliminary Examination in Criminal Juries', *Journal of Empirical Legal Studies* 4, no. 2 (2007) 273.

[6] Neil Vidmar and Shari S. Diamond, 'Juries and Expert Evidence', *Brooklyn Law Review* 66, no. 4 (2001) 1121.

[7] Blake M. McKimmie, Emma Antrobus, and Chantelle Baguley, 'Objective and Subjective Comprehension of Jury Instructions in Criminal Trials', *New Criminal Law Review: An International and Interdisciplinary Journal* 17, no. 2 (Spring 2014) 163.

[8] See Ian Freckelton, *The Trial of the Expert* (Melbourne: Oxford University Press, 1987).

[9] Richard E. Petty and John T. Cacioppo, 'The Elaboration Likelihood Model of Persuasion', in *Advances in Experimental Social Psychology*, vol. 19, edited by Leonard Berkowitz (New York: Academic Press, 1986).

functional, and using them is normal because they help us deal with a large amount of information in our day-to-day lives. However, because they can sometimes be inaccurate, they can lead to less than optimal outcomes.

Heuristics are the quick-decision rules or shortcuts that we learn from experience. We will examine how stereotypes, schemas, and heuristics may influence jurors' decisions because this provides an indication of their comprehension of expert evidence: the more that these cues influence jurors' perceptions, the less they are relying on the content of the expert's message, and so comprehension is more likely to be impaired. We expect that complex expert evidence will make a range of extra-legal cues more influential in jury deliberations. **5.07**

In considering the research on juror comprehension, it is important to understand that we are not implying that jurors are not conscientiously doing their job. Rather, the point we are making is that jurors are people, and that people are affected by schemas, stereotypes, and heuristics. The reason that it is important to study use of stereotypes, schemas, and heuristics in the context of jury decision-making is not to criticize jurors, but to understand how these normal aspects of social-cognitive functioning affect jurors in their role as the decider of fact in a criminal trial. **5.08**

Armed with this knowledge, it may be possible to provide support to jurors and structure their task in such a way as to limit any adverse effect on their decisions. It can be thought about in this way: the research helps us to identify possible problems with how jurors are asked to perform their duties, not problems with individual jurors. It is important to remember that the single biggest influence on jurors' decisions is the strength of the evidence against the defendant.[10] So, generally, jurors do a competent job, but there are ways in which they could be better supported, because research shows that factors beyond the evidence alone affect their decisions. **5.09**

(3) Models of jury decision-making

To identify the factors that influence jurors' decisions, it is useful to consider how jurors *make* their decisions. One of the leading models that describe how jurors make their decisions is the cognitive story model. According to this model, jurors construct narratives during the trial to organize and interpret the evidence.[11] Jurors then evaluate and interpret all subsequent evidence, as it is presented, in line with the story. Jurors' schemas and stereotypes are useful in forming the story, especially to understand missing elements of the story—these schemas and stereotypes provide templates for what certain types of people and events are like, so jurors can fill in any missing details. **5.10**

Another set of models is also used to understand juror decision-making, and take into account the influence of extra-legal information on their decisions. These are the elaboration likelihood[12] and heuristic systematic models.[13] Both are known as dual process models[14]: they **5.11**

[10] Neil Vidmar, 'Expert Evidence, the Adversary System, and the Jury', *American Journal of Public Health* 95, suppl. 1 (2005) 137.

[11] Nancy Pennington and Reid Hastie, 'Evidence Evaluation in Complex Decision Making', *Journal of Personality and Social Psychology* 51, no. 2 (August 1986) 242.

[12] Pennington and Hastie, 'Evidence Evaluation in Complex Decision Making', 242.

[13] Shelly Chaiken, Akiva Liberman, and Alice H. Eagly, 'Heuristic And Systematic Information Within and Beyond The Persuasion Context', in *Unintended Thought*, edited by James S. Uleman and John A. Bargh (New York: Guilford Press, 1989).

[14] See Shelly Chaiken and Yaacov Trope, *Dual Process Theories in Social Psychology* (New York: Guilford Press, 1999); Eliot R. Smith and Jamie DeCoster, 'Dual Process Models in Social and Cognitive Psychology: Conceptual Integration and Underlying Memory Systems', *Personality & Social Psychology Review* 4, no. 2 (2000) 108.

describe two ways in which decisions or evaluations are made. The models were originally developed to understand persuasion and attitude change, but have since been adapted to the jury context, because thinking about a jury trial as a series of persuasive messages is a productive way to answer questions about how jurors make their decisions. While there are some fine distinctions between the two models, they generally make the same predictions, so for our purposes we will focus on the elaboration likelihood model.[15]

5.12 This model describes two distinct modes or routes to persuasion—the central and peripheral routes. Each of these involves different amounts of thinking. The central route involves more effortful thinking, while the peripheral route involves less thinking. We refer to the amount of thinking in terms of how much a person elaborates about a persuasive message. Elaboration is measured by looking at the number of positive and negative thoughts generated about a message. If a substantial number of pros and cons are generated when a person is given a persuasive message, we would say that a high level of elaboration is being shown.

5.13 For the central route, the amount of favourable elaboration about the message influences persuasion. The more that you think of benefits, as opposed to costs, the more you will be persuaded. For the peripheral route, the strength of the message content is less important; you are more likely to be persuaded if the message is associated with other things that are positively evaluated. If you have a positive stereotype about the type of person giving you the message, you will be more persuaded by the message. For example, if you generally think that scientists are trustworthy, then you are more likely to evaluate the evidence of a scientist positively, regardless of the actual content of that evidence.

5.14 We use the central route when an issue is important to us, and when we have the time and cognitive capacity to think about the issue. We tend to use the peripheral route when there is limited time to think about the message, when we are distracted, or when the issue is not so important.

5.15 One of the assumptions underlying all of the models of jury decision-making is that people like to put in the minimum amount of cognitive effort possible. This has led to some people referring to perceivers as 'cognitive misers'[16] or 'mental sluggards'.[17] An alternative perspective on these findings is that we use stereotypes strategically to maximize the amount of information that can be stored in our brains under taxing conditions.[18] Stereotypes help us encode some of the information so that we can then turn our attention to other features of the information.

5.16 According to this latter perspective, perceivers try to engage in as much thinking about unexpected, or stereotype-inconsistent information as possible.[19] For instance, in one study participants spent more time reading and thinking about stereotype-inconsistent behaviours, and consequently recalled a greater number of these behaviours than stereotype-consistent behaviours. When perceivers made use of stereotypes to encode information, those perceivers were then able to allocate more of their thinking capacity to other cognitive tasks.[20] Findings

[15] Petty and Cacioppo, 'The Elaboration Likelihood Model of Persuasion'.

[16] Susan T. Fiske and Shelley E. Taylor, *Social Cognition: Topics in Social Psychology* (New York: Random House, 1984).

[17] Daniel T. Gilbert and Gregory J. Hixon, 'The Trouble of Thinking: Activation and Application of Stereotypic Beliefs', *Journal of Personality and Social Psychology* 60, no. 4 (April 1991) 509.

[18] Blake M. McKimmie and others, 'Stereotypical and Counterstereotypical Defendants: Who is He and What was the Case Against Her?', *Psychology, Public Policy and Law* 19 (2013) 343.

[19] Leonard D. Stern and others, 'Processing Time and the Recall of Inconsistent and Consistent Behaviors of Individuals and Groups', *Journal of Personality and Social Psychology* 47, no. 2 (August 1984) 253.

[20] Neil C. Macrae, Alan B. Milne and Galen V. Bodenhausen, 'Stereotypes as Energy-Saving Devices: A Peek Inside the Cognitive Toolbox', *Journal of Personality and Social Psychology* 66, no. 1 (January 1994) 37.

such as these have been interpreted as a strategy to maximize or optimize the amount of information encoded. Our cognitive resources can be conserved by encoding stereotype-congruent targets relatively effortlessly in terms of the relevant stereotype, allowing more effortful thinking to be used in relation to stereotype-incongruent targets.[21]

Sometimes jurors will be influenced by the content of the evidence presented at trial, and sometimes they might be influenced by some attributes that are independent of the content of the evidence. In the following sections we consider how both the format of expert evidence and also the characteristics of the expert can influence how expert evidence is received by jurors. To do this, we look at how jurors make sense of probabilistic evidence in the context of DNA evidence (a topic explored in more detail in chapter 6 of this volume). **5.17**

(4) The impact of the form of expert evidence

Concern has been expressed by various courts that evidence including probabilities could unduly influence jurors.[22] A review of the research showed, however, that jurors actually undervalue statistical evidence when it is presented in the context of other evidence.[23] Other research suggests that while jurors are susceptible to some fallacies when reasoning about probabilities, these tend to favour the defence, not the prosecution.[24] In one study, 480 people called for jury service viewed a 70-minute film of a simulated trial that included mitochondrial DNA (mtDNA) evidence. The expert stated that only one in 5,072 Caucasian men had the mtDNA type that matched the sample from the crime scene. Participants then deliberated to reach a verdict in groups of eight. The results suggested that the jurors were not unduly persuaded by the probabilities, generally coped with the evidence, and, if anything, were conservative in estimating the likelihood that the sample came from the defendant.[25] **5.18**

The presentation format used by the expert can make that evidence more or less persuasive. Three experiments manipulated the form in which statistical evidence was presented. When evidence was presented one way, decision-makers were convinced that the suspect was almost certainly the source of the DNA sample; but when it was presented another way, a substantial portion concluded that the suspect could not have been the source.[26] **5.19**

These studies tested whether the cognitive availability of coincidental match exemplars determines what jurors conclude about guilt. If we can easily think of examples of other people who might match the DNA sample by chance, we think the defendant or suspect is less likely to be guilty. It was then made more easy or more difficult for people to think of such exemplars by changing the framing of the statistical information. The probability of a match was presented either as a percentage in relation to a single target, such as 0.1% likelihood of a chance match with this specific defendant, or an equivalent frequency in relation to multiple **5.20**

---

[21] Jeffrey W. Sherman and others, 'Stereotype Efficiency Reconsidered: Encoding Flexibility under Cognitive Load', *Journal of Personality and Social Psychology* 75, no. 3 (1998) 589; Jeffrey W. Sherman, Frederica R. Conrey and Carla J. Groom, 'Encoding Flexibility Revisited: Evidence for Enhanced Encoding of Stereotype-Inconsistent Information under Cognitive Load', *Social Cognition* 22, no. 2 (April 2004) 214.

[22] See e.g. *Doheny & Adams v The Queen* [1997] 1 Cr App R 369; *R v Adams* [1996] 2 Cr App R 467; *R v T* [2010] EWCA Crim 2349, [2011] 1 Cr App R 9.

[23] Jonathan J. Koehler, 'When Are People Persuaded by DNA Match Statistics?', *Law and Human Behavior* 25, no. 5 (2001) 493.

[24] David H. Kaye and others, 'Statistics in the Jury Box: How Jurors Respond to Mitochondrial DNA Match Probabilities', *Journal of Empirical Legal Studies* 4, no. 4 (2007) 797.

[25] David H. Kaye and others, 'Statistics in the Jury Box: How Jurors Respond to Mitochondrial DNA Match Probabilities', 797.

[26] Jonathan J. Koehler, 'When Are People Persuaded by DNA Match Statistics?', 493.

targets; one in 1,000 people in the specific city where the accused lived. In the latter case, the reference group included 1,000 people, compared to a single person in the former.

5.21 The first presentation is designed to make it difficult to think of examples of other chance matches to the DNA sample—the probability that it is a chance match seems like a very small number, close to zero, so the defendant must be the source of the DNA. With the second form of presentation, it is easy to reason that if the probability of a chance match is one in 1,000, and we assume there are one million people in the city, that means there are about 1,000 people who would match the DNA by chance alone. Since it is reasonably easy to think of someone who matches the sample by chance, it is also quite possible that the defendant matches the sample by chance, not because he or she is the actual source of the DNA. Despite the fact that both statistical presentations of probabilities in these examples are equivalent, the first was much more persuasive and led people to conclude that the defendant was the actual source of the DNA.

5.22 However, this presentation effect disappeared as the probabilities became smaller and smaller. As the size of the reference group used to describe the probabilities approaches the size of the population in the context, it becomes harder to imagine chance matches. For example, if the probability is one in a million, and we present that as either 0.0001% likelihood that the sample matches the defendant by chance, or alternatively that the sample would match one person in the city of a million by chance, there is very little difference in the persuasiveness of each frame. It seems very hard to imagine matches by chance alone with either form of presentation.

5.23 While presentation format has an effect on the persuasiveness of probabilistic statistical expert evidence under some conditions, other extra-legal factors associated with expert evidence have a more pervasive influence.

(5) The influence of expert characteristics on juror comprehension

5.24 In one of the first studies to examine the influence of expert characteristics, participants watched a video recreation of a trial in which two scientists gave expert evidence about one aspect of the case. The plaintiff's expert was described as having either strong or weak credentials, and gave his evidence using either simple or complex language. As predicted, the extra-legal cue of the expert's credentials influenced the participants—they were more persuaded when the expert had strong credentials—but only when the expert's evidence was complex. When the evidence was simple, participants were influenced by what the expert said, rather than the expert's credentials. This finding suggested that the participants were using the cue of the expert's credentials when they could not directly evaluate the content of what the expert said because the language was too difficult to understand.[27]

5.25 An expert's gender can have a similar effect to credentials as a cue that influences how persuasive the expert is in the eyes of perceivers. Some earlier research suggested that female experts were more persuasive than male experts,[28] but subsequent research showed that when an expert's gender matched the domain about which they were testifying, their evidence was evaluated more positively and mock jurors awarded more monetary damages.[29] For example,

[27] Joel Cooper, Elizabeth A. Bennett and Holly L. Sukel, 'Complex Scientific Testimony: How Do Jurors Make Decisions?', *Law & Human Behavior* 20, no. 4 (1996) 379.

[28] Rodney A. Swenson, David L. Nash and David C. Roos, 'Source Credibility and Perceived Expertness of Testimony in a Simulated Child-Custody Case', *Professional Psychology: Research and Practice* 15, no. 6 (December 1984) 891.

[29] Blake M. McKimmie and others, 'Jurors' Responses to Expert Witness Testimony: The Effects of Gender Stereotypes', *Group Processes and Intergroup Relations* 7, no. 2 (April 2004) 131; Regina A. Schuller, Deborah Terry and Blake M. McKimmie, 'The Impact of Expert Testimony on Jurors' Decisions: Gender

if a male expert testifies about a commercial price-fixing agreement in the context of business engaged in rock crushing, he will be more persuasive than a female expert giving exactly the same evidence; whereas a female expert would be more persuasive giving the same price-fixing evidence for businesses of perfume suppliers. This line of research also suggests that expert gender is used as a heuristic cue, as the effect is greatest when evidence is complex and difficult to understand,[30] as is the case with expert credentials. The effect of expert gender is also explored in more detail in chapter 8 when the factors that contribute to expert credibility are analysed.

The type of language used by an expert can also be relied on as a heuristic cue by mock jurors.[31] This is because perceivers have expectations about how men and women typically use language—we expect men to use more complex language than women.[32] In one study, male experts were found to be more persuasive than female experts when they used complex language and perceivers were under high levels of cognitive demand.[33] Similarly, an expert presenting evidence using more complex statistical language was viewed as having greater expertise, even though their testimony was rated as less clear.[34] It seems that jurors expect experts to use complex testimony, especially when they are men. **5.26**

(6) The impact of expert remuneration

It is not just an expert's credentials and gender that matter. Whether an expert testifies in court frequently and is identified in court as paid for his or her services also affects how jurors think about the expert's evidence. This is known as the 'hired gun' effect[35] and is a criticism often brought against the operation of the adversary system.[36] In one United States study, three experiments examined whether jurors fall back on cognitive shortcuts in the context of the gun for hire.[37] If an expert appears to be a gun for hire by testifying relatively frequently for a fee, their evidence might be less convincing because it appears as though they are just in it for the money. Participants who heard from a well-paid expert who frequently testified viewed that expert as less trustworthy and were subsequently less persuaded by that expert's evidence. The results of this study suggested that this was indeed the result of a cognitive shortcut—the effect was present when the evidence was presented in complex, but not simple, language. As in other studies, shortcuts such as heuristics are most prominent when perceivers are not able to think through the information context systematically. The complex language made it difficult for participants to evaluate the expert's evidence systematically, so **5.27**

of the Expert and Testimony Complexity', *Journal of Applied Social Psychology* 35, no. 6 (June 2005) 1266; Regina A. Schuller, Deborah Terry and Blake M. McKimmie, 'The Impact of an Expert's Gender on Jurors' Decisions', *Law and Psychology Review* 25 (2001) 59.

30 Regina A. Schuller, Deborah Terry and Blake M. McKimmie, 'The Impact of Expert Testimony on Jurors' Decisions: Gender of the Expert and Testimony Complexity', *Journal of Applied Social Psychology* 35, no. 6 (June 2005) 1266.

31 Blake M. McKimmie and others, 'Stereotypical And Counterstereotypical Defendants: Who is He and What was the Case Against Her?', 343.

32 Sheila Brownlow, Julie A. Rosamond and Jennifer A. Parker, 'Gender-Linked Linguistic Behavior in Television Interviews', *Sex Roles* 49, nos 3–4 (2003) 121.

33 Blake M. McKimmie and others, 'Stereotypical And Counterstereotypical Defendants: Who is He and What was the Case Against Her?', 343.

34 Shari S. Diamond and Jonathan D. Casper, 'Blindfolding the Jury to Verdict Consequences: Damages, Experts, and the Civil Jury', *Law and Society Review* 26, no. 3 (1992) 513.

35 Joel Cooper and Isaac M. Neuhaus, 'The "Hired Gun" Effect: Assessing the Effect of Pay, Frequency of Testifying and Credentials on the Perception of Expert Testimony', *Law and Human Behavior* 24, no. 2 (2000) 149.

36 See e.g. Margaret A. Hagen, *Whores of the Court* (New York: Regan Books, 1997).

37 Joel Cooper and Isaac M. Neuhaus, 'The "Hired Gun" Effect: Assessing the Effect of Pay, Frequency of Testifying and Credentials on the Perception of Expert Testimony', 149.

they resorted to a shortcut—if the expert is motivated by money, he or she is a hired gun and should not be trusted as much.

(7) The influence of media portrayals of forensic experts

5.28 How the media portray expert evidence, in particular that of a scientific nature, may influence how jurors perceive an expert's evidence. Often, these effects are called the 'CSI effect'. This label has been used to describe a range of related but different effects. The three possible ways to define this effect were described by Podlas:

1. That *CSI* just increases the lay public's interest in forensics and science;
2. That *CSI* creates unreasonable expectations about forensic evidence in the minds of the jurors, making a conviction less likely; and
3. That *CSI* raises the credibility of scientific evidence so that it is seen as almost infallible, making a conviction more likely.[38]

5.29 In the last category there is a related effect that refers specifically to specialists who create profiles of suspects—'The Hollywood Effect'. In coining this term, David Canter was referring to unproven theories and methods gaining credibility and acceptance in jurors' minds due to being portrayed in popular movies and so being more familiar.[39]

5.30 What research evidence is there for the effect of watching CSI-related television shows? A survey of 306 university students asked them to report how often they viewed CSI-related television shows and consider a hypothetical case of rape before reaching a verdict. The results suggested that there was no difference in verdicts for those who watched CSI-related television shows compared to those who did not watch them. Thus, it was concluded that there was no effect of watching CSI-related shows (in terms of the first two definitions as described by Podlas).

5.31 In contrast, other researchers used a very similar paradigm and found that watching CSI and crime programmes made participants more critical of expert evidence in some circumstances, such as when that evidence was ambiguous.[40] Those studies used university students pretending to be jurors. It is reasonable to ask whether such findings also reflect the experiences of actual jurors. One such United States study making use of actual jurors as research participants found that watching CSI-type shows did not influence verdicts.[41] That sometimes we find evidence of a CSI effect and sometimes do not suggests that other factors might be involved in the relationship between watching CSI shows and outcomes such as conviction rates. One possibility is that CSI exposure raises expectations about the nature of the evidence, and it is these expectations that influence verdicts.

5.32 This possibility was tested in a survey of 1,027 actual jurors in the state of Michigan in the United States.[42] Participants read about three different cases and indicated how willing they would be to convict a defendant when there was no scientific evidence and

[38] Kimberlianne Podlas, 'The "CSI Effect": Exposing the Media Myth', *Fordham Intellectual Property, Media and Entertainment Law Journal* 16 (2006) 429.

[39] David V. Canter and others, 'The Organized/Disorganized Typology of Serial Murder: Myth or Model?', *Psychology, Public Policy and Law* 10, no. 3 (September 2004) 293.

[40] N. J. Schweitzer and Michael J. Saks, 'The CSI Effect: Popular Fiction About Forensic Science Affects the Public's Expectations About Real Forensic Science', *Jurimetrics* 47, no. 3 (2007) 357.

[41] Donald E. Shelton, Young S. Kim and Gregg Barak, 'A Study of Juror Expectations and Demands Concerning Scientific Evidence: Does the "CSI Effect" Exist?', *Vanderbilt Journal of Entertainment & Technology Law* 9 (Winter 2006) 331.

[42] Young S. Kim, Gregg Barak and Donald E. Shelton, 'Examining the "CSI-Effect" in the Cases of Circumstantial Evidence and Eyewitness Testimony: Multivariate and Path Analyses', *Journal of Criminal Justice* 37, no. 5 (2009) 452.

only (a) circumstantial evidence; or (b) eyewitness evidence. Participants also reported how often they watched CSI drama shows, along with their expectations about receiving scientific evidence of some kind. Watching CSI shows had an indirect effect on convictions by raising expectations about scientific evidence, but only when circumstantial evidence was presented.[43]

In sum, jurors do seem to be able to make sense of some evidence that is complex and difficult to understand, and do not seem to be too badly misled by media portrayal of forensic evidence or statistical information; but sometimes they rely on shortcuts when the decision-making becomes more difficult. **5.33**

C. Are Jurors, Experts, and Judges Aware of the Issues Around Expert Evidence?

Juror comprehension research, as discussed in section B of this chapter, suggests a number of ways in which jurors have difficulties with expert evidence, and some of the legal and extra-legal factors that they might find influential. It is not clear whether jurors' self-reported confidence that they understand expert evidence reflects a lack of awareness of these factors, or whether jurors are attuned to the difficulties that expert evidence poses. A related question is: how do criminal justice professionals, including expert witnesses, lawyers, and judges, evaluate jurors' comprehension? Are they able to identify the difficulties that expert testimony poses to jurors? Doing so would be an important first step in being able to provide appropriate assistance to jurors. **5.34**

The ensuing analysis of the results of this project first focuses on the interview responses concerning jurors' comprehension of expert evidence; 108 jurors, 79 experts, 102 lawyers, and 40 judges responded to questions used in this analysis. The second part of the analysis focuses on data obtained from 298 jurors that were surveyed as part of the project. The juror survey data are compared and contrasted with the responses of the 79 experts, 103 lawyers, and 40 judges. **5.35**

(1) Method of analysis

To conduct a systematic analysis of participants' responses to the interview questions we used a software package called Leximancer, which allows researchers to identify emergent patterns from free-text responses. Leximancer works through three steps to generate a concept map. First, the program identifies frequently occurring words in the text. These frequently occurring words are used as concept seeds. Then 'thesaurus learning' occurs, whereby the program searches the text for the concept seeds, and also for bits of text that occur around the concept seeds to generate concepts. Then concepts are displayed on the concept map. Grey circles on the concept map represent a concept discovered by Leximancer. Concept names (as shown on the map) are the frequently used words Leximancer has identified and used as concept seeds. **5.36**

Leximancer engages in both conceptual (content of text) and relational (structure of text) content analysis, so on the concept map the size of the concepts and distances between concepts can be interpreted. On the concept map, the size of the grey circles for each concept represents the number of comments that belong to that concept. The larger the grey **5.37**

[43] Young S. Kim, Gregg Barak and Donald E. Shelton, 'Examining the "CSI-Effect" in the Cases of Circumstantial Evidence and Eyewitness Testimony', 452.

circle representing the concept, the more frequently this concept was discussed by interview respondents. In terms of the relationships between concepts, those concepts located closely on the map were closely related in the interview responses. The absolute location of the concepts on the map has no meaning.

(2) Analysis strategy

5.38 For each participant group (jurors, experts, lawyers, and judges were treated as separate groups), the responses to several questions about the jury's comprehension of expert evidence were entered simultaneously into Leximancer and analysed as one set of text. A data-driven (grounded theory) analysis has been undertaken for each data set—this is where the concepts and links between concepts are based on the content of the data. The concept maps constructed by Leximancer are stable for each participant group, with the ten most frequent concepts on the map holding formation through ten re-clustering iterations of the map.

(3) Limitations of the data analysis

5.39 There are three main limitations of the content analyses of juror, expert, lawyer, and judge interview responses about juror comprehension. First, unfortunately the judge interview data are restricted in the volume of content available—judges were either extensive in their responses or provided single-sentence responses. When volume of text is low, the text coded into concepts extracted by Leximancer can be disparate, and therefore concepts can be difficult to define. Second, concepts in Leximancer are not exclusive—a unit of text can be coded into multiple concepts so the meaning of concepts is not mutually exclusive. Third, concepts do not necessarily have directional meaning. Positive, negative, and neutral opinions about an issue (e.g. the use of technical language by the expert) are often clustered in a single concept. Despite these limitations, however, Leximancer content analysis provides an impartial and data-driven exploration of juror, expert, lawyer, and judge interview responses about juror comprehension.

D. Results

(1) Interview responses of the jurors

5.40 Jurors were asked whether they found the evidence presented by each expert difficult to comprehend. The majority of jurors indicated they did not find the evidence difficult to understand. When asked about the first expert who presented expert evidence, 80.6% said they did not find the evidence difficult and the remaining 19.4% said they did find the evidence difficult. When asked about the second expert, 74.1% said they did not find the evidence difficult to understand and 25.9% said they did find the evidence difficult to understand.

(a) What aspects of expert evidence were difficult to understand?

5.41 Jurors were asked a series of questions about their comprehension of the expert evidence presented by each expert. Responses from two questions—'Were there any parts of the expert evidence that you had difficulty understanding?' and 'Overall, what helped you the best to understand this expert's evidence?'—were extracted from the interview data analysed using Leximancer (see Figure 5.1 and Table 5.1 for the concept map and content of the concepts on the map).

(b) Findings

5.42 Broadly, jurors indicated that many experts competently explained their evidence in a clear manner (e.g., see the concepts 'clear' or 'easy' in Table 5.1). When discussing whether there were parts that they found hard to understand, jurors generally identified overuse of technical

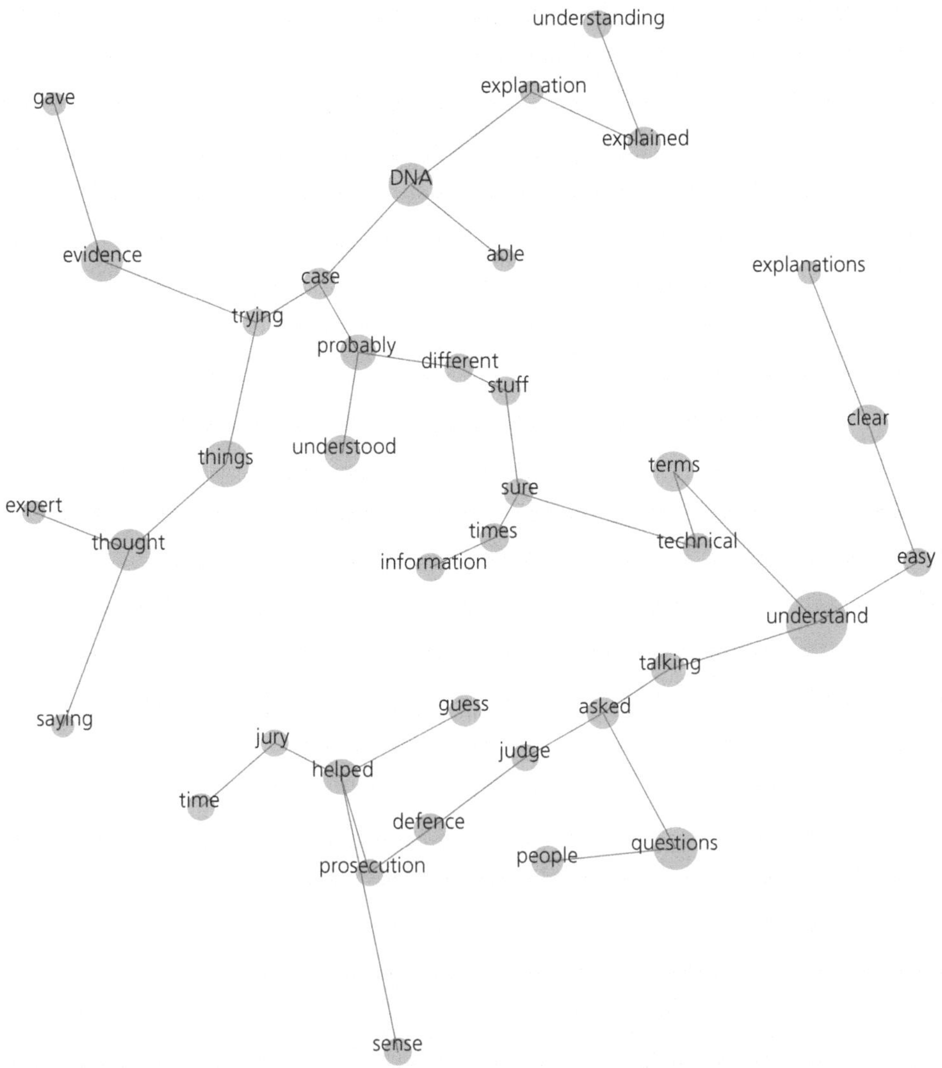

Figure 5.1 Concept map of jurors' evaluations of expert evidence.

language as a barrier (see 'terms' or 'technical' concepts); one juror responding, 'Yes, sometimes when he said more scientific words I couldn't understand.'

DNA evidence was identified as complex, but was often described as well-explained by the expert (see 'DNA' concept). Sometimes the presentation style of the expert, for example talking too quickly or not being confident, was identified as a barrier to comprehension (see 'guess' concept). Lengthy presentation of expert evidence was identified as a barrier to easy comprehension (see 'time' concept). **5.43**

Jurors frequently identified the experts' explanations as helpful in understanding the expert evidence (see 'explained' and 'explanations' concepts). Jurors also identified judges' questions to the expert to further explain aspects of their evidence as useful assistance for their comprehension (see concepts 'helped' or 'judge'). As one juror explained; 'I mean, he was asked to clarify a couple of technical terms that he was using. The judge, he did quite a good job there of saying, excuse me, you're making reference to a particular piece of jargon, or what have **5.44**

Table 5.1 Concept content from jurors' responses about comprehension.

Concept name	Concept description	Frequency[44]
understand	Features of evidence that helped or hindered jurors' comprehension (e.g., jargon, common sense, previous experience)	66
things	Jurors' experience of expert evidence during the trial	43
clear	Jurors' perception of expert evidence clarity	39
thought	Opinions on the expert's performance and impact on comprehension	36
evidence	Influence of presentation strategies on comprehension	35
DNA	DNA evidence including complexity, comprehension, and use of diagrams, jargon, and statistics	33
questions	Questioning style of counsel and questions jurors wanted to ask the expert	33
terms	Benefits of using lay language for comprehension	28
probably	Jurors expressing uncertainty about their opinions	26
talking	Reflections on the jurors' own level of comprehension	26
helped	Tactics the expert employed which assisted understanding	24
explained	Expert evidence was well explained	24
people	Inferences about what others on the jury may have thought about the expert	24
understood	Statements affirming the juror understood the expert evidence	23
time	Recalling their experience of the evidence on the day or opinions about duration of expert evidence	22
guess	Jurors expressing uncertainty about the expert evidence	21
sense	Common sense was necessary to comprehend the expert evidence	21
understanding	Capacity to comprehend the expert evidence	20
defence	Defence barrister's examination of expert assisted juror comprehension	18
technical	Technical language hindered understanding and plain language explanations assisted juror comprehension	18
case	Relevance or importance of expert evidence in relation to the case	17
information	Mechanisms by which expert evidence was understood	16
easy	Expert evidence was easy to understand	16
jury	Jury's use of the expert evidence during deliberations	16
gave	Understanding of specific information in expert evidence	16
asked	Questioning style of counsel	15
judge	Judge intervention to encourage the expert to be clearer, use less jargon, or slow down	15
trying	Reflections on jurors' attempts to interpret evidence	15
expert	Usefulness of the expert's explanations	15
sure	Usefulness of prosecution, defence, and judge interventions to elicit clearer explanations from the expert	14

(Continued)

[44] Please note: frequency represents the number of text segments Leximancer has coded into the concept. Leximancer does not code text segments into concepts exclusively. This means that one segment can be coded into multiple concepts, i.e., the concept frequencies are not independent.

Table 5.1 *Continued*

Concept name	Concept description	Frequency
stuff	Reflections on jurors' own knowledge of expert's area of expertise	14
explanations	Expert's explanations were helpful	14
saying	Expert's demeanour while presenting evidence	14
times	Elements of evidence that were repeated or emphasised by the expert	13
different	Contradictory statements made by the expert	13
prosecution	Prosecution interaction with the expert	13
able	Reflections on capacity of jurors generally to comprehend expert evidence	13

you [said] there, can you clarify to the jury what that means.' Cross-examination of experts by defence counsel was identified as useful assistance (see concepts 'defence' in Table 5.1).

(2) Interview responses of the experts

Expert witnesses were asked several questions about the delivery of their evidence and their opinion of the jury's level of comprehension of their evidence. **5.45**

(a) What experts say about how they delivered their evidence

In response to a question about whether their evidence had been delivered in the best way to inform the jury, about two thirds of experts said yes (64.7%), one quarter (26.5%) said they did not feel that their evidence had been delivered in the best way to inform the jury, and 8.8% of experts were unsure. In response to the question about visual aid use, the overwhelming majority of experts reported that they had not used visual aids to support their evidence (80.0%) with the remaining experts stating that they had. Experts were also asked whether the jury received a copy of their expert report. Most expert witnesses did not know (74.6%), with the remaining experts stating that the jury had not been given a copy of the report (18.3%), and only a small proportion of experts stating that the jury had been given a copy of their report (7.0%). **5.46**

(b) What experts say about juror comprehension

Experts were also asked about whether they thought there were parts of their evidence that were difficult for the jury to understand. Over one third of experts agreed that they thought there were parts of their evidence that were difficult for jurors to understand (38.2%), and the same proportion thought that their evidence was not difficult for jurors to understand (36.8%). One quarter of experts (25.0%) said that they did not know whether the jurors had difficulty understanding their evidence or not. **5.47**

Expert witnesses were also asked about whether they were asked any questions by the jury. Most expert witnesses (95.8%) were not asked any questions by the jury. Only 1.4% of experts stated that they were asked questions by the jury and 2.8% of experts could not remember if they were asked questions by the jury in the trial. **5.48**

Experts were asked several questions about their perspective on juror comprehension of their evidence. Responses to two interview questions 'Were there parts of your evidence which you think the jury had difficulty understanding?' and 'How reasonable is it to expect the jury in this trial to understand the matters you testified about?' were extracted from the interview data and input into Leximancer (see Figure 5.2 and Table 5.2 for the concept map and content of concepts for this analysis). **5.49**

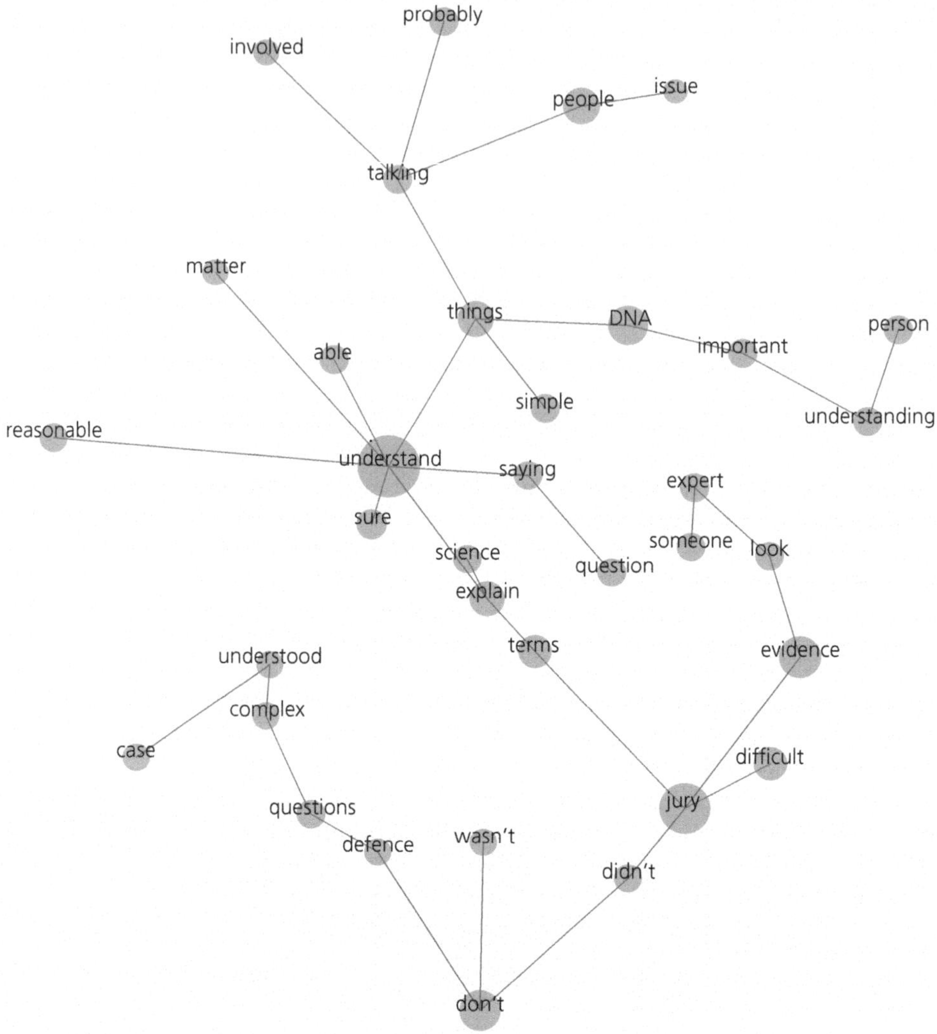

Figure 5.2 Concept map of experts' evaluations of juror comprehension.

(c) Findings

5.50 Generally, there were three common perspectives from experts about juror comprehension of their evidence. These three perspectives are summarized in the following example interview responses from three experts:

(a) 'Oh, I think they could have been able to understand what I was talking about; they weren't very technical or complex issues.'
(b) 'But I don't know whether they understand it or not. They don't get an opportunity to ask questions and say "Excuse me, I didn't understand that".'
(c) 'Always, as I say, very difficult to know what they do understand or don't understand. Obviously if there was some stuff that they didn't understand then it's my fault, not explaining it adequately.'

5.51 While experts generally agreed that jurors could comprehend their evidence and that it was reasonable to expect jurors to do so (see 'reasonable' concept), they also acknowledged that particular elements of their evidence might be difficult for the jury to interpret. Like jurors,

Table 5.2 Concept content from experts' responses about jury comprehension.

Concept name	Concept description	Frequency
understand	Jury's understanding of the expert's evidence broadly (positive, neutral, or negative)	68
jury	Strategies used to encourage and gauge jury understanding	65
don't	Assertions that the jury understood the expert evidence	52
evidence	Nature of expert evidence in the expert's area of expertise generally	36
DNA	Reasons that DNA evidence is complex for jurors to understand	33
people	Lay perceptions of the expert's area of expertise	32
difficult	Elements of the expert's evidence that were easy or difficult for the jury to understand	32
things	Ideas within the expert's evidence that the expert identified as complex	23
explain	Aspects of the expert's evidence that required explanation	22
questions	Questioning style of counsel	21
reasonable	Affirming it is reasonable for jurors to understand expert evidence	21
able	The jury's capacity to understand expert evidence and the expert's ability to communicate their evidence	20
understanding	Expert's confidence that the jury understood their evidence	20
case	General reflections on the trial	20
terms	Use of lay terminology and jargon	19
sure	Uncertainty about the jury's comprehension	19
didn't	Inability to receive feedback from the jury on the expert's presentation of evidence	19
person	Lay comprehension of complex concepts in specified areas of expertise	18
complex	Complex elements of their testimony	18
expert	General procedure for expert evidence	17
question	Specific questions asked by counsel or the jury about the expert's evidence	16
understood	Opinion on the jury's level of understanding	15
probably	Uncertainty about the expert's opinion	15
talking	Discussion of elements of the expert's evidence	14
simple	Parts of the expert's evidence that were simple	13
saying	Inferences that the jury were required to make based on the expert's evidence	12
look	Visual evidence used by jurors	12
important	Relative importance of expert evidence generally in trials or specifically in the current trial	12
defence	Defence use of expert evidence	12
wasn't	Aspects of the expert's evidence that were not critically important to the case	12
someone	Strategies that may assist jurors' comprehension	11
issue	Contested facts that the expert's testimony addressed	10
science	Difficulties in communicating science information in the expert's evidence	9
matter	Reflections on the case in general	9
involved	Influence of parties involved in the criminal trial process	7

experts identified DNA evidence as potentially complicated (see 'DNA' concept). More broadly, experts often reported identifying one or more aspects of their evidence as complex and generating strategies to make this aspect clearer for the jury (see 'difficult', 'things', 'explain', and 'complex' concepts).

5.52 Two general strategies for presenting evidence emerged from the content analysis. Expert witnesses reported that thinking about lay understanding of their area of expertise and addressing misleading perceptions of their expertise when presenting evidence (see 'people' or 'person' concepts) were useful for communicating their evidence. Experts also reported avoiding technical jargon to assist the jury in understanding their evidence (see 'terms' concept). On using non-technical language, one expert remarked, 'I think the jury understands. I always go to great pains to use non-technical language to describe medical issues in non-technical terms, so I think when I was describing injuries and the mechanism I thought happened they should have known how to understand that.'

5.53 Experts were also interested in whether they had been understood by the jury. Some experts were frustrated by a lack of direct feedback from the jury about whether they understood the evidence provided by the expert (see 'understand' concept). Other experts reported attempting to read jurors' body language for an indication of how their evidence was being comprehended, even at the basic level of whether members of the jury were attending to them during testimony (see 'jury' concept). In the words of one expert, 'I always look at the jury; I try to look as little as possible at the bar table, and you can tell by people's reactions whether they are taking in what you said. That's why I do it; because my job is to help them understand.'

(3) Interview responses of the lawyers

(a) Do lawyers think jurors understand expert evidence?

5.54 Lawyers were asked, for each expert who presented evidence in the case, whether they thought that the jurors had difficulty understanding that expert's evidence. In relation to the first expert, 59.1% of lawyers thought jurors did not have difficulty understanding the expert's evidence, 30.1% thought jurors did have difficulty understanding the evidence, and 10.8% were unsure about jurors' comprehension in this regard. In relation to the second expert, 52.4% of lawyers thought jurors did not have difficulty understanding the expert's evidence, 18.4% thought jurors did have difficulty understanding the expert's evidence, and 8.7% were unsure of jurors' comprehension of it.

(b) What lawyers say about jury comprehension

5.55 During the project interview, lawyers were asked several questions about how they perceived jurors' comprehension of expert evidence at trial. Responses to three questions, 'Were there any parts of this expert's evidence which you think the jury had difficulty understanding?' (asked for each of the two experts) and 'Was there any expert evidence in this trial that was complex for jurors?' were extracted from the interview data and analysed using Leximancer (see Figure 5.3 and Table 5.3 for the concept map and content of concepts for this analysis).

(c) Findings

5.56 Lawyers generally thought that the jury understood expert evidence (see 'understood', 'understand', 'don't', and 'didn't' concepts). Like jurors and expert witnesses, lawyers also identified that DNA evidence has the potential to be complicated for jurors to understand (see 'DNA' concept). In the words of one lawyer, 'I think DNA evidence is always a little bit difficult for juries to understand.' In addition, and as expert witnesses did, lawyers commented on

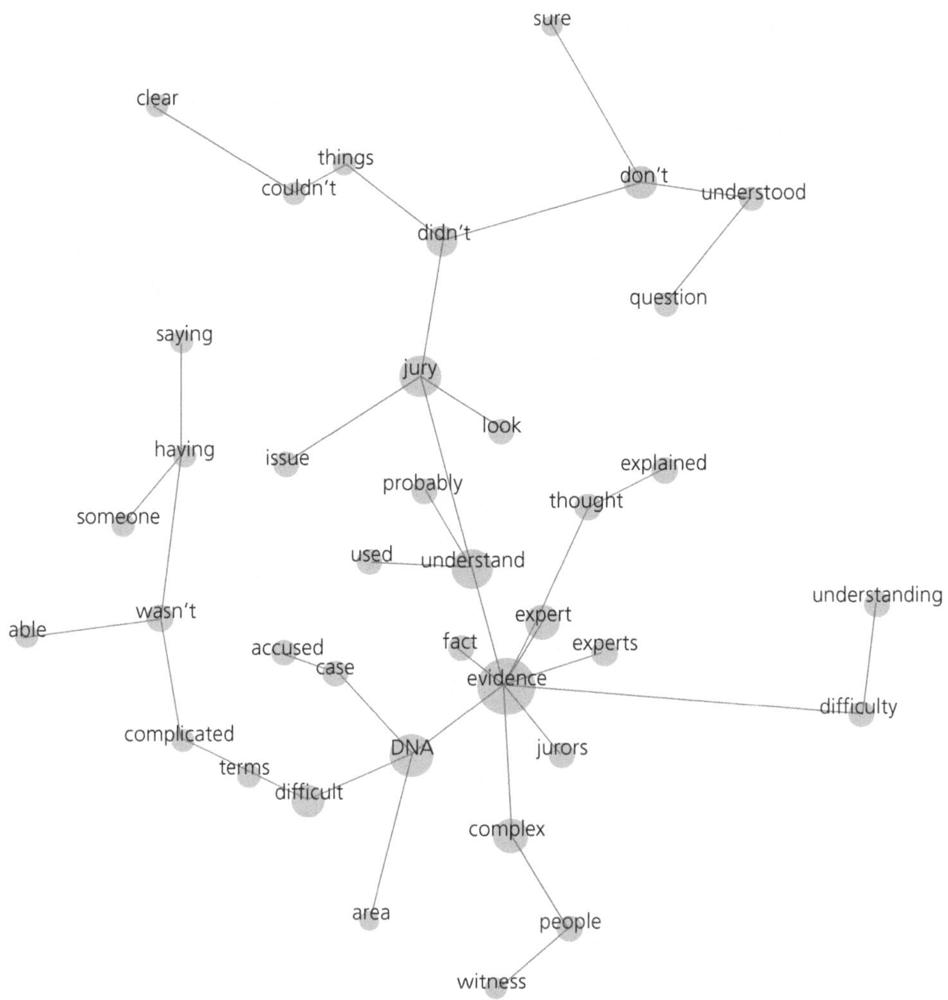

Figure 5.3 Concept map of lawyers' evaluations of juror comprehension.

technical language as a barrier to comprehension (see 'terms' concept). Lawyers also reflected on lay understanding of areas of expertise as part of making inferences about the jury's relative level of understanding (see 'people' concept).

Lawyers mentioned some additional considerations that they thought influenced jurors' comprehension. Many were barristers and therefore professional speakers. They commented on the manner and style that experts adopted on the witness stand as relevant to comprehension (see 'used' concept). One lawyer remarked, 'Well, he used a lot of slightly unusual expressions, but I think that's just his personality. So possibly they did [understand], but maybe not.' Lawyers were also concerned that the questioning style of opposing counsel reduced comprehension of the expert's evidence (see 'question' concept) and wondered whether the opposing counsel had been able to undermine the expert in cross-examination. **5.57**

In discussing jury comprehension, lawyers referenced the relevance of expert evidence on disputed issues at trial (see 'issue' concept). **5.58**

Table 5.3 Concept content from lawyers' responses about jury comprehension.

Concept name	Concept description	Frequency
evidence	Complexity of expert evidence presented in the trial	147
jury	Lawyers' ability to evaluate jury comprehension and discussion of the jury's level of comprehension	85
DNA	Influence of DNA evidence on the jury and challenges to encouraging jury comprehension	81
don't	Assertions that expert evidence is not difficult for juries to understand	74
complex	Identification of expert evidence that was simple or complex for jury comprehension	64
understand	Opinions about the level of the jury's comprehension	62
difficult	Aspects of expert evidence that were complex for the jury to understand	52
expert	Challenges to comprehension posed by the expert's area of expertise or evidence presentation	46
didn't	Identification of expert evidence that was not complex	37
thought	Admissions about the lawyer's own comprehension and opinions about the jury's comprehension	32
wasn't	Reflections on information not communicated in expert evidence	31
explained	Opinions about specific explanations provided by an expert	27
understood	Assertions about whether the expert evidence was understood	27
issue	Relevance of expert evidence to contentious facts for the jury to determine	26
terms	Use of jargon or lay language by experts	26
difficulty	Relative complexity of elements of an expert's evidence	25
case	General reflections on expert evidence presented at trial	24
people	Challenges of lay understanding of expert evidence	24
experts	Comparing presentations by experts who gave evidence at trial	23
able	Information an expert was willing to provide in their evidence	23
probably	Estimations of the level of the jury's comprehension	22
used	Experts' experience in testifying and lawyers' experiences at trial with particular experts	21
clear	Clarity of the expert's evidence	21
jurors	Opinions about the jury's likely interpretation of expert evidence	21
complicated	Elements of expert evidence that were not complicated	20
understanding	Opinion about the jury's difficulty understanding the expert evidence	20
question	Questions asked by the lawyer or opposing counsel	18
accused	Expert evidence about the accused	17
look	Emphasis used to identify key issues in relation to jury comprehension	17
fact	Importance of expert evidence to contentious facts for the jury	16
area	Identification of specific areas of expertise likely to cause confusion for the jury	16
things	Explanation of specific facts during expert evidence	16
saying	Presentation style of particular experts	14
sure	Expert evidence that the lawyer was confident the jury understood	13
having	What the jury's experience of the expert evidence might have been	12
someone	Lay understanding of expert evidence	11
couldn't	Information that would have been uncertain for the jury after expert evidence	10
witness	Presentation strategy of experts	8

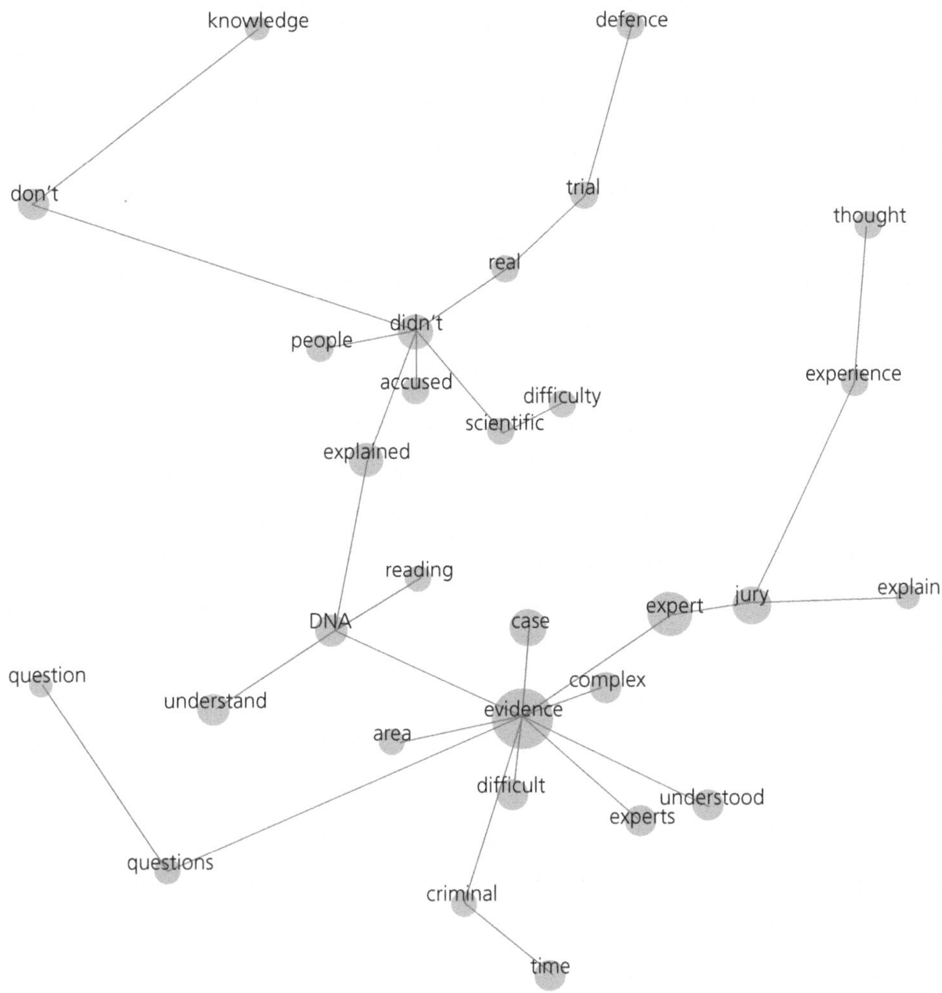

Figure 5.4 Concept map of judges' evaluations of juror comprehension.

(4) Interview responses of the judges

(a) Do judges think jurors understand expert evidence?

Judges responded to a series of questions about jurors' comprehension of expert evidence.[45] **5.59** These included 'Were there any parts of this expert's evidence which you think the jury had difficulty understanding?' and 'Which parts of their evidence presented difficulty?' (about each expert) and 'Do you have any other comments or concerns about this expert, or any other expert in this case?' (see Figure 5.4 and Table 5.4 for concept map and concept content for this analysis). Responses from forty interviews with judges are included in this analysis.

(b) Findings

Interview responses from judges were shorter and fewer in number than those provided by **5.60** jurors, expert witnesses, or lawyers. For this reason, the number of comments coded into the

[45] The answers given by the judges constituted an interesting point of comparison with the answers given by them on a similar subject in 1999: see Freckelton, Reddy, and Selby, *Australian Judicial Perspectives on Expert Evidence: An Empirical Study*.

Table 5.4 Concept content from judges' responses about juror comprehension.

Concept name	Concept description	Frequency
evidence	Challenges to jury comprehension of expert evidence in the case and the relative influence of expert evidence	42
expert	Opinions on expert performance	21
don't	Uncertainty about how expert evidence was perceived by the jury	17
jury	Inferences the judge made about the jury's perception of the evidence	16
case	Relevance of expert evidence in the case	12
I've	Reflections on the judge's own experience with expert evidence	12
didn't	Identification of parts of expert evidence the jury would have struggled to understand	10
explained	Extent of explanations provided by experts	10
thought	Opinions about particular experts	10
DNA	Complexity of DNA evidence for the jury	9
complex	Strategies for addressing complex expert evidence	9
understand	Influences on jury comprehension	9
time	Discussion of events at trial	8
understood	Parts of expert evidence that were understood	8
defence	Defence counsel interactions with experts	8
difficult	Relative difficulty of various expert evidence	7
criminal	General discussion of expert evidence in criminal trials	6
area	Common areas of expertise in expert evidence	6
people	Expert involved in the case	6
experts	Generic discussion of experts providing evidence	6
experience	Reflections on the judge's own experience with expert evidence across their career	6
question	Discussion of interview questions	6
difficulty	Difficult facts the jury had to determine in the case	5
scientific	Nature of scientific evidence	5
accused	Complexity of evidence about the accused's presence at the crime scene	4
trial	Opinions about how the trial was perceived by jurors	4
questions	Questioning style of counsel or questions asked by the jury	4
explain	Effectiveness of particular expert explanations	4
knowledge	Recognized areas of expertise and knowledge within these fields	4
reading	Statement evidence compared to testimony at trial	3
real	Usefulness of life experience in understanding expert evidence	3

concepts in this analysis is noticeably lower than in other analyses in this chapter. Judges, like jurors, expert witnesses, and lawyers, generally thought that jurors could understand expert evidence relatively well (see 'evidence' concept). Like jurors, experts, and lawyers, they conceded that DNA evidence could be complex depending on the explanation provided (see 'DNA' concept).

5.61 In contrast, judges were more concerned with the experience of the expert witness in testifying than any other stakeholder group (see 'expert' concept). As one judge explained, 'Oh, from time to time there's an expert witness who doesn't perform particularly well. Usually it's because they're not accustomed to it and often it will be young doctors who maybe spent a year or whatever period it might've been doing their internship in a hospital and so they come across this case and they have to come to court.' Judges referred to their personal experience in dealing with expert evidence on the bench and their experience examining witnesses as a barrister (see 'experience' concept) and commented on cross-examination of witnesses by defence counsel as a factor in the jury's comprehension of evidence, for better or worse (see 'defence' concept). One judge described the potential adverse impact of cross-examination as follows: 'No, look, I was concerned about the medical expert because I thought he was inexperienced, and I thought he allowed defence counsel to get away with propositions that they shouldn't have, and the problem is a judge can only intervene so far…'

(5) Influence of barriers to comprehension on the persuasiveness of the evidence

Do identified barriers to juror comprehension and expert characteristics influence jurors' reliance on expert evidence? The analysis of stakeholders' responses yielded consensus that overuse of technical language, lack of experience in providing evidence, and lack of confidence on the part of the expert witness are potential barriers to jurors' comprehension of evidence. However, it was not clear whether these potential barriers impacted on jurors' reliance on expert evidence in reaching a verdict. To explore whether the identified barriers to juror comprehension of expert witness evidence influenced jurors' reliance on expert evidence, correlational analyses of jury responses to the survey were undertaken. **5.62**

Jurors evaluated the presentation of expert evidence by each expert witness in the criminal trial in which they participated, and rated the relative strength of the prosecution and defence cases, as well as whether the expert evidence influenced their verdict decision and the extent to which they relied upon the prosecution and defence experts. **5.63**

The prosecution expert's gender was correlated with perceived prosecution case strength and influence of the expert on the verdict, such that when the expert was male the case was seen as being stronger and the expert had a greater impact. The perceived education level of the prosecution expert was also positively related to ratings of the strength of the prosecution case, negatively with difficulty comprehending prosecution expert evidence, and positively with reliance on prosecution expert witness evidence in reaching a verdict. The more that jurors perceived the expert to be highly educated, the more they rated the prosecution's case as strong, the more they thought they understood that expert's evidence, and the more they relied on that evidence. Jurors' perceptions of the prosecution expert as scientific or wise was negatively associated with difficulty in comprehending the evidence and positively so with reliance on the prosecution witness evidence (see Table 5.5 for correlations between evidence features and ratings of case strength and comprehension of or reliance on prosecution expert witness evidence). **5.64**

The confidence of the prosecution expert influenced jurors' reliance on the evidence. Ratings of the confidence of the prosecution expert were positively associated with evaluations of the prosecution case as strong, negatively so with difficulty comprehending the expert's evidence, and positively with reliance on the expert's evidence in reaching a verdict. That is, the more that the expert called by the prosecution was perceived as confident, the more jurors evaluated the prosecution's case positively, the more they thought they understood that expert's evidence, and the more they relied on that evidence. **5.65**

As in the analysis of juror interview responses, use of technical language was associated with difficulty in comprehending the expert's evidence. Similarly, ratings of the prosecution expert evidence as complex were positively associated with difficulty understanding the evidence. Thus, technical language and the complexity of evidence may be barriers to comprehension of expert witness evidence. Despite the association of the use of technical language and complexity in prosecution witness evidence with difficulty understanding, both evidence features were associated with perceptions that the prosecution's case was stronger. **5.66**

Table 5.5 Prosecution expert features and jurors' self-reported reliance on the expert.

		Prosecution case strength	Defence case strength	Difficulty understanding prosecution expert	Influence of prosecution expert on verdict decision
	M	3.73	2.64	1.84	3.91
	(SD)	(1.12)	(1.06)	(1.01)	(1.16)
Expert gender		–.17**	.08	–.06	–.15*
Expert education	9.22 (1.26)	.16**	–.06	–.22***	.19**
Expert confidence	8.73 (1.47)	.16**	–.09	–.21***	.19**
Expert scientific	8.41 (1.67)	.14*	–.10	–.21***	.22***
Expert wise	8.91 (1.45)	.10	–.01	–.17**	.27***
Need for more simple explanation	2.42 (1.24)	–.04	–.01	.36***	–.02
Evidence clarity	4.08 (.96)	.05	–.12*	–.29***	.15*
Evidence complexity	3.07 (1.24)	.15*	–.00	.22***	.06
Evidence contained technical language	2.83 (1.25)	.13*	–.07	.14*	.08

Note: Probabilities indicated as * $p < .05$, ** $p < .01$, *** $p < .001$. Expert gender coded as 1 = male, 2 = female. *M* = mean; *SD* = standard deviation.

5.67 The perceived clarity of prosecution expert evidence was negatively associated with ratings of the defence case strength and difficulty in comprehending the prosecution expert witness. Clarity of evidence was positively associated with ratings of reliance on evidence,[46] suggesting that clear prosecution evidence may have influenced jurors' decision-making process.

5.68 Associations between jurors' evaluations of the defence witness evidence and jurors' self-reported ratings of comprehension and reliance on that evidence were also examined (see Table 5.6). We were not able to analyse the associations for the gender of the defence expert, as there were no female defence experts included in the sample. As in the case of prosecution experts, the perceived level of defence expert education was not associated with ratings of case strength, or comprehension of or reliance on defence expert evidence. Perceptions of the defence expert as wise or scientific were negatively associated with difficulty in comprehending the expert evidence. The perceived confidence of the defence expert was positively associated with ratings of the strength of the defence case. Clarity in the defence expert evidence was negatively associated with difficulty in comprehending that evidence. Jurors' perceptions that the defence expert evidence needed to be explained more simply were associated positively with difficulties in comprehending the defence expert evidence.

[46] In the 1999 judicial survey, clarity was identified by judges as the most persuasive factor when an expert gave evidence: Freckelton, Reddy, and Selby, *Australian Judicial Perspectives on Expert Evidence: An Empirical Study*. There was a similar outcome in the 2001 survey of magistrates: Ian Freckelton, Prasuna Reddy, and Hugh Selby, *Australian Magistrates' Perspectives on Expert Evidence: A Comparative Study* (Melbourne: AIJA, 2001).

Table 5.6 Defence expert features and jurors' self-reported reliance on the expert.

		Prosecution case strength	Defence case strength	Difficulty understanding defence expert	Influence of defence expert on verdict decision
	M	3.45	2.92	2.16	3.21
	(*SD*)	(1.30)	(1.21)	(1.21)	(1.20)
Expert gender		–	–	–	–
Expert education	9.15 (1.03)	.19	.08	–.15	.12
Expert confidence	8.57 (1.56)	–.21	.35**	–.23	–.01
Expert scientific	8.39 (1.62)	.01	.02	–.24*	.07
Expert wise	7.90 (1.78)	.12	–.02	–.36**	.01
Need for more simple explanation	2.51 (1.23)	.18	–.14	.59***	–.19
Evidence clarity	3.59 (1.13)	–.08	–.10	–.51***	.14
Evidence complexity	3.06 (1.21)	.19	–.04	.01	.12
Evidence contained technical language	2.86 (1.24)	.21	.07	.16	.11

Note: Probabilities indicated as * $p < .05$, ** $p < .01$, *** $p < .001$. *M* = mean; *SD* = standard deviation.

However, some key discrepancies emerged in the pattern of results for prosecution versus defence expert evidence. Critically, none of the identified barriers to comprehension were associated with jurors' reliance on defence expert evidence in reaching their verdict. In contrast, jurors' perceptions of the prosecution expert witness as confident, scientific, and wise, and the perception of the expert's evidence as clear, were all positively associated with jurors' reliance on the prosecution expert evidence in reaching a verdict. The more that the prosecution expert was perceived as confident, the more jurors evaluated the prosecution case positively, the more they thought they understood that expert's evidence, and the more they relied on that evidence to reach their verdict. However, defence experts who were seen as confident, evaluations of the defence case as positive, and greater self-report understanding of that evidence by jurors did not have any influence on jurors' reliance on the defence expert evidence to reach a verdict. **5.69**

E. Conclusions

Jurors, experts, lawyers, and judges generally agreed on the extent to which jurors understood the expert evidence, a finding reflected in both quantitative and qualitative analyses of interview responses. Of great interest is that all identified DNA evidence as potentially difficult for jurors to comprehend. **5.70**

Regarding the sources of complexity in expert evidence, jurors and expert witnesses identified technical jargon as a key barrier to comprehension. However, jurors often commented that technical jargon was not overused by experts, indicating that experts gave a satisfactory, jargon-free explanation of their evidence. In instances where expert witnesses used jargon, jurors **5.71** reported that judges had assisted by directing the witness to explain this jargon. Consistent with jurors' observations, expert witnesses reported that reducing use of jargon was a key method employed to ensure their evidence was comprehensible.

5.72 While judges and lawyers acknowledged that jargon could be a deterrent to comprehension, they implicated the questioning style of counsel as a barrier to jurors' comprehension of expert evidence. This finding is consistent with reports by judges that they intervene to ensure that the evidence of an expert is comprehensible when counsel fails to do so. Judges perceived that the level of experience an expert has of testifying in court could influence the clarity of communication by an expert providing testimony and accordingly the jury's comprehension of the expert evidence.

5.73 Jurors reported that several strategies helped overcome some of the challenges of understanding complex expert evidence. Jurors noted with approval the experts who used plain language. When experts lapse into technical jargon, jurors are appreciative of barristers and judges who ask the expert to explain the concept in plain language. This is particularly needed when presenting DNA evidence to the jury.

5.74 While this finding might suggest a realistic appraisal of the challenges posed by expert evidence, the correlational analyses imply that jurors continue, at least in part, to be influenced by many of the factors identified by earlier research as problematic, particularly in the case of the prosecution expert. Since more data were collected for prosecution than defence experts in the sample of cases included in this project, there was greater statistical power to detect effects for prosecution experts.

5.75 The credentials of prosecution experts were important for jurors' evaluations of the prosecution case and their verdicts. This was an interesting finding, as when judges in the 1999 survey were asked about what they considered as the most persuasive factor when experts were giving evidence, credentials rated very low.[47]

5.76 Expert gender was influential—male experts for the prosecution were associated with jurors' perceptions that the prosecution case was stronger, and they tended to rely more readily on male experts' evidence. The experts' demeanour was also influential. Complex language, identified as common in certain types of expertise, and identified in 1999 by almost a quarter of judges as the single most serious problem they encountered with expert evidence,[48] was perceived as more persuasive—despite its association with greater difficulties in understanding, and acknowledgement by jurors in the interviews of its problematic nature. Further evidence that these effects reflect the possible influence of heuristic cues and stereotypes via peripheral rather than central processing is that several of these factors were associated with jurors' evaluations of the opposing defence expert.

5.77 Jurors in criminal trials are faced with a complex task to understand and evaluate the evidence presented at trial and reach a decision on the guilt of the accused. The results of the qualitative and quantitative analyses presented in this chapter suggest that jurors are most able to understand expert evidence when it is presented to them in a way that uses simple explanations and avoids technical language.

[47] Freckelton, Reddy, and Selby, *Australian Judicial Perspectives on Expert Evidence: An Empirical Study*, p. 150.

[48] Freckelton, Reddy and Selby. *Australian Judicial Perspectives on Expert Evidence: An Empirical Study*, p. 144.

6

DNA PROFILING EVIDENCE

A. Introduction

An exponential increase in the use of DNA profiling evidence in criminal trials has occurred in all jurisdictions over the past 25 years, and Australian courts are no exception.[1] This trend was reflected in the fact that of the 55 criminal trials included in this project, across all three states, the most frequently encountered type of expert evidence was DNA profiling evidence. A total of 23 DNA experts appeared in 18 trials. Two-thirds of these trials proceeded in a Supreme Court and one third in District or County Courts. **6.01**

The impact of DNA profiling evidence at trial should not be underestimated. Prior to the advent of DNA evidence, in criminal trials involving forensic scientific evidence such as blood type matches, hair analysis, etc., the general consensus among evidence scholars was that jurors were prone to ignoring probabilistic statistics that were difficult to understand,[2] perhaps because this information is less vivid and memorable than other types of evidence.[3] **6.02**

---

[1] Patricia Weiser Easteal and Simon Easteal, 'The Forensic Use of DNA Profiling', *Trends & Issues in Crime and Criminal Justice*, no. 26 (November 1990) 1, <http://aic.gov.au/media_library/publications/tandi_pdf/tandi026.pdf>; Simon Walsh and others, 'DNA Profiling and Criminal Justice: A Contribution to a Changing Debate', *Australian Journal of Forensic Sciences* 36, no. 1 (January–July 2004) 34.

[2] Jane Goodman, 'Jurors' Comprehension and Assessment of Probabilistic Evidence', *American Journal of Trial Advocacy* 16, no. 2 (winter 1992) 361; William Thompson and Edward Schumann, 'Interpretation of Statistical Evidence in Criminal Trials: The Prosecutor's Fallacy and the Defence Attorney's Fallacy', *Law and Human Behavior* 11, no. 3 (1987) 167; Michael Saks and Robert Kidd, 'Human Information Processing and Adjudication: Trial by Heuristics', *Law and Society* 15, no. 1 (1980–1) 123.

[3] Jane Goodman-Delahunty, Thea Gumbert-Jourjon, and Sandra Hale, 'The Biasing Influence of Linguistic Variations in DNA Profiling Evidence', *Australian Journal of Forensic Sciences* 46, no. 3 (2014) 348;

6.03 However, DNA expert evidence is accompanied by extreme statistical probabilities of a magnitude that is hard to overlook, such as odds of one in a trillion.[4] Indeed, one expert in a trial in the project testified that the likelihood of a random match between the crime scene sample and the DNA profile of the defendant was one in ten billion (trial 35).

B. The Impact of DNA Profiling Evidence on the Criminal Justice System

6.04 DNA evidence derived from a direct match between a sample taken from a crime scene and a sample from a suspect is used in a diverse range of criminal investigations of crimes such as homicide, sexual assault, and burglary. In the present project, this diversity was reflected in that three-fifths of the trials (61.1%; $n = 11$) in which the DNA profiling evidence was used were murder trials, three were sexual assault trials (16.7%), and the remainder were armed robbery, reckless driving, and kidnapping/assault trials.

6.05 Archival studies of matched Australian trials of sexual assault and murder conducted with and without DNA evidence revealed that juries were 33 times more likely to convict in both types of trials when DNA evidence was admitted than in comparable trials without it.[5] Similarly, experimental studies revealed that the mere mention of a DNA match, without further details of the comparison, increased the conviction rate compared to parallel trials in the absence of this information.[6] One of the experts whom we interviewed favoured bench trials over jury trials for precisely this reason:

> I would generally think a judge for a defendant would be better because of what we call the CSI effect. That is, if someone says there's a match to DNA, they don't really listen to where it is, or what it is. That's almost in my experience in a jury's mind what it thinks. That maybe a false interpretation, but that's what I think (expert 2, trial 43).

6.06 Interviews with defence counsel have revealed the view that in some sectors DNA evidence is regarded as unassailable, thus is less likely to be contested than are other types of expert evidence, including other forms of forensic scientific evidence.[7] Without cavil, the least contentious use of DNA profiling evidence in an investigation is to rule out a suspect, i.e., DNA test results can provide conclusive exculpatory evidence when the crime scene sample and a sample from the defendant yield a non-match.[8] In this project, in a murder trial involving multiple defendants (trial 40), DNA evidence was introduced to exclude certain defendants from consideration on specific charges.

David Kaye, 'Probability, Individualization, and Uniqueness: What's the Difference?', *Law, Probability & Risk* 8, no. 2 (2009) 85; Jonathan Koehler, 'One in Millions, Billions and Trillions: Lessons from *People v Collins* (1968) for *People v Simpson* (1995)', *Journal of Legal Education* 47, no. 2 (1997) 214.

4 Jane Goodman-Delahunty and Ben Newell, 'One in How Many Trillion?' *Australasian Science* 25, no. 7 (August 2004) 14. See too *R v Cannell* [2012] SADC 80; *R v Lindsay* [2013] SASCFC 95.

5 Michael Briody, 'The Effects of DNA Evidence on Murder Cases in Court', *Australian and New Zealand Journal of Criminology* 37, no. 2 (August 2004) 231; Michael Briody, 'The Effects of DNA Evidence on Sexual Offence Cases in Court', *Current Issues in Criminal Justice* 14, no. 2 (2002) 159, <http://www.austlii.edu.au/au/journals/CICrimJust/2002/25.pdf>.

6 Stephanie Dartnall and Jane Goodman-Delahunty, 'Enhancing Juror Understanding of Probabilistic DNA Evidence', *Australian Journal of Forensic Sciences* 38, no. 2 (2006) 85.

7 Kate Cashman and Terese Henning, 'Lawyers and DNA: Issues in Understanding and Challenging the Evidence', *Current Issues in Criminal Justice* 24, no. 1 (2012) 69.

8 Ian Freckelton and Hugh Selby, *Expert Evidence: Law, Practice, Procedure and Advocacy*, 6th edn. (Sydney: Thomson Reuters, 2016).

(1) 'Cold hit' cases

A contemporary trend attributable to the availability of DNA evidence is its use to prosecute 'cold hit' cases, or trials in which no adequate evidence to link a suspect to the crime scene was available at the time of the offence, but a subsequent test between a DNA sample from the crime scene and a reference sample in a police analysis databank yields a match. These cases often proceed to trial many years after the crime scene samples were gathered. **6.07**

The DNA profiles aggregated in a police databank come from other investigations and trials. The largest DNA databases maintained in the United States (Combined DNA Index System) and the United Kingdom (National DNA Database) contain many millions of DNA profiles. The National Criminal Investigation DNA Database, in partnership with all nine Australian police agencies, contains approximately one million DNA profiles and is used for kinship matching and familial searching, as well as rapid and direct profile matching.[9] **6.08**

Three of the trials in the present project were 'cold cases', able to be prosecuted on the basis of cold DNA hits. One was a trial of violent sexual assault, and two were murder trials (trials 22, 35, and 39). **6.09**

(2) DNA evidence and errors

When DNA profiling evidence is used in an inculpatory way to support the inference that the defendant was at the crime scene, and the crime scene sample yields a direct match, this proof is regarded as the 'gold standard' among many types of forensic scientific evidence.[10] DNA evidence attained this status because of a body of reliable published scholarly scientific research underpinning the forensic techniques used in generating a DNA profile. Moreover, the expression of the test results in a probabilistic manner is compatible with the approach used in most other physical and social sciences, i.e. in terms of the likelihood of an error or random match between the crime scene sample and the sample of DNA from the defendant. **6.10**

DNA profiling evidence is rarely challenged. One defence lawyer in the present project articulated the view that while DNA evidence is not irrefutable, the primary source of problems with DNA profiling evidence was the way the information was presented: **6.11**

> [DNA scientists] don't have the capacity to explain it very well. It is a very vexed science, and can be presented in a way that makes it overwhelming, when it is not (defence lawyer, trial 25).

DNA profiling evidence is not impervious to human error. Official acknowledgement of the potential for errors occurring in the preparation DNA profiling evidence has been slow, and often conceded only in the face of irrefutable evidence of laboratory errors.[11] **6.12**

In a 2008 trial in the Victorian County Court, jurors suspected a mix-up of DNA samples might have produced the expert evidence that a DNA profile linked a young black male suspect to the crime scene of a sexual assault at a nightclub with middle-aged white clientele. The defendant credibly denied ever attending. The jury sent queries to the court **6.13**

---

[9] CrimTrac, *Annual Report: 2013–2014* (Canberra: Commonwealth of Australia, 2014), <http://www.crimtrac.gov.au/documents/CRIMTRACAnnualReport2013_14.pdf>.

[10] Committee on Identifying the Needs of the Forensic Sciences Community, National Research Council, *Strengthening Forensic Science in the United States: A Path Forward* (Washington: The National Academies Press, 2009); Joel Lieberman and others, 'Gold Versus Platinum: Do Jurors Recognise the Superiority and Limitations of DNA Evidence Compared to Other Types of Forensic Evidence?', *Psychology, Public Policy, and Law* 14, no. 1 (2008) 27.

[11] *R v Domaszewicz* (Supreme Court of Victoria, 4 December 1998) (unresolved kidnap and homicide of a toddler); *Murdoch v The Queen* [2007] NTCCA 1, (2007) 167 A Crim R 329.

about sampling error, based on their qualms about the reliability of the prosecution's DNA evidence. So iron-clad is the reputation of DNA evidence that the judge and legal counsel dismissed the jury questions and instructed jurors to rely on the admitted DNA evidence. The ensuing false conviction of the defendant, Farah Jama, was ultimately overturned following an inquiry which revealed that contaminated samples gathered from a medical office with substandard hygiene procedures had produced this match.[12] As a consequence, the Victorian Chief Commissioner of Police suspended DNA testing and analysis until a review was completed of DNA reporting practices by the Victoria Police Forensic Services Division, and new national standards for DNA analysis were in place.[13]

6.14 Despite this dramatic series of events compelling the acknowledgement of errors in the routine gathering and processing of DNA profiling evidence in Australian courts, forensic experts do not take into account the potential for a laboratory error when making their statistical computations of the likelihood of a random match between the suspect and the crime scene.[14] Inclusion of information about known errors rates in scientific procedures has been shown to reduce the probative weight of the DNA evidence,[15] and is mandatory in some United States jurisdictions,[16] but is not required in the United Kingdom, Canada, or Australia. Jury simulation studies revealed that jurors appropriately gave less weight to DNA evidence if they considered that a sample had been corrupted or an error made in the laboratory.[17]

(3) Other factors affecting DNA evidence reliability

6.15 Aside from known error rates, other factors such as the amount and nature of the available DNA sample can have an impact on the probative value of the resulting DNA profile. For example, a recent development in DNA profiling technology is the use of low-template, low-copy, or touch DNA (LTDNA), by means of which a profile is generated from minute quantities of DNA; just a few cells. Partial DNA profiles generated in this way have been admitted into evidence internationally, for instance in the United Kingdom,[18] and by the South Australian Supreme Court.[19] The English Court of Appeal has emphasized that a DNA match derived from low-copy number analysis should not comprise the sole basis of charging a suspect.[20] It established guidelines as to the limits of the admissibility of LTDNA, and requires the jury to be informed of its limitations and instructed on how to evaluate the partial DNA profile.[21]

---

[12] Katherine Rayment, 'Faith in DNA: The Vincent Report', *Journal of Law, Information and Science* 20 (2009–10) 214.

[13] Jim Fraser, John Buckleton, and Peter Gill, 'Review of DNA Reporting Practices by Victoria Police Forensic Services Division', *Victoria Police News* (April 2010) 3.

[14] Conversation between Simon Walsh, Australian Federal Police, and Jane Goodman-Delahunty (18 December 2014) concerning laboratory procedures; conversation between Fabio Guarino, Victoria Police Lab, and Jane Goodman-Delahunty (20 July 2012).

[15] Studies by Jonathan Koehler, Audrey Chia, and Samuel Lindsey, 'The Random Match Probability (RMP) in DNA Evidence: Irrelevant and Prejudicial?', *Jurimetrics Journal* 35, no. 2 (winter 1995) 201, although jurors may not always make such fine-grained distinctions, as shown in Stephanie Dartnall and Jane Goodman-Delahunty, 'Enhancing Juror Understanding of Probabilistic DNA Evidence', 85, when lab error rates were specified.

[16] Those which adhere to the standards articulated in *Daubert v Merrell Dow Pharmaceuticals Inc*, 509 US 579 (1993).

[17] Jason Schklar and Shari Seidman Diamond, 'Juror Reactions to DNA Evidence: Errors and Expectancies', *Law and Human Behavior* 23, no. 2 (1999) 159.

[18] *R v Bates* [2006] EWCA Crim 1395 (Application for Leave to Appeal).

[19] *R v Priestley* [2012] SASC 119. Cp *DPP v Tangaloa* [2013] VCC 621.

[20] *R v Ogden* [2013] EWCA Crim 1294.

[21] *R v Reed* [2009] EWCA Crim 2698, [2010] 1 Cr App R 23.

Previously, profiles derived from partial or mixed DNA samples were regarded as too small to generate intelligible results and were inadmissible as evidence due to their complexity and unreliability. Ongoing research and refinements to the DNA sampling and testing technology in recent decades have enabled partial or mixed DNA samples to generate individual DNA profiles. Australian courts have accepted the admissibility of mixed DNA samples as long as this DNA evidence is not considered inculpatory in the absence of other evidence.[22] Thus, the Australian High Court held that a match from a mixed DNA profile taken from a single blood spot on a didgeridoo found in the home of a murder victim with a sample taken from the defendant, in the absence of other incriminating evidence placing the defendant at the crime scene, was insufficient to sustain a conviction. This evidence was inadequate to meet the criminal standard of proof of the defendant's guilt beyond a reasonable doubt.[23] None of the DNA trials included in this project involved no other proof linking the defendant to the crime aside from DNA evidence. **6.16**

Nonetheless, heated contention in the scientific community persists as to the reliability[24] and interpretation of, and reliance on, mixed DNA profiles.[25] For this reason, although the exculpatory DNA evidence in Trial 40 in the project was not the central scientific evidence in that trial, because the DNA profiles were based on tests of mixed DNA profile samples, this evidence was presented by opposing DNA experts. Unsurprisingly, they disagreed about aspects of the interpretation of the results of the mixed samples. **6.17**

Since March 2013, in all Australian states and territories, except Tasmania and the ACT, a new software package called STRmix, developed by a team of scientists from Australia and New Zealand, has been in use to estimate the likelihood that a DNA profile obtained from the crime scene sample would match that of the accused versus that of an unknown person chosen at random from the relevant population. Through an iterative Markov chain Monte Carlo process, based on random number generation, STRmix produces alternative explanations for a tested profile, and weightings that can take into account the low-template DNA or mixed samples that yield incomplete profiles. Moreover, because the Markov chain process is random, the statistical likelihood ratio that is generated when the process is repeated will vary. Although the statistics are not precisely reproducible upon repetition, the variances in the statistics are typically extremely small in magnitude.[26] In a recent Victorian case, *Tuite v The Queen*,[27] in which the accused was charged with aggravated burglary, rape, indecent assault, and intentionally causing injury, the reliability of this novel method was unsuccessfully challenged. The likelihood ratios generated by this software are notably high. For example, in that case, using STRmix, the expert stated that it was estimated to be **6.18**

---

22 *R v Hillier* [2007] HCA 13, (2007) 228 CLR 618, *R v Priestley* [2012] SASC 119.

23 *Fitzgerald v The Queen* [2014] HCA 28, (2014) 88 AJLR 779. The High Court unanimously held that the prosecution's main contention, that the appellant's DNA in the sample obtained from the didgeridoo derived from his blood, was not made out beyond reasonable doubt. Further, the recovery of the appellant's DNA from the didgeridoo did not raise any inference about the time when or circumstances in which the DNA was deposited there. The Court held that it could not be accepted that the evidence relied on by the prosecution was sufficient to establish beyond reasonable doubt that the appellant was present at, and participated in, the attack. The jury, acting reasonably, should have entertained a reasonable doubt as to the appellant's guilt. As the evidence was not capable of supporting the appellant's conviction for either offence, no question of an order for a new trial arose.

24 David Bentley and Peter Lownds, 'Low Template DNA', *Archbold Review* 1 (February 2011) 6; David Bentley and Peter Lownds, 'DNA-Analysis of Complex Mixed Profiles: The New Frontier?', *Archbold Review* 8 (September 2012) 5.

25 See *Clarke v Western Australia* [2011] WASC 285; *R v Berry* [2007] VSCA 202, (2007) 17 VR 153.

26 Duncan Taylor, Jo-Anne Bright, and John Buckleton, 'The Interpretation of Single Source and Mixed DNA Profiles', *Forensic Science International: Genetics* 7, no. 5 (September 2013) 516: p. 521.

27 *Tuite v The Queen* [2015] VSCA 148.

2.7 sextillion times more likely that a mixed DNA sample from three contributors taken from a shoelace used to attach a blindfold to the complainant 'would occur if the DNA originated from the accused, the complainant and one unknown person than if it originated from the complainant and two unknown people chosen at random from the Australian Caucasian population.'[28]

6.19 To ensure that DNA evidence is appropriately used and to avoid wrongful identification or conviction, the premise that not all DNA evidence is equal is vital. Thus, lawyers and judges need to be cognizant of the limitations of particular forms of DNA profiling evidence, such as those derived from LTDNA and mixed samples, and to differentiate these from other types of DNA profiles, to appreciate that there are limitations to the probative value of DNA profiling evidence.

C. Project Findings

(1) Prosecution use of multiple forensic experts

6.20 One consequence of heightened jury expectations that trials will include DNA profiling evidence, as was noted in chapter 2 in paragraph 2.19, is a concomitant increase in the use of DNA evidence in criminal trials—even in trials in which it is not the central inculpatory evidence—because prosecutors view their cases as more persuasive when DNA profiling evidence is adduced to meet jury expectations. As a result, backlogs developed in some state laboratories to process the mounting DNA crime scene samples gathered by investigators to meet this new trial demand.[29]

6.21 Scrutiny of the use of DNA profiling evidence in the present project showed that it addressed a central or key issue in relatively few (22.2%; $n = 4$) of the 18 trials in which it was introduced, i.e., three murder trials and one sexual assault trial. This finding raised a question as to the necessity of introducing less contentious or uncontested DNA evidence, and of calling experts for this purpose, in the majority of the trials in which it was introduced.[30]

6.22 Since DNA profiling evidence is typically introduced by the prosecution, unless this evidence is central to disputed issues in the trial, counsel for the defendant often prefer to rely on cross-examination to challenge this evidence rather than to call an independent rebuttal expert. Most typically in criminal trials, a single expert guides the jury through the DNA evidence.[31] A further feature of this contemporary practice is that the prosecution often calls a series of expert witnesses. This view was endorsed by one prosecutor who was interviewed, who commented about forensic scientific expert evidence that 'It's quite important these days... more so than it used to be years ago, especially with DNA evidence' (prosecutor, trial 43).

---

[28] *Tuite v The Queen* [2015] VSCA 148 [19].

[29] Jenny Wise, 'Providing the CSI Treatment: Criminal Justice Practitioners and the CSI Effect', *Current Issues in Criminal Justice* 21, no. 3 (March 2010) 383, <http://www.austlii.edu.au/au/journals/CICrimJust/2010/3.pdf>. In 2010, the New South Wales backlog was over 7,000 cases, as the demand exceeded the processing capacity; Peter Achterstraat, *Managing Forensic Analysis: Fingerprints and DNA* (Auditor-General's Report, February 2010), <http://www.audit.nsw.gov.au/ArticleDocuments/142/195_Managing_Forensic_Analysis.pdf.aspx?Embed=Y>.

[30] Oriola Sallavaci, *The Impact of Scientific Evidence on the Criminal Trial: The Case of DNA Evidence* (New York: Routledge, 2014).

[31] Mark Findlay, 'Juror Comprehension and the Hard Case: Making Forensic Evidence Simpler', *International Journal of Law, Crime and Justice* 36, no. 1 (2008) 15.

The strategy of 'expert stacking' by the prosecution can create an impression of a powerful trial, and an uneven playing field in court, as the defence has access to fewer resources, and relies primarily on cross-examination or lay, not expert, witnesses. In most trials in which DNA evidence was presented, the prosecution called additional experts (71.2%), only one of whom was designated as a DNA profiling expert. The other forensic experts on whom the prosecution relied presented physiological evidence (e.g., a forensic pathologist), or another type of expert evidence, such as ballistics, blood-spatter evidence, or podiatry. In only two trials (11.1%) (one in which the defendant was charged with committing assault, and the other with committing three armed robberies), the prosecution presented a single expert at trial, whose DNA evidence was challenged only by means of cross-examination by counsel for the defence. **6.23**

These findings confirmed that the more likely situation was that jurors were exposed to multiple experts (in support of the case for the prosecution), and to experts who appeared only on behalf of the Crown prosecutor. Details of trial 35 are elaborated in this chapter as an example of a trial litigated with multiple unrebutted prosecution experts, including DNA profiling experts. **6.24**

Of the 23 experts who presented DNA evidence in the trials in the present project, only three (13.6%) appeared on behalf of the defendant. An unexpected finding was the reliance by defence counsel on cross-examination to challenge the DNA experts, even in a trial in which the prosecution called more than one DNA expert. The defence called independent rebuttal DNA experts in only 16.7% of the trials; two of these were trials of sexual assault, and one was a murder trial. This finding that jurors are rarely exposed to competing DNA experts has significant implications about traditional safeguards in criminal trials to test expert evidence, for the way jurors understand and use the expert evidence, and for the roles of defence counsel and the judge in these criminal trials. **6.25**

(2) Jury expectations and susceptibility to the 'CSI/tech effect'

General consensus exists among forensic scientists, trial judges, and lawyers that *CSI* and similar popular crime-scene television programmes have led jurors to believe that expert evidence is used frequently in criminal investigations and to expect this evidence to yield a high probative value in criminal trials.[32] These shows portray forensic scientists solving crimes in less than an hour, setting up unrealistic expectations of the complex nature of real crimes and real evidence,[33] fostering the impression that incontrovertible scientific evidence will be available. The pervasive concern is that the CSI effect biases jurors' decision-making and that in its absence, *CSI* viewers will not convict, potentially leading to unjust verdicts.[34] Judges whom we interviewed echoed these concerns: **6.26**

> Juries send in notes saying 'Where is the forensics?' So they're expecting forensic evidence, and they think it's going to be the solution to everything. And if there's no forensic evidence, it means there's no case... I think the jury expectation was you'd expect DNA of the

[32] Simon Cole and Rachel Dioso-Villa, 'Investigating the "CSI Effect" Effect: Media and Litigation Crisis in Criminal Law', *Stanford Law Review* 61, no. 6 (April 2009) 1335; Tom R. Tyler, 'Viewing CSI and the Threshold of Guilt: Managing Truth and Justice in Reality and Fiction', *The Yale Law Journal* 115, no. 5 (2006) 1050.

[33] Michael Mann, 'The "CSI Effect": Better Jurors through Televisions and Science?', *Buffalo Public Internet Law Journal* 24 (2005–6) 211; Jane Goodman-Delahunty and Hielkje Verbrugge, 'Reality, Fantasy and the Truth about CSI Effects', *InPsych: The Bulletin of the Australian Psychological Society* 32, no. 4 (2010) 18, <http://www.psychology.org.au/publications/inpsych/2010/august/goodman/>.

[34] '"CSI" Earth's No. 1 Show', *New York Post*, 17 June 2008, <http://nypost.com/2008/06/17/csi-earths-no-1-show/>.

> accused to be on it. If it wasn't there, then that was pretty good evidence that he hadn't used it, and that was really the way the evidence was left for the jury. That, to me, is a distortion (judge, trial 19).

A defence lawyer in our project who expressed a similar view anticipated that judicial instructions would effectively cure this problem:

> My problem with DNA evidence is all that alarmist stuff about one in 450 billion can tend to throw them off the issue... You know, they watch a lot of CSI, and they can be influenced by that sort of evidence as being determinative of the whole trial. But, there are directions designed to accommodate that (defence lawyer, trial 39).

6.27 Contrary to popular beliefs, the vast majority of studies of *CSI*-viewing uncovered no significant link between jurors' television viewing habits and their verdicts.[35] Accordingly, some legal commentators view the CSI effect as a baseless twenty-first-century construct emanating from contemporary legal, scientific, and media distrust of the jury system,[36] just as advocates in the 1960s blamed the 'Perry Mason effect'[37] and the 'white coat syndrome' for their courtroom losses. Empirical studies demonstrated that the CSI effect is more of a 'tech' effect resulting from the convergence of rapid advances in technology and uses of this technology in the criminal justice system.[38,39] Frequent viewing of CSI programmes has increased juror expectations of readily available and incontrovertible scientific evidence,[40] and possibly made them better-informed than non-*CSI* viewers about concepts of proof,[41] and more sceptical about certain types of expert evidence.[42]

6.28 Some support for the 'tech effect' in Australia came from ground-breaking studies of actual jurors who were interviewed at the close of trials in which DNA evidence was introduced. Results confirmed that jurors tended to overrate the value of DNA evidence in circumstantial trials.[43] The reluctance of jurors to contemplate a guilty verdict absent DNA evidence was confirmed in jury interviews.[44] Defence lawyers have exploited this bias to their advantage using the absence of DNA evidence as a reason for the jury to acquit the defendant.[45] While

---

35 See, e.g., N. J. Schweitzer and Michael Saks, 'The CSI Effect: Popular Fiction About Forensic Science Affects the Public's Expectations About Real Forensic Science', *Jurimetrics* 47, no. 3 (2007) 357; Young S. Kim, Gregg Barak, and Donald E. Shelton, 'Examining the "CSI-Effect" in the Cases of Circumstantial Evidence and Eyewitness Testimony: Multivariate and Path Analyses', *Journal of Criminal Justice* 37, no. 5 (2009) 452; Jane Goodman-Delahunty and Lindsay Hewson, *Improving Jury Understanding and Use of Expert DNA Evidence: Technical and Background Paper No. 37* (Australian Institute of Criminology, 2010).

36 Tom R. Tyler, 'Is the CSI Effect Good Science?' *The Yale Law Journal* (February 2006), <http://www.yalelawjournal.org/forum/is-the-csi-effect-good-science>.

37 Perry Mason was a TV show lawyer who solved crimes within 30 minutes. Wendy Brickell, 'Is It the CSI Effect or Do We Just Distrust Juries?', *Criminal Justice* 23, no. 2 (summer 2008) 10.

38 Donald E. Shelton, Young S. Kim, and Gregg Barak, 'An Indirect-Effects Model of Mediated Adjudication: The CSI Myth, the Tech Effect, and Metropolitan Jurors' Expectations for Scientific Evidence', *Vanderbilt Journal of Entertainment & Technology Law* 12, no. 1 (autumn 2009) 1.

39 Donald E. Shelton, Young S. Kim, and Gregg Barak, 'A Study of Juror Expectations and Demands Concerning Scientific Evidence: Does the "CSI Effect" Exist?', *Vanderbilt Journal of Entertainment & Technology Law* 9 (winter 2006) 331.

40 Shelton, Kim, and Barak, 'An Indirect-Effects Model of Mediated Adjudication', 1.

41 Kimberlianne Podlas, 'The "CSI Effect": Exposing the Media Myth', *Fordham Intellectual Property, Media and Entertainment Law Journal* 16 (2006) 429.

42 Schweitzer and Saks, 'The CSI Effect', 357.

43 Australian jurors were interviewed following six criminal trials where forensic evidence featured in circumstantial cases; Mark Findlay, 'Juror Comprehension and the Hard Case', 15.

44 Rhonda Wheate, 'The Importance of DNA Evidence to Juries in Criminal Trials', *International Journal of Evidence & Proof* 14, no. 2 (2010) 129: p. 144.

45 Jane Goodman-Delahunty and David Tait, 'DNA and the Changing Face of Justice', *Australian Journal of Forensic Sciences* 38, no. 2 (2006) 97.

scientific evidence may assist with circumstantial proof, in the vast majority of criminal trials, scientific evidence is incapable of resolving contentious evidence, such as the issue of consent in many sexual assault trials, or motives in murder trials.

In the present project, in addition to looking for evidence of a possible CSI effect, a bivariate correlation was conducted between jurors' mathematics and science exposure via formal study during and after high school and the number of hours spent watching crime TV shows, and the expected frequency of and trust in forensic science. No indication emerged that CSI exposure increased juror knowledge or scepticism about forensic scientific evidence. **6.29**

To explore the influence of jurors' pre-trial attitudes about forensic science in juror decision-making further, a British team of psychologists developed a questionnaire called the Forensic Evidence Evaluation Bias Scale.[46] This measure distinguished two types of attitudes held by mock jurors about forensic scientific evidence. A pro-prosecution series of items incorporated beliefs in the infallibility and conclusiveness of forensic science. The pro-defence items measured jurors' high expectations for forensic science and reliance on scientific evidence for conviction (unwillingness to convict in the absence of forensic science). **6.30**

The same researchers conducted a murder trial simulation with ambiguous DNA evidence. Mock jurors who believed the DNA evidence had high probative value were more likely to convict. A subsequent simulation study of robbery and sexual assault trials was conducted in which weak DNA evidence was either present or absent. The evidence was weak because an innocent explanation for the DNA traces at the crime scene existed. DNA evidence was the only significant predictor of probability of guilt in the robbery trial and the strongest predictor of guilt in the sexual assault trial. Stronger pro-prosecution beliefs predicted strong probative weight or perceived strength of the DNA evidence; mock jurors with pro-defence attitudes gave the circumstantial evidence in the absence of DNA evidence very low strength ratings.[47] These analyses not only illustrate the relationship between DNA and proclivities to convict, but also assist in explaining the different types of attitudes related to CSI effects, and why those earlier studies in which both sets of attitudes were confounded did not yield clear effects. In other words, the perceived strength of the DNA evidence in the trials was predicted by and varied depending on the jurors' pre-trial attitudes to forensic science. **6.31**

In the present project given jurors' high expectations that forensic scientific evidence might resolve issues in criminal trials, they sometimes found the evidence disappointing. After trial, some jurors commented that, unlike what they saw in TV shows, DNA evidence did not provide absolute proof. As one juror put it 'DNA is not like a fingerprint, it is not 100%' (juror E, trial 35). Another juror expressed this view: **6.32**

> I found that a little bit disappointing in a way because, and that's probably my own...you know you sort of hear on TV and all that about DNA and how by itself it's like fingerprinting; it's so absolute. Well, the way it was presented, and her interpretation, in some ways the DNA didn't add any value to this case (juror F, trial 7).

(3) The nature of DNA profiling evidence

The now commonplace presentation of biological evidence in criminal trials is divided into two major parts. The experts commence by outlining how DNA samples are gathered, **6.33**

---

46 Lisa L. Smith and Ray Bull, 'Identifying and Measuring Juror Pretrial Bias for Forensic Evidence: Development and Validation of the Forensic Evidence Evaluation Bias Scale', *Psychology, Crime and Law* 18, no. 9 (2012) 797.

47 Lisa L. Smith and Ray Bull, 'Validation of the Factor Structure and Predictive Validity of the Forensic Evidence Evaluation Bias Scale for Robbery and Sexual Assault Trial Scenarios', *Psychology, Crime and Law* 20, no. 5 (2014) 450.

managed, and processed to generate a 'profile' from a section of the DNA strand. This description is essentially procedural, but can become technically complex, especially when crime scene traces yield mixed samples, or specific types of DNA, such as mitochondrial DNA (mtDNA) evidence. The expert's description usually concludes with depictions in graphical form of tandem repeat sequences showing the peaks and valleys in a segment of a DNA strand, identified by alphabetical strings.

6.34 Proportionately, this evidence is reasonably well understood by jurors and takes longer to convey than the second part of the expert evidence, which is essentially abstract, mathematical, and probabilistic, and entails assessing the prevalence of the relevant population group in the geographical locale to which the suspect belongs, and the likelihood that the match observed (between the suspect and the crime scene sample) would occur on a random or chance basis in that group. A common source of contention is the selection of the target population[48] and the degree of subjectivity in the procedures used by the expert to generate the likelihood of a random match in that population.

6.35 One prosecutor who was interviewed in the present project summarized the explanation provided by experts on this aspect of a positive DNA match as follows:

> They acknowledge that the DNA is not unique, and explained it along these lines: 'DNA is not unique, but that the chances of there being a DNA profile, or the likelihood that someone else has the same DNA profile as the accused, was one in ten billion, a billion being a thousand million, and as we know, there are perhaps six billion people on earth.' It was explained to the jury that the population that they talk about of ten billion is in fact, hypothetical. It includes everyone who has ever existed, and everyone who is going to exist, so that's why the likelihood ratio is expressed in that way, of one in ten billion (prosecution, trial 39).

6.36 This part of the expert testimony is typically brief and somewhat formulaic. Experts tend to adopt a uniform and invariant method to express the likelihood, to avoid inadvertently making an error by paraphrasing this information. One of the defence lawyers interviewed in this project emphasized the point that the statistics were not fixed, or a given, but were subject to variation and manipulation: 'Stats don't carry with them conclusions. They're stats. They can be manipulated' (trial 8).

6.37 The expert who appears in court is rarely the same person who gathered the samples from the crime scene. While it is common for two different police agency employees to conduct parts one and two, in Australian courts, most typically the expert who testifies is familiar with the sampling and amplification procedures to generate the profile, and relies on other laboratory technicians to do that work, or oversees it. The scientifically trained DNA expert may have less formal training and expertise in statistics, and limited facility in conveying the probabilistic statistical outcomes. Nonetheless, part of the DNA profiling process includes generating the probabilistic statistical information to describe the outcomes of a positive match between samples from the suspect and crime scene. Regarding the tendency of experts to stray beyond their expertise when testifying in court, one prosecutor noted that in DNA trials, what is 'really contentious [is] whether the scientist can give the expert evidence on the statistics or whether you need a statistician' (trial 22).

(4) Comprehension of probabilistic statistical evidence about a random match

6.38 A substantial body of research has established that jury comprehension of the probabilistic statistical evidence used to express the outcome of the DNA comparative sample matching is

[48] *Forbes v The Queen* [2010] HCATrans 120 (18 May 2010).

poor. Of some concern has been the additional finding that lack of understanding has not made jurors reluctant to vote to convict. A study of 571 Australian high school students and their parents showed they achieved a generally accurate understanding of the science of DNA, but were insensitive to stark variations in the statistical evidence, voting to convict equally often when presented with random match probabilities (RMPs) of one in 4,000 versus 400,000, although the conviction rate was higher when the RMP was specified as one in 4,000,000.[49]

Interviews with several Australian jurors who served on criminal trials revealed that they, too, convicted based on weak circumstantial evidence.[50] Prior simulation studies have shown that some jurors confuse the RMP with the likelihood that the defendant is guilty of the crime charged, i.e., mock jurors did not distinguish between an inference of guilt and the information that a DNA sample from the defendant and that from the crime scene matched, substituting the likelihood of a random match for the likelihood of reasonable doubt in the defendant's culpability. A strong positive match, however, can occur for innocent reasons. For instance, if the defendant visited the crime scene and left DNA traces, but had an innocent reason for the visit, or if a test was conducted with a sample contaminated with traces of the defendant's DNA, then a strong positive match would not be probative of guilt of the crime charged.[51] The danger here is that the very small likelihood of a random match is transposed into a strong likelihood of guilt. This erroneous reasoning is known as the 'prosecution fallacy' because it favours the prosecution case.[52] This issue persists. For instance, our post-trial interviews with a juror who was a biologist revealed some concern over erroneous inferences drawn by fellow jurors in one trial: **6.39**

> I watched in the jury room as people quoted evidence that was 99% certain, which is clearly the wrong...you know, that's the lay interpretation of what [the expert] said. It is clearly 99% probability from a DNA rating into the billions if not trillions. It was sort of taken by a lay group as she was 99% certain. So I'm not sure that the ultimate scientific interpretation translates to a complete understanding (juror D, trial 28).

A related but opposite error in reasoning known as the 'defence counsel fallacy' arises when too much weight in isolation is given to the number of people in the target population group whose DNA potentially matches that found at the crime scene, and an inference is made that because there are multiple possible sources of a DNA match, this comprises reasonable doubt of the guilt of the defendant. This simplistic reasoning does not take into account the weight of other evidence in a trial that might distinguish the defendant from other persons in the target population, such as a motive, a relationship with the victim, observed presence at the crime scene, etc. Since DNA evidence is rarely the sole evidence linking the defendant to the alleged crime, jurors have to weigh the DNA evidence along with the additional facts to reach a verdict. The task of integrating probabilistic evidence and non-probabilistic evidence has been shown to challenge some mock jurors.[53] Some indication that certain juries **6.40**

---

[49] Rhonda Wheate, 'Jury Comprehension and Use of Forensic Science' (PhD dissertation, Australian Defence Force Academy, University of New South Wales, 2007), pp. 96–101. Similar results emerged from studies of juror comprehension of probabilistic scientific evidence regarding matching blood type samples in the era preceding the advent of DNA profiling evidence. Jane Goodman, 'Jurors' Comprehension and Assessment of Probabilistic Evidence', 361.

[50] Mark Findlay, 'Juror Comprehension and the Hard Case', 15.

[51] *Rv Hillier* [2007] HCA 13, (2007) 228 CLR 618.

[52] Thompson and Schumann, 'Interpretation of Statistical Evidence in Criminal Trials', 167; *R v Doheny and Adams* [1997] Cr App R 369.

[53] Jane Goodman, 'Jurors' Comprehension and Assessment of Probabilistic Evidence', 361; David H. Kaye and Jonathan Koehler, 'Can Jurors Understand Probabilistic Evidence?', *Journal of the Royal Statistical Society: Series A (Statistics in Society)* 154, no. 1 (1991) 75; Thompson and Schumann, 'Interpretation of Statistical Evidence in Criminal Trials', 167.

simply ignore the probabilistic information emerged in a post-trial interview in the present project in which a juror reported that the expert had testified that: 'There was a one in 13,000 chance. We paid no attention to it in our deliberation' (juror E, trial 12).

(5) The persuasive force of DNA profiling evidence

6.41 Researchers have observed that DNA profiling evidence can appear infallible to jurors, who may be 'blinded' by its scientific aura and fail to scrutinize the evidence thoroughly.[54] Other jurors who are less scientifically sophisticated or less familiar with mathematical probabilities may be susceptible to what has been termed the 'white coat syndrome'; in other words, uncritical acceptance of scientific evidence. One prosecutor, in reflecting on presenting DNA profiling evidence to juries, acknowledged the propensity of DNA profiling evidence to have this effect: 'DNA is not unique.[55] Getting that point across, and explaining that whilst it's not unique, it is nevertheless a very powerful piece of evidence, capable of compelling persuasion…' (prosecution, trial 4).

6.42 Other legal professionals expressed concern that limited understanding of statistics would lead to over-reliance on the DNA evidence even in trials where the DNA evidence had limited probative value. A defence lawyer said: 'The stuff's got the potential to send a jury off on false issues due to the "one in a billion" stuff…We seem to have got by without it for hundreds of years, and now all of a sudden, it seems to be the be all and end all of everything' (defence lawyer, trial 9). The persuasive force of the extreme probabilities attested to by the expert was a factor in the decision-making of one juror in the present project, who commented: 'Parts where he said "extremely strong", and then the statistic—it was strong evidence for me' (juror D, trial 24).

6.43 As was noted in Chapter 5 in paragraphs 5.05 to 5.17, regarding research on persuasion, heuristic processing of expert evidence by jurors can arise for several reasons. Firstly, the jury may assume that once a witness is allowed to testify in court with the added status as a designated 'expert' this signifies that the evidence has been pre-screened for its accuracy and reliability, and that they are therefore justified or expected to accept it as reliable. Indications that jurors distinguish between expert and non-expert evidence on this basis come from jury simulation research in the United States, where the reduced scrutiny afforded to expert evidence was attributed to what the researchers identified as the 'gatekeeper' effect.[56]

6.44 These findings established that jurors were operating on the assumption that all vetting of the quality of the expert evidence had already occurred outside their presence, and that by the time the expert testified in court, this was, in essence, pre-approved evidence. Moreover, jurors often do not realize that an expert is in any sense partisan, and presume that expert witnesses appear on behalf of the court, i.e., are approved by the judge, as if court-appointed. References by the courts and lawyers to witnesses as 'experts', and judicial directions explaining that these witnesses are entitled to convey their opinions to the jury, tend to reinforce these presumptions.

6.45 A second factor, more particular to the persuasive force of DNA profiling evidence and that may induce heuristic rather than systematic processing of the evidence, is the apparent objectivity of scientific methods, which can inspire more confidence in that evidence, compared, for example, to eyewitness testimony or other 'naked' circumstantial evidence. Third, the

[54] See too *State of Western Australia v Muller* [2015] WASC 199 [40] (Simmonds J).

[55] David Bentley and Peter Lownds, 'Low Template DNA', 6.

[56] Michael Saks and Dawn McQuiston-Surrett, 'The Testimony of Forensic Identification Science: What Expert Witnesses Say and What Factfinders Hear', *Law and Human Behavior* 33, no. 1 (2009) 436.

impressive credentials of expert witnesses may lead jurors to apply a less stringent threshold in attending to the evidence, and to accept the bottom-line opinions expressed. Social scientific research confirms that persuasive messages from apparent authorities or experts are typically processed more peripherally than information imparted by individuals who are not presented as authorities.[57]

Since most expert evidence admitted at trial is proffered by the prosecution, jurors may regard that evidence as more reliable than evidence presented by an independent defence expert, because the prosecution witnesses are affiliated with law-enforcement authorities.[58] In Australia, most of the forensic scientific experts are employees of the state or federal police agencies. This imprimatur may imbue the prosecution experts with a badge of authority unavailable to defence experts, even when the latter have comparable educational and professional credentials. **6.46**

Finally, both jurors who have and who lack a scientific training and education may give the evidence more weight and apply less scrutiny to the content of DNA expert evidence, for different reasons. Jurors who have not studied mathematics and/or physical science at high school or university may not follow the scientific and mathematical content as readily as others who have that background. One juror stated: 'A science degree puts you at an advantage in understanding the statistics' (juror B, trial 24). Some experts in our project thought that differences in juror educational background were critical to the accessibility of the information presented: 'It depends on education level of juror' (expert 58, trial 8). Innumeracy may prompt some jurors to defer to the expertise of a witness with specialized qualifications and competencies. **6.47**

Interestingly, more than one lawyer anticipated that jurors would be defeated if they tried to understand the evidence in depth, and presumed that they would rely on heuristic strategies regarding this evidence, but did not view this as an obstacle to their decision-making: **6.48**

> If they wanted to understand the science I think they had difficulty. But if they accepted it as an article of faith, that the DNA... that he's an expert and those were the probabilities, I thought they'd have no difficulty. It depends what a jury decides to do. I certainly don't think that they would try and understand it; they would just accept it as an article of faith that an expert's given evidence (prosecution, trial 25).
>
> It comes down to the presentation of the evidence and tables. . . People possibly are overwhelmed with numbers and just accept it (defence lawyer, trial 4).

One judge who clearly anticipated that jurors would resort to heuristic strategies commented that the persuasive force of the DNA evidence was not determined by the statistics but by the attributes of the individual expert: 'It is not the clash about the probability ratio, rather it is about the credentials of the expert themselves' (judge, trial 19). **6.49**

Research has shown that some jurors (and even some legal professionals) may have only a limited and naive understanding of the meaning of probability, believing that it always means a 50:50 chance or likelihood;[59] not realizing that chance can have many instantiations and degrees of likelihood. Comparisons of individual and group understanding and **6.50**

---

[57] Robert Cialdini, *Influence: The Psychology of Persuasion* (New York: William Morrow and Company Inc, 2006); Robert Cialdini and others, 'Managing Social Norms for Persuasive Impact', *Social Influence* 1, no. 1 (2006) 3; Robert Cialdini and Noah Goldstein, 'Social Influence: Compliance and Conformity', *Annual Review of Psychology* 55, no. 1 (2004) 591.

[58] See chapter 4 discussion of perceptions that experts who are 'guns for hire' apply to defence experts and not prosecution experts.

[59] Simon Walsh, 'Evaluating the Role and Impact of Forensic DNA Profiling on the Criminal Justice System' (PhD dissertation, University of Technology, Sydney, 2009).

of performance by mock jurors in simulated trials have been conducted. For instance, the comprehension levels of mtDNA evidence by 480 jury panel members, allocated to 60 juries of eight persons, revealed that the collective jury was capable of comprehending and applying the evidence, although errors and doubts about the evidence arose. Jurors who had studied tertiary-level mathematics or science had the highest comprehension. Jurors who had more reservations about the scientific reliability, such as contaminated samples, had the lowest comprehension levels.[60]

6.51 Conversely, jurors who are more scientifically and mathematically literate may feel so comfortable with this type of evidence that they do not examine it as closely, because it seems familiar and trustworthy, and thus is given more weight than other non-scientific, less objective evidence. Jurors in this project who had studied mathematics or science at a senior high school level or tertiary level had significantly higher levels of trust in expert evidence presented in criminal trials.[61]

6.52 In other words, a lack of thorough scrutiny of the evidence can arise through relaxation of critical standards or criteria for different reasons. Based on findings of this nature, many scholars and practitioners regard the challenge for lawyers and courts as not to eliminate jurors without a mathematical or scientific educational background, but to engage jurors sufficiently to motivate them to respond with systematic rather than heuristic processing of the content of the DNA profiling expert evidence.

(6) Jury understanding of the DNA profiling evidence

6.53 The pervasive use of DNA profiling evidence has heightened concerns amongst the judiciary,[62] members of the bar, and legal academics[63] regarding the ability of juries to understand complex scientific concepts and the ability of defence counsel to understand it well enough to challenge it, and whether the use of DNA profiling evidence is a benefit without compromise to justice. The closest observers of juries in the project trials were the presiding judges, the legal professionals, and the DNA experts themselves. Their views of jury responses are relevant because if there are gaps between their views and jury performance, this is an indication to the justice system that over-reliance should not be placed on their views, which have been the major source of information to date used to develop jury policies. In other words, so long as reforms are reliant on input from these professionals, in the absence of any validation of their perspectives, proposed reforms may be misguided. This project sought to provide some triangulation of the issue by including the perspectives

---

60 Valerie Hans and others, 'Science in the Jury Box: Jurors' Comprehension of Mitochondrial DNA Evidence', *Law and Human Behavior* 35, no. 1 (2011) 60.

61 Jurors who had studied maths or science at high school were significantly more likely to trust forensic evidence ($M = 4.62$, $SD = 0.63$) than jurors who did not study maths or science at senior high school level ($M = 4.42$, $SD = 0.71$), $t(118.95) = -2.20$, $p = .030$ (equal variances not assumed). There was no difference in expectations for forensic experts to be involved in criminal trials between jurors who had studied maths or science at senior high school ($M = 7.71$, $SD = 2.87$) and those who had not ($M = 7.99$, $SD = 2.80$), $t(260) = 0.68$, $p = .498$. Jurors who had studied maths or science at tertiary level were significantly more likely to trust forensic evidence ($M = 4.68$, $SD = 0.57$) than jurors who had not studied science or mathematics at tertiary level ($M = 4.49$, $SD = 0.71$), $t(286.74) = -2.54$, $p = .012$ (equal variances not assumed). Again, there was no difference in expectations for forensic experts to be involved in criminal trials between jurors who studied maths or science at a tertiary level ($M = 7.91$, $SD = 2.79$) or jurors who did not study maths or science at tertiary level ($M = 7.71$, $SD = 2.87$), $t(260) = -0.59$, $p = .584$ (equal variances assumed).

62 New South Wales Law Reform Commission, *Jury Directions: Report No. 136* (Sydney: New South Wales Law Reform Commission, 2012).

63 Gary Edmond, 'Actual Innocents? Legal Limitations and their Implications for Forensic Science and Medicine', *Australian Journal of Forensic Sciences* 43, no. 2 (2011) 177; Gary Edmond and Mehera San Roque, 'The Cool Crucible: Forensic Science and the Frailty of the Criminal Trial', *Current Issues in Criminal Justice* 24, no. 1 (2012) 51.

on the same trials of all stakeholders, as well as some in-depth studies of individual trials. Typically, the observations gathered in surveys are not verifiable in any way, nor compared with others in the same trial.[64]

(a) Perceived jury difficulties by members of the legal profession

Across the 18 trials involving DNA expert evidence, 13 judges were interviewed. Of this group, more than two thirds (69.2%) thought that DNA expert evidence was difficult for jurors to comprehend due to the complexity of the evidence itself. About the same proportion of the lawyers who examined and cross-examined the experts (71.8%) rated the DNA expert testimony as difficult for jurors to understand because of the complexity of the forensic testing procedures, technical and scientific terminology, or probabilistic statistics. In sum, both prosecutors and defence lawyers regarded the DNA evidence as intrinsically difficult for jurors: **6.54**

> DNA evidence is extremely difficult when you're talking about likelihood ratios and all this sort of stuff (prosecutor, trial 3).
>
> I suppose one thing that I myself thought about a fair bit and the jury might have, is to what extent the DNA evidence can satisfy you beyond reasonable doubt and sort of comparing, you know, how you can use the statistical probability to fit within what the law calls 'beyond reasonable doubt' (defence lawyer, trial 22).

Considerable consensus emerged between the judges (69.2%) and the lawyers (71.8%) about jury difficulties in understanding the DNA evidence. By comparison, substantially fewer (40.5%) of the DNA experts believed the jury had difficulties understanding their testimony. The smaller proportion of experts who perceived juror difficulties may be due to the fact that experts viewed the content of their evidence with which they were familiar as more accessible than did the judges and lawyers, who were less familiar with the topic. One third of experts estimated that the judge and/or lawyers had difficulty understanding their testimony. This perception was not unfounded. For example, one defence lawyer stated: 'Frankly, I found it somewhat difficult' (defence lawyer, trial 40). **6.55**

(b) Jurors' self-reported understanding of the DNA evidence

The number of jurors interviewed per DNA trial in the present project ranged from zero to seven. A total of 39 juror interviews about DNA expert evidence were conducted. As might be expected, a high proportion of jurors (73.9%) believed that when listening to expert testimony they did not have difficulties understanding DNA evidence; i.e., just over one quarter of the jurors reported difficulty with this type of expert evidence. Psychological studies of self-reports show that these are typically more self-serving and favourable than the reports of others,[65] i.e. their self-reported comprehension far exceeded that perceived by judges and lawyers who closely observed the jurors at trial. **6.56**

(c) Jury responses to DNA profiling evidence

Regarding the scientific procedure used to gather DNA samples and amplify them to develop a DNA profile, comments from the stakeholders revealed that this was an anticipated and actual source of jury difficulty. For instance, a lawyer noted that most people are unfamiliar with the process, which is mysterious and not readily comprehensible (defence lawyer, trial 4). To some degree, the explanation of the process remained obscure because of the use by the **6.57**

[64] Gary Edmond, 'Judging Surveys: Experts, Empirical Evidence and Law Reform', *Federal Law Review* 33, no. 1 (2005) 95.

[65] Ruth Wylie, *The Self-Concept: Theory and Research on Selected Topics*, vol, 2, rev. edn. (Lincoln, Neb: University of Nebraska Press, 1979); Dale H. Schunk and Judith L. Meece, *Student Perceptions in the Classroom* (Hillsdale, N.J.: Lawrence Erlbaum, 1992).

expert witnesses of unfamiliar terms: 'Technical words such as 'alleles' and 'loci' were difficult to understand without any study into what they are' (juror A, trial 9). Another juror commented: 'I am science/biology trained and wonder how a non-scientific person could manage this material?' (juror H, trial 28).

6.58 Jurors reported that they experienced some difficulty with this information, especially when it was presented orally without any accompanying visual aids: 'I had a lot of difficulty with understanding the process of all the extraction and amplification, etc. There wasn't any graphics' (juror B, trial 8) and 'Because none of us knew about how to go about doing it, it was difficult to understand at first. He explained the process without showing images' (juror A, trial 8).

6.59 Despite these difficulties, jurors offered some critique of the methods and approaches outlined in the expert evidence. For instance, one juror suggested that the expert should have provided more contextual information to assist the jury in interpreting the scientific information: the expert 'could have quoted acceptable methods, certification, work ethics, etc.' (juror D, trial 22).

(d) Responses to the evidence of the probability of a random DNA match

6.60 While some experts thought that all aspects of their testimony were difficult for jurors—'DNA, the stats and verbal equivalent' (expert 1, trial 21)—most of the experts agreed that the statistics, calculations, and sampling were the hardest aspects of their evidence for jurors, judges, and lawyers to comprehend, and in particular, that the likelihood 'ratio and propositions would've been difficult' (expert 1, trial 19). Lawyers perceived the same challenges in the expert testimony for jurors: 'It is due to the scientific basis and statistical calculation' (defence lawyer, trial 4), but anticipated that 'The jury had the most difficulty with the blindingly large numbers' (prosecutor, trial 24).

6.61 In interviews, jurors were specifically asked how well they understood the expert evidence. Responses revealed that without prompting a total of 41% of jurors raised issue with statistical probabilities in expert evidence (16/39 jurors). Many jurors reported difficulties understanding the calculations and statistics related to the RMP. One juror stated simply that it was difficult to understand the application of the probability ratio (juror B, trial 19).

6.62 The hypothetical nature of the probabilities was identified as a particular source of confusion: the source of 'difficulty lies in statistics, as you are not talking real numbers of people' (expert 1, trial 28). Jurors echoed this sentiment: 'I felt frustration with the way in which DNA accuracy was expressed, i.e., the expert saying "it is 120 million times more likely DNA matched", than simply that it matched a certain sample' (juror B, trial 23). Similarly, following the presentation of DNA profiling evidence in a murder trial, a juror reported difficulty understanding the expert's 'calculations and the number 1 in 14 billion. Then, she changed the number to make it a more calculable amount, and confused me' (juror G, trial 8).

6.63 Jurors who could recall the evidence and reproduce the numbers were none the wiser as to what to make of them, as is shown in the similarity of the following comments from jurors who served in different trials:

> For us, there was 200 times more chance that someone else, that two random people had touched the weapon as opposed to the defendant, and another random person... there was a little bit about a ratio... I didn't truly get it (juror B, trial 19).
>
> DNA sample was something less than 1 in 10 billion which is actually 1 in 270 billion, I understood. Why she did it, to relate it to the population of the planet? (juror K, trial 8).

Experts justified their selection of a target population as a basis to compute the probability of a random match. **6.64**

> Stats give a default likelihood ratio. So if it's a single source profile we give a default for the Australian Caucasian population like a ratio of 120 million which is more understandable by people (expert 3, trial 16).

One judge was critical of reference to a Caucasian rather than an Aboriginal population. The judge was dissatisfied with **6.65**

> the appropriateness of the use of the database of the Australian Caucasian population and not the Aboriginal population given that the defendant indicated that he had 1/16 Aboriginal heritage (judge, trial 22).

In another trial, jurors questioned the relevance of the probabilities regarding DNA tests which had yielded only a partial profile, not because they did not understand the method applied, but because the expert's choice of population seemed inappropriate. This mismatch between the defendant and the relevant target population left them frustrated, as the weight of the DNA evidence could not properly be considered. One judge sophisticated in scientific understanding explained: **6.66**

> The probability assessment done was that it was 208 times more likely that the contributors to the DNA were two people other than the defendant, drawn at random from the Caucasian population. That was a problem because the defendant wasn't Caucasian, or at least I don't think he fits within the range of what would normally be described as Caucasian—he's Assyrian (judge, trial 19).

In another trial, a juror also questioned the relevance of the basis of the computations:

> The way that those statistics were presented... where a calculation was made about likelihood of a false positive due to insemination from a family where cousins always married... I said 'this is complete stupidity' (juror K, trial 8).

(7) Steps taken by the court, legal counsel, and the experts to assist the jury

Despite the omnipresence of DNA evidence, remarkably little has been accomplished in terms of ensuring the effective presentation of this form of expert evidence in criminal trials. Notwithstanding awareness of the issues, most lawyers regarded the presentation as a problem. For instance, a defence lawyer commented: 'Often it is not simplified sufficiently for jurors' (defence counsel, trial 16). Accordingly, the findings of this project offer an important opportunity to examine trends and problems with the presentation of DNA profiling evidence in criminal trials. **6.67**

Several interviewees noted the importance of taking action prior to trial in order to ensure that the presentation of DNA profiling evidence at trial is enhanced; others focussed on actions to take during the trial itself. **6.68**

(a) Before trial

Pre-trial conferencing was a solution proposed by a number of project interviewees in different states. Lawyers favoured conferencing with experts before trial in order to streamline the presentation and issues: 'It is important to present DNA evidence properly. It is important to conference them beforehand' (prosecutor, trial 43). The 'answer is to conference to assist you to understand it, and then to call them as a witness' (prosecutor, trial 21). **6.69**

(b) At trial

Many lawyers appeared preoccupied with how the presentation of DNA expert evidence might be improved. Some saw their role and responsibility to enhance the expert presentation **6.70** as primary: 'It is down to me as the prosecution to phrase questions that are understood by all parties and to introduce the science' (prosecutor, trial 40).

6.71 Another prosecutor prepared a jury 'cheat sheet' naming and describing the identity of each witness, and relating the name to each aspect of the DNA evidence, to make it easier for jurors to follow the complex trial evidence (prosecutor, trial 39). Defence counsel, who of course had no say in selecting the experts proffered by the prosecution, and had to cross-examine them, were critical of the DNA scientists, whom they observed often lacked the capacity to explain the evidence very well (defence counsel, trial 25). At least one defence lawyer commented that the DNA experts needed to have more statistical training so they could properly explain the evidence (defence lawyer, trial 24). The experts themselves felt that the 'difficulty lies in explaining a ratio' (expert 3, trial 16). The lawyers held the view that the experts 'need to provide more than just numbers, but a degree of opinion as to the nature of the numbers' (trial 8). Lawyers and experts noted that the experts could express the match outcomes far more simplistically, and that complications arose because of the conservative manner in which they chose to express their opinions that the DNA science or match was not perfect (prosecutor, trial 21).

(c) The role of the expert to assist the jury

6.72 Many of the scientific experts regarded it as their responsibility to make the information accessible to non-experts: 'the onus is on me to explain it in a clear and reasonable way for them to understand' (prosecution expert 1, trial 3). 'Scientists have to take greater responsibility for scientific evidence which is presented in the courts due to that lay person's interpretation of the presentation of the evidence' (defence expert, trial 22). They anticipated that jury understanding was facilitated by the effort they put into breaking the information down into simpler components making it 'reasonable for them to understand due to the simplistic level at which DNA is evidence is explained' (expert 1, trial 41).

6.73 The efforts expended by the experts made a difference to some jurors, as reflected in comments such as: 'It was the explanation by the expert that assisted with the understanding' (juror K, trial 10; juror B, trial 12), and 'I could understand what she was saying even though I had no scientific background. Her clear explanation assisted' (juror G, trial 10). Researchers exploring different ways to express probabilistic scientific evidence more effectively have focussed on visual and linguistic variations.

6.74 A series of studies of the language or form of expression used by the expert to present statistical probabilities to juries have shown that although mathematically equivalent, certain verbal formulations are more readily accessible than others.[66] For example, the phrase '0.1% match by chance' using a likelihood ratio and '1 in 1,000 match by chance' using a frequency both express the same mathematical probability, but the former is more incriminating and the latter is easier for jurors to understand and apply in the context of a criminal trial. Jurors who served on one trial complained specifically that the verbal form of the probabilistic evidence was oblique and opaque and should have been converted to a percentage likelihood. They objected that they were 'never told a percentage of DNA involved. And 8.6 as a fraction of 10 I found confusing... I didn't really understand that very well but they called it trace—they didn't put a percentage of DNA, and nothing... it was hard to understand' (juror L, trial 7). The Australian High Court, in

[66] A simple example of the way statistics can baffle is presented by Oxford Mathematician, Marcus du Sautoy, 'Testing Out the Monty Hall Problem', YouTube, 4 November 2009, <http://www.youtube.com/watch?v=o_djTy3G0pg&feature=related>. See also Jonathan Koehler, 'When Are People Persuaded by DNA Match Statistics?', *Law and Human Behavior* 25, no. 5 (2001) 493.

Aytugrul v The Queen[67] where the question arose whether the RMP was expressed in an unfairly prejudicial manner when the judge stated that 99.9% of people other than the defendant would not be expected to have this DNA profile, has not endorsed probabilistic presentations to jurors expressed in frequencies rather than an odds ratio or likelihood ratio.

An awareness from the community of forensic scientific experts that the likelihood ratio is controversial, both in terms of how it is calculated and because of the low comprehension or high propensity for misinterpretation,[68] has led to imperatives to offer alternative verbal expressions of the significance of the information: Certain DNA experts recommended avoiding the likelihood ratio entirely, and substituting phrases such as 'strong', 'moderate', or 'weak' likelihoods in order to convey the information to jurors in a more transparent and accessible fashion.[69] On the topic of providing verbal equivalent descriptors, one expert commented that barristers did not seem to favour this approach: they 'don't seem to like the verbal equivalent descriptors', e.g., 100–1,000 is 'moderately strong' and 1,000–10,000 is 'strong.' This expert was also opposed to their use, as 'you are reducing the value of the actual statistic. You cannot go from a descriptor of 99, then have a likelihood ratio of 99, then a likelihood ratio of 101' (expert 4, trial 21). **6.75**

(d) Use of visual aids at trial

A wide range of visual aids was used in a number of DNA trials by the experts to illustrate the content of their testimony. In most trials, these illustrative aids were prepared by the experts. For instance, a diagram of DNA processing was applied in trial 39, visual images depicting the method of testing DNA were used in five trials, and PowerPoints were used in a further three. One laboratory scientist had developed a PowerPoint presentation specifically for members of their staff to use in testifying about the DNA testing procedures, but, as one expert reported, this was not always used in court, even when the expert thought it might assist (expert 1, trial 16). A video was played for jurors in one trial. In another, the expert brought in models and photographs, and these were described by the jury as helpful (trial 21). **6.76**

In four trials, jurors commented that the visual aids were not necessarily edifying due to the clarity in the expert's explanation. In other trials, the jurors were enthusiastic about the extent to which the aids assisted them, for instance, in understanding how DNA samples are interpreted: **6.77**

> Yes, if there was more visual stuff and samples of the tools or whatever are used in the lab or whatever, then I think it would help the jury to understand much quicker (juror B, trial 8).
>
> Anything extra [visual aids, diagrams, and PowerPoints] can help, I think (juror J, trial 10).
>
> The expert could have presented his evidence better by using visual aids on the comparison of DNA profiles (juror H, trial 24).
>
> A PowerPoint slide would have been really, really good (juror I, trial 9).

Jurors commented that these aids were especially helpful for some persons: **6.78**

> Some people are visual and need to see things and for a jury where you've got 12 different people, they all look at things in different ways and that's why we're all there. But some people are very visual and need to see more than just the exhibits (juror I, trial 4).

[67] [2012] HCA 15, (2012) 247 CLR 170 [31]–[34].

[68] See *Doheny and Adams v The Queen* [1997] 1 Cr App Rep 369; *Latcha v The Queen* (1998) 127 NTR 1; 104 A Crim R 390.

[69] Loene Howes, 'A Step Towards Increased Understanding by Non-Scientists of Expert Reports: Recommendations for Readability', *Australian Journal of Forensic Sciences* (2015).

6.79 A jury simulation study in which a tutorial presenting the DNA expert evidence with multimedia to explain the basis of DNA profiling and the significance of random match increased juror scepticism about DNA infallibility. Additionally, this method reduced convictions by less knowledgeable mock jurors. When the same DNA evidence was presented traditionally, in oral examination and without visual aids, mock jurors with a lower level of DNA knowledge were more prone to convict than their more knowledgeable counterparts.[70] Results of this study indicated that a carefully sequenced expert presentation was effective in increasing jury understanding and reducing unsafe convictions.

(e) Judicial clarification of expert testimony at trial

6.80 Judges were asked whether they took any affirmative steps to assist the jurors to understand the DNA expert evidence. Quite a few indicated they were proactive in this regard. For instance, one judge responded: 'I intervened in the questioning, and then attempted to identify what was really in issue, and what the evidence was related to it' (trial 19). This action was appreciated by jurors, as is reflected in comments received from a juror in that trial who reported that after the judge intervened, the expert 'answered it better—about probabilities' (juror F, trial 19). Jurors in trials 7, 19, and 25 all reported that they benefited from judicial assistance in questioning the experts: 'I found the scientific explanation of DNA quite hard to follow until [he] repeated himself more clearly under direction from the judge' (juror A, trial 25).

6.81 Whether the statistics were fully understood or well explained by experts was an issue in one trial, in which a juror said: 'It appeared she did not thoroughly understand the calculations leading to the likelihood ratio—when pressed by the judge' (juror B, trial 21, commenting about the Crown DNA expert).

6.82 Although lawyers and judges were supportive of the practice of encouraging jurors to ask questions, and thought it was 'useful for jury members to be allowed to ask questions about the evidence' (prosecutor, trial 39), no examples were identified.

(8) The level of reliance on DNA expert evidence by jurors

6.83 Despite the presence of DNA expert evidence, for some jurors this proof was still inadequate. For instance, a juror in trial 19 said, 'I do believe there should have been more evidence' (juror B).

6.84 However, there was variability in whether the jury accepted (and therefore relied on) the DNA expert evidence in reaching a verdict, depending on the extent to which the expert evidence was considered contentious or critical in the trial, among other items of evidence. Some jurors clearly articulated the central role of the evidence and engaged in a thorough evaluation, showing systematic analysis: For instance in trial 22, a juror reported: 'The DNA evidence was the most important aspect of this trial so we had to truly believe that this was a true and reliable piece of evidence. The defence attorney agreed that the DNA evidence was reasonably correct, but had to try to prove that there was a fault in the gathering of that evidence' (juror G).

6.85 In other trials, other evidence and expert testimony had a more significant role. For example, jurors in trial 39 reported that, regarding the DNA evidence:

> Well the DNA evidence certainly was important. Without that DNA evidence I don't think the jury could have convicted him (juror T).
>
> Like, because we don't know anything about firearms, or entry and exit wounds, or DNA, the DNA identification process, or any of those things. Like, one of the experts who did the

[70] Goodman-Delahunty and Hewson, *Improving Jury Understanding and Use of Expert DNA Evidence.*

> post mortem, we were talking about the blood splatter. We referred to the experts' opinions when they told us, just the things that they told us, to give us a better understanding of what really might have happened at the crime scene (juror J).

The jury interviews demonstrated that jurors integrated the DNA expert evidence with other evidence admitted in court. A majority of jurors who were interviewed reported that they regarded the DNA expert evidence as important, and that it assisted in resolving the main issues before them in the trials they heard. For instance one juror stated about trial 22: 'I think the whole defence's argument was that the DNA is insufficient to provide identification, and that was the whole crux of [the case's issue] so definitely the DNA was a big factor' (juror E). **6.86**

Jurors commented that the amount of deliberation time reportedly spent discussing expert testimony ranged from 5% to 70%. **6.87**

> It probably, I would guess, covered 20 to 30%. The major reason for that was that the defence case against the DNA evidence, we thought, was quite weak. So the jury relatively quickly accepted that the DNA brought by the prosecution was pretty much agreed on by everyone, and then we went from there onto other things (juror K, trial 39).
>
> Probably a third of the deliberations. Not so much the forensic because there was only a trace of DNA, but the actual beating, the doctor's testimony about the photos and that was discussed quite a lot (juror K, trial 39).
>
> I think it played probably up to 70%, because based on the evidence that we were given, the DNA were the only thing that we could work on (juror L, trial 7).

The estimate of a lower percentage of time was in some instances attributed to the greater clarity of the explanation provided by the expert in that trial. **6.88**

Most jurors (74.3%) confirmed that the DNA expert evidence was important in their deliberations. This result indicated that ignoring the statistical evidence was an infrequent and unlikely occurrence in the jury room. **6.89**

(9) Responses to DNA profiling evidence from a rebuttal defence expert

A total of three trials in the project (Trials 21, 22, and 40) included testimony from rebuttal DNA profiling experts. The lawyers in these three trials anticipated that jurors would struggle to distinguish the details presented by the competing experts: 'When experts disagree it is difficult for the jury to resolve these discrepancies/disputes between the experts' (defence lawyer, trial 22).[71] The jurors from these trials reported that they believed that they benefited from exposure to opposing evidence, rather than becoming more confused: **6.90**

> There seemed to be a few points of disagreement between the expert witnesses—over methodology and the possibility of contamination. It was easier for the jury to appreciate debate about the possibility of contamination than it was the intricacies of experiment/testing methodology. It was ironic that it was the defence expert witness who helped us to understand the science better (juror J, trial 22).

In several instances, the jurors reported enhanced understanding of the second expert's evidence due to the learning process and greater familiarity derived from the first expert's evidence, even though there was difficulty in understanding what was said. This was a type of 'practice' effect. **6.91**

---

[71] This can constitute a basis for the overturning of a jury decision: *Velevski v The Queen* (2002) 76 ALJR 402 [85]; *R v Juric* [2002] VSCA 77, (2002) VR 411.

6.92 Presentation of evidence by competing experts did not automatically result in reliance on credentials rather than the content of the evidence, or heuristic strategies. As juror J in trial 22 explained:

> We ultimately chose to believe in the integrity of [the prosecution expert's] data, for reasons that he had made clear. [The defence expert] could not rule out the possibility that [the prosecution expert's] results were accurate. The defence was not able to convince the jury that contamination was a reasonable possibility, given all the other circumstantial evidence.

6.93 In trial 21 there was disagreement between the experts over the statistical portion of the evidence. The DNA expert for the defence took issue with some of the certainty in the statistics. The prosecution expert testified that the likelihood was 9,700 times stronger that the accused had deposited the sampled biological material at the crime scene, and interpreted this as moderately supportive of a positive match. The defence expert took issue with this interpretation of the numbers, saying: 'It should not be classified as moderately supportive of a match' (defence lawyer, trial 21).

6.94 One expert remarked that 'It would have been beneficial if we could have sat down to see if there was any common ground rather than have two experts presenting two different opinions' (expert 1, trial 40).

6.95 A comparison of the three trials where competing DNA expert evidence was provided to the jury with the other 15 trials where no rebuttal DNA expert was called revealed that the jurors with access to a rebuttal expert made fewer complaints or requests for assistance in understanding the DNA evidence. Jurors exposed to competing DNA experts complained less about the experts' terminology, the level of detail provided, and the pace of questioning. They became more confident in their abilities to interpret the expert evidence, but still sought visual aids. Jurors in single DNA expert trials were more inclined to ask for comprehension aids such as a basic summary of DNA processing. Exposure to rebuttal experts assisted the jurors to engage with the content of the experts' evidence.

(10) Jury responses to single vs. competing DNA expert evidence

6.96 In the present project, 72% of trials with DNA experts involved a single DNA expert who presented evidence on behalf of the prosecution. The defence relied on cross-examination to test this evidence. Jury responses to a trial in which no rebuttal expert was called are examined in more detail in the following section, which uses trial 35 as an example.

D. Case Study: Unopposed DNA Evidence

6.97 In one of the cold case DNA murder trials (trial 35), the prosecution called two DNA profiling experts and three other forensic experts. The defence called no independent expert witnesses but stated that 'pretty much everything was in dispute'. The defence case theory, regarding DNA evidence, was that 'even if the jury concluded that the mixed sample DNA was from the defendant, and was not transferred by contamination or secondary transfer, but was on the victim's clothing as a result of the earlier altercation, they could not be satisfied that he committed the fatal injury as death was consistent with a fatal punch, and someone else was observed punching the victim.' Arriving at the verdict was not straightforward, given the availability of evidence that someone other than the defendant was observed punching the deceased. The trial lasted several weeks. The jury deliberated for a total of 24 hours after the trial ended. It returned a verdict finding the accused guilty.

Prior to the trial, both DNA experts met jointly with counsel for the prosecution and defence, for about two hours, and also separately with the prosecutor. Two DNA experts were called because each had conducted relevant DNA tests at different times. The first expert was highly experienced and did the earlier DNA testing. The second expert was less experienced in giving evidence in court; that expert conducted the tests against the state analytical database that yielded the cold hit, and computed the statistic of one in 10 billion likelihood of a random match, leading to the arrest of the defendant. **6.98**

The first DNA expert stated that his testimony in this trial lasted a total of four hours, and was one of the longest examinations in his experience. He conceded there had been some contamination of the crime scene evidence. The victim's pants (from which samples were taken), the shoes bearing the critical blood spot that matched the victim (which had been stored in an unsealed bag), and some crime scene exhibits that were recorded in police logs were no longer available. In his view, the major issue in the case was how the victim's blood got on the shoes alleged to belong to the accused, not really whether it was the accused's DNA. The expert in this trial provided diagrams of the clothing showing jurors precisely where the DNA samples were derived. 'He could show directly on the exhibit from where he took these DNA samples' (juror G, trial 35). This concrete demonstration in visual form was found very persuasive by jurors and made the match evidence appear stronger. The prosecutor used a table with coloured squares to illustrate precisely where the matching points were. The defence theory was not that the match was erroneous, but that the match did not establish that the accused was the perpetrator, i.e., that innocent explanations for the presence of the DNA traces were viable. It was conceded by the prosecution that approximately 20 people had handled the various samples, and that multiple tests were carried out. The prosecutor also provided 'the jury with a cheat sheet or a schedule of the identity of each of the witnesses relating to each piece of the DNA evidence'. **6.99**

The first expert expressed some doubt that the jury understood the defence theory. He thought the prosecutor's examination-in-chief could have been shortened, and that its length had increased potential jury confusion. The judge consulted with counsel after the examination of the expert, and then, in the presence of the jury, directed a number of questions to the expert following the cross-examination. These focussed on the potential for secondary transfer. The defence theory raised the possibility that DNA was transferred from the defendant to the deceased in a scuffle that occurred between him and the deceased the same evening that the deceased was punched fatally, and that the fatal blows were administered by one of three men observed punching the victim by another individual, and that therefore, the presence of the defendant's DNA on the clothing of the defendant was innocent. The expert commented that **6.100**

> The judge asked many clarifying questions regarding the amount of time lapse between sample and collection and testing, and how this may have increased the risk of sample contamination and/or DNA transfer. I think the judge and lawyers maybe should have asked more questions on how they thought contamination might have occurred.

The jury members understood that they could have asked questions of the judge, but did not. As the trial proceeded, jurors had access to the exhibits, such as clothing from which DNA samples had been extracted. They also had access to four copies of daily trial transcripts, and any judicial directions, but not the expert reports or the judge's summing up. **6.101**

The jurors reported that they spent 'at least half of the [deliberation] time looking at exhibits, using the expert testimony' (juror I) and that at times they did go back over portions of the expert testimony in the transcripts, especially after the cross-examination by the defence raised issues about the evidence-in-chief: 'The defence asked pretty pointed questions to which the expert answered yes or no. The defence doing that often makes you go back and read the transcript again to get a better view of that "no" answer or that "yes" answer' (juror E). **6.102**

6.103 The second expert described the DNA testing that commenced in 2008 and the match with the defendant's reference sample that resulted in the 'one in 10 billion' statistic. This was computed from a calculation of all possible combinations of the 739 individual DNA samples in the state analytical database. The illustrative table used in this expert's evidence during the trial was prepared by the defence and given to the second expert to demonstrate that the peak readings on the mixed DNA profile were not high enough—that they were inconclusive. The expert testified with an air of confidence, knew where the cross-examination was directed, and, according to the defence, answered the defence questions in as helpful a manner as possible to the prosecution.

6.104 The defence lawyer thought the jurors were less likely to be confused about the DNA evidence in this trial than in others, based on the way it was presented and the fact that two experts for the prosecution appeared. Nonetheless, jurors were unable to articulate the RMP or statistical evidence in their post-trial interviews. Some indication that jurors did not fully understand the secondary transfer theory put forward by the defence emerged when jurors reported in interviews that because the defendant had been arrested several years ago, his DNA could not have been secondarily transferred or have been placed on samples maintained in police custody. Accordingly, the jury concluded that this defence was simply a 'red herring'. In other words, jurors did not entertain the defence theory of secondary transfer or contamination. They rejected any secondary transfer by police.

6.105 Interviews with the jurors revealed that some jurors saw this as a close trial, because of weaknesses in the non-expert evidence, given the elapsed time and the fact that the witnesses had been drinking heavily on the night in issue (juror E). The jury had concerns about lay testimony by other witnesses regarding who struck the fatal blows. Jurors scrutinized the trial transcript to resolve this issue. They reported that they 'went through transcripts, read it out on occasions, out loud for everybody' (juror I) especially to resolve the issue of the defendant's presence at the time of the fatal blow to the deceased.

6.106 The jurors understood that the trial was built around the testimony of the two DNA experts, and that the DNA was 'the bedrock issue as far as the trial was concerned' (jurors G and E). Some jurors were very satisfied with the way the evidence fitted together; others less so, primarily because of the lack of evidence placing the defendant at the scene when fatal blows were delivered to the victim.

6.107 The jury accepted that the DNA from the crime scene was that of the defendant. Jurors viewed the DNA experts as key, their evidence as central, and regarded it as 'solid'. The jurors perceived the DNA expert evidence as incontrovertible, even though they understood the match was imperfect. They relied on the DNA evidence to place the accused at the crime scene, and that was the key. However, this did not mean that the content was analysed in depth: 'You know, we're not scientists, and we didn't pretend to be, so we just had to take it on the facts' (juror A).

6.108 This set of responses to the expert evidence was consistent with the 'white coat syndrome'. Regarding the first expert, the jurors were aware that he was a repeat player in court: 'I thought he had obviously done this before... and he did it very, very well' (juror A). Jurors also commented that he was 'a very good scientist', 'very knowledgeable', and 'certainly knew what he was talking about'.

6.109 Jurors' comments reinforced that their evaluations were focussed on attributes of the expert's presentation rather than the content: He 'left a good impression', was 'very interesting in explaining DNA', 'very contained and controlled in answers', and 'experienced in giving evidence'. Other comments about the second expert included: 'very well spoken', 'very good language to deliver his knowledge', 'explained in simple terms what he did, how he did it, why he did it', and that he successfully used visual aids: 'diagrams about DNA helped us a lot', and 'they were giving us diagrams and then visuals to show us where he puts his DNA tests'. However, the jury did acknowledge that 'The testimony helped us a lot to make our decision, and puts a clarity, more clarity into making our decision' (juror G).

The jurors discussed how they dealt with missing and inconclusive evidence, namely that they set those issues aside and worked at reaching a verdict in the trial based on the conclusive evidence before them. This decision strategy may have led them to avoid construing unresolved issues as a basis for reasonable doubt, and instead to dismiss consideration of unresolved issues. The jurors said they assessed the evidence in light of the reasonable doubt instructions, and believed they did a very careful and thorough job, having first concluded there was a positive DNA match of victim in a bloodstain on the shoes of the defendant, and that this was acquired during the fatal assault on the victim. **6.110**

Cross-examination, in this case by a highly skilled defence counsel, was ineffective in persuading jurors of the potential for secondary transfer of DNA in the course of a scuffle, and of innocent reasons for the presence of DNA traces on the clothing of the deceased. Jurors were impressed by the DNA experts' responses to cross-examination, and their confidence, and this made them confident in their verdict to convict. **6.111**

The combination of two solid DNA experts, the series of visual aids for jurors that emphasized the matching samples, and the extreme probability statistic, in the context of a sympathetic victim (a young man killed on a night out), eclipsed the weaknesses of the case—the lapse of time between the murder and the trial, the eyewitness evidence that was unreliable due to alcohol and the potential innocent explanations for the presence of DNA samples from the defendant. The jurors gave little weight to evidence from lay witnesses about another group of assailants who had been observed assaulting the victim after someone resembling the defendant left the scene, but whose DNA evidence was not available in the database. **6.112**

E. Semantic Analysis of Participant Interview Responses

To conduct a systematic analysis of transcripts of participants' free-text verbal responses to interview questions about the forensic scientific evidence, we applied a similar method of analysis to that described in chapter 5 in paragraphs 5.36 to 5.39. For this analysis, the interview responses of all participants who attended a project trial in which DNA profiling evidence was presented were used. In many of those trials, the DNA profiling evidence was not the major or central expert evidence in the case, and the DNA expert may have been one among several prosecution experts, or several forensic scientific experts appearing on behalf of the prosecution. Leximancer software was used to generate a conceptual map of the content of the interview responses by counting the most frequently occurring words across all interviews. In addition, Leximancer was used to generate a relational concept map (details of the method are set forth in chapter 5). **6.113**

The results of these analyses revealed that in all 18 trials in which a DNA expert was called, DNA evidence eclipsed all other forms of expert evidence. The five most commonly discussed concepts associated with DNA in these trials, in descending order of frequency, were 'evidence', 'expert', 'case', jury', and 'DNA'. Synonyms are listed together. The full set of frequently mentioned concepts is presented in Table 6.1. **6.114**

By using the sentiment lens analysis feature of Leximancer, we were able to distinguish whether participants mentioned the DNA evidence in a favourable or an unfavourable manner. The results of this analysis, as shown in Table 6.2, indicated that, in most instances when DNA was mentioned by participants, their comments were negatively valenced (60%; $n = 193$). **6.115**

Table 6.1 Frequency count of concepts mentioned in trials with DNA expert evidence.

Concept name	Frequency
evidence	3,418
(expert, experts) expert*	3,268
(juror, jury, juries) jury*	3,075
(case, cases) case*	1,920
(question, questions) question*	1,720
DNA	1,473
trial	1,406
testimony	1,298
issues	987
defence	875
(people, person) person*	753
parts	750
(prosecution, crown) prosecution*	714
judge	712
things	676
time	672
witness	525
transcript	503
report	501
forensic	486
difficult	457
issue	457
relation	456
probably	444
general	438
accused	391
terms	389
particular	367
better	364
fact	356
criminal	347
court	340
information	328
course	265
blood	238
area	230
work	215
example	190
interview	142
police	122
car	115

Note: *denotes a compound concept.

Examples of the unfavourable comments about DNA expert evidence were centred on its content. Many of these remarks referred to its complexity for all trial participants, the fact that it was not well explained in court, and that both the testing procedures and the outcomes in terms of the RMP statistic were inherently complicated. Other comments about the content of the DNA evidence were more evaluative. For instance, a number of participants stated that the weight of the probative value of the DNA evidence was overestimated. Although a substantial amount of in-court time and other resources were devoted to the DNA expert evidence, its probative value in terms of resolving the disputed issues in the criminal trial was relatively low.

Table 6.2 Description of shared content between 'DNA' and other concepts mentioned in trials with DNA expert evidence.

Related concept	Description of content shared by DNA concept and related concept	Frequency
unfavourable	Complex for judges, lawyers, and jurors to understand (e.g. not explained well, testing procedures inherently complicated, match probabilities inherently complicated). Probative value of DNA evidence is overestimated (e.g. often not informative about key issues in dispute, a lot of time and effort goes into explaining the evidence in court and has small impact on case).	193
favourable	DNA evidence was well explained (e.g. with visual aids, without jargon, expert explained things in an interesting/engaging way).	130
evidence	Jurors' experiences of listening to the DNA evidence in court (e.g. it was long/boring/confusing/helpful). Content of DNA testimony (e.g. testing process, location of samples, inferences able to be made on the basis of the analysis). Barriers to comprehension (e.g. misperceptions about DNA evidence/CSI effect, complexity of subject matter).	697
expert*	Identifying who the DNA expert(s) were in the case, their qualifications (and how these were communicated to the jury), what they testified about, exhibits/aids associated with their evidence, role of DNA experts at trial, and aspects of evidence competing DNA experts disagreed on.	472
jury*	Expert/lawyer/judge perceptions of the jury's understanding of the DNA evidence, reasonableness of expecting the jury to understand, opinions about how the jury relies on DNA evidence, jurors' experiences using DNA evidence in deliberations, lawyers' perspectives on jurors' experience of the DNA evidence in court, techniques that may assist juries to understand DNA evidence, opinions about what aspects of DNA evidence juries respond to.	368
case*	Identifying the expert's role in the case (i.e. being there to present DNA evidence), the relative importance of the DNA evidence to the case being made by prosecution/defence, talking about experience with other (non-project) trials/cases involving DNA evidence.	333
trial	How DNA evidence related to facts in dispute at trial.	159
question*	Opinions about how well the DNA expert performed during questioning and particularly during cross-examination. Questions jurors asked of DNA experts. DNA experts' views on answering these questions and their importance. Factual questions that the jury had to answer in relation to the DNA evidence to arrive at a verdict. Aspects of the DNA evidence that were unconvincing.	159
person*	Lay understanding of DNA or the scientific processes used to test DNA: 'Basically, because what people believe about DNA evidence, which comes from television, is just wrong. It doesn't in any way reflect the truth of the situation, so that's why I think it is more complex than people actually realize.' Discussion of the DNA expert's clarity and lay understanding of the DNA match to complainants, victims, or defendants.	149
issues	Problems with the DNA evidence (e.g. contamination during testing, sample being too small to re-test, technician error during testing). Whether DNA evidence supported contentious facts/issues at trial (e.g. whether the accused was at the scene/held the weapon used to cause injury).	147
accused	Whether the DNA evidence taken from the crime scene was able to be accurately matched to the accused (includes discussion of comprehension difficulties and statistical probabilities used for DNA evidence).	138

(Continued)

Table 6.2 *Continued*

Related concept	Description of content shared by DNA concept and related concept	Frequency
testimony	Important parts of the DNA evidence presented by the expert. How the DNA evidence was discussed during deliberations/relied on to reach verdict.	135
parts	Elements/aspects of DNA evidence that were or were not explained well (difficult to understand: e.g. the extraction process, match probabilities, understanding what is not a match/well-explained: e.g. structure of DNA using PowerPoint). Important parts of the DNA evidence (e.g. ability to match samples to accused, location of samples at crime scene).	121
prosecution*	Name-like concept: How DNA evidence was used by the Crown to make a case. Relevance of DNA evidence to critical facts in the prosecution case.	112
defence	How DNA evidence was relevant to the defence case. Strategies the defence used to rebut or challenge the DNA evidence called by the prosecution (e.g. critiquing methods used to analyse samples, capitalizing on human error, playing on the match statistics, arguing the sample could have been left by secondary transfer).	111
things	Interpretations of what the DNA evidence means, misperceptions brought into the courtroom (e.g. DNA is always conclusive about who committed the crime on TV).	99
difficult	Statement by participant that DNA evidence is difficult to understand.	96
issue	Identifying aspects of the DNA evidence that were or were not contentious, e.g.: 'Obviously not, because they convicted. There was no issue about whether there was a match in the sample, because it was... when all ten sites in the DNA molecule were examined, it was consistent with the profile of the victim, so that wasn't an issue.'	95
terms	Challenges of understanding DNA evidence jargon. Challenges of understanding what DNA evidence tells the audience about facts in the case (or understanding the relevance of DNA evidence to the facts).	86
blood	DNA evidence drawn from blood samples. Methods used to infer blood was present. Impact of integrating DNA and blood spatter evidence.	79
forensic	Challenges of understanding DNA and forensic evidence more generally.	79
fact	How DNA evidence was informative to establish necessary facts at trial.	77
time	How lawyers and DNA experts spent preparation time prior to trial. Probative value of DNA evidence analysed years prior. Length of DNA evidence at trial.	72
particular	Opinions about communicating information about testing procedures to the court. Specific issues with some kinds of DNA analysis and samples.	71
probably	Inferences about how others may have understood the DNA evidence and what the DNA evidence could tell the court: 'And everyone sort of assumed that the DNA on the airbag that was male would probably be X, because he was in the middle and he was her boyfriend. So everyone was quite surprised when it came out, I was quite surprised when it came out to be Y.'	71
general	Expert's use of a general introduction to DNA evidence as part of their testimony.	59
relation	Connection between DNA evidence and various aspects of the case.	59
judge	Lawyer and expert preferences for judge-alone trials. Strategies/interventions the judge used to make the DNA evidence more simple for the jury. Perceived competence of the judge to understand the DNA evidence. Instructions the judge gave about the DNA evidence.	59

(Continued)

Table 6.2 *Continued*

Related concept	Description of content shared by DNA concept and related concept	Frequency
witness	Role of the expert witness at trial. Discussion of demeanour/competence of DNA witnesses.	58
course	Things that happened during EIC or cross-examination that might have influenced comprehension of DNA evidence. Obvious conclusions that could be drawn from the DNA evidence.	43
example	Tactics used by DNA experts on the stand to illustrate points in their evidence.	40
better	Strategies that were implemented or could be implemented to improve comprehension of DNA evidence.	36
report	Contents of report provided by DNA experts. Expert perspectives on preparing the report. Opinions on whether jurors should have access to DNA expert reports.	34
car	DNA samples drawn from vehicles of victims, complainants, and defendants.	32
information	Identifying information about DNA that prosecution or defence wanted from the DNA expert or information the jury wanted from the DNA expert.	30
court	Views on DNA expert's demeanour during evidence. DNA expert's perspectives on their experience giving evidence in court.	30
area	Contentious areas of DNA evidence (e.g. 'shedding', 'allele drop-out'). Limitations of some witnesses' expertise.	28
work	How DNA evidence works for the prosecution/defence in a case. Work experience of DNA experts.	25
criminal	Value of DNA evidence in criminal trials. Issues with using DNA evidence in criminal trials.	24
police	Police role in commissioning/gathering DNA evidence.	19
transcript	Instances in which the jury was, or was not, provided with the transcript of the DNA expert evidence.	17
interview	Statements made by the interviewer that a DNA expert is being interviewed.	4

Note: *denotes a compound concept. Frequency counts based on text units loaded into both DNA and related concepts.

Examination of these concepts in conjunction with the frequencies revealed that the participants were not 'blinded by science' but were sensitive to problems with the DNA evidence. For example, a high proportion of units in the discussion by participants ($n = 147$) noted one or more potential sources of error in the DNA profiling analysis, such as contamination of the DNA source sample, the small size of the DNA sample (low copy numbers), technical errors, or contamination during testing. **6.116**

By comparison, the favourable comments about DNA evidence (40%; $n = 130$) focussed on the presentation of the expert evidence rather than its content. For instance, participants noted that the evidence was conveyed in a clear way, with visual aids or without technical jargon, and was interesting and engaging to hear. **6.117**

Table 6.2 provides in some detail the content of the discussions about DNA in relation to other concepts mentioned in the participants' interview responses. To some degree, these frequencies provide insight into the manner in which the expert evidence was assessed and evaluated by the stakeholders. Issues of jury understanding dominated much of the discussion in relation to several of the highest-frequency words used in relation to this **6.118**

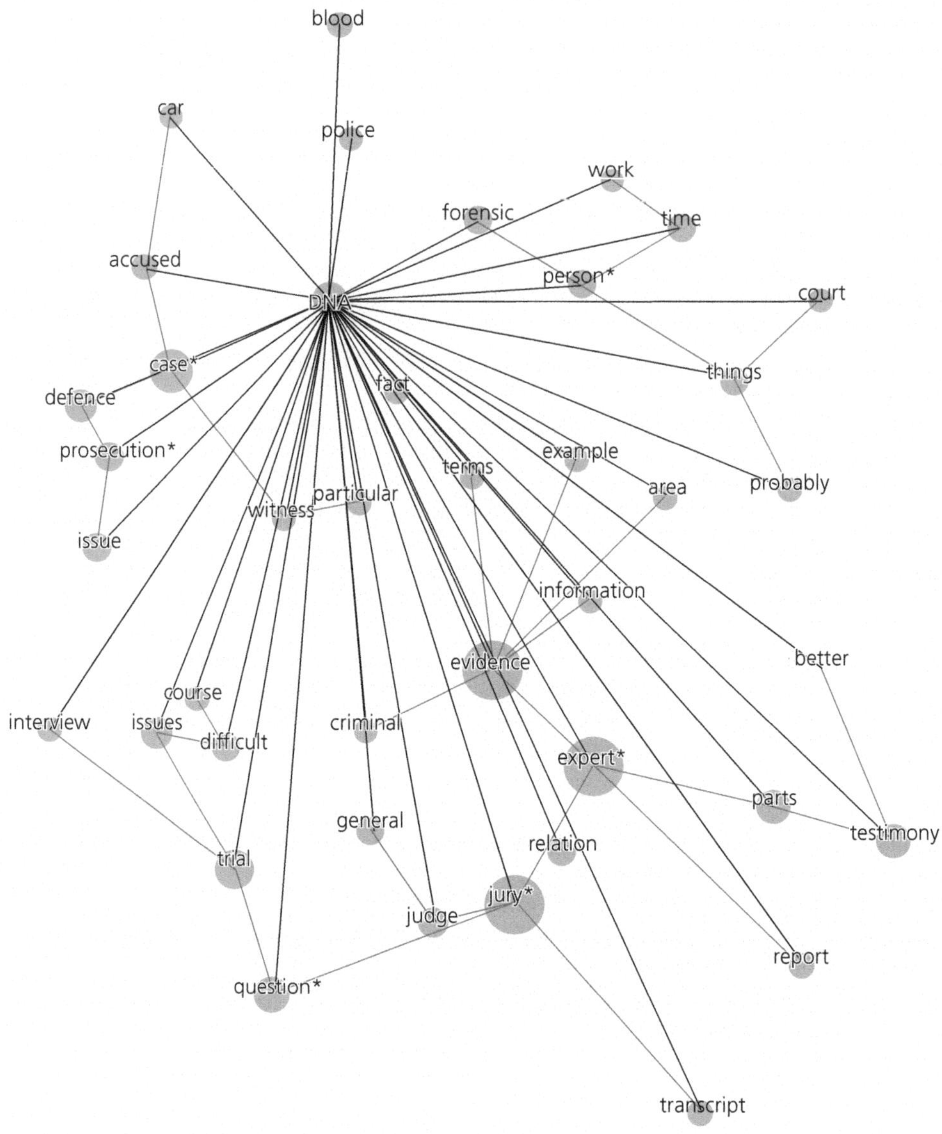

Figure 6.1 Shared content between 'DNA' concept and other concepts.

evidence (e.g., evidence, expert, jury), and the word 'understand' on its own received 200 mentions.

6.119 In terms of discerning efforts by the participants to assess the content or meaning of the expert evidence as opposed to peripheral cues related to the expert's appearance or credentials, it was encouraging to find that far more participants discussed how the DNA evidence related to the case facts ('trial', 'accused', 'case') than discussed the individual expert, the expert's credentials, or their presentation in court. In other words, the participants were practical, and were primarily focussed on the significance of the DNA evidence to the case at hand.

6.120 Reference to the frequency table and the conceptual map in Figure 6.1 revealed that participants commented on the nature of the DNA evidence (whether it was lengthy, confusing, helpful, etc.), the procedures involved in generating a DNA profile (such as the location of the samples) and the inferences that could be drawn from it, and barriers to the comprehension of this evidence.

F. Conclusions

The overall results indicated that the key participants in these trials, the jurors, the legal professionals, and the experts, agreed that somewhere between 26% and 72% of the jurors had difficulty understanding evidence intended to assist them in resolving disputed issues in serious criminal trials involving issues such as murder, armed robbery, and sexual assault. What is most striking in these results is the extent of the disparity, showing a lack of convergence or consensus regarding jury comprehension. Given that in a trial no objective comprehension tests, such as a multiple-choice questionnaire on the content of the expert evidence, can be administered to all participants, these findings raise a number of issues. While the reliability of both the professionals' perceptions of jury comprehension and the jurors' self-reported comprehension is questionable, a dominant theme in relation to the DNA evidence that emerged from the Leximancer analysis concerned the comprehensibility of the evidence. These findings point to the need for far more communication in criminal trials between the judge and the jury about what is and is not understood, and place a premium on better communication mechanisms between judges, lawyers, experts, and jurors about expert evidence. **6.121**

Adequate comprehension should not be left to the chance that some empanelled jurors will have a scientific background, or that a proactive judge will intervene on their behalf, or that a particular expert will be especially committed to communicating effectively in court. A more systematically co-ordinated approach is required to advance criminal justice policy and enhance jury comprehension. In part, this has not been undertaken because of judicial reluctance to look too closely at jury decisions in these trials.[72] As a consequence, rather than intrude to ascertain jury comprehension, judges and lawyers engage in the fiction that everything can be cured by yet another jury direction. Efforts to facilitate jury comprehension by implementing more pre-trial management of the trials have been resisted by members of the defence bar for strategic reasons.[73] **6.122**

The findings of this project are important because they provide some insight into the extent of the difficulties that jurors experience and the problems these can cause. Some of these problems are not addressed by counsel, the experts, or the presiding judge because of poor communication between them about what is really understood by jurors. The confusion generated by the use of likelihood ratios was extensive. Drawing on the literature, which shows that frequencies and percentages are more accessible, a verbal modification should be implemented to use frequencies and percentages instead of fractional ratios (to which they are mathematically equivalent). **6.123**

The findings indicated that in some instances, particularly when the DNA evidence interacted with jurors' interpretation of what 'beyond reasonable doubt' means, jury comprehension issues have the potential to lead to miscarriages of justice. In some trials, there was evidence that other factors compensated, reducing the likelihood of an unsafe verdict—for example, when: **6.124**

(a) jurors who had scientific and mathematical education were able to guide other, less knowledgeable jurors;

---

[72] Gary Edmond and David Mercer, 'The Politics of Jury Competence', in *Participation and Technology*, edited by Brian Martin (Wollongong: University of Wollongong, 1998); Dan Simon, *In Doubt: The Psychology of the Criminal Justice Process* (Cambridge, Mass.: Harvard University Press, 2012).

[73] New South Wales Law Reform Commission, *Jury Directions: Report No. 136*.

(b) lawyers and experts met in advance of the trial and collaborated to prepare a range of visual aids and exhibits to assist jurors;
(c) the judge was pro-active in seeking clarification of the expert evidence.

6.125 Regarding the presentation of DNA evidence, both the experts and legal professionals acknowledged that more could be done, but were not always certain what steps to take to improve the presentations. More regular and systematic procedures are advisable to expand the range of visual aids, to provide these in the jury room, and to encourage jury questions.

6.126 The comments by many jurors, and especially those elaborated in the cold case study discussed above, showed that some jurors will engage in peripheral as opposed to central processing of the content of the expert evidence, and will be susceptible to the persuasive features of cues such as expert credentials, demeanour, and confidence, i.e., will base their judgements on the communicator effects—the messenger rather than the message. The influence of communicator effects regarding DNA expert evidence may be exacerbated by the alliance of the expert with the police and prosecution, and misunderstandings of the extent to which the evidence is pre-screened before it is presented at trial. In other words, this evidence is viewed as akin to court-appointed expert evidence, which is processed peripherally because it is perceived as more neutral and reliable or credible than other expert evidence.

6.127 In contrast with the outcomes of the single case study, the Leximancer systematic analyses of the responses from the participants revealed a substantial number of comments acknowledging the weaknesses of DNA evidence, such as the potential for error by contamination of the samples, secondary transfer, the ambiguity that can arise from using very small or mixed DNA samples, ethnic differences in population databases versus samples, etc. These comments demonstrated a far more sophisticated grasp of the nature of the DNA evidence among all participant groups than might have been expected. The extent of the comments in the interviews about the limitations on the probative value of the DNA profiling evidence and the appropriate inferences to draw from a reported match suggested that many juries and legal professionals have entered a new era of sophistication in terms of understanding and using DNA profiling evidence. Jurors are not outpaced by technological advances and the sometimes complicated nature of this scientific evidence, provided it is well-presented in criminal courts.

6.128 The foregoing findings are consistent with the view of the Victorian Court of Appeal in a case in which the reliability of very high likelihood ratios derived from a newly developed DNA software package, known as STRmix, was challenged. The accused sought to exclude the evidence in part on grounds that the probative value of the expert evidence was outweighed by the danger of unfair prejudice in terms of the particular DNA sample (low template DNA and mixed samples), and the general complexity of the expert evidence, which might mislead or confuse the jurors. Following an extensive 22-day pre-trial hearing in which four DNA experts provided testimony, the trial judge first determined that the evidence proffered by the Crown was admissible. Next, the trial judge determined that the potential for unfair prejudice could be averted by careful presentation of the evidence, recommending that (a) the jury be provided with visual and other aids, (b) the evidence be led logically and sequentially, (c) expert conclusions be tested on cross-examination, and that these be supplemented by (d) a strong judicial direction advising the jury not to 'act on the STRmix conclusions unless they are wholly satisfied that they are soundly based in the evidence that they have heard and understood.' The Victorian Court of Appeal commended the trial judge for discharging 'her "gatekeeper" function with exemplary care and thoroughness', and affirmed her decisions both on admissibility and the matter of unfair prejudice, noting that they accorded with prior views expressed about the capacity of a jury to decide between competing DNA expert opinions.[74]

[74] *Tuite v The Queen* [2015] VSCA 148.

7

HEALTH PRACTITIONER EVIDENCE

A. Introduction

Evidence by health practitioners is the most common form of opinion evidence provided by experts to the courts. In the 1999 survey of Australian judges and the 2001 survey of Australian magistrates that constituted earlier phases of this project, health practitioner evidence figured very prominently, not just because of its ubiquity but as an area identified as problematic for decision-making by courts.[1] **7.01**

The present project builds upon those earlier studies through the scrutiny of the evidence given in criminal trials in three Australian states by a variety of health practitioner experts. These experts came from a number of different health practitioner categories, including physicians, forensic pathologists, psychiatrists, and psychologists. There was major diversity in the subject matter of the evidence given by the health practitioner experts, including the potential for epileptic seizures to impact upon volition, the possibility for the accused to have been acting while sleepwalking, the mental state of the accused at the time of homicides, and the cause of death of victims of homicide. **7.02**

The approach of this chapter is to capture some significant perceptions of the judges, lawyers, expert witnesses, and jurors interviewed in relation to health practitioner evidence. The quotations from interviewees do not purport to be representative of the sample of those interviewed or of the judicial, legal, or medical communities more generally—the sample was **7.03**

[1] See Ian Freckelton, Prasuna Reddy and Hugh Selby, *Australian Judicial Perspectives on Expert Evidence: An Empirical Study* (Melbourne: AIJA, 1999), where 15.97% of judges identified psychiatric evidence that they had been unable to evaluate effectively, 13.03% psychological evidence, and 10.50% medicine/surgery evidence; Ian Freckelton, Prasuna Reddy and Hugh Selby, *Australian Magistrates' Attitudes Toward Expert Evidence: A Comparative Study* (Melbourne: AIJA, 2001), where 15.96% of magistrates identified psychiatric evidence that they had been unable to evaluate effectively, 10.64% psychological evidence, and 18.09% medicine/surgery evidence.

not large enough to enable this. Rather, they afford an interesting opportunity to identify and contextualize issues of concern and controversy in the area.

7.04 After categorizing the types of health practitioner evidence our project captured, we then present a case study of a typical trial that involved competing health practitioner evidence. The case study provides a useful context within which to discuss the common issues raised by the trial participants in relation to the presentation of such evidence.

B. Types of Health Practitioner Evidence

7.05 We identified from our sample three major groups of health practitioner experts that regularly gave evidence in court.

(1) Forensic pathologists

7.06 Forensic pathologists were called to give evidence about cause of death in eleven of the trials studied, including eight trials in which the prosecution called multiple experts. Forensic pathologists were called by both the prosecution and the defence in just the one trial. This may well be reflective of the shallow pool of forensic pathologists available to be commissioned by the defence in Australia.

7.07 In recent years, forensic pathology has been one of the more controversial forms of expert evidence in Australia because, as in the United Kingdom, there have been high-profile cases which have involved contentious issues relating to whether deaths may or may not have been attributable to sudden infant death syndrome (SIDS)[2] and also as to whether deaths were self-inflicted.[3]

(2) Psychiatrists and psychologists

7.08 Psychiatrists were called in ten trials in the project. Five of these trials included competing psychiatric evidence. In Australia,[4] as elsewhere,[5] expert evidence about the mental state of the accused arises with regularity both at trial and at sentencing, often prompting different perspectives from psychiatrists called for the prosecution and the defence, as well as between psychiatrists and psychologists.

7.09 Notably, very few psychologists were called—on one occasion a clinical neuropsychologist in an indecent assault trial and on one occasion a child psychologist in a child sexual assault trial. Part of the reason for the comparative rarity of psychologists in our sample is likely to be the fact that in both the United Kingdom[6] and Australia[7] significant reservations have been

---

[2] See e.g. *R v Clark* [2000] EWCA Crim 54; *R v Folbigg* [2005] NSWCCA 23, (2005) 152 A Crim R 35; *R v Matthey* [2007] VSC 398, (2007) 17 VR 222.

[3] See e.g. *Velevski v The Queen* (2002) 76 ALJR 402; *Wood v The Queen* [2012] NSWCCA 21, (2012) 84 NSWLR 581.

[4] See Arlie Loughnan, *Manifest Madness: Mental Incapacity in the Criminal Law* (Oxford: Oxford University Press, 2012); Stephen Yannoulidis, *Mental State Defences in Criminal Law* (Aldershot: Ashgate, 2012).

[5] See recently Asne Seierstad, *One of Us: The Story of Anders Breivik and the Massacre in Norway* (London: Hachette, 2015); Calvin A. Colarusso, *The Psychiatric Witness in Court: What Mental Health Professionals Need to Know* (New York: Rowman & Littlefield, 2014); John Gunn and Pamela Taylor, *Forensic Psychiatry: Clinical, Legal and Ethical Issues*, 2nd edn. (London: CRC Press, 2014); Keith Rix, *Expert Psychiatric Evidence* (London: RC Psych Publications, 2011).

[6] See eg *R v MacKenney* (1983) 76 Cr App R 271, 275.

[7] See eg *Klimoski v Water Authority of Western Australia* (1989) 5 SR (WA) 148; *R v Peisley* (1990) 54 A Crim R 42, 52; *R v Kucma* [2005] VSCA 58, (2005) 11 VR 472. See also *R v Ching* [2011] NSWDC 232 [28]. However, contrast *R v Whitbread* (1995) 78 A Crim R 452; *Nepi v Northern Territory* [1997] NTSC 153.

expressed on occasion by superior courts about the entitlement for psychologists to diagnose mental disorders (save post-traumatic stress disorder in the context of criminal injuries compensation applications);[8] accordingly, where there is a question of pathology, psychiatrists tend more commonly to be called. However, in a range of other non-diagnostic domains psychologists are the expert witnesses of choice.[9] In particular, where a question of intellectual disability arises or where evidence is required in relation to child development,[10] the extent and effects of brain injuries, the impact of criminal assaults, family relationships, parenting skills, or reactions to physical or sexual assault, it is common for evidence from psychologists to be adduced.[11] It is comparatively rare for psychologists, or any other expert, to be permitted to give evidence in Australia or New Zealand, as in the United Kingdom, in relation to matters such as the risks of erroneous eyewitness identification or in relation to the operation of memory.[12]

(3) Other health practitioners

A variety of other health practitioners—physicians, neurosurgeons, toxicologists, and neuropharmacologists—were called in eleven trials. In two of these trials experts were called by both sides, but it was more common for such evidence to be called by the prosecution only. **7.10**

Injuries are often sustained in assault crimes and it is the forensic medical officer who commonly is the first person to assess the injured person(s). This type of evidence tends to be more factual and less contentious than psychiatric or pathology evidence. Eight forensic medical officers were called to give evidence and two general practitioners also gave evidence as to their treatment of the injured person(s). None of this evidence was countered by an opposing expert. **7.11**

The fact that those who provide treatment to patients are called from time to time to give evidence in respect of their treatment or the observations/diagnoses that they have made of their patient has often engendered confusion in relation to the role of treaters giving evidence and on occasion it has led to their evidence being relegated to second-class status. There was no indication that this was so from the perspective of jurors in our project. However, in trial 55 a treating doctor who was not accustomed to giving evidence admitted to feeling uncomfortable, and queried: **7.12**

> Do you think that the court, or somebody, had a responsibility to me to explain to me, first off that I was an expert witness, and what was expected, not of me in the case, but what is expected of me as an expert witness?. . . They asked me all these open-ended questions about the disorder, so they obviously considered me an expert, but I wasn't considering myself an expert. It was confusing.

Evidence given by treaters has the potential to be in the form of both evidence of fact and opinion evidence, although more often it is in the form of an account of what occurred during treatment and as to what, as a matter of fact, were the form of presentations and **7.13**

See Ian Freckelton, 'The Diagnostic Expertise of Psychologists', *Psychiatry, Psychology and Law* 4, no.1 (1997) 73; Ian Freckelton, 'Psychologists' Entitlement to Diagnose', *Psychiatry, Psychology and Law* 5, no.1 (1998) 159.

[8] See Ian Freckelton, *Crimes Compensation: Law, Practice and Policy* (Sydney: LBC Information Services, 2001).

[9] See Jack White, Andrew Day, Louisa Hackett, and J. Thomas Dalby, *Writing Reports for Court: An International Guide for Psychologists Who Work in the Criminal Jurisdiction*, 2nd edn. (Brisbane: Australian Academic Press, 2015).

[10] See e.g. pursuant to Evidence Act 1995 (Cth), s. 79(2).

[11] See Roger Kennedy, *Psychotherapists as Expert Witnesses* (London: Karnac, 2005), pp. 10–12.

[12] See Ian Freckelton, 'Eyewitness Identification Law Reform: The Need for Persistence', *Journal of Law and Medicine* 20, no. 3 (2013) 503.

diagnoses.[13] It can be particularly valuable in that it can provide a longitudinal and highly informed perspective upon a person's clinical condition.[14] The first principle of such evidence is that, properly viewed, it is expert evidence provided by a person possessed of specialized knowledge, in spite of the fact that it is given by a treater, so it is subject to the ordinary rules about admissibility of expert evidence when it takes the form of opinion evidence.[15] The second principle is that, although giving evidence in such circumstances may be regarded as generating 'role conflict',[16] once a treating health practitioner enters the courtroom forum, they are subject to obligations, by which their paramount duty is to the court, not any longer to act as an advocate for their patient/client.[17] Significantly, though, there have been suggestions that the discrepancy between diagnoses provided by treaters compared to independent assessors is only very modest;[18] put another way, any bias that might occur due to the treating role does not appear to have a major influence on diagnoses.

C. Case Study

(1) Summary of the facts

7.14 Like four other trials in this project, trial 44 featured competing expert evidence about the diminished mental capacity of the defendant. We interviewed four jurors, the judge, the prosecutor and her instructing solicitor, the defence barrister and her instructing solicitor, and the psychiatrists that gave evidence in relation to the defendant's mental capacity at the time that the offence was committed.

7.15 Three psychiatrists gave evidence; two for the defence and one for the prosecution. Our discussion focusses on the prosecution expert and one defence, due to the confines of the study but also because these are the two experts that were said by jurors to be most influential over the verdict and consequently featured the most in the interviews.

7.16 The jurors reported that the psychiatric evidence dominated the jury deliberations. The jurors wrestled with the mental capacity issue for about three quarters of the one-and-a-half day deliberation time. As juror G said, it was hard, *'but we had to come to a decision. We probably could've sat in that room for another week and disputed.'* Whilst there was disagreement in the deliberation room, there was no suggestion from the jurors that this was unusually fraught. A verdict was reached.

---

13 The General Medical Council uses slightly different terminology: 'Witnesses of fact (also known as professional witnesses) provide professional evidence of their clinical findings, observations and actions, and the reasons for them.' General Medical Council, *Acting as a Witness in Legal Proceedings* (2013), para. 8, <http://www.gmc-uk.org/guidance/ethical_guidance/21188.asp>.

14 See Collins Greaves, 'The Expert Witness', in *The Expert Medical Witness*, edited by Rosalind Winfield (Sydney: The Federation Press, 1989).

15 See e.g. *Bland v Verizon Wireless*, 538 F 3d 893, 897 (8th Cir, 2008): 'A treating physician's expert opinion is subject to the same standards of scientific reliability that govern expert opinions of physicians hired solely for purposes of litigation.' See e.g. in Supreme Court of Victoria, *Practice Note No. 2: Expert Evidence in Criminal Trials* (25 June 2014).

16 See Larry H. Strasburger, Thomas Gutheil, and Archie Brodsky, 'On Wearing Two Hats: Role Conflict in Serving as Both Psychotherapist and Expert Witness', *American Journal of Psychiatry* 154, no. 4 (1997) 449; Michael L. Commons and others, 'Forensic Experts' Perceptions of Expert Bias', *International Journal of Psychiatry* 35, nos 5–6 (2012) 362.

17 See e.g. Steven C. Bank, 'From Mental Health Professional to Expert Witness: Testifying in Court', *New Directions for Mental Health Services*, no. 69 (spring 1996) 5.

18 See Matthew Large, Olav Nielssen, and Gordon Elliott, 'The Reliability of Evidence about Psychiatric Diagnosis after Serious Crime: Part II. Agreement between Experts and Treating Practitioners', *Journal of the American Academy of Psychiatry and Law* 38, no. 4 (2010) 524.

The jurors were universal in their preference for the prosecution expert's evidence over the defence expert's evidence, even though the comprehension difficulties that they reported arose only in respect of the prosecution expert's evidence. Qualifications of the experts did not feature as a way used by the jurors to distinguish between the evidence. 7.17

(2) Jurors' perceptions of the prosecution expert

The jurors were consistent in their description of the prosecution expert as 'honest and open' and 'most believable'. Juror B explained: 7.18

> He spoke clearly and he spoke at a layman's level... I found him easy to understand comprehensively like that. His explanations were clear and I guess his statement relied very heavily on the questions he was being asked by the Crown and those questions were logical and well thought out, obviously.

Juror D was most impressed by the prosecution expert, as 7.19

> he was the one that fully explained what paranoid schizophrenia is, and what the differences between delusions and hallucinations are. So he was very knowledgeable about his areas of expertise.

Juror D appreciated the fact that the prosecution expert conceded points: 7.20

> He actually had views that also supported the defence for mental illness in the first—what do you call it?—indictment. So he sounded as if he'd considered both sides; he didn't sound as if he was fully on the Crown's side and wanted to prosecute and find a guilty verdict.

The jurors all reported difficulties in comprehending the alternative hypothetical scenarios that the prosecution expert explained. Juror A wanted to ask questions about the hypotheticals but did not. Juror D explained: 7.21

> There were moments when we'd walk away during our break in session and think to ourselves: 'Well if only we could put our hands up and ask a question', but we also thought that it was because... it was very high level and it was things that we weren't familiar with. We thought that if we had waited until we got the transcript and the transcripts were available to us, that we'd be able to fill in our own gaps.

This juror wanted to ask the prosecution expert about why certain assumptions were made and what pieces of the accused's statement were not incorporated when creating the hypotheticals. 7.22

The jury relied upon the transcript to help them make sense of the hypotheticals. The jurors were given the transcript of the medical evidence and some referred to this frequently, particularly in relation to the hypothetical cases described by the prosecution expert. Two jurors commented that they would have found it more useful to have been given an electronic version of the transcript. Juror D explained: 7.23

> If they had been available in an electronic format, we could have actually done a search of certain words that we were looking for during deliberation. Unfortunately because we only had paper, we had to pore over it again and again and again to try and find what people had written in their notes, and people had come out and said 'This is how I support my decision'... people needed to back up their own decision by having to trawl through the paper transcript—if it was, say, in like a PDF, Acrobat format, we could have at least... done a 'control find' or we could have found the keywords that we were looking for.

Juror B, who expressed frustration with not being given an electronic transcript, resorted to his notes.

7.24 Juror D pointed to the scenarios that provided the most realistic options for the jury, and yet 'the scenarios were quite difficult to follow because it was like a load of information all at the same time and it wasn't until later on with the transcripts that we could actually read them at our own pace and actually understand.' The self-reports of these jurors tend to suggest that they chose not to engage with peripheral processing when the evidence became complex but engaged with the issues through the transcript in their own time.

(3) Jurors' perceptions of the defence expert

7.25 Three of the four interviewed jurors thought that the defence expert lacked confidence and thought that the prosecutor 'demolished' him. Juror B explained: 'After [the defence expert] spoke I remember going to the jury and saying to the guys "Boy I really bet the defence is regretting bringing him in"... a lot of the things that he said weren't consistent.' Juror G disagreed with the other jurors and thought this expert performed adequately but acknowledged that the expert had limited factual knowledge of the matter as he was brought in so late.

7.26 What was most damaging to this expert's evidence was the fact that the expert's report:

> was made a day after the trial began so it was really like a last minute thing and the fact that he had interviewed the accused at such a late time after the event just made most of what he said for us quite unbelievable. We more or less wrote it off because there was such a long time period between the event and when he did his statement.

7.27 In spite of dismissing the defence expert's opinion, the juror did indicate that the jury engaged with the evidence provided before dismissing it:

> He clearly stated at one stage that the accused would've known that what he was doing was right or wrong and he would've... what was the other element of that? Two of the elements that had to be proven, he actually negated them when he was talking and I wrote it down and highlighted it. So for me he was meant to be the defence expert but he ended up confirming... you know for the Crown. But anything else he said... I didn't really give much weight to it, actually.

7.28 The self-reports of two of the jurors tend to suggest that these jurors chose not to engage with peripheral processing when the evidence became complex; however, the other jurors pointed to jurors taking mental shortcuts.[19] Juror G reflected on the way the jurors handled the complex evidence: 'It was hard. I was trying to look at the whole picture and I think a lot of the jury was taking portions of what they wanted to take out and just sort of sticking with that.'

7.29 One of the jurors reported that the jury was offended by the language used by one the defence experts who 'referred to the murders as a "tragic accident" because of the fact that he [the defendant] had a mental illness and that really put all of us offside quite a bit.'

(4) The weight of the evidence

7.30 Despite the expert evidence going to the heart of the issue in the trial, juror B thought that the reason why the jury:

> didn't put that much weight on what the experts said was for all three of them the length of time between when the event happened and when the accused was interviewed... So while we took some things on board, really it was just the length of time. I don't know why they let that amount of time go, maybe it would've been in the Crown's interest to let that amount of time go, but yeah, that was the main factor. For all three of them we sort

[19] Peripheral processing is discussed in more detail in chapter 5.

> of treated them as okay, well we'll look at it and we'll listen but we're not going to give it that much weight.

Overall, the jurors who were interviewed did not respond favourably to the certainty of opinion offered by the defence experts. They preferred the uncertainty of the prosecution expert on the basis that due to the fact that none of the psychiatrists saw the defendant around the time of the murder and the nature of the illness, it was unrealistic for the defence experts to offer such certainty. **7.31**

(5) Perceptions of the other stakeholders

The judge and lawyers in trial 44 all agreed that the psychiatric evidence in this case was hard for the jury to understand. The judge and prosecutor agreed with the jurors that the reasoning of the psychiatrist called by the prosecution, particularly around the hypotheticals, 'seemed quite confused.' **7.32**

The prosecutor was not overly impressed with the expert's inability to convey a conclusive opinion: **7.33**

> He generally equivocates a lot on giving an opinion and he hedges it a lot with a lot of cautions and so I've got a high opinion of him as an expert to describe these symptoms and how such a mental illness manifests itself but in applying it to the factual matters or to consider all the facts, I have some reservations about his ability to do that and come to conclusive opinions. In this case he struggled to come to the conclusive opinion, so overall not impressed.

Notably, the prosecutor spent only about an hour with this expert in preparation. For a murder trial where this evidence was key to the case, this was a surprisingly brief interaction; there are many indications that it was inadequate.

By contrast, the judge and lawyers all appreciated that the psychiatrists called by the defence were clear and unequivocal in their opinion. **7.34**

The prosecution lawyer emphasized that the task for the jury was not one of choosing between the experts or determining which was the more convincing: 'it was them making an assessment of the facts themselves and then applying it to the type of illness that this person is said to have had.' The defence lawyer expressed similar views, observing that the challenge for the jury was that the experts came from different perspectives in terms of whether the accused man was mentally ill: 'I think that was what was very confusing for the jury.' The defence lawyer was right in her observation that the fact that the medical assessments occurred so long after the events impacted upon the jury's decision: **7.35**

> I just don't think the jury got it one little bit, and it had absolutely nothing to do with preferring the opinions of the experts. I think they thought that the experts were not capable in the factual scenario of this case of proffering any opinion one way or the other as to the operation of mental illness because they didn't get to see the accused until a year or two years or three years after the event.

(6) Common themes

This case study serves to highlight the following features of competing expert evidence that were also common themes in other trials: **7.36**

(a) the jurors' emphasis on the helpfulness of clarity of the expert's opinion;
(b) how jurors deal with conflict of expert opinion;
(c) the impact of timing of medical assessments; and
(d) experts who make sensible concessions.

These themes are discussed in further detail in the following sections D to G.

7.37 The case study also highlights important aspects of witness credibility from the perspective of the jurors. For example, the experts' qualifications did not feature heavily in the juror interviews that were conducted as part of the case study. However, in other trials, qualifications were compared and discussed by jurors. For example, a juror from trial 50 referred to a medical expert's qualifications as having been found to be impressive by jurors, along with 'her talk and sense of character'. It appeared that it was a combination of factors that included credentials, delivery, and appearance of integrity that impressed the juror. This contrasts interestingly with the views of judges in the 1999 study where clarity of explanation was identified by 27% of judges as a persuasive factor, and impartiality by 26%. In addition, experience in the field (22%) and familiarity with facts (19%) were prominent answers but experience as an expert witness (3%) and qualifications (2%) did not figure prominently.[20] When judges were pressed to identify the single most persuasive factor in an expert's oral evidence, the outcome was even more pronounced: clarity of explanation was deemed most persuasive (52%), then impartiality (24%), experience in the field (13%), and familiarity with facts (8%), with only 2% identifying experience as an expert witness and 1% qualifications.[21]

7.38 Many factors that can impact upon whether witnesses are or should be regarded as convincing or credible. Psychology enables legal practitioners to harness juror expectations and a variety of considerations to impugn and sometimes to enhance the `believability' of witnesses, including expert witnesses, although identification of specific factors that contribute to persuasiveness and credibility can be complex. These matters are discussed further in chapter 8.

7.39 Some lawyers expressed concern about whether the evidence as it emerged was sufficiently comprehensible for jurors. An example given was resort to technical terms that may not be readily understood by lay persons, such as the use of names for pharmaceutical drugs. Along similar lines, a lawyer expressed a level of frustration about the inaccessibility of the evidence given by a psychiatrist: 'I would've preferred if he had borne in mind that the rest of us don't know psychiatry the way he does and so you need to explain things in more detail . . . a better trained psychiatrist would elaborate more.'

7.40 However, otherwise lawyers did not identify particular concern about the inaccessibility of health practitioner evidence. This may or may not be correlated with the forensic skills in communication on the part of the health practitioners called to give evidence in the trials which were studied during the project.

7.41 In trial 4, the suggestion was made by a defence lawyer that the task of the jury was eased by the quality of the evidence given by an expert called on behalf of the accused: 'A very considered witness that just didn't go straight into answers, and provided significant explanation and foundation for her answers.' It was observed that the way in which the expert's evidence was adduced—leading general evidence about battered woman syndrome and then reviewing how the general principles applied to the accused woman—assisted the exercise in educating the jury. This issue of the role of the expert as an educator of those with limited knowledge of an area of specialized knowledge is one that has often been remarked upon as fundamental to the forensic role.[22] As with all areas of pedagogy, the effectiveness of communication is partly a product of high levels of technical knowledge, but also the capacity to be interesting, memorable, clear, and likeable.

[20] Ian Freckelton, Prasuna Reddy, and Hugh Selby, *Australian Judicial Perspectives on Expert Evidence*, p. 47.

[21] Ian Freckelton, Prasuna Reddy and Hugh Selby, *Australian Judicial Perspectives on Expert Evidence*, p. 48.

[22] Richard Eggleston, *Evidence, Proof and Probability*, 2nd edn. (London: Weidenfeld and Nicolson, 1983). See too Stanley Brodsky, *The Expert Expert Witness: More Maxims and Guidelines for Testifying in Court* (Washington DC: American Psychological Association, 1999), p. 52.

D. Clarity of Opinions

Whilst the jurors from the case study found the prosecution expert's use of hypothetical scenarios was difficult to follow, they did note that the particular expert delivered his evidence with clarity. The delivery of the complex hypotheticals was perceived by the jurors to be an overload of information rather than lacking in clarity. Jurors were keen to ask questions but resorted to referring to the transcript to enable them to read at their own pace and fully engage with what the expert was explaining. In contrast, the definitive presentation of the defence experts was perceived as too simplistic and did not impress the jurors. **7.42**

The jurors' perceptions in the case study contrasted with views on the same witnesses expressed by the judge and the lawyers. The judge and lawyers noted their frustration with the unsatisfactory and inconclusive presentation by the prosecution expert and commended the defence expert for his clear presentation. A result of the earlier 1999 and 2001 AIJA studies was that a quality valued more than any other in an expert's oral evidence by both judges (51.91%, n = 122) and magistrates (43.08%, n = 84) is clarity—on the basis that the decision-making task is facilitated by an expert being 'clear' as to what their opinions are and in expression of them, the latter enabling comparison and contrast with any opinions which are to the contrary, as well as an understanding as to how opinions are derived from basis material.[23] **7.43**

The case study was not the only trial where the unwillingness of a health practitioner expert to be definitive caused frustration for the lawyers, who would have preferred that the expert was clearer in relation to the mental state of the accused at the relevant time. This has two significant aspects to it. The first is that the cause may well have been that the expert was not comfortable embracing the kind of unequivocal opinion that the lawyer had hoped the expert would. This may simply have been an ethical and proper response to ambiguity on the part of the expert. This appears to have worried the lawyers more than the jurors in the case study. Second, the lack of adequate pre-trial preparation of the prosecution expert in the case study is likely to have contributed to the complexity of the presentation by the prosecution expert. This common factor linked to complex presentations has been discussed in more detail in chapter 4. **7.44**

In trials in which there had been considerable expert evidence by health practitioners, including from doctors who had conflicting opinions, jurors indicated that they devoted a large amount of time to trying to evaluate the expert evidence. The case study in this chapter provides an example of this. **7.45**

The mechanisms by which jurors attempt to engage with the expert evidence varied. The jurors in the case study relied heavily upon the transcript and their notes to make sense of the complex evidence. In trial 13 the jury made it clear that they valued access to a transcript of proceedings, too. Juror A from this trial noted that the judge had the transcript of the evidence made available to jurors: 'We were going to ask for it but the judge realized that it was a difficult one so he gave us all the transcript from the three expert witnesses.' **7.46**

Other jurors referenced their use of their own notes during deliberations, particularly given that there was no efficient search function provided with the transcript. Juror G from the case study also suggested that it would be helpful to be given a list of questions to consider as they listen to the expert evidence that would enable them to focus on aspects of the expert evidence that relate to the ultimate questions that they must answer. **7.47**

---

[23] It may also be that judges and magistrates particularly valued clarity because of the assistance that it gave for the task of writing reasons for their decisions.

7.48 Jurors were generally appreciative of the questions asked by the judge, which often served to fill a gap of understanding for them. However, as in the case study, jurors would have liked to have asked questions but refrained from doing so.

7.49 Clarity of evidence was often linked by jurors to the presentation style of the expert. Juror B believed that the prosecution expert's evidence in the case study was clear because of his use of layman's language. When experts resorted to technical terms that may or may not be readily understood by lay persons, such as the use of names for pharmaceutical drugs, this was sometimes perceived as a barrier to clarity in the evidence they gave. Along similar lines, a lawyer in trial 26 expressed a level of frustration about the lack of detail in the evidence given by a psychiatrist: 'I would've preferred if he had borne in mind that the rest of us don't know psychiatry the way he does and so you need to explain things in more detail.... a better trained psychiatrist would elaborate more.'

7.50 It is often difficult to identify what it is that renders a person credible or persuasive. This subject is examined further in chapter 8. Although psychology provides a number of insights into what makes a person apt to be believed, disaggregation of particular aspects of presentation is often difficult. A juror from trial 1 found an eminently qualified psychiatrist to be 'a little bit long-winded in some of his answers, not that there was anything wrong with that or not; but it would've been nice if he could've said it a little bit shorter. I don't know whether it's some sort of academic thing.' Again, this is consistent with earlier findings from 1999 and 2001 which suggested that the 'mere' possession of particular qualifications (such as postgraduate degrees), beyond those necessary for the person to be found to be an expert, or the fact that an expert had authored learned articles are not regarded by judges and magistrates in Australia as particularly persuasive; rather, knowledge of the relevant facts and command of the expert area in question are regarded as the most persuasive attributes for an expert witness.

7.51 In part, such approaches may be particularly characteristic of Australian attitudes - that who people are and the credentials that they possess is not as important as their practical experience in the area in question. It may be too that what is perceived as pretentiousness or a failure to be straightforward is particularly alienating for jurors (and judges) in Australia.

7.52 A number of observations were made of the skill in evidence delivery by the health practitioner witnesses. A psychiatrist in trial 13 was described as 'very knowledgable and... charismatic and he has a good energy, a good benevolent energy'; a combination of features that the prosecution lawyer suspected discouraged the defence barrister from cross-examining him lest the witness exert additional impact upon the jury.

7.53 In trial 4, it was noted by a defence lawyer that the provision of explanations and bases for the views held by the expert, rather than just the expression of opinions, assisted the task of the jury in evaluating the strength of the witness's evidence. It was observed that leading general evidence about battered woman syndrome and then reviewing how the general principles applied to the accused woman was constructively educative. As is generally the case, a number of diverse considerations bear upon the effectiveness of communication, be they from experts or any other source. Presentation style is further explored in chapter 8.

E. Exceeding Parameters of Expertise

7.54 A further issue that was identified as troubling was where health practitioners moved beyond their range of competence. This theme is covered in more detail in chapter 4. Notably, the issue manifested starkly in trial 16 in respect of a medical practitioner called by the prosecution. He trespassed so problematically into the field of ergonomics without skills or qualifications in engineering that a no case submission on this basis ultimately brought about the end of the trial. As the judge observed:

> In my view, he didn't have the relevant expertise and if it had been challenged I might well have said 'Look, I don't think he's got the expertise'. He had a degree in, apart from medicine, electrical engineering, [but] he'd never actually practised as an engineer. He said he had given evidence four or five times before on movement of passengers in a major impact type collision, [but] he couldn't remember the last time he had, and he agreed that a mechanical engineer would be far more competent to give the type of expert opinion he was expressing.

In trial 18, a case in which an issue in contention was the effects of a drug, a health practitioner gave evidence in reply to a prosecution expert, although he lacked qualifications on the subject. This led the judge to observe both that his evidence may not have qualified as expert evidence in the first place and also that it went beyond what should have been appropriate, given his qualifications: **7.55**

> What he was doing was repeating what he'd read on the internet…I didn't think he was qualified as an expert to speak about the effects of the drug, even though he was a highly qualified expert.

F. Overly Broad-Based Evidence

Risks in terms of credibility are run when experts purport to have a wide range of forms of expertise. It was this that generated a number of the difficulties in the evidence given by the main police-employed forensic expert, Sergeant Cocks, in South Australia's Royal Commission in relation to Edward Charles Splatt.[24] **7.56**

On occasion, health practitioner experts in the study were cross-examined about the parameters of their expertise. As the General Medical Council has identified, it is an ethical obligation for expert witnesses to confine themselves within the scope of their expertise: **7.57**

> You must only give expert testimony and opinions about issues that are within your professional competence or about which you have relevant knowledge including, for example, knowledge of the standards and nature of practice at the time of the incident or events that are the subject of the proceedings. If a particular question or issue falls outside your area of expertise, you should either refuse to answer or answer to the best of your ability but make it clear that you consider the matter to be outside your competence.[25]

This issue arose in this project where the evidence was specialized and a generalist expert had been called. An instance of this phenomenon occurred when a forensic pathologist was called by the defence about the issue of cigarettes having been applied to the body of the victim and having caused injury marks. By contrast with the expert called by the prosecution who had unimpeachable expertise in the sexual assault area, the defence expert was questioned at some length by counsel for the prosecution about the extent and nature of his expertise. The question that was being addressed was the parameters of the expert's expertise as to the causation of particular forms of injury. The question of whether it is possible for an expert **7.58**

---

[24] Carl Shannon, *Royal Commission Report Concerning the Conviction of Edward Charles Splatt*, vol. 1 (Adelaide: Government Printer of South Australia, 1984), p. 16.

[25] General Medical Council, *Acting as a Witness in Legal Proceedings* (2013), <http://www.gmc-uk.org/guidance/ethical_guidance/21188.asp>. See also Nicholas Wall, *A Handbook for Expert Witnesses in Children Act Cases*, 2nd edn. (Bristol: Jordans, 2007).

to be confident as to whether wounds are self-inflicted has been the subject of a number of significant superior court and appellate decisions.[26] The issue identified by the juror was as to whether a generalist medical expert had sufficient expertise in this niche area for their opinions to be accorded significant weight.

G. Conflict in Expert Evidence

7.59 Jurors are not bound to accept unchallenged expert evidence uncritically.[27] Similarly, juries are not free to reject unchallenged expert evidence uncritically when it relates to a matter calling for scientific expertise.[28] However, they receive limited guidance in terms of how they should handle conflicts between experts in discerning between different evidence, sometimes using different terminology, on the same area.

7.60 It has been held that a jury can find a case proved in spite of such disagreement. Lord Chief Justice Widgery in *R v Sodo*,[29] for instance, was straightforward on the issue:

> Basic to the issues before us today is the proposition which one hears a great deal nowadays, namely that if experts differ there must be a reasonable doubt in the jury's mind which will lead to an acquittal. This is heresy, and the more often it can be pointed to as heresy the better. To apply such a principle would be to have trial by expert instead of trial by jury. The truth of the matter is that juries are perfectly entitled, when experts before them differ, to decide, if they think fit, that one expert is telling them the right and proper answer and the other is not, and if they reach such a conclusion beyond reasonable doubt it is proper for them to act on the opinion of one expert although that is contradicted by another expert.

7.61 Likewise the fact that expert evidence is uncontradicted does not require that a jury accept it,[30] provided that the rejection of the evidence is not capricious.[31]

7.62 Decision-making by a jury where there is conflicting expert evidence is not a matter of preferring one witness over another; it is a more sophisticated exercise which involves evaluating expert evidence placed before a court and determining whether, in conjunction with other evidence, it amounts to what is necessary to find a case proved to the requisite level. However, the fact that genuine and profound differences exist between expert witnesses may create a reasonable doubt in a criminal case before a jury, but this does not necessarily follow. It has been held that particular care must be exercised by judges when expert witnesses have disagreed about key issues.[32]

7.63 These principles have given rise in Victoria to the following model directions in respect of expert opinion evidence:

> In the course of giving evidence, these witnesses expressed their conflicting opinions about…
>
> Ordinarily, witnesses are not allowed to give their opinions in court. They must confine their evidence to their own observations. This is because it is you who are the judges of facts, and so usually it is only your opinion that is relevant.

---

[26] See eg *Velevski v The Queen* (2002) 76 ALJR 402; *Wood v The Queen* [2012] NSWCCA 21, (2012) 84 NSWLR 581.

[27] *Lanfear* (1968) CAR 176; *Brennan v The Queen* [2014] EWCA Crim 2387, [2015] Crim LR 290 [47]; *R v Klamo* [2008] VSCA 75, (2008) 18 VR 644 [44].

[28] *Anderson v The Queen* [1972] AC 100.

[29] (1975) 61 Cr App R 131, 133.

[30] See e.g. *R v Klamo* [2008] VSCA 75, (2008) 18 VR 644.

[31] See e.g. *R v Hall* (1988) 36 A Crim R 368, 370; *R v Klamo* [2008] VSCA 75, (2008) 18 VR 644; *K v Western Australia* [2010] WASCA 157 [43], [126]; *R v Rodriguez* [2010] NSWSC 198 [45].

[32] See *Nicholas v The Queen* (1989) 45 A Crim R 299, 311.

> However, the law says that people with specialised knowledge or training are allowed to give their opinions about matters within their field of expertise, if that may assist you in making your decision.
>
> In this case... evidence may assist you in determining [explain permissible uses of the expert evidence and any limitations on use].
>
> It is for you to determine whose opinion, if any, to accept, and how to use that opinion. You are the judges of fact in this case, and even though these witnesses are experts in their field, their opinions are merely a piece of evidence like any other, which you may accept or reject.
>
> When assessing evidence given by experts, you should consider factors such as the witnesses' qualifications, their demeanour, the way they expressed their opinions, and how they responded to cross-examination. You should also consider whether the witnesses appeared objective, or whether they seemed biased and overstated their evidence.
>
> You should also examine the quality of the reasons offered for an opinion, and the facts that support that opinion. A witness's opinion is only valuable if the facts on which it is based are true.[33]
>
> [If there is a dispute about the factual bases of the experts' evidence, explain the dispute to the jury and summarise the relevant arguments.]
>
> [If resolution of the conflict is likely to determine the accused's guilt, add the following section.]
>
> While it is for you to determine which evidence to accept, I remind you that it is for the prosecution to prove the accused's guilt beyond reasonable doubt. This means that you may only accept [insert name of prosecution witness] opinion that [describe opinion] if you are satisfied beyond reasonable doubt that his/her opinion is correct.
>
> In this case part of the dispute between the witnesses is about scientific matters. [Summarise dispute.] If you find that you cannot resolve this conflict by considering the witnesses' evidence, then you must give the accused the benefit of your doubt, and reject [insert name of prosecution witness] evidence. You can only accept that evidence if you find there to be a good reason to reject [insert name of defence witness] evidence.

An important issue that arose in some answers given by jurors in other trials was the extent **7.64** to which they simply compared the evidence from different experts and decided which they preferred, rather than focussing upon whether, by reference to all of the evidence adduced, the case had been proven to the requisite level. For instance, a juror in trial 2 commented: 'The experts both had different views and you had to see which one you, you understood more and you believed more.' A risk hereby exists of a misconceptualization by jurors of the role of experts and thereby that experts will be given an excessive role in resolution of contested issues. It highlights the importance of a suitable trial direction on the issue.

Interviewees were asked about their perceptions of conflict between experts. The juror inter- **7.65** views from the case study suggest that, whilst the jurors engaged with the conflicting evidence, this jury may not have ultimately accepted either side's expert evidence as to mental capacity. Some of the jurors suggested that the fact that the defendant was not assessed by all psychiatrists in a timely manner undermined all of the expert evidence.

In murder trial 26, the experts disagreed on whether the accused's psychotic illness deprived **7.66** him of the capacity to reason with a moderate degree of sense and composure in terms of whether he knew that his actions were wrong and thus whether he suffered from mental impairment. The prosecution lawyer interviewed expressed the view that it was hard for the jury to choose between the opinions of the psychiatrists—it took them three and a half days to bring in their verdict: 'I think they were probably grappling with it but at the end of the

[33] See *R v NCT* [2009] VSCA 240, (2009) 26 VR 247.

day weren't satisfied that the defence had made out that defence on the balance of probabilities.' Interestingly, the defence lawyer had a different perspective, expressing the view that the jury did not have major difficulties. This difference of view may well have been the product of the opposing perspectives.

7.67 A juror from trial 48, which also featured competing psychiatric expert evidence addressing mental capacity, summarized the challenge:

> I was a bit concerned when these witnesses were put up because I thought, well, if they disagree and given that the science of the mind is not an exacting science, we could be faced with a dilemma when we've got diametrically opposed views on this sort of stuff. So, where do we go as twelve ordinary people?

Thus, the issue clearly arose as to the inference that this juror believed should be drawn when there was irreconcilable difference between learned persons in an area of specialized knowledge about which the jurors knew little.

7.68 It was apparent that conflict between two learned professionals troubled some jurors, leaving them a little flummoxed as to how they should discern between different views. In trial 2, for instance, a juror commented: 'Basically the experts would have counteracted each other,...as their evidence would have been as useless as the other in the end, because it was so contradictory.'

7.69 An aspect of difficulty for jurors when experts disagreed was identified in one case as the complexity of the evidence. An example was competing evidence about the causation of an injury that caused death—whether the tear of the vertebral artery could only have been caused by a rotational stretching force or whether it could also have been caused by simple blunt force trauma (trial 50). The prosecution lawyer expressed the view that this would have posed difficulties for the jury 'because it's not so well understood'. The defence lawyer disagreed (in hindsight) on the basis of the speed with which the jury returned its verdict of not guilty—there was no evidence of a punch, so that relieved the jury of the need to grapple with it.

7.70 Mechanisms for discerning between conflicting views of experts can involve resorting to irrelevant considerations, such as the experts' appearances, or to collateral knowledge such as that arising from jurors' personal experience. To expect jurors to abandon all collateral sources of knowledge when an evaluative task is important and complex may be naive, especially in the Internet era when resort to Google is an ordinary incident of life for most people.[34] A juror in trial 50 gave an insight into the risk in this regard:

> I was in a tricky situation that I had a relative who had actually cut their vertebral artery through a fall so that turned me completely off the Crown expert witness. She was a mere pathologist who tried to present herself as a researcher in the field which she wasn't—there was no evidence of any published papers of research that she'd done, that she was opinionated...I knew she was wrong because of personal experience which I can't take out of my own head, not that I disclosed that to the rest of the jury at the time, though.

H. Timing of Medical Assessments

7.71 A number of jurors expressed the view that the sooner that psychiatrists could interview the accused after the commission of the index offence, the more valuable their opinions were

[34] See Jacqueline Horan, *Juries in the 21st Century* (Sydney: The Federation Press, 2012), pp. 150–64; Carol Myers Morrison, 'Can the Jury Trial Survive Google?', *Criminal Justice* 25, no. 4 (2011), <http://www.americanbar.org/content/dam/aba/publications/criminal_justice_magazine/cjw11jurytrial_google.authcheckdam.pdf>.

(e.g., the case study). Again, it is likely that the common-sense view being expressed was that a forensic evaluation of mental state at the time of the commission of an offence accrues greater authenticity by its proximity to the index event. The interesting inference in this regard is that the probative value of the *ex post facto* reconstruction of an accused's mental state a significant time later by a forensic assessor may be perceived as of limited value.

I. Impressiveness of Expert

In trial 49, although competing opinions were expressed to some extent, one of the defence lawyers expressed the view that the demands for the jury were ameliorated by the fact that there was a contrast between on one hand a clearly expert psychiatrist called by the defence, and, on the other, a prosecution expert who had not seen the accused. The prosecution expert was viewed by one of the defence lawyers as not really understanding his role, and by another as inappropriately prepared to express views about whom he believed. Whilst none of the jurors brought up the fact that the prosecution expert had not seen the accused, the jurors did describe this witness as having 'little impact', and being 'unmemorable' and 'confusing.' In agreement with the lawyers, the jurors were impressed with the defence expert. As juror A described: 'Well, his whole presentation was very, very, very good; very, very emphatic. Just his list of credentials and list of experience—there was a book he'd written, etc.—was very impressive.' Whilst this trial featured competing expert evidence over the complex issue of battered woman/person syndrome, the impressive performance of the defence expert appears to have made the decision much easier for the jury. **7.72**

J. Preparedness to Make Concessions

It has been suggested in commentaries on the giving of evidence by expert witnesses that preparedness to make concessions or to admit a lack of knowledge on an abstruse point or acquaintance with a text may accrue to a witness's credibility.[35] Some of the jurors from the case study suggested that they were more inclined to accept the prosecution psychiatrist's evidence because he showed that he was even-handed and prepared to concede points, as he accepted the defence expert's opinions to a certain extent. **7.73**

The dynamic nature of the trial process cured some of the difficulties that might otherwise have existed concerning disagreements amongst expert witnesses. An example was trial 2, in which an issue in contention was whether the accused had a history of sleepwalking. There was extensive evidence on the subject, but ultimately, after hearing all the expert evidence, the prosecution made a concession on the issue so the jury was relieved of the burden of having to form a final view arising from the expert evidence adduced. **7.74**

One of the pathologists from a state pathology laboratory also explained that, before the hearing, they always informally invite pathologists employed by the defence to come and view the body and discuss any pathological issues associated with the death. In at least one case, this resulted in the prosecution expert conceding an issue to the defence and modifying/clarifying his opinion. This resulted in the defence pathologist no longer being called to give evidence. This process proved to be both efficient and promoted clarity of evidence for the jury. **7.75**

---

[35] See e.g. Ian Freckelton and Hugh Selby, *Expert Evidence: Law, Practice, Procedure and Advocacy*, 6th edn. (Sydney: Thomson Reuters, 2016).

7.76 An expert from trial 2 expressed a measure of frustration about the adversarial processes, when commenting on the capacity to respond to the issues raised by the expert called by the defence, whether by way of disputing issues or conceding them:

> You almost felt like there should have been a round-table-debate-style thing because I think there were lots of areas of overlap and lots of areas where you could create controversy, but there wasn't any great controversy.... So I think that's an area that could be improved.

Such a comment provides a level of support for the advantages in greater use of both expert conclaves and concurrent evidence (see chapter 3 for a more detailed consideration of this point).

K. Experts' Views of Other Experts

7.77 In general, health practitioner experts reported that they felt that they had had the opportunity to respond adequately in the witness box to the opposing expert evidence. On occasion they did identify questions that they thought that counsel for the party calling them should have asked the expert on the other side. An example was a psychiatrist called for the defence who commented that: 'I would have been going in a bit harder around the diagnostic issue, I think.'

7.78 No major significance should be attributed to such an observation, but it does highlight the different perspectives that inevitably exist between legal practitioners, endeavouring to secure a particular objective on behalf of their client, and expert witnesses, who will generally have a significantly more informed (and hopefully less partisan) perspective on the technical issues being traversed.

7.79 Even though guarantees of confidentiality were given to the medical experts who were interviewed, they were hesitant to be critical of professional colleagues. A psychiatrist from trial 48, however, commented that a psychiatrist on the other side 'lost it a bit. I thought his poise and demeanour suffered'. He said that he got the impression that when the opposing expert was put under pressure, he did not like the manner of questioning and 'it was like he was feeling he was being criticized and he tried to make up for it by becoming curt, saying: "I've already answered that question".' The comment was made that the opposing expert lost credibility when he became combative and 'looked a bit sulky'. He reflected: 'You've just got to stay in control and maintain that sort of calm demeanour even if you are rankled by the fact that people are questioning you.' This is consistent with advice frequently given to forensic experts by those who have engaged in training of expert witnesses.[36]

7.80 It is clear that a facility whereby feedback could be provided to expert witnesses about how they performed in giving oral evidence would be a valuable mechanism with the potential to enhance skills in testifying. However, in practice this seldom occurs.

[36] See e.g. Richard Rogers and Daniel W. Shuman, *Fundamentals of Forensic Practice: Mental Health and Criminal Law* (New York: Springer, 2005); Jack V. Matson, *Effective Expert Witnessing: Practices for the 21st Century* (Boca Raton: CRC Press, 2004); Stanley L. Brodsky, *Testifying in Court: Guidelines and Maxims for the Expert Witness* (Washington, DC: American Psychological Association, 2013); Stanley L. Brodsky, *Coping with Cross-Examination and Other Pathways to Effective Testimony* (Washington, DC: American Psychological Association, 2004); Kenneth S. Cohen, *Expert Witnessing and Scientific Testimony: Surviving in the Courtroom* (Boca Raton, Florida: CRC Press, 2007); Thomas G. Gutheil, *The Psychiatrist as Expert Witness*, 2nd edn. (Washington, DC: American Psychiatric Publishing, 2009); Freckelton and Selby, *Expert Evidence: Law, Practice, Procedure and Advocacy*.

L. Conclusions

The various perspectives provided by judges, lawyers, experts, and jurors reinforced the complexity and diversity of the task of jurors in evaluating expert health practitioner evidence. In general, there was confidence that jurors were managing the role effectively. It was evident that, when there was conflicting evidence on the same topic or when evidence was unclearly delivered or convoluted in its complexity, there was reason for concern about the effectiveness of the decision-making process by jurors. In trials involving complex competing evidence, such as the five trials where psychiatric witnesses gave contrasting opinions about whether the accused was mentally impaired, if the issues were sharply delineated and the assumptions made by the experts were clearly identified, we can be cautiously optimistic that the jury managed to evaluate the differences between the experts adequately. **7.81**

This analysis highlights the importance of both sound pre-trial preparation by expert witnesses, and training so that they can optimize their evidence during criminal trials and the reasons for the views that they hold. As discussed in chapter 4, if barristers spent adequate time with their experts in pre-trial preparation, this would give experts a better opportunity to raise technical medical issues that might well be useful for the party calling them—whether that be in the form of questions asked of the expert or of the opposing expert. There is no reason why experts should not be proactive in this regard and request such conferences. **7.82**

While the trial system exhorts jurors to use their common sense and their everyday experience, it is a conundrum, and probably experienced by many as anomalous and artificial, that jurors are precluded from accessing ordinary sources which could assist them in acquiring context, clarifying misconceptions, and understanding better the knowledge that they have. This is not to argue against the proposition that jurors should be instructed to refrain from their own research and to take into account only the evidence adduced in the trial, but it is to observe that the task imposed upon them requires them to discharge an important role in a way which is different from how they would discharge other important decision-making roles that they undertake in their non-juror lives. Empowering jurors to feel that they can ask questions of experts and providing the transcript of expert evidence in searchable form are logical next steps to improving juror comprehension of such evidence. **7.83**

The views of the jurors suggest that health practitioner experts should feel comfortable with conceding points as the jurors looked favourably upon experts who did so, if the concession was delivered by a confident witness. Even-handed expert evidence delivered with confidence was perceived as more important by the jurors who were interviewed than any disparity between the experts' qualifications. **7.84**

The timing of assessment featured in the feedback from the jurors. It would be helpful for police investigators and prosecutors to do what is reasonably open to them to ensure that psychiatric/psychological assessments, particularly as to mental capacity at the time of an index act, are performed as close as possible to the events in issue at the trial. Reports that are commissioned much later, or during the trial, run the risk of being given little weight. **7.85**

8

EXPERT WITNESS CREDIBILITY

A. Introduction

Within legal systems that follow the adversarial model of the common law, a premium is placed on the oral presentation in court of evidence by lay and expert witnesses called on behalf of the prosecution and defence. The role of the jury in assessing and evaluating this evidence is a critical function of jury decision-making before rendering a verdict of guilty or not guilty. The evidence from a witness whose testimony is rated as credible will usually be given weight and relied upon by the jury over that of a witness whose evidence is rated low in credibility. However, credibility is not often clearly defined.[1] The growing body of research on this topic indicates that a precise definition is still a work in progress. However, contemporary researchers often distinguish the believability of a witness, which is associated with the demeanour and presentation style of the witness, from the plausibility and veracity of the content of the evidence of the witness. In other words, a witness can be believable and likeable[2] but dishonest. With respect to expert witnesses, the plausibility is often referred to as the reliability and the validity of the expert evidence, a subject discussed in chapter 2. One problem in much of the legal doctrine in the common law is that believability (credibility) and honesty are presumed to be synonymous, and therefore that careful scrutiny of witness demeanour (the messenger) can inform the finder of fact as to whether or not a witness is truthful (the message). **8.01**

This chapter examines how the credibility of expert witnesses is evaluated. For example, when a rebuttal opposing expert witness is called by the defence, does the resulting battle **8.02**

[1] Not very helpfully 'credibility of a witness' is defined in the Dictionary to the Evidence Act 1995 (Cth) as 'the credibility of any part or all of the evidence of the witness, and includes the witness's ability to observe or remember facts and events about which the witness has given, is giving or is to give evidence.'

[2] See Stanley L. Brodsky and others, 'Credibility in the Courtroom: How Likeable Should an Expert Witness Be?', *Journal of the American Academy of Psychiatry and Law* 37, no. 4 (2009) 525.

of experts edify jurors and facilitate their comprehension, or do two well-qualified and well-credentialed experts 'neutralize' each other's persuasive influence?[3] Many commentators have theorized that jurors will ignore the disputed content and resolve the battle by relying entirely on their general impressions of the expert's character and veracity.[4] In this chapter, we examine how existing beliefs contribute to the perceived trustworthiness of expert witnesses, what jurors and legal professionals say they base their evaluation of expert credibility upon, and also the factors associated with jurors, experts, and presentation style that are actually related to credibility. As part of the latter analysis, we consider the extent to which individual jurors agree in their ratings of expert credibility, and also whether their views are consonant with those of legal professionals, to ascertain whether expert credibility is associated with socially shared beliefs about the experts, or is due to differences in the perceptions of lay versus legal professionals, or idiosyncratic criteria applied by individuals in all groups.

(1) Framework for credibility analysis

8.03 The general framework for this analysis is described by the elaboration likelihood model[5] and other dual-process models of persuasion. As was explained in chapter 5 in paragraphs 5.11 to 5.16, these models suggest that there are two general pathways or routes to evaluate a persuasive message. A high cognitive effort or central route involves careful scrutiny of the strengths and weaknesses of the content of a persuasive message. Because the content of the message is the primary determinant of persuasion, a strong message (or strong evidence in the case of an expert witness) will be most influential. This mode is primarily engaged when a juror has the time, ability, and motivation to engage in substantial effort to think about the content of the message.

8.04 The alternative, less effortful peripheral route involves evaluating the message based on decision rules (called heuristics), or associations between the message and positive or negative cues that are not directly related to the content of the message. In this instance, a message (or evidence) will be more persuasive when it is associated with a cue that we evaluate positively, such as an expert's credentials, rather than the content of the message itself. Peripheral route processing occurs mainly when a juror is unwilling or unable to think carefully about a message, for example when a message is complex and difficult to understand, or a juror is tired. In chapter 5 in paragraphs 5.05 to 5.07 and 5.18 to 5.33, we reviewed existing literature that has identified a range of different peripheral cues that have been identified to influence perceivers' perceptions, including credentials, expert gender, and case domain. Before proceeding, we consider additional factors that have specifically been identified as related to the assessment of credibility.

(2) Factors associated with credibility

8.05 Lawyers will often coach experts as to how they should present their evidence at trial.[6] Experts, and the lawyers preparing experts for trial, may be advised about a number of factors that are believed to affect the credibility of the expert. For example, some advice emphasizes

[3] Jane Goodman-Delahunty and Kosuke Wakabayashi, 'Adversarial Forensic Science Experts: An Empirical Study of Jury Deliberation', *Current Issues in Criminal Justice* 24, no. 1 (July 2012) 85.

[4] Dennis J. Devine and others, 'Jury Decision Making: 45 Years of Empirical Research on Deliberating Groups', *Psychology, Public Policy and Law* 7, no. 3 (September 2001) 622.

[5] Richard E. Petty and John T. Cacioppo, 'The Elaboration Likelihood Model of Persuasion', in *Advances in Experimental Social Psychology*, vol. 19, edited by Leonard Berkowitz (New York: Academic Press, 1986), pp. 123–205.

[6] Anthony Champagne, Daniel Shuman, and Elizabeth Whitaker, 'Expert Witnesses in the Courts: An Empirical Examination', *Judicature* 76, no. 1 (1992) 5.

the importance of non-verbal behaviours for expert credibility. In particular, maintaining an open posture, using expansive gestures, being friendly and relaxed, and making eye contact with the jury are all seen as important in promoting perceptions of credibility.[7] Other advice reinforces the importance of eye contact and good posture, as well as communication skills such as pausing before answering, avoiding slang and jargon, speaking clearly, and not arguing. Essentially, the way an expert can appear credible in terms of non-verbal behaviour is to be as natural as possible and focus on appearing believable.[8] Advice of this nature appears sensible given common behavioural stereotypes about what constitutes deceptive behaviour that might undermine perceptions of credibility.[9]

Others suggest that the content of the evidence itself is most important for perceptions of credibility. In particular, if the content of the evidence is too complex and jurors cannot readily comprehend it, they will be less willing to engage in efforts to understand that evidence. This potentially leaves the testimony open to counter-arguments suggested by the opposing side. One study of jury behaviour determined that the most important factor was global comprehensibility.[10] This suggested that, unlike a mechanical lie-detection machine, witness credibility evaluations are not typically assessed utterance by utterance, but are more comprehensive or global determinations. The tone of the content of the evidence is also seen as important in determining credibility. In particular, appearing to be impartial or neutral, rather than clearly advocating for one side or the other is important if an expert does not wish to be dismissed as partisan or a 'hired gun'.[11] **8.06**

This advice appears to be consistent with what lawyers believe is associated with a credible witness. In particular, research suggests that lawyers think that experts who demonstrate trustworthiness, knowledgeability, and communication skills will be seen as credible. Lawyers further thought that duration and type of experience were important, in addition to the actual content of the evidence provided.[12] A focus on the content of the evidence (and avoiding a tentative or hesitant manner) is consistent with how lawyers actually prepare expert witnesses for trial.[13] **8.07**

Some lawyers also apparently believe that expert gender is an important factor in credibility assessments. The observation that a greater number of male than female expects are selected to provide evidence led some scholars to conclude that lawyers think that jurors perceive male experts as more credible.[14] **8.08**

The research examining the issue of expert credibility partially confirmed this advice, and provided further insight into the factors that drive credibility assessments. Two broad themes emerged from the reported research. The first is the relative importance of the content and **8.09**

[7] The Synchronics Group, 'Five Imperatives for Expert Witnesses: Effective Non-Verbal Skills Can Be Learned', <http://www.synchronicsgroup.com/articles/articles_5imperatives_p.htm>.

[8] Marcus T. Boccaccini and Stanley L. Brodsky, 'Believability of Expert and Law Witnesses: Implications for Trial Consultation', *Professional Psychology: Research and Practice* 33, no. 4 (2002) 384.

[9] Blake M. McKimmie, Barbara M. Masser, and Renata Bongiorno, 'Looking Shifty But Telling the Truth: The Effect of Witness Demeanour on Mock Jurors' Perceptions', *Psychiatry, Psychology and Law* 21, no. 2 (2014) 297.

[10] Dorothy K. Kagehiro, 'Jurors Keenly Assess Experts' Credibility', *The National Law Journal* 24, no. 11 (5 November 2001) B14.

[11] The Synchronics Group, 'Five Imperatives for Expert Witnesses: Effective Non-Verbal Skills Can Be Learned', <http://www.synchronicsgroup.com/articles/articles_5imperatives_p.htm>.

[12] Hayley J. Wechsler and others, 'Attorney Beliefs Concerning Scientific Evidence and Expert Witness Credibility', *International Journal of Law and Psychiatry* 41 (2015) 58–66.

[13] Champagne, Shuman, and Whitaker, 'Expert Witnesses in the Courts', 5.

[14] Amina Memon and Daniel W. Shuman, 'Juror Perception of Experts in Civil Disputes: The Role of Race and Gender', *Law & Psychology Review* 22 (1998) 179.

style of the expert evidence and features associated with the messengers, the experts themselves. The findings on this point are generally consistent with the dual-process models of persuasion described earlier (addressed in detail in chapter 5, paragraphs 5.11 to 5.16).

8.10 Essentially, mock jurors attempt to assess the credibility of the evidence based on its content, but when that content becomes complex and difficult to understand, they tend to revert to peripheral cues, such as positive or negative features associated with the experts themselves, to assess credibility. For example, an expert with strong credentials will be more persuasive compared to an expert with weak credentials.[15] Likewise, in some contexts, a male expert will be more persuasive than a female expert,[16] or an expert who appears to be a hired gun will be seen as less credible than one who testifies less frequently.[17] This conclusion is somewhat at odds with the advice that complex expert evidence is more susceptible to rebuttal and thus less credible due to difficulties in comprehension.[18] Rather, it suggests that the criteria for perceptions of credibility change as a function of the complexity of the evidence. While some research has concluded that jurors form expert-specific evaluations based on 'rational criteria' rather than the attributes or the demeanour of the expert or the juror,[19] that research has focussed exclusively on surface-level features such as expert and juror occupation, and omitted consideration of a range of extra-legal factors identified by other research.

8.11 The second theme to emerge from the body of research on credibility is a focus on specific factors that contribute to credibility, rather than the manner in which credibility is assessed. These include a range of factors associated with the expert and the way in which the evidence is presented that are important to ensure that an expert is perceived as credible. For example, findings of experimental research suggested that the expert's demeanour was an important contributor to perceived credibility. In particular, it is important for an expert to be likeable in order to be credible. For some groups of perceivers, such as women, a likeable witness is particularly important.[20] Confidence is also an important attribute, as moderate levels of confidence were associated with the highest level of credibility—too much confidence undermines a witness's credibility in the eyes of mock jurors.[21]

8.12 Aspects of non-verbal behaviour are important for credibility, and the importance of non-verbal behaviours is reinforced in training for experts.[22] Experts who make eye contact are rated as more credible,[23] perhaps because averting one's gaze is stereotypically seen as a cue to deception.[24] Expert gender moderates the influence of certain non-verbal behaviours.

---

15 Joel Cooper, Elizabeth A. Bennett, and Holly L. Sukel, 'Complex Scientific Testimony: How Do Jurors Make Decisions?', *Law & Human Behavior* 20, no. 4 (1996) 379.

16 Regina A. Schuller, Deborah Terry, and Blake M. McKimmie, 'The Impact of Expert Testimony on Jurors' Decisions: Gender of the Expert and Testimony Complexity', *Journal of Applied Social Psychology* 35, no. 6 (June 2005) 1266.

17 Joel Cooper and Isaac M. Neuhaus, 'The "Hired Gun" Effect: Assessing the Effect of Pay, Frequency of Testifying and Credentials on the Perception of Expert Testimony', *Law and Human Behavior* 24, no. 2 (2000) 149.

18 Dorothy K. Kagehiro, 'Jurors Keenly Assess Experts' Credibility', B14.

19 Daniel W. Shuman, Anthony, Champagne and Elizabeth Whitaker, 'Assessing the Believability of Expert Witnesses: Science in the Jurybox', *Jurimetrics* 37, no. 1 (1996) 23.

20 Stanley L. Brodsky and others, 'Credibility in the Courtroom: How Likeable Should an Expert Witness Be?', 525.

21 Robert J. Cramer, Stanley L. Brodsky, and Jamie DeCoster, 'Expert Witness Confidence and Juror Personality: Their Impact on Credibility and Persuasion in the Courtroom', *Journal of the American Academy of Psychiatry and the Law* 37, no. 1 (March 2009) 63.

22 Marcus T. Boccaccini and Stanley L. Brodsky, 'Believability of Expert and Law Witnesses', 384.

23 Charles I. Brooks, Michael A. Church, and Lance Fraser, 'Effects of Duration of Eye Contact on Judgments of Personality Characteristics', *Journal of Social Psychology* 126, no. 1 (February 1986) 71.

24 McKimmie, Masser, and Bongiorno, 'Looking Shifty But Telling the Truth', 297.

For instance, eye contact appears to have greater importance for male expert witnesses.[25] This finding is potentially due to different gendered expectations for behaviour, and consistent with research findings indicating that the most effective style of language for an expert depends at least in part on the expert's gender.[26] Communication style more generally has been shown to affect perceived credibility. For example, experts who use powerful speech, deliver their evidence in a narrative format, and avoid hyper-correct or overly formal speech are rated as more credible.[27]

The conclusions drawn from interviews with jurors in a series of international studies are consistent with the experimental research findings on perceptions of expert credibility. Interviews with jurors in New Zealand indicated that witness credibility was higher when the witness had relevant professional experience, appeared unbiased, gave evidence in a clear manner, was confident, and made eye contact. Academic qualifications were noted as important.[28] Other interviews with American jurors suggested that jurors did not uncritically accept expert evidence but instead considered both the content of the evidence as well as features of the experts themselves when assessing credibility. Experts rated as most credible might be called 'sound teachers' with 'acceptable motives'. Having strong credentials contributed to perceived credibility. Consistent with the findings from interviews conducted with New Zealand jurors, an expert's communication style was important, and clear, unbiased communication enhanced credibility ratings. Jurors further indicated their concerned about experts who were repeat players in court and frequently gave evidence, indicating that they were sensitive to repeat player effects and hired guns.[29] The latter point was confirmed by other research.[30] **8.13**

(3) Measuring credibility

Increasingly, research on expert witness credibility makes use of a measure called the Witness Credibility Scale.[31] This 20-item measure assesses four dimensions of expert credibility: knowledge, likeability, trustworthiness, and confidence. The knowledge dimension focuses on aspects of the expert: whether the expert is logical, informed, wise, educated, and scientific. The likeability dimension assesses the positivity of the impression of the expert as kind, friendly, pleasant, respectful, and well-mannered. The trustworthiness subscale measures whether the expert's evidence can be relied upon by asking whether the expert is truthful, trustworthy, honest, and dependable. The final dimension, confidence, asks about the presentation style of the evidence: whether the expert was self-assured, well-spoken, confident, poised, and relaxed. In other words, two dimensions focus on the demeanour of the messenger (likeability and confidence), and two focus on the plausibility or reliability of the content or message of the expert (knowledge and trustworthiness). Given the range of factors assessed by this measure and their alignment with the existing **8.14**

[25] Tess M. S. Neal and Stanley L. Brodsky, 'Expert Witness Credibility as a Function of Eye Contact Behavior and Gender', *Criminal Justice and Behavior* 35, no. 2 (2008) 1515.

[26] Blake M. McKimmie and others, 'It's Not What She Says, It's How She Says It: The Influence of Language Complexity and Cognitive Load on the Persuasiveness of Expert Testimony', *Psychiatry, Psychology and Law* 20, no. 4 (2013) 578.

[27] William M. O'Barr, *Linguistic Evidence: Language, Power, and Strategy in the Courtroom* (New York: Pergamon, 1982).

[28] Suzanne Blackwell and Fred Seymour, 'Expert Evidence and Jurors' Views', *Psychiatry, Psychology, and Law* 22, no. 5 (2015) 673.

[29] Sanja Kutnjak Ivković and Valerie P. Hans, 'Jurors' Evaluations of Expert Testimony: Judging the Messenger and the Message', *Law and Social Inquiry* 28, no. 2 (2003) 441.

[30] Marcus T. Boccaccini and Stanley L. Brodsky, 'Believability of Expert and Law Witnesses', 384.

[31] Stanley Brodsky, Michael P. Griffin, and Robert J. Cramer, 'The Witness Credibility Scale: An Outcome Measure for Expert Witness Research', *Behavioral Sciences and the Law* 28, no. 6 (2010) 892.

research about perceptions of expert credibility, it is a useful tool to examine credibility assessments in relation to expert witnesses.

8.15 One unresolved issue in the extant research is a lack of clarity as to whether the credibility of a witness is a function of shared social beliefs about different types of witnesses—that is, whether certain witnesses are inherently more credible—or whether perceptions of credibility are due to idiosyncratic beliefs held by individual jurors about experts and their attributes. This distinction is important, because it has implications for whether the jury deliberations will either counteract or accentuate the influence of beliefs about extra-legal factors, such as expert gender. Past research suggested that socially shared beliefs tended to become the focus of group discussion,[32] and that the effect of shared beliefs is often accentuated or magnified in the course of jury deliberations.[33] The proposed corrective effect of jury deliberation would only emerge if jurors' credibility assessments were relatively idiosyncratic in nature, and not socially shared.

8.16 This project uniquely allowed the comparison of the views of different types of perceivers, both experienced and novice, to address the question of expert witness credibility. The project incorporated multiple ratings of each expert to allow the variability in ratings for each expert to be analysed. In a few instances, experts who happened to testify in one project trial were called to give evidence in a second project trial. In these instances, we were able to compare the ratings of jurors, judges, and legal advocates of the same expert in separate trial contexts. Fortuitously, these two features of our study permitted us to test whether perceptions of witness credibility were socially shared or idiosyncratic.

8.17 While it is true that the analysis in this chapter is focussed on factors extraneous to the content of the evidence, this does not imply that jurors and legal professionals are not alert to the quality and content of the experts' evidence. This focus was pragmatic because it was difficult to derive an objective measure of evidence quality. We used jurors' reliance on non-content-related factors to estimate the extent to which perceived credibility was based on the quality of the evidence or other factors; the more that jurors relied on other factors, the less they were assessing credibility on the basis of the content of the expert evidence.

8.18 In this chapter we consider not only the factors that jurors and legal professionals said they used to evaluate expert evidence, but also objective factors associated with experts and jurors that may be correlated with ratings of expert credibility. The reason for considering both sets of factors is that while jurors may be able to report coherently on how they arrived at an evaluation, they might not be fully aware of all of the factors that contributed to that evaluation. The reported factors may be post hoc justifications for an evaluation made on other grounds. One of the reasons people use peripheral route processing is because it is an efficient way to make use of limited cognitive resources. Evaluations may be derived in an automatic manner outside of conscious awareness. For this reason, it is important to consider both sets of factors in examining the way that expert credibility is assessed by jurors, as this analysis may uncover factors that are not explicitly mentioned in interviews or surveys. We start with a case study examining the views of jurors and legal professionals about the credibility of opposing experts who testified in trial 22.

---

[32] Li Lu, Y. Connie Yuan, and Poppy Lauretta McLeod, 'Twenty-Five Years of Hidden Profiles in Group Decision Making: A Meta-Analysis', *Personality and Social Psychology Review* 16, no. 1 (February 2012) 54.

[33] Martin F. Kaplan, 'Discussion Polarization Effects in a Modified Jury Decision Paradigm: Informational Influences', *Sociometry* 40, no. 3 (1977) 262; Daniel J. Isenberg, 'Group Polarization: A Critical Review and Meta-Analysis', *Journal of Personality and Social Psychology* 50, no. 6 (1986) 1141.

B. Case Study: Assessments of Opposing DNA Profiling Expert Evidence

To compare the credibility-related comments of various participants in a single trial, a case study of trial 22 was conducted. The defendant in this trial was charged with historical sexual assault, alleged to have occurred many years before it was reported to the police. The case proceeded when a positive DNA match of a crime scene sample was made to the defendant. Central to the case was the DNA profiling expert evidence which corroborated a range of circumstantial evidence connecting the defendant to the crime. The defence theory was that the positive match was the result of a contaminated DNA sample and did not support an inference of guilt on the part of the defendant. The judge, prosecutor, two defence barristers, and both experts were interviewed for the project. Eight juror surveys were completed and three of those jurors expanded upon their responses in interviews. In this case study, we draw on responses to questions about their impressions of the adversarial forensic science experts, and how they resolved the battle of the experts. **8.19**

The jurors in trial 22 were asked what thoughts came to mind while listening to the testimony of each expert. Five of the eight jurors who completed the survey provided written comments about the respective experts' performance (see Table 8.1). **8.20**

The jurors described the prosecution expert as having an honest and 'non-threatening' demeanour. One suggested that he could have been more forceful. This view was consistent with that of the judge, who rated the prosecution expert as too non-committal. The less engaging performance of the prosecution expert was described by juror B as making their job harder and slower: 'We liked the fact that he was just quiet and methodical, but the defence witness did give us, or to use an analogy, that was a bit of an 'ah-ha' moment for us all. And that if the prosecution could have done that, we would've had the 'ah-ha' a day or two earlier.' **8.21**

The jurors were alert to the charismatic performance of the defence expert. One juror astutely observed: 'He was a bit like a great actor, working with really bad lines.' However, the integrity **8.22**

Table 8.1 Jurors' perceptions of opposing expert witnesses in trial 22.

Juror	Prosecution expert	Defence expert
B	'Very honest, never felt he was in any way biased.' 'Outstanding in his field.'	'A little too self-assured, a bit of a "show-pony".' 'Felt a bit like he was putting up a 'smoke-screen' to sow doubt, but failed to do so.'
D	—	'Understood his point. But I felt he was trying to find fault everywhere (striking it blind).' 'At one point his own arguments seemed suspicious.'
G	'He was very mild mannered but could have been more forceful in his pronouncements of his findings.'	'Thought that as he was called by the defence he would act on their behalf to skew results or place doubt on results.'
J	'He had a manner which was non-threatening and he was not at all arrogant, which can be an occupational hazard for some experts.'	'He was arrogant. This was problematic when it became clear he only testifies for the defence—that weakened his credibility.' 'Ultimately, his testimony did not undermine the jury's view about the integrity of the prosecution expert's data.'
K	—	'Bias—represented mostly defendants, not Crown.'

of the prosecution expert impressed the jurors. Juror B explained 'He wasn't nearly as charismatic a performer as the defence expert, but he plodded along methodically and carefully, and left me very impressed.'

8.23 The jurors acknowledged that the defence expert was a very experienced court performer. However, his arrogance contributed to the jurors' perception of bias in this expert. Juror B expanded on this, during his interview:

> I had an impression that, let's say [the defence expert] had a stake in the outcome, in terms of this is a blow to his ego if this doesn't go his way, whereas with the prosecution witness, we never felt that. He was quite dispassionate about the whole thing, and I think it added to his professionalism. It just felt like he was giving us hard facts.

8.24 The same juror respected the expert's qualifications, but, along with misgivings about the defence expert's motivation, the juror was underwhelmed by the expert's capacity to provide a sufficiently persuasive argument:

> I think the defence expert's role, I guess from the defence point of view, was to raise reasonable doubt in our minds, and we just don't think he did it. We think he tried really hard, and we think he's very expert and very qualified, which was kind of more compelling for us in the end, because we thought, if this guy's as good as he seemed to be, but for us, he was still unable to refute the evidence that the prosecution expert brought to us. So despite clever questioning by the defence, and despite being very, very highly qualified, we felt that if this is his best shot, it's actually not that compelling.

8.25 Juror J agreed with this sophisticated observation:

> It was ironic that it was the defence expert witness who helped us to understand the science better. But we ultimately chose to believe in the integrity of [the prosecution expert's] data, for reasons that he had made clear. [The defence expert] could not rule out the possibility that [the prosecution expert's] results were accurate. The defence was not able to convince the jury that contamination was a reasonable possibility, given all the other circumstantial evidence.

8.26 Consideration of the viewpoints of the different participants in this trial revealed similarities between the views of the jurors and those of the lawyers and the judge. Moreover, the jurors demonstrated a nuanced understanding of the role of the defence expert within an adversarial system. Whilst they identified arrogance in the defence expert, this did not prevent them from appreciating the value of his evidence and the assistance that it offered them.

8.27 Juror B explained his thought processes in assessing the defence expert's evidence:

> I actually had to work pretty hard to put my feelings aside of it all, in order to concentrate on what he was saying, because he came across as a little too cocky. Gee, I'm trying to be careful with what I say here, but as a little too... we'll leave it at 'cocky', hey? So by the time he had finished, we just felt that it had just been a big smoke screen.

8.28 This description provided insight into how this juror imposed a structure on his decision-making that distinguished the message from the messenger. Although he disliked this expert's performance and communication style, he consciously attempted to put his reactions to those aspects aside, in order to concentrate on the content of the expert's evidence rather than its delivery—clear indications of cognitively effortful central processing. Comments by juror J suggested that his response to the expert evidence was similar. In all, credibility-related comments from participants in trial 22 revealed that the attitude and demeanour of the expert were factors that participants attended to in determining the credibility of the experts.

The jurors surveyed and interviewed in trial 22 did not perceive the case as a 'battle between the experts'. The jurors accepted that both experts were well-qualified and well-credentialed but did not describe their evidence as 'neutralizing' each other's persuasive influence. The jurors reported that they grappled with the disputed content and did not resort to their general impressions of the experts' character and veracity. **8.29**

Rather, the jurors heard the prosecution expert first and reported that they accepted his evidence as honest and trustworthy. The defence expert evidence was not perceived by the jurors as an alternative to accept or reject. The defence expert evidence was used to test the prosecution evidence that they had already deemed to be reliable. The jurors acknowledged that the adversarial process of having the defence expert critique the prosecution expert's evidence assisted them greatly in understanding the evidence of the prosecution expert. This finding suggested that the expert who gives evidence first might have an advantage, in that the jurors used the second or subsequent experts merely to critique the first expert. **8.30**

Whilst the non-committal demeanour of the prosecution expert and the overly committed demeanour of the defence expert did not please some of the jurors, the descriptions of their assessments of their evidence suggested that the jurors actively tried to put their subjective reactions to the personalities of these witnesses to one side, and engaged with the contents of their evidence. In the next section, we explored in more detail how viable this is for finders of fact. **8.31**

C. Dimensions and Indicators of Expert Credibility

When assessing the credibility of expert witnesses, it was the demeanour of the expert that the participants often identified in their responses to interview questions as the basis for their evaluations. In eleven of the 22 trials where the participants viewed the expert evidence as problematic in terms of credibility, the demeanour and language used by the expert was used to explain the perceived problems. The demeanour and language used by novice experts were the factors that left jurors with the impression that the expert lacked conviction and was uncertain about the opinion expressed in court, leading them to discount the strength of the evidence provided. Experts can undermine the credibility of their evidence by an over-confident or under-confident demeanour. **8.32**

Overall, six factors were repeatedly mentioned by the participants when discussing an expert's credibility, namely **8.33**

(a) an arrogant demeanour,
(b) defensiveness,
(c) use of emotive language,
(d) evasiveness,
(e) extent of experience, and
(f) the manner of delivery of the evidence.

Examples of each are discussed in the next section.

(1) Experts with an arrogant demeanour

Of the seven highly experienced experts who were identified as susceptible to the repeat player effect, six were perceived by the participants as having an arrogant demeanour. The most extreme example, where the expert's demeanour notably undermined his credibility, was the defence expert in trial 1, a murder trial. The judge described this expert's demeanour **8.34** as 'bombastic'; the prosecutor described him as 'histrionic'. The three jurors who were interviewed after the trial were initially impressed by the qualifications of this highly experienced expert. At the outset, they were sympathetic to the defence case, but after observing his courtroom presentation, the expert had convinced them that 'he had an agenda to push' and 'he was on an ego trip'. Juror A explained the impact of this expert's egotistical demeanour on his consideration of the evidence:

> I was probably on his side... and he was saying these things that were convincing to me, but as he kept on going... he was not wavering at all. He was trying to say there was no other possible explanation at all. He sort of started to lose me after about an hour or so of listening to him. So I think: hang on, you've got to be wired up a bit on both sides. You can't be that definitive about something.

Ultimately, the jury in this trial returned a guilty verdict.

(2) Experts with a defensive attitude

8.35 When experts were intransigent in their opinions and were unable to listen and respond thoughtfully to contrary views, this diminished jurors' trust in the expert's opinion. Juror A from trial 1 explained: 'he didn't waver on his line, but he gave the impression to me that "How can you doubt what I'm saying is wrong?—Because I'm saying it, it must be true"'. This has been described by judges as an 'oracular pronouncement' or an *ipse dixit* by an expert.[34]

8.36 Similarly, the attitude of the prosecution expert in trial 50 was described as intransigent because he refused to engage with the alternative viewpoint. This expert's defence was to use humour to obfuscate his unwillingness to engage with any issues that controverted his opinion. The inappropriate use of humour in this manslaughter trial was noted by the judge, defence counsel, and a juror during interview. The defence lawyer explained:

> His response, when I put [a possible alternative scenario]... and he went 'oh never heard of it, that's bizarre. You know, if such a thing happened I'd get all my colleagues and we'd write a paper.' I was really quite horrified at that because it was not farfetched or fanciful what I was putting. I was putting something that had clearly emerged on the evidence and it had emerged on the evidence of more than one witness, so I think there were three witnesses who said that, plus it was supported by the type of injuries he had across the left side of his head. When someone is, you know, a medical practitioner and therefore trained in science, and a scientist, I expect them to behave like a scientist.

8.37 When asked how well the prosecution expert in trial 21 performed under cross-examination, juror L said 'I think there were times when—I don't think he became flustered; I think he became almost annoyed with the sorts of questions that he was being asked.' The defence expert and judge shared the same opinion of this expert: 'well qualified but very defensive and a bit frazzled and reluctant to accept criticism, but defensive is probably the best adjective... He wasn't an appealing personality.' The judge explained the problem she encountered with the intransigence of the prosecution expert in that trial:

> I thought he was a quite difficult witness in the sense that like a lot of expert witnesses, they become quite resentful if they get the impression that their opinion or their expertise is

[34] See e.g. in *Makita (Australia) Pty Ltd v Sprowles* [2001] NSWCA 305, (2001) 52 NSWLR 705 [59], [86], where Heydon JA applied the view of Lord President Cooper in *Davie v Magistrates of Edinburgh* [1953] SC 34, 39–40, that the 'bare *ipse dixit*' or 'oracular pronouncement' of an expert witness can carry little weight, and he observed (at [59]) that if an expert's report is to be 'useful', it is necessary for it to comply with 'a prime duty of experts in giving opinion evidence: to furnish the trier of fact with criteria enabling evaluation of the validity of the expert's conclusions'.

> being in any way challenged. He did seem to have that air about him that 'I am an expert, and therefore you must accept what I say' which makes his direction to the jury all the more important. They need to understand that experts are witnesses like every other witness and just because they're qualified in a particular area doesn't mean the jury must accept what they say.

(3) Use of emotive language

Emotive language used by the expert was identified by the participants as inappropriate (perhaps as inconsistent with expectations of professional detachment) and consequently undermining the strength of the expert evidence. The judge in trial 22 gave a specific example of the unprofessional language used by a forensically experienced (repeat player) expert to describe the samples used for the DNA testing: 'I thought he sort of lacked sensitivity. I thought his use of terminology such as "grubby little stains", when you're talking about a really awful sexual assault of a child, was insensitive.' **8.38**

In trial 50, both counsel and one juror criticized the prosecution expert for his use of inflated language when describing the defence's alternative scenario. Even the prosecutor regretted the inappropriate language of this expert: **8.39**

> My only criticism perhaps is in the language he used when finally rejecting the defence's proposition . . . People have different personalities, and he revealed some of his personality. It's not a problem. We explained it in our closing address, that if something absurd is suggested to someone who's an expert, they're entitled to say that. He did use that word, though, which is perhaps a more emotive term than I would've liked in an expert. But it depends on juries; jurors are people, human beings. But I have this suspicion that juries expect experts to be a bit less emotional.

The barrister's suspicions were correct. One juror commented that this expert made fun of the opposing barrister, and described the expert as: 'very confident in what he said, but to me, that confidence became a negative'. **8.40**

(4) Evasive responses

Experts who avoided answering the questions posed in cross-examination, and used this as an opportunity to say what they wanted to impart, rather than respond to what the barrister asked them to address, were not seen as helpful by the jurors: 'When the question wasn't going to go towards what he wanted to say, he just tended to avoid it. That was the major thing, and that's one of the reasons why I ended up going the other way . . . I found him to be a little bit evasive' (juror C, trial 1). **8.41**

The impact of this evasive behaviour was further explained by another juror in that trial: **8.42**

> I felt that he wouldn't give a straight answer and, it was mentioned in court, that he answered a question with a question . . . I felt in the end, he was all over the shop . . . He was a little bit of a smart ass . . . Some of us discussed that he didn't help the defence at all. He did not help, and if that's all they had, 'phoof' . . . . One thing that I would like to say to someone like him was 'If you're talking to lay people and you are addressing us, as far as I'm concerned, we're the ones that are going to make this damned decision'. So if I was them, and they've got to direct it at us, I would make it as simple and as easy to understand, and as convincing, as possible. Instead, he confused the hell out of us, which in hindsight, might have hurt big time (juror B, trial 1).

(5) Extent of courtroom experience

Seven novice experts were identified to lack an effective presence in court and to deliver uncomfortable courtroom performances. Their lack of confidence manifested in nervousness and defensiveness, in all probability a product of their discomfort and lack of familiarity with the curial **8.43** environment. Three of the novices were described as nervous. For example, the jurors in trial 49 found the novice prosecution expert to be nervous and lacking in confidence. The lawyers agreed that this expert was '*nervous*' and '*fidgety*', '*hesitated a lot*', and was '*a little bit defensive*'.

8.44 Four of the novice experts exhibited defensive behaviour under cross-examination. Some of the opposing counsel described these novice experts as biased due to such behaviour. However, the judge and other lawyers regarded this defensive behaviour as a normal reaction to the unfamiliar and confronting nature of cross-examination. There was no evidence that the jurors perceived these experts as biased. For example, in trial 47, the defence counsel thought the expert 'came across, I thought, as biased... and was prepared to give evidence about areas where he later said he wasn't an expert.... I think it got to the point where the jury couldn't trust him.' A response that can occur when an expert is stressed or anxious is a retreat into dogmatism—usually consistent with the opinions expressed in the report commissioned by the party calling the expert. In the one juror response obtained for this trial, the juror contradicted the defence lawyer's perception of the expert's performance:

> He gave very articulate answers, presented as 'an expert', and deflected argument well under what seemed extreme pressure.... [He] appeared to me to be responding/coping well despite constant misdirection and twisting of the defence's questions.

8.45 The expert admitted to getting 'tongue-tied' during cross-examination; he became very frustrated when he commented on a journal article that was presented to him but was later admonished for talking about the article, as the topic was outside of his area of expertise. He felt that the article should not have been put to him if it was inappropriate for him to comment on it. The prosecutor perceived the expert as:

> Not experienced in giving evidence and I think he got hung up on the idea that this was an attack on him... in [his] own field. Doctors come in here, and they hate giving evidence, unless that's their natural thing, because they're well respected in their field. They come into someone else's field—the court, which is run by lawyers—and they have to play by someone else's rules, and they are attacked in a way that would not be permissible in general life.... He gets stroppy about that, and is distracted, and therefore doesn't make as good an impression as he should. He's very competent. He's clear. If you ask him a question, he can explain it. But then, when he's put under pressure in that cross-examination, he wasn't coming across as clearly.

(6) Manner of delivery of the expert evidence

8.46 Participants observed that certain characteristics of an expert's evidence contributed to the credibility of their evidence. For example, in trial 16, a DNA profiling expert presented his evidence by reading it from his written report at a very rapid pace:

> The DNA evidence... I found that very difficult to follow. The witness—we'd had him on a voir dire just before the jury was empanelled— and I found it pretty hard to follow the technical nature of it then. And then, when he presented it to the jury, quite a bit of it was—he was reading it, and reading it fairly fast, and I had to tell him to slow down,... I said 'Hold on, we're all trying to absorb this', and then the prosecutor said 'Look, I'm having trouble understanding what you're saying, I don't quite understand this'. And I was having trouble—and I know a little bit about DNA, I've had cases before with it—so I thought 'Well if I'm having those problems, what about the jury?' (judge, trial 16).

8.47 Thus, not only was it the method of presentation, reading from the written report which was not available to the jury, that was perceived as ineffective communication, but also the speed of the presentation of evidence, and the technical nature of the language used (the latter was identified as a potential barrier to comprehension in chapter 5).

D. Context of Jurors' Ratings of Experts

To provide a context in which to interpret the witness credibility ratings presented next in this chapter, we first examined how jurors evaluated experts relative to other participants in the trial, including other lay witnesses. This provided a picture of how easy or difficult it was for jurors to evaluate an expert's testimony and also how much they personally relied on that evidence in reaching a verdict. The dual-process models of persuasion introduced in chapter 5 and at the start of this chapter predict that the more difficult it is for jurors to understand an expert's evidence, the more likely it is that factors other than the content of that expert's testimony will contribute to the evaluation of the expert's credibility. Next we report findings derived from a comparison of experts for the prosecution and defence in terms of their relative influence on the jury members in the project trials. **8.48**

Jurors rated how difficult it was to understand the judge, expert witnesses, and lawyers in the trial, using a five-point scale (1 = *not at all*; 5 = *very difficult*). A one-way repeated measures analysis of variance yielded significant differences in the perceived difficulty of understanding across those target speakers.[35] Surprisingly, it was not the expert witnesses who were rated as most difficult to understand. As shown in Table 8.2, lay witnesses called by the prosecution were rated as the most difficult to understand, along with the lay witnesses called by the defence, and the defence experts. The prosecution experts were the next most difficult group of speakers to understand in court. The prosecutors were rated as easier to understand than the prosecution experts, and the group of speakers rated as most easy to understand was the judges. **8.49**

A series of one-sample t tests comparing ratings of the mean difficulty of understanding against the scale mid-point (3) indicated that all average difficulty ratings fell below the mean, $p < .001$, which suggested that jurors did not perceive any of the groups of speakers as particularly difficult to understand overall. **8.50**

One possible explanation for the observed differences in the perceived difficulty ratings is the role that each of these legal speakers plays in court. The prosecutor must prove a case by presenting clear evidence of the culpability of the accused. The judge has the role of providing clear instructions as to the law and trial procedures. The role of defence counsel is not to provide clear evidence—for example, in a typical case where the prosecution bears the **8.51**

Table 8.2 Perceived difficulty in understanding speakers in court.

Speaker group	Mean	Standard deviation
Prosecution witnesses	2.05_a	1.07
Defence witnesses	2.04_{ab}	1.09
Defence counsel	2.01_{ab}	1.13
Defence expert	1.89_{ab}	1.03
Prosecution expert	1.86_b	1.04
Prosecutor	1.60_c	0.86
Judge	1.44_d	0.79

Note: Means with different subscripts are significantly different, $p < 0.05$.

[35] $F(6, 972) = 13.79$, $\eta_p 2 = 0.08$.

Table 8.3 Perceived influence of courtroom speakers on jury verdict.

Speaker group	Mean	Standard deviation
Prosecution expert	3.85_a	1.20
Judge	3.84_a	1.28
Prosecutor	3.81_a	1.02
Prosecution witnesses	3.74_a	1.06
Defence counsel	3.25_b	1.18
Defence expert	3.11_b	1.25
Defence witnesses	3.06_b	1.30

Note: Means with different subscripts are significantly different, $p < .05$.

onus of proving the case beyond reasonable doubt, a strategic decision by defence counsel and the defence expert may be to introduce complexity in an effort to 'muddy the waters' or obfuscate and thereby to create elements of doubt about the prosecution case. Perhaps the fact that lay eyewitnesses, whether called by the prosecution or the defence, were rated as the most difficult to understand was because these witnesses have had little prior experience communicating with a jury.

8.52 The surveyed jurors reported the perceived level of influence of all trial protagonists on their decisions. There were significant differences, although relatively modest, in how influential each of the groups of speakers in court were perceived to be.[36] As displayed in Table 8.3, the prosecution expert, judge, prosecutor, and prosecution witnesses were the most influential speakers. These were followed by the defence counsel, and defence expert. The lay witnesses called by the defence were the least influential.

8.53 Jurors reported their understanding of how they were meant to make use of the expert evidence as set out in the judges' instructions. In a typical jury trial, just before the first expert gives evidence, the presiding judge will instruct the jury that they are free to reject any or all of the expert's evidence. Jurors rated the extent to which they were free to reject the evidence of the expert witness (1 = *not at all*; 5 = *very much*). The average score on this measure was 3.60, which was significantly higher than the mid-point of the scale,[37] suggesting that jurors generally understood this direction. The median was 4 on the five-point scale; thus about half of the jurors reported that they were completely free to reject the expert evidence.

E. Witness Credibility Scale Ratings

8.54 To compare what jurors and legal professionals said they relied on when evaluating the credibility of expert witnesses with the factors actually related to witness credibility, we asked study participants to complete the Witness Credibility Scale described in section A of this chapter (paragraph 8.14).[38] The following results focus primarily on the overall global average scores on the scale. Higher scores reflect greater perceived credibility.

8.55 To compare how different groups of study participants perceived the expert witnesses in terms of the witness credibility scale, we grouped jurors' ratings and legal professionals'

36 $F(6, 834) = 20.95, p < .001, \eta_p^2 = .13$.
37 $t(284) = 8.46, p < .001$.
38 Brodsky, Griffin, and Cramer, 'The Witness Credibility Scale', 892.

Table 8.4 Jurors' and legal professionals' overall ratings of expert witnesses.

Type of expert witness	Jurors' ratings	Legal professionals' ratings	*N*
Forensic scientists	8.57 (0.72)	7.98 (1.10)	25
Medical doctors	8.48 (0.48)	8.36 (0.82)	8
Psychiatrists/psychologists	8.51 (1.37)	7.83 (0.96)	9
Overall mean	8.54 (0.84)	8.02 (1.02)	42

Note: Mean ratings on the Witness Credibility Scale. Standard deviations are in parentheses.

(lawyers' and judges') ratings for each expert. To ensure there were sufficient ratings from each group, we analysed ratings of the first prosecution expert who gave evidence in all cases, as every trial in this study involved at least one prosecution expert. This enabled correlations of features of the expert, the expert's testimony, and the study participant groups with ratings on the witness credibility scale, and an assessment of the degree of consensus amongst groups of study participants.

(1) Is witness credibility associated with experts or perceivers?

As a preliminary matter, we considered whether views as to an expert's credibility were attributable to some feature of the expert or the expert's testimony or whether perceptions of credibility were idiosyncratic and depended on how each individual perceiver viewed that expert. If the latter were the case, considerable variation in ratings of the same expert on the witness credibility scale would be evident, derived from each perceiver's personal beliefs and conclusions about expert credibility. If it were the former, then perceivers' ratings should generally reflect agreement. **8.56**

To test these two possibilities, we examined differences between the overall witness credibility ratings by jurors and legal professionals of each of the three main types of experts included in the project (apart from accountants, as there were insufficient ratings to include this expert type), and the extent of variation in these ratings. The only significant effect was for participant group, showing that on average, jurors rated experts as more credible than did legal professionals (see Table 8.4).[39] **8.57**

We further examined whether there was more or less consensus in the ratings of expert credibility by comparing the extent of rating variation (standard deviation) for jurors with that for legal professionals.[40] Overall, there was a reasonable level of agreement in jurors' scores; more so than for legal professionals.[41] These analyses suggested that ratings of credibility were associated with the experts and with the experts' evidence, and were not idiosyncratic predilections of the jurors and legal professionals. In the next section this possibility is examined in more depth. **8.58**

[39] Main effect of rater type, $F(1, 39) = 4.45$, $p < .05$, $\eta^2 = .10$.

[40] The standard deviation of a measure indicating the extent to which scores on that measure vary around the mean or average score. A large standard deviation suggests that there is more variability in scores and therefore less agreement amongst raters. A repeated measures t test indicated that there was more agreement in credibility ratings amongst jurors (*M*SD = 0.99, SDSD = 0.54) than legal professionals (*M*SD = 1.38, SDSD = 0.78), $t(38) = -2.48$, $p = .018$. Given that the witness credibility scale is a ten-point scale, a standard deviation of 0.99 for jurors' ratings indicated that approximately 68% of jurors' scores fell between 7.54 and 9.54 on the scale.

[41] This finding might partly reflect the greater number of observations from jurors, as standard deviations tend to become smaller with larger numbers of observations.

Table 8.5 Expert witness presentation style and perceived witness credibility.

Presentation style	Mean WCS score (*SD*)	Correlation with WCS
Inconsistency	1.69 (.56)	–.47**
Clarity	4.06 (.55)***	.30*
Complexity	2.99 (.70)	.21
Confusing	1.95 (.56)***	–.20
Use of jargon	2.80 (.70)	–.08
Lengthy	2.47 (.84)***	–.24
Fast-paced	1.85 (.50)***	–.15

Note: $^{*}p < .05$, $^{**}p < .01$, $^{***}p < .001$. Means tested against scale midpoint (3). WCS = Witness Credibility Scale; *SD* = Standard deviation.

(2) Consistency and perceived credibility of expert evidence

8.59 Previously we reported the finding that study participants were influenced by the consistency of the experts' evidence when evaluating that evidence. We compared the perceived inconsistency of the experts' evidence with ratings on the witness credibility scale. The more that jurors thought an expert's evidence contained inconsistencies, the less credible they found the expert (see Table 8.5).[42]

(3) The influence of expert presentation style on perceived credibility

8.60 Next, we correlated other dimensions of the presentation style of the expert witness with ratings on the Witness Credibility Scale. As shown in Table 8.5, the more that jurors thought the experts' evidence was clear, the higher the experts' perceived witness credibility was. Thus, presentation clarity, as noted earlier in this chapter, was an important factor associated with perceptions of witness credibility. Consideration of the mean, or average, scores in these dimensions overall provided insight into whether jurors thought that the expert evidence was particularly poorly or well presented. Jurors' mean credibility scores were compared to the midpoint of the Witness Credibility Scale. Scores that were significantly higher or lower than the midpoint (as indicated in Table 8.5) suggested that a particular dimension characterized the nature of evidence given by experts in this project. The results revealed that expert evidence was viewed as being relatively clear, not very confusing, not too lengthy, and not too fast-paced. Contrary to many suppositions about jury responses to expert evidence, overall, jurors' evaluation of the presentation of the expert evidence was positive.

(4) Expert characteristics

8.61 In chapter 5, in considering whether jurors were alert to a variety of extra-legal factors that might influence their perceptions, we discussed experimental research findings which suggested that expert characteristics such as credentials, gender, and repeated appearances in court can affect whether the expert is perceived to be credible or not (in paragraphs 5.18 to 5.33). Experts who were unused to giving expert testimony were perceived more negatively, potentially because, amongst other things, they have not performed as well because of anxiety or lack of awareness of how they should conduct themselves in a curial environment. To examine whether characteristics associated with the experts have an impact on their perceived credibility, we compared the correlations of jurors' ratings and legal professionals' ratings, and the extent of agreement in those ratings, on various characteristics of the experts.

[42] $r = -0.47$, $p = .001$, $n = 47$.

Table 8.6 Expert witness characteristics and perceived credibility.

Expert characteristic	Jurors: correlation with WCS (and with WCS *SD*)	Legal professionals: correlation with WCS (and with WCS *SD*)
Gender (1 = male, 2 = female)	−.38* (.33*)	−.29 (.03)
Age	−.07 (.20)	.01 (.15)
Experience (years)	−.10 (.03)	−.01 (.29)
Frequency of appearances	−.23 (.41*)	.00 (-.12)
Number of reports per year	−.09 (.24)	−.10 (-.15)

Note: **p* < .05, ***p* < .01, ****p* < .001. WCS = Witness Credibility Scale; *SD* = Standard deviation.

As shown in Table 8.6, the sole expert characteristics that were significantly related to witness credibility were expert gender and the frequency of past expert appearances in court. Male experts were rated as more credible than female experts. In addition, the presence of a female expert was associated with greater variation in ratings on the witness credibility scale, reflecting less consensus about the credibility of female experts. A similar effect emerged for the frequency of appearances in court over the previous year—the more that the expert had appeared in court, the greater the disagreement in jurors' ratings of the credibility of that expert. **8.62**

Table 8.7 Expert witness gender and perceived witness credibility.

WCS subscale	Jurors: correlation with expert gender (1 = male, 2 = female)
Confident	−.09
Likeable	−.37*
Trustworthy	−.27
Knowledgeable	−.29

Note: **p* < .05, ***p* < .01, ****p* < .001. WCS = Witness Credibility Scale.

To examine the effect of witness gender in more detail, we correlated expert witness gender with each of the four subscales of the witness credibility scale: confidence, likeability, trustworthiness, and knowledgeability. As shown in Table 8.7, the gender of the expert witness was significantly correlated only with ratings of likeability, i.e., male experts were rated as more likeable. Thus, perceptions of the role of expert gender in determining expert credibility seemed to derive primarily from a more positive affective response to male than female experts, rather than any inference about the possible knowledge domains of male versus female experts. **8.63**

(5) Jurors' characteristics and their perceptions of expert credibility

Next, we examined whether features of the jurors themselves were associated with how credible they perceived the experts to be: in other words, whether perceptions of credibility are idiosyncratic, varying based on differences between jurors, or as a function of something to do with the expert themselves. Unlike the initial analyses presented at the start of this chapter, these correlations examined the finer grain of how specific juror attributes might relate to perceptions of credibility. Jurors' gender, age, use of English as a first language, time spent watching forensic-science-related television programmes, and education in science **8.64**

Table 8.8 Jurors' characteristics and witness credibility.

Juror characteristic	Correlation with WCS	Correlation with WCS *SD*
Gender	.28	–.15
Age	–.07	–.26
English as first language	.15	–.44**
Time spent watching CSI TV	.13	–.13
Education in science and maths	–.08	.22

Note: * $p < .05$, ** $p < .01$, *** $p < .001$. WCS = Witness Credibility Scale; *SD* = Standard deviation.

and mathematics were aggregated. For example, the gender score reflected the overall proportion of men and women in the jury, with higher scores reflecting the presence of more women in the jury.

8.65 As can be seen in Table 8.8, there were very few significant correlations, suggesting once again, and consistently with our initial analyses, that jurors' ratings of witness credibility did not appear to be idiosyncratic. The only significant effect was for level of agreement in ratings as a function of whether English was a first language for jurors. A greater proportion of jurors who had English as a first language on a jury was associated with less disagreement about the witness's credibility. This might suggest that differences in interpreting expert evidence—and evaluating the credibility of the expert—might be most apparent when jurors come from different language backgrounds.

(6) Jurors' expectations and perceived witness credibility

8.66 While jurors' characteristics might not be strongly related to whether they see an expert as credible or not, their beliefs about experts might be particularly important when evaluating expert credibility. As part of the juror survey, jurors were asked some preliminary questions designed to elicit their expectations about the expert evidence. In particular, they were asked about typical expected characteristics of expert witnesses from different professions, and which experts were seen as most trustworthy. One of the reasons why it was of interest to understand jurors' expectations about expert witnesses is because these expectations can influence how jurors perceive a specific witness who gives expert evidence. For example, previous research suggested that jurors might have expectations about an expert's gender, and when the expert who ultimately presents evidence in court does not match those expectations, the expert is perceived by jurors as less persuasive.[43] These expectations appear to be relied on more extensively when testimony is complex and difficult to understand.[44]

(a) Juror expectations as to the gender of expert witnesses

8.67 Jurors were asked to indicate what proportion of the experts in each of the four main fields of expertise they anticipated would be male and how many would be female. Overall, jurors expected more male than female experts.[45] However, this effect was qualified by the type of expertise. As can be seen in Table 8.9, jurors expected significantly more male

[43] Regina Schuller, Deborah Terry, and Blake McKimmie, 'The Impact of an Expert's Gender on Jurors' Decisions', *Law and Psychology Review* 25 (2001) 59.

[44] Regina A. Schuller, Deborah Terry, and Blake McKimmie, 'The Impact of Expert Testimony on Jurors' Decisions: Gender of the Expert and Testimony Complexity', *Journal of Applied Social Psychology* 35, no. 6 (June 2005) 1266.

[45] A 2 (expert gender) by 4 (expert type) repeated measures analysis of variance yielded a main effect of expert gender, $F(1, 729) = 124.44$, $p < .001$, $\eta_p^2 = .34$.

Table 8.9 Proportion of anticipated experts by type and gender per 100 criminal trials.

Type of expertise	Proportion of female experts	Proportion of male experts
Forensic science	43.06_a (13.87)	56.58_b (14.37)
Medicine	44.59_a (11.70)	55.50_b (12.13)
Psychiatry/psychology	49.59_a (12.35)	49.92_a (12.72)
Accounting	39.87_a (15.24)	58.56_b (16.27)

Note: Standard deviations from the mean in parentheses. Pairs of means with different subscripts are significantly different $p < .001$.

Table 8.10 Perceived trustworthiness of experts by type of expertise.

Type of expertise	Mean	Standard deviation
Forensic science	4.57_a	0.66
Medicine	4.29_b	0.81
Psychology/psychiatry	3.75_c	0.94
Accounting	3.59_d	1.02

Note: Means with different subscripts are significantly different $p < .01$.

experts than female experts in each field of expertise except for mental health professionals (psychiatrists and psychologists), where they anticipated an equal proportion of male and female experts.[46]

(b) Expectations as to the trustworthiness of expert evidence

Jurors were asked to rate how much they trusted each of the four types of experts (1 = *not at all*; 5 = *very much*). Jurors rated the evidence of forensic scientists as the most trustworthy, followed by that of medical doctors, then of psychiatrists/psychologists, with the evidence of accountants perceived as the least trustworthy of the four disciplines.[47] The perceived trustworthiness of the four different types of expert evidence are reported in Table 8.10. **8.68**

To examine the possible influence of jurors' expectations on the perceived credibility of the expert witnesses, we compared jurors' beliefs about the expected gender of experts and their trust in experts with their ratings of expert credibility. While there were no consistent effects as a function of the expected gender of the types of expert included in this study, we did find consistent effects for jurors' expectations about how much they would trust the different types of experts (see Table 8.11). The more that jurors expected to trust all of the different types of experts, except for psychiatrists and psychologists, the more that they rated the expert in their specific trial as credible. Similarly, the more that they expected to trust all of the types of experts, except medical experts, the more consensus there was in their credibility ratings. This finding clearly suggests that jurors relied on their pre-existing beliefs about types of experts in evaluating the credibility of any particular expert who gave evidence before them in court. **8.69**

46 A significant, although smaller, interaction emerged with expert type, $F(3, 729) = 33.41$, $p < .001$, $\eta_p^2 = .12$.

47 A one-way repeated measures analysis of variance yielded differences in how trustworthy each field of expertise was perceived to be, $F(3, 870) = 137.65$, $p < .001$, $\eta_p^2 = .32$.

Table 8.11 Jurors' expectations and perceived witness credibility.

Jurors' trust in types of expertise	Correlation with WCS	Correlation with WCS *SD*
Forensic experts	.52***	–.48**
Medical experts	.33*	–.13
Accountants	.37*	–.41**
Psychiatrists/psychologists	.04	–.42**

Note: * $p < .05$; ** $p < .01$, *** $p < .001$. WCS = Witness Credibility Scale.

F. Conclusions

8.70 The foregoing qualitative analysis comparing what jurors and legal professionals said contributed to their evaluation of expert credibility emphasized that the demeanour of experts could undermine their credibility. The quantitative analysis, however, emphasized the importance to credibility of consistency and clarity when giving expert evidence. Notably, several other factors that previous research had identified as important contributors to credibility, such as avoiding the use of jargon, speaking slowly, and avoiding complex explanations, did not emerge as significant correlates of credibility.

8.71 The language used by experts was highlighted in chapter 5 (paragraph 5.66) as a barrier to juror comprehension—more complex language was associated with lower levels of comprehension, but paradoxically, and of some concern, higher levels of perceived expertise. Clarity of evidence was positively associated with higher perceived witness credibility. The difference between these two findings is possibly due to the distinction between complexity and clarity. Evidence of a complex nature could be explained. It is noteworthy that perceptions of evidence complexity were unrelated to perceived credibility. Given these findings, an expert may improve the receptiveness of jurors to their evidence by focussing on clear explanations, even if their testimony is conceptually complex, rather than over-emphasizing simplification of the content of the testimony.

8.72 This strategy on the part of the expert would have the added benefit of potentially reducing differences in the interpretation of the evidence when the jury is comprised of jurors from diverse language backgrounds. As a related point, it would be a poor strategy to attempt to select jurors with a homogeneous language background (e.g., all English as first language) with the goal of increasing the perceived credibility of the expert. A variety of research studies suggest that diverse groups are potentially more effective decision-makers in terms of how they process and combine information, and work together as a group.[48]

8.73 Together, the foregoing analyses highlighted a range of factors that influenced perceptions of credibility of which the respondents were unaware, namely expert gender, language composition of the jury, and jurors' pre-existing beliefs about the trustworthiness of experts.

[48] Jasmine Rijnbout and Blake McKimmie, 'Deviance in Organizational Group Decision-Making: The Role of Information Processing, Confidence, and Elaboration', *Group Processes & Intergroup Relations* 15, no. 6 (2012) 813; Samuel Sommers, Lindsey Warp, and Corrine Mahoney, 'Cognitive Effects of Racial Diversity: White Individuals' Information Processing in Heterogeneous Groups', *Journal of Experimental Social Psychology* 44, no. 4 (2008) 1129; Stefan Schulz-Hardt and others, 'Biased Information Search in Group Decision Making', *Journal of Personality and Social Psychology* 78, no. 4 (2000) 655. Brian Mullen and others, 'Group Cohesiveness and Quality of Decision Making: An Integration of Tests of the Groupthink Hypothesis', *Small Group Research* 25, no. 2 (1994) 189; Rod Bond, 'Group Size and Conformity', *Group Processes and Intergroup Relations* 8, no. 4 (2005) 331.

Lawyers who have a choice in the expert they opt to use in a trial should be conscious of these influences. Overall, the average expectations about the trustworthiness of experts were relatively high. However, as was highlighted in chapter 2 in relation to the reliability of expert evidence, some of this trust may be misplaced, given the absence of any systematic screening in Australian courts of the reliability and validity of the proffered expert testimony.

As was suggested in chapter 2, further work is needed to assess the reliability and validity **8.74** of different types of expert evidence better, and to increase the plausibility and veracity of the content of expert evidence. One component of that research should examine ways to communicate to jurors the level of trustworthiness of the expert evidence. Moreover, in the absence of any pre-trial screening of the reliability and validity of the expert evidence admitted in court, perhaps jurors should be advised or directed that their duty includes an assessment of this aspect of the evidence, so they do not mistakenly presume that the judge has performed a gate-keeping function in this regard and accord undue weight to the evidence without engaging in a critical and evaluative process. A goal of future research should be to enable jurors to calibrate their evaluations of expert credibility in a more sophisticated way. Advice or instruction on this point should not simply take the form of yet another judicial instruction to the jury, as there are concerns about the extent to which jurors can absorb, understand, and follow advice on the quality of the evidence provided at the conclusion of the trial.[49]

The general absence of any effects as a function of variations in the perceptions of witness **8.75** credibility strongly suggested that jurors perceived the experts in a similar way, i.e., they agreed on how credible an expert was as a function of characteristics of the expert and of the evidence analysed in this chapter. Notwithstanding an absolute difference in how jurors and legal professionals rated credibility (the former were more positive than the latter), these findings indicated that credibility assessments were founded more on the basis of socially shared beliefs than on jurors' idiosyncratic evaluations and reactions to the expert witnesses. The implication of this finding is that jury deliberation is likely to exacerbate the effect of factors such as expert gender and clarity and consistency of evidence.

In interpreting the foregoing project findings, it is important to have regard to the fact that **8.76** the size of the correlations was modest at best, suggesting that the quality of the experts' evidence was still important in evaluating the credibility of the respective expert witnesses. At most, about one fifth of the variance in credibility ratings was accounted for by any one factor. This finding does not imply that the remaining four fifths of variation was attributable to the quality of the evidence (as this would imply that the factors that we assessed overlapped perfectly with each other). In this project, we did not specifically examine the simultaneous contribution of multiple factors to perceived witness credibility, but it is likely due to the observed shared variance between these factors that a substantial percentage of the variation in credibility ratings was due to the content of the specific evidence presented in court. Further experimental research is needed to distinguish the relative contribution of evidence quality and other factors to the evaluation of expert credibility.

Further, based on results from trials where jurors were exposed to competing expert evidence **8.77** (such as in trial 22 discussed above) there is reason to dispute the theory that jurors who encounter a 'battle of the experts' on complex matters such as DNA evidence resolve the battle by relying on their general impressions of the experts' character and veracity. The jury

---

[49] Blake M. McKimmie, Emma Antrobus, and Chantelle Baguley, 'Objective and Subjective Comprehension of Jury Instructions in Criminal Trials', *New Criminal Law Review: An International and Interdisciplinary Journal* 17, no. 2 (spring 2014) 163.

interviews conducted in this project revealed that jurors actively engaged with the subject matter of the expert evidence. Lengthy deliberation times of over a day, in the majority of the trials where there was competing expert evidence, and reliance upon the transcript during deliberations, supported the finding that the jurors were actively engaged with the content or message conveyed by the two competing experts.

8.78 The results of this project identified a new concern about the way in which jurors assess expert evidence based on the sequence of the presentation of the expert evidence. Some of the jurors explained that they either accepted or rejected the evidence of the first expert witness (in compliance with the standard judicial direction on this topic) after hearing that evidence. If the jurors accepted that evidence, then all expert evidence that followed was used by these jurors merely to test the first opinion. As a consequence, expert evidence that is not the first to be heard might suffer from its use as a tool for critique of the first opinion rather than an alternative opinion accorded equal footing with the first opinion. This phenomenon requires further evaluation and research.

9

CONCLUSION

The aim of the project reported in this volume was to gain a broader understanding of the use of expert evidence in the contemporary jury trial. By studying and comparing the views of jurors, judges, trial lawyers (both barristers and litigation solicitors), and the experts themselves, we sought to build on the experimental laboratory work in this area as well as the arguments and anecdotal views reported in the literature. **9.01**

This study included 55 criminal trials conducted before juries in three jurisdictions in Australia between 2011 and 2012. We canvassed views on a range of topics related to expert evidence, from admissibility and reliability to presentation, comprehension, and credibility. We specifically focussed on DNA evidence and medical and psychiatric/psychological evidence to explore the particular challenges posed by these types of evidence, as well as jurors' responses to them. **9.02**

In considering the views of the various participant groups, we were able not only to examine these individual issues, but also to look more broadly at system-level issues. Through this analysis, we identified a number of practical recommendations for practitioners in terms of the issues likely to impact (positively and negatively) on eliciting evidence from expert witnesses and ensuring that experts are held accountable for the views that they express in criminal trials before juries. We also highlighted a range of avenues for useful future research. **9.03**

A. Major Findings

(1) The role of jurors

We ask a great deal of jurors in criminal trials. Not only do we require them to give up time from their work and everyday lives, but we call upon them to make important decisions that they know will impact powerfully upon accused persons' liberty and reputations. To arrive at their verdicts they must listen to vast amounts of information, much of it often distressing, work with eleven other people whom they did not previously know, and come to grips with **9.04** areas of technical discourse that are unfamiliar to them. And they have to get their conclusions right. A juror in trial 44 of our project summed up the pressures tellingly:

> Serving on a jury was pretty full on. It was only a two-week trial, but I went to work the next day and felt like really, really spacey—like quite removed from everything. We have counsellors available at work so I went and talked to somebody that evening and she said what I was experiencing was like a post-traumatic sort of experience after immersing yourself in all the horrible details of the case, which was quite ghastly really, and when you're in it it's very intellectually stimulating and you're concentrating and you're in this little world of your own but then when it stops it's like...yeah, it takes you a few days to process.

9.05 The capacity of jurors to grapple effectively with complex and sometimes conflicting expert evidence is controversial and far from clear.[1] It depends upon a number of factors. In the United Kingdom in 1986, the Fraud Trials Committee Report, chaired by Lord Roskill, recommended that complex fraud trials be removed from juries, in part because of the complexity of the expert evidence involved[2] In Australia, Justice McLellan of the New South Wales Supreme Court observed that judges experience real difficulties in resolving disputes between experts, and commented:

> these difficulties will be greater for a jury of lay people. Many criminal trials involve medical issues or the sophisticated expertise of forensic scientists. Increasingly, the prosecution of white-collar and financial crimes involves accounting issues and an understanding of market transactions. The complexities can be significant, and the issues perplexing, even for experts in the relevant field.[3]

Justice Stuart Morris of the Victorian Supreme Court has advanced a similar hypothesis: '...jurors may not understand complex, conflicting expert evidence; or they may be misled by the myth that the expert is wholly independent from the party engaging them; or the very role of the jurors may be usurped by evidence which trespasses into their domain.'[4] Deputy Commissioner Nick Kaldas of the New South Wales Police contended that modern criminal trials are often too complex for juries to understand the evidence.[5] Academic commentators have contributed to the discussion.[6]

9.06 Roberts and Zuckerman have identified that 'the distinctive nature of the facts to which experts testify presents a fundamental choice in the reception of scientific evidence between juror education and juror deference.'[7] This involves either focussing upon the threshold decision of which expert evidence is permitted before jurors by a sophisticated enunciation of exclusionary rules of admissibility or enhancing the capacity of jurors by procedural reform to undertake their role and trusting them to do it adequately, or both.[8]

---

[1] See e.g. Neil Vidmar and Shari S. Diamond, 'Juries and Expert Evidence', *Brooklyn Law Review* 66, no. 4 (2001) 1121.

[2] Eustace W. L. Roskill, *Fraud Trials Committee Report* (London: HMSO, 1986).

[3] Peter McClellan, 'The Future Role of the Judge: Umpire, Manager, Mediator or Service Provider'. *New South Wales Judicial Scholarship*, no. 44 [2011]: <http://www.austlii.edu.au/au/journals/NSWJSchol/2011/44.html>.

[4] Stuart Morris, 'Getting Real about Expert Evidence' (lecture, National Environment Law Conference, Canberra, 13 July 2005), <http://www.austlii.edu.au/au/journals/VicJSchol/2005/14.pdf>.

[5] See Matthew Clayfield, 'Modern Trials Too Difficult for Juries', *The Australian*, 10 October 2008, <http://www.theaustralian.com.au/archive/news/modern-trials-too-difficult-for-juries/story-e6frg6o6-1111117712224>.

[6] See e.g. Mike Redmayne, 'Theorising Jury Reform', in *The Trial on Trial: Volume 2: Judgment and Calling to Account*, edited by Antony Duff and others (London: Bloomsbury Publishing, 2006).

[7] Paul Roberts and Adrian Zuckerman, *Criminal Evidence*, 2nd edn. (Oxford: Oxford University Press, 2010), p. 473.

[8] See Oriola Sallavaci, *The Impact of Scientific Evidence in the Criminal Trial: The Case of DNA Evidence* (New York: Routledge, 2014); see also Fiona Cownie, Anthony Bradney, and Mandy Burton, *English Legal System in Context* (Oxford: Oxford University Press, 2013).

Studies have documented jurors' difficulties in evaluating conflicting testimony by expert witnesses, with some suggesting under-utilization of such evidence[9] and others suggesting undue deference to it.[10] It may be that jurors are more persuaded by highly complex expert evidence and that when testimony is less complex, jurors are able to focus more upon the substance of evidence and less on extraneous factors such as expert credentials.[11] However, the findings of the current project suggest that jurors are generally aware of the potential challenges posed by expert testimony, and that extraneous extra-legal factors play at most a modest role in influencing jurors' evaluations of that testimony. Experts themselves appear to be aware of the problems posed by complex evidence and actively attempt to minimize the difficulties for jurors. This has outcomes in how they write their reports and the way in which they give oral evidence in court. Judges reported intervening when evidence was expressed in a manner that they thought impacted adversely on the capacity of jurors to understand and evaluate the evidence. Thus, the findings of this project indicated that most jurors were capable of deciding complex cases involving expert evidence as long as they received appropriate support from the court. **9.07**

We have some perspective, too, on how judge-alone criminal trials in the adversary system function by contrast with those with juries, as a result of the 'Diplock courts' in Northern Ireland.[12] It is fair to say that some commentators favour judges as uniquely placed to be deciders of fact: **9.08**

> Impartiality is a capacity of mind—a learned ability to recognize and compartmentalize the relevant from the irrelevant and to detach one's emotions from one's rational facilities. Only because we trust judges to be able to satisfy these obligations do we permit them to exercise power and oversight.[13]

Neil Vidmar outlined how legal training and the constraints placed on judges by precedents in previous cases contribute to making judges' decision-making potentially different from that of lay jurors.[14] Having noted some of the difficulties in studying judicial decision-making, he turned his attention to what the scientific research says about the decisions of judges compared to jurors, and, consistent with the conclusions of others, concluded that the view that judges are better placed than jurors to decide matters of fact in an impartial manner is contradicted by the systematic scientific research. **9.09**

Research has consistently demonstrated that both inexperienced and experienced decision-makers, including jurors and judges, are largely susceptible to the same judgemental biases **9.10**

---

[9] See e.g. David L. Faigman and A. J. Bagkioni Jr, 'Bayes' Theorem in the Trial Process: Instructing Jurors on the Value of Statistical Evidence', *Law and Human Behavior* 12, no. 1 (1988) 1.

[10] See e.g. Laurence H. Tribe, 'Trial by Mathematics: Precision and Ritual in the Legal Process', *Harvard Law Review* 84, no. 6 (1971) 1329.

[11] See Joel Cooper, Elizabeth A. Bennett, and Holly L. Sukel, 'Complex Scientific Testimony: How Do Jurors Make Decisions?', *Law & Human Behavior* 20, no. 4 (1996) 379; Daniel A. Krauss and Joel D. Lieberman, *Jury Psychology: Social Aspects of Trial Processes Psychology in the Courtroom*, vol. 1 (Dartmouth: Ashgate, 2012), p. 193.

[12] See John Jackson and Sean Doran, *Judge Without Jury: Diplock Trials in the Adversary System* (Oxford: Clarendon Press, 1995); Paul Roberts and Jill Hunter, eds., *Criminal Evidence and Human Rights: Reimagining Common Law Procedural Traditions* (London: Bloomsbury, 2012). See also Vicki Waye, 'Fact-Finding: Trial by Judge Alone in Serious Criminal Cases', *Melbourne University Law Review* 27, no. 2 (August 2003) 423.

[13] Robert F. Peckham, 'Judicial Response to the Cost of Litigation: Case Management, Two-Stage Discovery Planning and Alternative Dispute Resolution', *Rutgers Law Review* 37 (winter 1985) 253: p. 262.

[14] Neil Vidmar, 'The Psychology of Trial Judging', *Current Directions in Psychological Science* 20, no. 1 (2011) 58.

and heuristics,[15] which is perhaps unsurprising as these tend to be functionally adaptive and a fundamental component of human cognition.[16] For example, in one study both the judges and the community members (acting as jurors) were negatively influenced by inadmissible prejudicial information, and an instruction to disregard the prejudicial information had little effect on both judges and laypersons.[17] Findings of this nature are consistent with additional research demonstrating that judges were vulnerable to most of the cognitive biases that affect lay decision-makers when evaluating information in a legal context.[18] Jurors may be preferable fact-finders, however, because they are exposed to less inadmissible evidence and pre-trial information than are judges. Moreover, it is easier to remove an apparently biased juror from a case than a judge.

(2) Selecting experts and admitting expert evidence

(a) Expert characteristics

9.11 In terms of experts who are selected by the parties to criminal litigation our findings revealed that the domain of expert witnesses remains male-dominated; well over two thirds of the witnesses sampled in the current project were men. One possible reason for the disproportionate selection of male experts may be the gender composition of the professions included as experts, although we do not have data on the proportion of men and women in the professions of medicine, forensic science, psychiatry, and psychology to assess this possibility. A second reason, which the project findings did address, was the perception of male experts as more influential. Aside from community stereotypes and prejudices, there may be a number of reasons for this, including witness confidence, speaking styles, and customary eye contact, as well as other features related to demeanour,[19] all of which have the potential to impact upon perceptions of credibility, trustworthiness, and reliability.

9.12 The analysis of jury comprehension and evaluations of evidence in chapter 5 and jury perceptions of credibility in chapter 8 supported this notion. Although participants did not explicitly say that they found male experts more credible than female experts, the correlations between expert gender and scores on the Witness Credibility Scale showed that male experts were generally perceived to be more credible.

9.13 Before selecting experts based on gender with the goal of maximizing the credibility of an expert witness, however, it is worth considering research showing that the influence of expert gender on the persuasiveness of an expert witness is dependent on a range of other factors, as discussed in chapter 5, paragraphs 5.05 to 5.07 and 5.18 to 5.33. For example, when an

---

[15] Rocio Garcia-Retamero and Mandeep Dhami, 'On Avoiding Framing Effects in Experienced Decision Makers', *The Quarterly Journal of Experimental Psychology* 66, no. 4 (April 2013) 829; Chris Guthrie, Jeffrey Rachlinski, and Andrew J. Wistrich, 'Inside the Judicial Mind', *Cornell Law Review* 86, no. 4 (May 2001) 777; Jeffrey Rachlinski, 'Heuristics and Biases in the Courts: Ignorance or Adaptation?', *Oregon Law Review* 79, no. 1 (spring 2000) 61; Ian Weinstein, 'Don't Believe Everything You Think: Cognitive Bias in Legal Decision Making', *Clinical Law Review* 9, no. 2 (spring 2003) 783; Birte Englich, Thomas Mussweiler, and Fritz Strack, 'Playing Dice with Criminal Sentences: The Influence of Irrelevant Anchors on Experts' Judicial Decision Making', *Personality & Social Psychology Bulletin* 32, no. 2 (February 2006) 188.

[16] Gerd Gigerenzer, *Gut Feelings: Short Cuts to Better Decision Making* (London: Penguin Books, 2008).

[17] Stephan Landsman and Richard Rakos, 'A Preliminary Inquiry into the Effect of Potentially Biasing Information on Judges and Jurors in Civil Litigation', *Behavioral Sciences & the Law* 12, no. 2 (1994) 113.

[18] Andrew J. Wistrich, Chris Guthrie, and Jeffrey J. Rachlinski, 'Can Judges Ignore Inadmissible Information? The Difficulty of Deliberately Disregarding', *University of Pennsylvania Law Review* 153, no. 4 (2005) 1251. Jeffrey Rachlinski and others, 'Does Unconscious Racial Bias Affect Trial Judges?', *Notre Dame Law Review* 84, no. 3 (March 2009) 1195. Chris Guthrie, Jeffrey Rachlinski, and Andrew Wistrich, 'Judging by Heuristic: Cognitive Illusions in Judicial Decision Making', *Judicature* 86, no. 1 (July–August 2002) 44.

[19] Elaine D. Ingulli, 'Trial by Jury: Reflections on Witness Credibility, Expert Testimony, and Recantation', *Valparaiso University Law Review* 20 (winter 1986) 145.

expert's gender matches the inferred knowledge domain of the case itself, then the expert will be more persuasive, even if that knowledge domain is not the area of expertise for that expert.[20] Likewise, use by the expert of a language style that is more consistent with gender-related stereotypes about language can increase an expert's persuasiveness.[21] Simply selecting male experts to maximize the credibility of the expert evidence is not recommended.[22] The full context of the expert evidence needs to be taken into account in relation to the gender of the expert.

Expert credentials and experience in the courtroom were important in determining how receptive jurors were toward experts and expert evidence. Jurors were more positively disposed toward experts who were perceived to have stronger credentials (see chapter 5, paragraph 5.64). The more highly educated the prosecution expert was, the more that jurors thought the prosecution had a strong case, the less difficulty jurors reported in understanding the expert, and the more that jurors thought the expert's evidence had an impact on their verdicts. These findings differed from what judges reported in the 1999 AIJA survey, where only 3.44% of judges ($n = 13$) thought that experts' educational qualifications were amongst the three most persuasive factors to jurors in assessing oral expert evidence.[23] These two sets of findings are not necessarily inconsistent. Due to the expectations associated with the role of being a juror, there is social pressure for jurors to appear attentive to the evidence as it is given, and so observers such as judges may arrive at a misplaced belief in what jurors are attending to and being influenced by. This issue has been acknowledged and studied regarding judicial perceptions of jury understanding of jury directions.[24] It may bear further evaluation and examination. **9.14**

The influence of a related expert attribute—level of experience in the courtroom—was less straightforward. Again, this was an issue that received minimal priority in the 1999 survey of judges, with only 7.94% of respondents ($n = 30$) numbering prior experience as an expert witness amongst the three most persuasive factors for jurors when experts give evidence. Interviewees in the present project made a slightly different point: some reported concerns about the ability of experts with limited experience to give expert evidence effectively in the courtroom. Judges, too, made the subtle observation that the level of experience an expert has, in testifying in court, could influence the clarity of communication of the expert in delivering in-court testimony[25] and accordingly the jury's comprehension of the expert evidence. Interviewees noted, however, that many of the problems associated with less experienced experts seemed to originate from the way the experts were questioned by counsel. **9.15**

---

[20] Regina A. Schuller, Deborah J. Terry, and Blake M. McKimmie, 'The Impact of Expert Testimony on Jurors' Decisions: Gender of the Expert and Testimony Complexity', *Journal of Applied Social Psychology* 35, no. 6 (June 2005) 1266. Cf James V. Couch and Jennifer N. Sigler, 'Gender of the Expert Witness and the Jury Verdict', *The Psychological Record* 52 (2002) 201.

[21] Blake M. McKimmie and others, 'It's Not What She Says, It's How She Says It: The Influence of Language Complexity and Cognitive Load on the Persuasiveness of Expert Testimony', *Psychiatry, Psychology and Law* 20, no. 4 (2013) 578.

[22] See Kimberly McCall, 'When Choosing an Expert Witness, What's Important? Gender or Expertise', *Attorney At Law Magazine* (2015): <http://www.attorneyatlawmagazine.com/las-vegas/when-choosing-an-expert-witness-whats-important-gender-or-expertise/>.

[23] Ian Freckelton, Prasuna Reddy, and Hugh Selby, *Australian Judicial Perspectives on Expert Evidence: An Empirical Study* (Melbourne: AIJA, 1999) 152.

[24] Blake M. McKimmie, Emma Antrobus, and Chantelle Baguley, 'Objective and Subjective Comprehension of Jury Instructions in Criminal Trials', *New Criminal Law Review: An International and Interdisciplinary Journal* 17, no. 2 (spring 2014) 163.

[25] This was the characteristic regarded as most valuable by judges (36.51%, $n = 138$) in expert evidence in the 1999 AIJA survey.

9.16 Concerns about the performance of some of the more experienced experts emerged, including their ability to confine their opinions to their area of expertise, and how they responded to questioning. The analysis of the credibility ratings suggested that experience in the courtroom (frequency of appearances over the previous twelve months) was unrelated to higher or lower ratings of credibility, but was related to the amount of disagreement in jurors' ratings of credibility. Importantly, and in some respects counter-intuitively, the more appearances that an expert had, the greater disagreement there was about the expert's credibility. Experts with a moderate level of experience in the courtroom were best received. The total number of years that the expert had worked in their profession had no influence on perceptions of their credibility, nor did the expert's age.

(b) Reliability and admissibility

9.17 The reason so much attention is focussed on the admissibility of expert opinion evidence and the characteristics of expert witnesses who may appear before fact-finders, especially jurors, is the potential for experts to be highly influential, sometimes too influential, on trial outcomes. As Marshall JA of the Newfoundland Supreme Court put it:

> There is always the underlying concern in admitting expert evidence that the aura surrounding the requisite specialized knowledge and the expert's credentials may result in the opinion being accorded more weight than warranted by the proven facts. Thus, cases speak of apprehension that expert testimony, cloaked as it generally is in scientific language, will acquire a mystical air of infallibility that technical vocabularies often communicate to those not versed in the expert's discipline. The fear is, therefore, rather than assist laypersons in forming judgments, that the use of expert evidence will usurp the function of the trier of fact and distort the proceedings by bolstering the evidence of parties and overwhelm a jury.[26]

9.18 This gives rise to a number of dynamics. First, it prompts caution on the part of judges in terms of their preparedness to allow expert evidence to go before jurors if it is regarded as unlikely to assist fact-finding. This is reflected in the application of the exclusionary rules of expert evidence. A consequence is that expert evidence that does not comprise specialized knowledge is excluded from trial. However, for Australia, although the United States *Daubert* definition of 'knowledge', which applies to 'any body of known facts or to any body of ideas inferred from such facts or accepted as truths on good grounds', has been endorsed, what these notions import has not yet been explicated. In addition, the concepts that lie within 'knowledge' being 'specialized' are far from clear. How recondite or abstruse must it be? It is clear that if the knowledge resides within facts that are generally known within the community or can readily enough be observed and evaluated by jurors, expert evidence will not be permitted, as it does not constitute knowledge with the required degree of specialization. It may also be regarded as unfair, or apt to mislead, confuse, or consume undue time.

9.19 Community discourse and the reasoning of many judges have had resort to the concept of reliability when identifying characteristics of expert evidence that ought to be permitted to go before jurors. The many notorious problematic decisions, together with the historical reality that prosecutions have often drawn upon newly emerging fields of scientific and medical endeavour (latterly, including lip-reading, gait analysis, and low-weight DNA), compel an approach that identifies expert opinions that have enough probative value to go before jurors.

9.20 These realities have generated rules of evidentiary admissibility—the exclusionary rules. They differ from country to country. However, as of 2015/16 what can be said for the first time is that an international consensus is emerging: that the notion of reliability of expert opinions

[26] *R v C(G)* (1996) 110 CCC (3d) 233, 259 (Newfoundland CA).

ought to be a lynchpin of evidentiary admissibility. This accords with Popperian views of epistemology,[27] is consistent with empiricist approaches within psychology, and provides a bridge between medico-scientific values and legal needs.

The proposition that reliability should constitute the principal tool for discerning the acceptable from the unacceptable in expert evidence was initiated in 1993 by the United States Supreme Court in *Daubert v Merrell Dow Pharmaceuticals, Inc.*, and has since been followed in Canada, New Zealand, India, and England and Wales. It has also been mooted in Ireland.[28] While the *Daubert* calculus of four indicia—(1) falsifiability; (2) peer review in publication; (3) error rate identification; and (4) general acceptance within the relevant intellectual marketplace—has been applied variably, the essence of the reliability approach is becoming one of evidence law orthodoxy. Australia has yet to commit itself to such a course in the form of statute, court rules, statutory interpretation, or common law development. After the 2014 Rules of Criminal Procedure and Practice Directions in England and Wales, such an evolution verges on the inevitable. **9.21**

(3) Presentation of expert evidence

(a) Pre-trial conferences with legal counsel

Responses in this project from judges and trial counsel and litigation solicitors identified inadequate preparation of expert witnesses in the form of pre-trial conferences as problematic. In some instances this was the product of lack of industry; in others it seemed reflective of usual practice. Some on the defence side ascribed it to the fact that pre-trial conferencing was not paid for by legal aid services and a few indicated that expert witnesses were not as amenable to consultation as would be preferable. Whatever the cause, if counsel calling an expert witness is not adequately apprised of the subtleties or shades of grey in an expert's opinions, or even the fact that the expert may, to some degree, have reconsidered their views in light of the passage of time, or reading the reports of other experts, problems will emerge at trial. **9.22**

These situations were shown to be highly adverse (and potentially embarrassing) for the party calling the witness or, more subtly, may result in the expert being unable to communicate their views or reasons for them effectively, because the appropriate questions are not asked. Further, if counsel have not taken the time to understand the nuances of the expert evidence by pre-trial conferences with their own expert, let alone the expert(s) for the other side, as they can on the basis of there being no property in a witness, they are less likely to be able to formulate a strong case theory or undertake the process of cross-examination as effectively as they should. **9.23**

(b) Sequencing of the evidence of expert witnesses

The familiar and orthodox methods of adducing expert evidence have come under scrutiny. In the civil domain the options of court-appointed experts, single experts, and referees have continued to be mooted.[29] In criminal trials, though, such a level of intrusion by judges into **9.24**

---

[27] See Karl Popper, *The Logic of Scientific Discovery* (London: Routledge, 1992).

[28] Irish Law Reform Commission, *Expert Evidence: Consultation Paper No. 52* (Dublin: Irish Law Reform Commission, 2008), para. 2.406, <http://www.bailii.org/cgi-bin/markup.cgi?doc=/ie/other/IELRC/2008/cp52.html&query=daubert&method=boolean>.

[29] See generally Ian Freckelton and Hugh Selby, *Expert Evidence: Law, Practice, Procedure and Advocacy*, 6th edn. (Sydney: Thomson Reuters, 2016). This is far from new; see Carol A. G. Jones, *Expert Witnesses* (Oxford: Oxford University Press, 1994); Ian Freckelton, *The Trial of The Expert* (Melbourne: Oxford University Press, 1987); Tal Golan, *Laws of Men and Laws of Nature* (Cambridge, Mass.: Harvard University Press, 2007).

the rights of the parties, in particular accused persons, has been regarded as inappropriate. However, the need for courts to be more efficient in their processes, to ensure a 'fair playing field' and to facilitate the capacity for sound decision-making by jurors, has generated an impetus for change.

9.25 A number of procedural responses have been forthcoming. Translation of codes of ethics for experts from the civil area into the criminal, with necessary adjustments, is inevitable. The Victorian County and Supreme Court Rules of 2014 are an example of such provisions. They have the merit of clearly identifying obligations that expert witnesses owe to the court in terms of their paramount duty, their responsibility to give reasons for their opinions, and the need to be clear about the assumptions that they make and the data that they take into account. These are constructive ways of enhancing both the quality of evidence and its transparency, in turn assisting jurors to be able to understand expert opinions better and to evaluate them more effectively during their deliberations.

9.26 However, more lessons are being learned from the civil area. The potential for trial judges to order experts to confer and crystallize the issues upon which they agree and disagree (the so-called conclave option) cannot be said to encroach upon the rights of the accused. It is an efficiency that has been employed for the improvement of the functioning of civil trials for some years. It is being imported into a number of jurisdictions for criminal trials and has the real likelihood of encouraging better pre-trial preparation of the expert evidence and removing unhelpfully obfuscating tactics from the defence arsenal. Such improvements would ultimately shorten trials and assist the decision-making of jurors.

(c) Jurors' attention to the content of expert evidence

9.27 Analysis of jurors' interview and survey responses suggested that they engaged in in-depth central processing of the content of the expert evidence and were engaged by their task. There was limited evidence of reliance on extra-legal cues, such as stereotypes and preconceptions, with the possible exception of some cases involving the presentation of DNA profiling evidence. As was the case in previous research, analysis of jurors' comprehension of expert evidence suggested that a range of extra-legal factors were influential; however, the magnitude of the correlations was small to modest. Jurors' preconceptions remained influential in the assessment of expert credibility. The more jurors expected to trust certain types of expert witnesses, the more they perceived the specific expert witnesses in the particular case on which they were empanelled to be credible. Overall, their expectations about the trustworthiness of experts were relatively high. However, as was highlighted in chapter 2, some of this trust may be misplaced, given the lack of pre-trial screening of much expert testimony for reliability and validity.

9.28 Further potential evidence that jurors were engaging in central processing of the expert evidence emerged in the correlational analyses of witness credibility. The largest correlation in those analyses was moderate in magnitude, which suggested that the majority of variation in perceptions of witness credibility was attributable to other factors that were not captured in those analyses. For practical reasons, it was not possible to assess directly the influence of evidence content on jurors' perceptions, but these analyses implied that perceptions of credibility may be based largely on the quality of the evidence given by experts.

9.29 Jurors, experts, lawyers, and judges generally agreed on the extent to which jurors understood the expert evidence and reported that the majority of jurors were able to understand the expert evidence adduced in criminal trials. This finding was reflected in both quantitative and qualitative analyses of their interview responses. Of great interest, though, is that all identified DNA evidence as potentially difficult for jurors to comprehend.

(d) The impact of language used by experts

There were two general aspects of expert language that were considered in this project. The first was the ability of jurors to comprehend expert evidence as a function of the language style used to present that evidence. The second was how aspects of that language style were related to perceptions of expert credibility. **9.30**

Technical jargon was described as a key barrier to comprehension by both jurors and expert witnesses. This perception was consistent with the views of trial judges, as expressed in a prior phase of this study in 1999.[30] Nonetheless, jurors reported that experts did not tend to overuse technical jargon when giving evidence, and that when jargon *was* used, judges intervened by asking for further explanation of the evidence. In addition, experts indicated that they actively tried to reduce their use of jargon in an attempt to make their evidence more comprehensible. Judges thought that the use of jargon was problematic, and that the questioning style of counsel was a major barrier to comprehension of expert evidence.[31] **9.31**

The correlational analysis suggested that, while more complex language was reported as more difficult to understand, it was also paradoxically a potential cue to perceived accuracy and precision. As the evidence of a prosecution expert increased in complexity and incorporated more technical language, it became more influential and strengthened the case against the defendant, even though those features were associated with greater difficulty in understanding. Consistent with this, when a prosecution expert appeared to be scientific, presumably due to their use of technical scientific terms, the prosecution case was perceived to be stronger, and the evidence had a larger reported impact on the verdict. **9.32**

Consistent with the findings related to the use of jargon and complex evidence, perceptions that the prosecution witnesses' evidence was clear were negatively correlated with prosecution case strength and difficulty in understanding the evidence. While evidence that was perceived to be clear was reported to be easier to understand, it was also associated with jurors' perceptions that the prosecution case was weaker and had a greater impact on the verdict. This finding was somewhat at odds with the analysis of the credibility scores. In those analyses, clarity of evidence was positively correlated with credibility—the more clear the expert's evidence was, the more credible the ratings of the expert. **9.33**

This latter finding suggested that perceptions of credibility were reliant on the content of the testimony—the more it could be understood, the more the expert was seen in a positive light. The findings on clarity and perceived strength of the prosecution case implied that some extra-legal cues might be at play, as it was then that the evidence appeared most scientific. One reason why these findings might also appear to be contradictory is that clarity and complexity/use of jargon may not be opposite sides of the same coin. For instance, it is possible for complex evidence that appears to be scientific (and so more influential because it matches possible expectations about expert evidence) to be expressed in either a clear or an unclear manner. When that evidence is expressed clearly, jurors are better able to evaluate the credibility of that information because they comprehend the content more readily, even when the concepts expressed are complex. **9.34**

---

[30] See Freckelton and Selby, *Expert Evidence: Law, Practice, Procedure and Advocacy*, p. 143.

[31] See Freckelton and Selby, *Expert Evidence: Law, Practice, Procedure and Advocacy*; Stephen Lubet and Elizabeth Boals, *Expert Testimony: A Guide for Expert Witnesses and the Lawyers Who Examine Them*, 3rd edn. (Boulder, Co: Lexis Nexis/NITA, 2014); Douglas L. Field, *The Expert Expert: The Path to Prosperity and Prominence as an Expert Witness* (iuniverse, 2013); Stanley L. Brodsky, *Testifying in Court: Guidelines and Maxims for the Expert Witness* (Washington, DC: American Psychological Association, 2013); Dan Poynter, *The Expert Witness Handbook: Tips and Techniques for the Litigation Consultant*, 3rd edn. (Santa Barbara, CA: Para Publishing, 2007).

9.35 Use of clear language has the side-benefit of potentially reducing differences in interpretations of the evidence when a jury is comprised of citizens with different language backgrounds. Jurors reported that several strategies helped overcome some of the challenges in understanding complex expert evidence, and in particular, noted with approval the experts who used plain language. This confirmed the value ascribed to clarity and accessibility of expert opinions by judges in the 1999 study.[32]

(e) The influence of expert demeanour

9.36 Both jurors' and legal professionals suggested that an expert's demeanour could undermine the credibility of their evidence. The risks of drawing inferences too readily or utilising inappropriate preconceptions in interpreting demeanour are well known to the courts.[33] Whether they are effectively implemented, especially by jurors, is another matter.

9.37 While over-confidence was mentioned as one cause for concern, confidence, on the part of the prosecution witness at least, was viewed positively. Greater confidence was associated with reporting from jurors that the expert's evidence was easier to understand. It was also correlated with more influence as the prosecution case was perceived as stronger and had a greater impact on the verdict. Consistent with this finding, the perception that the expert was wise was associated with greater ease of understanding and an increase in the impact of the expert's evidence on understanding.

(f) Jury responses to DNA, medical, and psychiatric/psychological evidence

9.38 A concern with expert evidence presented by forensic scientific experts and medical experts is that their evidence is viewed as akin to court-appointed expert evidence, because it is perceived as more neutral, reliable, and credible than other evidence, and is thus scrutinized less intensively by jurors, and processed peripherally. This would be an indicator of the 'white coat' effect associated with the identity of the communicator, when that person is a scientific expert. Juror susceptibility to communicator effects regarding DNA expert evidence and health practitioner expert evidence may be exacerbated by their misperception that the expert evidence is pre-screened for reliability and validity before it is presented at trial. The fact that prosecution experts presenting DNA profiling evidence were rarely successfully challenged by skilled defence barristers on cross-examination served to reinforce perceptions of this type of expertise as inviolate. Lawyers who have difficulty understanding the evidence, and are unconfident or ill prepared to conduct cross-examinations about scientific evidence,[34] may convey these cues to jurors.

9.39 Findings in the project indicated that there were specific issues that arose in jury responses to both DNA profiling evidence and evidence presented by medical and mental health experts, but that these issues were not due to white coat effects per se.

9.40 DNA profiling evidence was generally cited as potentially difficult for jurors to understand, in part because the presentation of the evidence regarding the random match probability was typically jargonistic and formulaic. This inflexible style on the part of the experts, adopted

[32] Ian Freckelton, Prasuna Reddy, and Hugh Selby, *Australian Judicial Perspectives on Expert Evidence: An Empirical Study*, p. 146.

[33] See e.g. *CSR Ltd v Della Maddalena* (2006) 224 ALR 1; *Fox v Percy* (2003) 214 CLR 118; Peter McClellan, 'Who Is Telling the Truth? Psychology, Common Sense and the Law', paper presented to the Local Courts of New South Wales Annual Conference, 2 August 2006: <http://www.austlii.edu.au/au/journals/NSWJSchol/2006/14.pdf>; Robert Fisher, 'The Demeanour Fallacy', (2014) *New Zealand Law Review* 575.

[34] Gary Edmond and others, 'How to Cross-Examine Forensic Scientists: A Guide for Lawyers', *Australian Bar Review* 39, no. 2 (2014) 174.

in an effort to avoid errors in expressing the results of probabilistic statistical calculations, was not adapted to convey the meaning of the random match to jurors in the most effective manner. Faced with the complexity of DNA profiling evidence and this presentational style, reliance by jurors on peripheral cues may be a particular issue in response to certain DNA expert evidence. Traditional adversarial system legal safeguards to test this evidence, such as (a) the presence of opposing expert opinions, (b) vigorous cross-examination, (c) jury directions, and (d) jury deliberation, were either unused or were found to be ineffective in testing the DNA profiling evidence reviewed in some of the trials examined in this project. As a consequence, some jurors dealing with this kind of evidence engaged in peripheral, as opposed to central, processing of the content of the expert evidence, and were more susceptible to the persuasive features of cues such as expert credentials, demeanour, and confidence; that is to say, they based their judgements on the communicator effects—the messenger rather than the message.

The potential for jury confusion generated by fractional ratios used to present the likelihood of a random match was extensive, as has been shown in many experimental laboratory studies. Recommendations flowing from psychological research on the greater accessibility to juries of expert presentations of this information by using a mathematically equivalent verbal modification in the form of frequencies and percentages should be implemented, although the confusion engendered by the use of vague descriptors in the United Kingdom, as highlighted in *R v T*,[35] needs to be avoided. **9.41**

The project results revealed extensive disparities, ranging by as much as 50%, amongst key participants about the extent to which jurors understand complex DNA profiling expert evidence. This disparity could be reduced if judges were more proactive in communicating with juries about what is really understood, and if juries were encouraged and permitted to seek clarification when they did not understand the expert evidence. If this communication gap remains unaddressed, particular difficulties that jurors experience in these cases will persist. **9.42**

The findings indicated that, in some instances, poor jury comprehension could lead to miscarriages of justice, particularly when the forensic scientific evidence interacted with jurors' misinterpretation of the meaning of 'beyond reasonable doubt'. In other trials where similar expert scientific evidence was presented, there was evidence that other factors compensated, and reduced the likelihood of an unsafe verdict. For example: **9.43**

(a) Jurors who had scientific and mathematical education were able to guide other, less knowledgeable jurors.
(b) Lawyers and experts who met in advance of the trial collaborated to prepare a range of visual aids and exhibits to assist jurors.
(c) The judge was pro-active in seeking clarification of the expert evidence.

The various perspectives provided by judges, lawyers, experts, and jurors reinforced the complexity and diversity of the task of jurors in evaluating expert evidence from health practitioners. In general they expressed confidence that jurors were managing their role effectively. **9.44**

More frequently than other types of expert evidence, medical evidence, and mental health evidence presented by experts, especially that on the defendant's state of mind at the time the **9.45**

[35] [2010] EWCA Crim 2439, [2011] 1 Cr App R 9. See Colin Aitken, Paul Roberts, and Graham Jackson, *Fundamentals of Probability and Statistical Evidence in Criminal Proceedings: Practitioner Guide No 1* (London: Royal Statistical Society's Working Group on Statistics and the Law, 2010).

crime in issue was committed, was rebutted by an opposing defence expert, exposing jurors to a 'battle of the experts', and conflicting expert evidence.

9.46 When jurors were confronted by conflicting expert evidence on the same topic, such as the five trials in which psychiatric witnesses gave contrasting evidence about whether the accused was mentally impaired, or the expert evidence was unclearly delivered or convoluted in its complexity, at times the effectiveness of the decision-making process by jurors was a cause for concern. In trials involving complex competing evidence, if the issues were sharply delineated and the assumptions made by the experts were clearly identified, jurors managed to evaluate the differences between the experts adequately. On balance, we can be cautiously optimistic about jurors' abilities in these cases. An important finding in this project was that a battle of experts did not inevitably lead juries to ignore the content and resort to reliance on peripheral cues in evaluating the expert evidence.

9.47 One common feature of much psychiatric and psychological expert evidence is the retrospective nature of the expert assessments. Jurors found it difficult to assess expert evidence involving retrospective timeframes. Police investigators, lawyers, and experts should be mindful of this by making sure psychiatric and psychological assessments are carried out as soon as practical after the offending behaviour. Expert reports that are commissioned much later or during the trial run the risk of being accorded significantly less weight.

(4) **System-level issues**

9.48 The project findings suggested that the current system was working reasonably well. The vast majority of the expert evidence was perceived by the judges, litigation lawyers, experts, and jurors as appropriate and adequate. Evidence was perceived as less than optimal in just over a quarter of the trials analysed. In ascertaining the source of the difficulties with the expert evidence in these trials, no single prominent cause emerged. Experts who provided evidence that evoked dissatisfaction from the stakeholders fell predominantly into two groups: the first group was comprised of highly experienced professional experts, often repeat players in court, and at the other extreme was the group of novice experts who had little prior exposure to adversarial procedures and the demands of the courtroom.

9.49 Our findings further suggested that the Australian criminal justice system was not dealing adequately with the repeat player effect on experts, in spite of lessons that should have been learned from the many high-profile miscarriages of justice attributable to unfounded expert opinions. Lawyers and experts need to be more vigilant about the scope of the evidence provided by experts who are experienced and confident in court.

9.50 Several neophyte experts were perceived to provide inadequate evidence that lacked clarity. The overwhelming response to this evidence was that it wasted precious court time, rather than undermined the ability of the criminal justice system to deliver a fair trial. The general agreement from stakeholders was that more courtroom experience for the novice experts and greater assistance from the lawyers who called them would go some way to redressing their inexperience and improve performance. Once again, pre-trial preparation of less experienced experts is key to ensuring that the evidence is of value to the process. An unexpected finding was the degree to which the trials in our project sample were dominated by prosecution experts, and often multiple or cumulative prosecution experts. By comparison, the defence rarely called rebuttal expert witnesses but did often use the prosecution expert to obtain evidence that they needed for their case. As a consequence of no defence expert being called, jurors were often exposed to a single expert witness on a factual issue in controversy. The impact on trial outcomes of exposure to (often multiple) unrebutted prosecution experts could not be systematically explored in this project with its limited sample of 55 trials. However, it is worthy of further analysis.

Similarly, we did not anticipate the project finding that defence experts who appear in court would be scrutinized more closely by jurors for bias compared to their counterparts appearing on behalf of the Crown, as they are presumed to be 'guns for hire'. Despite greater scrutiny for bias, the jurors did not ultimately perceive that the vast majority of defence experts were biased. A feature of the project was the modest emphasis on concerns about bias by contrast with the emphatic findings of the 1999 and 2001 studies. **9.51**

B. Recommendations

A number of recommendations for practitioners and researchers to enhance the effectiveness of uses of expert evidence in criminal jury trials emerged from the foregoing project findings. **9.52**

(1) Prepare experts to facilitate juror comprehension

The project findings highlight the fundamental importance of both sound pre-trial preparation by expert witnesses and training so that they can optimize their evidence during criminal trials and the reasons for the views that they hold. When expert evidence was identified as problematic by the stakeholders, it was usually apparent that the barristers had spent little time with the expert who provided inadequate evidence. This was equally the case for both the highly experienced professional experts and the novice experts. If barristers spent adequate time with their experts in pre-trial preparation, this would give experts a better opportunity to raise technical issues that might well be useful for the party calling them—whether that be in the form of questions asked of the expert or of the opposing expert. There is no reason why experts should not be proactive in this regard and request such conferences, even if they only take place on the telephone. **9.53**

Both the experts and legal professionals acknowledged that more could be done in relation to the presentation of DNA evidence, but were not always certain what steps to take to improve the presentations. More regular and systematic procedures are advisable to expand the range of visual aids in respect of expert evidence generally, and to provide these in the jury room to encourage jury questions. **9.54**

(2) Increase the pool of experts utilized in trials

Resistance to expert witnesses who give evidence remotely by audio-visual means is increasingly becoming anachronistic. As was identified by some participants in this project, remote witness participation has the advantage of going some way to redress shallow talent pools in terms of the availability of expert witnesses, in particular for the defence, in many areas of expert endeavour, especially those which are very specialized. **9.55**

However, if experts are to be allowed frequently or even routinely to give evidence from outside the courtroom, this will require adjustments to procedures and careful attention from prosecution and defence counsel alike to ensure that expert witnesses have access to materials they need during both examination-in-chief and cross-examination. **9.56**

The increasing use of remote witness evidence raises the issue of the ways in which experts can most effectively present their evidence so as to maximize their effectiveness remotely as providers of assistance to the courts. This topic could usefully be the subject of further research as the dynamics of giving evidence remotely are materially changed by both the physical absence of the witness and the mediation of the relevant technology. **9.57**

(3) Sequence expert evidence to facilitate juror comprehension

9.58 The potential for experts to present their evidence one after the other—known as 'consecutive evidence'—thereby facilitating the ability of jurors to understand better the differences in opinions that are expressed and thereby to discern between them, bears further consideration. On occasion, this procedure is already utilized, but only when the accused determines that from their point of view it is strategically advantageous.

9.59 The potential for consecutive evidence to enhance fact-finding raises the important question of whether enabling a trial judge to mandate consecutive evidence, for instance by requiring the defence to call their expert witnesses at the start of their case, is an acceptable intrusion upon the autonomy of the defence to call their witnesses at the time and in the order that it chooses. It is our view that giving the trial judge such a power is a reasonable compromise but that giving a trial judge the right to compel the accused to call its experts before the end of the prosecution case would unreasonably distort the balance of the trial process.

(4) Allow concurrent expert evidence where feasible

9.60 Another area in which the criminal trial could be adjusted in emulation of civil trials is by way of the use of concurrent evidence—hot tubbing. This kind of expert evidence in company, usually strongly judicially guided and allowing for a conversation amongst experts, has been enthusiastically embraced by many civil trial judges, especially in Australia, but also in Canada and the United Kingdom. It has been employed, with the consent of the defence, on a number of occasions in Australian criminal trials. The 2014 changes to criminal procedure rules in Victoria explicitly allowed for both consecutive and concurrent evidence in criminal trials.

9.61 In our view, this provision of procedural flexibility is a constructive means of assisting jurors to understand expert opinion evidence in a more sophisticated way. However, permitting trial judges to mandate such a method of adducing of expert evidence would probably be a step too far as it would distort the balance of the criminal trial process in favour of the prosecution. This is a matter for further research, discussion, and debate.

9.62 However, what can be seen from this sequence of Australian innovations, particularly from Victoria, is that there is potential for the criminal law to draw creatively in some respects upon civil law processes to ease the burden of jurors in relation to the evaluation of expert evidence. Further consideration of such options is worthwhile, as is evaluation of the success or otherwise of the initiatives utilized thus far.

(5) Support jurors in their role

9.63 The Lord Chief Justice in England and Wales has called for increased use of visual and multimedia aids.[36] While this reduces the orality of the court environment, it is consistent with ordinary experience in the Internet era. Indications from our project were that this was what was expected and appreciated by jurors. It needs to be further consolidated to enhance juror comprehension.[37]

9.64 The findings of this project suggested that jurors attempted to focus on the content of the expert's evidence and relied on few extra-legal cues when assessing expert credibility. Jurors

[36] Frances Gibb, 'Lord Judge Calls for Jury System that Caters for Computer Generation', *The Times*, 21 October 2009, <http://www.thetimes.co.uk/tto/law/article2215110.ece>.

[37] Jane Goodman-Delahunty and Sophie Rabone, 'Multimedia Evidence and the Jury: Applying Principles of Effective Communication' (lecture, 23rd Annual Conference of the Australian Institute of Judicial Administration, Wellington, New Zealand, 2005).

were most able to understand expert evidence presented by means of simple explanations, without overly technical language. To support jurors in performing their role as finders of fact, prosecutors and defence counsel can work more concertedly with expert witnesses to ensure that the expert evidence is presented in this form to jurors.

There are two caveats to this recommendation. First, it must be acknowledged that in some circumstances the defence may wish to adopt an obfuscatory strategy. To some degree this is legitimate but not where it is calculated to confuse or mislead a jury. Jurors evaluated an expert's evidence as more persuasive when the expert used more complex language, but complexity was not associated with increases in the perceived credibility of the expert—clarity of evidence appeared to be the key to credibility. Second, it must be acknowledged that jurors evaluate an expert's evidence as more persuasive when the expert uses more complex language. For the content of the expert's evidence to persuade jurors, however, the evidence must not be given in such a complex manner that the jurors cannot understand the actual content. **9.65**

The project findings suggested that perceptions of expert credibility were based both on the content of the expert's evidence and characteristics associated with the expert themselves. These findings were consistent with those of experimental laboratory studies and interviews with jurors in a variety of jurisdictions. Credibility assessments appeared to be based on socially shared beliefs and so not prone to disconfirmation during jury deliberation, and on an assumption of trust in expert evidence. This trust was most likely due to an inference that the reliability and validity of the expert evidence was already tested and endorsed by the court, as it was the court that admitted the evidence. **9.66**

As such, jurors currently do not appear to be particularly well equipped to assess the credibility of expert evidence. Assessing the credibility of expert evidence in the full sense should include not only an assessment of whether the expert is giving a credible performance in court and specifically what the expert says, but also an assessment of the underlying reliability of that type of evidence. This includes an assessment of the credibility of the entire chain of expert evidence—collection, storage, analysis, interpretation of data, and conclusion; with an acknowledgement of the role of human judgement in these stages—essentially a judgement about the reliability and validity of the evidence. **9.67**

As for other types of witnesses, such as child witnesses, jurors can be effectively educated about the issues relating to the underlying reliability and validity of their evidence by an expert witness.[38] While it is recommended that courts do more to ensure that the evidence that is admitted is reliable and valid, jurors can similarly be educated in the assessment of the underlying credibility of expert evidence with a view to shifting their credibility assessments to a sounder basis and, to the maximum extent possible, excluding from their evaluative processes irrelevant considerations that could distort or contaminate their decision-making. **9.68**

(6) Improve communication between judges, jurors, and experts

The overarching importance of effective communication between courts, litigation lawyers, experts, and jurors emerged as an important factor in the appropriate understanding and successful use by jurors of expert evidence. Adequate comprehension of expert evidence should not be left to the possibility that one or more empanelled jurors will have a scientific **9.69**

[38] Jane Goodman-Delahunty, Anne Cossins, and Kate O'Brien, 'A Comparison of Expert Evidence and Judicial Directions to Counter Misconceptions in Child Sexual Abuse Trials', *Australian and New Zealand Journal of Criminology* 44, no. 2 (2011) 196; Jane Goodman-Delahunty, Anne Cossins, and Kate O'Brien, 'Enhancing the Credibility of Complainants in Child Sexual Assault Trials: The Effect of Expert Evidence and Judicial Directions', *Behavioral Sciences & the Law* 28, no. 6 (2010) 769.

background, or that a proactive judge will intervene to enhance their comprehension, or that a selected expert will be especially effective as a communicator in relation to technical issues. A more concerted and systematically coordinated approach is required to advance criminal justice policy and procedures so as to enhance jury comprehension. This has an important role to play in maintaining community confidence in the ongoing relevance and competence of the jury as a trier of fact.

9.70 A commitment to undertake steps to meet this challenge is overdue, and should commence at the pre-trial stage. The current approach to rely almost exclusively on an ever-increasing number of judicial directions[39] to communicate with jurors needs to be reassessed in light of concerns about the abilities of jurors to understand and follow such instructions.[40] While the trial system requires jurors to use their common sense and their everyday experience, it is paradoxical, unrealistic, and anomalous that jurors are precluded from accessing ordinary sources of acquiring context, clarifying misconceptions, and understanding better the knowledge that they have. This is not to assert that jurors should be free to conduct their own research, but it is to observe that the task imposed upon them requires them to discharge an important role in a way which is different from how they would undertake other important decision-making roles in other parts of their lives.

9.71 Encouraging jurors to ask experts questions, and giving jurors the transcript of the expert's evidence, are the next logical steps to assist jurors to understand complex expert evidence. The project findings suggested that jurors are inhibited about asking questions, as most experts were not asked any questions by jurors.

9.72 We advocate that more written aids be made available to jurors in the deliberation room, including the transcript of the evidence in searchable form and written copies of judicial directions to aid in their comprehension and use of expert evidence. Given that jurors found the written expert reports very helpful and that their availability during deliberations saved time, we recommend that the assumption should be that expert reports are provided to the jury.

(7) Integrate credibility and persuasion findings and models

9.73 One possibly productive avenue for future research is to integrate the research findings and models on credibility with the cognate research findings and models on persuasion. To a large extent, these two areas have existed in parallel. Credibility research, with some notable exceptions, has tended to focus on the behaviour of experts and features of their evidence that result in the perception of experts as credible. This is entirely understandable given the pragmatic goals of much of that research, but it has resulted in a lack of development of a model to understand the process by means of which jurors assess credibility. However, the provision of expert evidence in court can be thought of as an attempt at persuasion—particularly as it is an attempt by a witness to communicate their views and the reasons why they hold them with a view to assisting the decision-making process of jurors.

9.74 There is an inevitable interplay between the probative value of evidence and the credibility of evidence, however. As McHugh J observed in *Palmer v The Queen*:

> The probability of testimonial evidence being true cannot be isolated from the credibility of the witness who gives that evidence except in those cases where other evidence confirms

---

[39] Accepting the important steps being made to simplify and streamline directions given to jurors in some jurisdictions: see e.g. Victorian Law Reform Commission, *Jury Directions: Final Report* (Melbourne: Victorian Government Printer, 2009); Jury Directions Act 2013 (Vic).

[40] McKimmie, Antrobus, and Baguley, 'Objective and Subjective Comprehension of Jury Instructions in Criminal Trials', 163.

its truth either wholly or partly. Furthermore, the conclusions drawn from that evidence are necessarily dependent on the credibility of the deponent. Zuckerman has correctly described the distinction between evidence as to the credibility of witnesses and evidence as to facts-in-issue as productive of absurdity.[41]

Consistent with the research on credibility, the research on persuasion generally considers factors associated with both the messenger (the expert) and the message (the evidence), along with a range of other factors, but unlike the credibility literature, it is not often conducted in an ecologically valid context vis-à-vis the courts. Psychological research on persuasion is characterized by models of underlying processes, and these are intrinsically related to questions of the credibility of the person giving us the message. By integrating these two frames for thinking about expert evidence, well-developed models of persuasion can be brought to bear on the issue of credibility assessments, to develop a deeper understanding of the underlying process. Such an integrated approach has the potential to identify ways to assist jurors to make credibility assessments on desirable, legally relevant factors instead of extra-legal factors (such as expert gender). **9.75**

A further issue that arises in this respect is when expert evidence should be allowed in respect of credibility or reliability.[42] This is a contentious area, but if there is value in enhancing jurors' capacity to evaluate witnesses' credibility generally, and if there is advantage in counter-intuitive evidence directed to enhancing jurors' discernment and capacity to evaluate, it may be that there is reason to consider this additional aspect of expert evidence in suitably circumscribed scenarios. **9.76**

(8) Evaluate recent reforms

Important changes have taken place in England and Wales in the 2014 Criminal Procedure Rules and Practice Directions, and in Victoria, Australia, in the 2014 County and Supreme Court Practice Note on Expert Evidence in Criminal Trials. The changes are both substantive and procedural in respect of the reception of expert evidence in criminal trials. It will be important to evaluate these groundbreaking reforms to determine whether they should be emulated, adjusted, or adapted by other jurisdictions. **9.77**

C. Concluding Remarks

This volume has provided rare insights into jury perceptions of expert evidence in criminal jury trials. The project outlined here was not intended as a critique of jurors or of the jury system, but rather an exercise in identifying the issues that jurors encounter in contemporary trials when expert evidence is presented, and ways to provide better support to jurors engaged in assessing and using expert evidence in their decision-making. **9.78**

Jurors' views of expert evidence from forensic science, medical, and mental health experts were examined from multiple perspectives. In examining the uses of expert evidence in jury trials, perspectives of the major participants in the trials were sought. Insights derived from such a cross-section of perspectives ensure that any intervention or reform is aimed at what the issue is for jurors and experts in giving their evidence, rather than at what others might (less informedly) perceive the issues to be. Consideration of the perspectives of judges and **9.79**

[41] [1998] HCA 2, (1998) 193 CLR 1, 22. See also Paul Roberts and Adrian Zuckerman, *Criminal Evidence*, 2nd edn. (Oxford: Oxford University Press, 2010).

[42] See generally Tony Ward, 'Usurping the Role of the Jury? Expert Evidence and Witness Credibility in English Criminal Trials', *International Journal of Evidence and Proof* 13, no. 2 (2009) 83.

litigation lawyers is fundamental for reforms and interventions, especially when their views differ from those of jurors and experts, because judges and legal practitioners are the stakeholders responsible for the adoption of these recommendations for reform.

9.80 Like all studies, this project was subject to a number of limitations that must be acknowledged and considered in interpreting the project findings. One of the challenges in conducting research in the field is access to the participants. This is a particular hurdle when studying aspects of the criminal justice system, as people's rights and liberty are at stake. To minimize potential disruptions to the legal cases, courts are reluctant to allow anyone, including researchers from outside the court system, to approach jurors and ask them about their experiences, and, in particular, their deliberations and decisions in criminal trials. While many of the participating legal professionals appreciated the significance of a study of this nature, and supported it, all were powerless to convey this to the juries in the cases which we tracked. Since participation was voluntary, interview and survey responses obtained were limited to those of the legal professionals and jurors who were willing to participate in the study.

9.81 A limitation in the methods used to study these trials (written surveys and oral interviews) is the inability to assess the ground truth (e.g., did the jurors actually understand the experts? Was the content of the expert testimony strong or weak, and simple or complex? Was the expert actually biased?) because of reliance almost exclusively on verbal reports from participants.[43] This limitation was offset by the triangulation of the responses of multiple participants with different perspectives on the expert evidence in each trial, including the participation of the object of the study, the expert witnesses themselves.

9.82 A notable strength of this project was the participation of researchers with expertise in multiple disciplines. One advantage of a multi-method, transdisciplinary approach is its capacity to go beyond interdisciplinary research, where only a shared understanding of the problems is achieved, and to generate innovation in terms of the insights and creative solutions to those acknowledged problems. The foregoing outcomes of this ground-breaking empirical study have yielded more nuanced answers than were previously available to some recurring questions about jury reactions to and evaluations of complex expert evidence in real cases. These findings may assist in reframing informed and innovative discussion surrounding expert evidence. Moreover, they provide an evidence-based foundation to support courts in adopting best practice and procedures to facilitate appropriate jury understanding and use of expert evidence.

[43] Timothy Wilson and Richard Nisbett, 'The Accuracy of Verbal Reports About the Effects of Stimuli on Evaluations and Behavior', *Social Psychology* 41, no. 2 (1978) 118; Richard Nisbett and Timothy Wilson, 'Telling More Than We Can Know: Verbal Reports on Mental Processes', *Psychological Review* 84, no. 3 (May 1977) 231; Peter White, 'Limitations on Verbal Reports of Internal Events: A Refutation of Nisbett and Wilson and of Bem', *Psychological Review* 87, no. 1 (1980) 105.

Appendices

APPENDIX 1

Juror Survey

Juries and Expert Evidence Survey

If you need additional space for any of your written responses, extra space is provided at the end of the survey. Please note the question number your response relates to next to any additional response.

These questions are about XXXXXX, the expert called by the prosecution.

1. **Instructions:** *Please rate the prosecution expert for the following items on the scale provided.*

Dressed formally	1	2	3	4	(5)	6	7	8	9	10	Dressed informally
This expert was...											
Unfriendly	1	2	3	4	5	6	7	8	9	10	Friendly
Disrespectful	1	2	3	4	5	6	7	8	9	10	Respectful
Unkind	1	2	3	4	5	6	7	8	9	10	Kind
Ill-mannered	1	2	3	4	5	6	7	8	9	10	Well-mannered
Unpleasant	1	2	3	4	5	6	7	8	9	10	Pleasant
Untrustworthy	1	2	3	4	5	6	7	8	9	10	Trustworthy
Untruthful	1	2	3	4	5	6	7	8	9	10	Truthful
Undependable	1	2	3	4	5	6	7	8	9	10	Dependable
Dishonest	1	2	3	4	5	6	7	8	9	10	Honest
Unreliable	1	2	3	4	5	6	7	8	9	10	Reliable
Not confident	1	2	3	4	5	6	7	8	9	10	Confident
Inarticulate	1	2	3	4	5	6	7	8	9	10	Articulate
Tense	1	2	3	4	5	6	7	8	9	10	Relaxed
Shaken	1	2	3	4	5	6	7	8	9	10	Poised
Not self-assured	1	2	3	4	5	6	7	8	9	10	Self-assured
Uninformed	1	2	3	4	5	6	7	8	9	10	Informed
Illogical	1	2	3	4	5	6	7	8	9	10	Logical
Uneducated	1	2	3	4	5	6	7	8	9	10	Educated
Unwise	1	2	3	4	5	6	7	8	9	10	Wise
Unscientific	1	2	3	4	5	6	7	8	9	10	Scientific

THE FOLLOWING QUESTIONS ASK YOU TO FOCUS ON THE CONTENT OF THE EXPERT TESTIMONY

Please mark the box that best represents your view about this testimony.

2. **The prosecution expert's testimony:**

	Strongly disagree 1	2	3	4	Strongly agree 5
Helped me understand the issues in the case	□	□	□	□	□
Should have been explained more simply	□	□	□	□	□
Went into more detail than was needed	□	□	□	□	□
Was neutralized by the cross-examination	□	□	□	□	□

Was important to deliberations	□	□	□	□	□
Was hard to understand	□	□	□	□	□
Changed my mind about the trial outcome	□	□	□	□	□
Contradicted itself	□	□	□	□	□
Was too fast-paced	□	□	□	□	□
Was lengthy	□	□	□	□	□
Was more important than any other witness	□	□	□	□	□
Was clear	□	□	□	□	□
Was complex	□	□	□	□	□
Was confusing	□	□	□	□	□
Contained a lot of technical language	□	□	□	□	□
Is difficult for me to remember now	□	□	□	□	□

3. We are interested in any and all thoughts that you remember coming to mind while listening to the testimony of the prosecution expert.

Please write your thoughts in the space provided below. Write only one thought per box.

Only include thoughts related to the expert testimony provided by <u>the prosecution expert.</u>

a) --

----

b) --

----

c) --

----

d) --

----

4. Could this expert have presented his/her evidence in a better way (e.g. with visual aids, PowerPoint slides, maps, models, diagrams, photographs, simulations)?

□ No □ Yes

→ In what way?

....

....

....

5. Did you have any questions that you wanted to ask this expert witness?

□ No □ Yes

→ Did you ask these questions?

□ Yes, all of them → If you asked your question(s), how
□ Yes, some of them → helpful was the response?
□ No

Not at all helpful 1 2 3 4 5 *Very helpful*

To what extent did the following factors influence your decision not to ask questions? *(Rate your agreement/disagreement with each one)*

	Strongly disagree 1	2	Neither 3	4	Strongly agree 5
i. I did not know jurors could ask questions	□	□	□	□	□
ii. I was worried they would not be allowed	□	□	□	□	□
iii. Someone else on the jury asked my question(s)	□	□	□	□	□
iv. The judge did not allow them	□	□	□	□	□
v. The other jurors explained it to me	□	□	□	□	□
vi. I didn't feel comfortable asking questions	□	□	□	□	□
vii. Other, specify:	□	□	□	□	□

....
....
....

These questions are about XXXXXX, the expert called by the defence

6. Instructions: *Please rate the defence expert for the following items on the scale provided.*

Dressed formally	1	2	3	4	(5)	6	7	8	9	10	Dressed informally
This expert was…											
Unfriendly	1	2	3	4	5	6	7	8	9	10	Friendly
Disrespectful	1	2	3	4	5	6	7	8	9	10	Respectful
Unkind	1	2	3	4	5	6	7	8	9	10	Kind
Ill-mannered	1	2	3	4	5	6	7	8	9	10	Well-mannered
Unpleasant	1	2	3	4	5	6	7	8	9	10	Pleasant
Untrustworthy	1	2	3	4	5	6	7	8	9	10	Trustworthy
Untruthful	1	2	3	4	5	6	7	8	9	10	Truthful
Undependable	1	2	3	4	5	6	7	8	9	10	Dependable
Dishonest	1	2	3	4	5	6	7	8	9	10	Honest
Unreliable	1	2	3	4	5	6	7	8	9	10	Reliable
Not confident	1	2	3	4	5	6	7	8	9	10	Confident
Inarticulate	1	2	3	4	5	6	7	8	9	10	Articulate
Tense	1	2	3	4	5	6	7	8	9	10	Relaxed
Shaken	1	2	3	4	5	6	7	8	9	10	Poised
Not self-assured	1	2	3	4	5	6	7	8	9	10	Self-assured
Uninformed	1	2	3	4	5	6	7	8	9	10	Informed
Illogical	1	2	3	4	5	6	7	8	9	10	Logical
Uneducated	1	2	3	4	5	6	7	8	9	10	Educated
Unwise	1	2	3	4	5	6	7	8	9	10	Wise
Unscientific	1	2	3	4	5	6	7	8	9	10	Scientific

THE FOLLOWING QUESTIONS ASK YOU TO FOCUS ON THE CONTENT OF THE EXPERT TESTIMONY

Please mark the box that best represents your view about this testimony.

7. The defence expert's testimony:

	Strongly disagree 1	2	3	4	Strongly agree 5
Helped me understand the issues in the case	☐	☐	☐	☐	☐
Should have been explained more simply	☐	☐	☐	☐	☐
Went into more detail than was needed	☐	☐	☐	☐	☐
Was neutralized by the cross-examination	☐	☐	☐	☐	☐
Was important to deliberations	☐	☐	☐	☐	☐
Was hard to understand	☐	☐	☐	☐	☐
Changed my mind about the trial outcome	☐	☐	☐	☐	☐
Contradicted itself	☐	☐	☐	☐	☐
Was too fast-paced	☐	☐	☐	☐	☐
Was lengthy	☐	☐	☐	☐	☐
Was more important than any other witness	☐	☐	☐	☐	☐
Was clear	☐	☐	☐	☐	☐
Was complex	☐	☐	☐	☐	☐
Was confusing	☐	☐	☐	☐	☐
Contained a lot of technical language	☐	☐	☐	☐	☐
Is difficult for me to remember now	☐	☐	☐	☐	☐

8. We are interested in any and all thoughts that you remember coming to mind while listening to the testimony of the defence expert.

Please write your thoughts in the space provided below. Write only one thought per box.

Only include thoughts related to the expert testimony provided by the defence expert.

a) --

----

b) --

----

c) --

----

d) --

----

9. Could this expert have presented his/her evidence in a better way (e.g. with visual aids, PowerPoint slides, maps, models, diagrams, photographs, simulations)?

□ No □ Yes

→ In what way?

....

....

....

10. Did you have any questions that you wanted to ask this expert witness?

□ No □ Yes

→ Did you ask these questions?

□ Yes, all of them → If you asked your question(s), how
□ Yes, some of them → helpful was the response?
□ No

Not at all helpful 1 2 3 4 5 *Very helpful*

↓

To what extent did the following factors influence your decision not to ask questions? *(Rate your agreement/disagreement with each one)*

	Strongly disagree 1	2	Neither 3	4	Strongly agree 5
i. I did not know jurors could ask questions	□	□	□	□	□
ii. I was worried they would not be allowed	□	□	□	□	□
iii. Someone else on the jury asked my question(s)	□	□	□	□	□
iv. The judge did not allow them	□	□	□	□	□
v. The other jurors explained it to me	□	□	□	□	□
vi. I didn't feel comfortable asking questions	□	□	□	□	□
vii. Other, specify:	□	□	□	□	□

General Views about the Trial

11. Overall, how strong was the...

	Not at all 1	2	3	4	Very 5
Prosecution case?.......................................	□	□	□	□	□
Defence case?..	□	□	□	□	□

12. Overall, how difficult was it to understand…

	Not at all difficult 1	2	3	4	Very difficult 5	Not applicable N/A
The expert(s) for the prosecution?	□	□	□	□	□	□
The testimony by other prosecution witnesses?	□	□	□	□	□	□
What the prosecution lawyer said?	□	□	□	□	□	□
The expert(s) for the defence?	□	□	□	□	□	□
The testimony by other defence witnesses?	□	□	□	□	□	□
What the defence lawyer said?	□	□	□	□	□	□
What the judge said?	□	□	□	□	□	□

13. How influential were the following in making your decision?

	Not at all influential 1	2	3	4	Very influential 5	Not applicable N/A
The expert(s) for the prosecution?	□	□	□	□	□	□
The testimony by other prosecution witnesses?	□	□	□	□	□	□
What the prosecution lawyer said?	□	□	□	□	□	□
The expert(s) for the defence?	□	□	□	□	□	□
The testimony by other defence witnesses?	□	□	□	□	□	□
What the defence lawyer said?	□	□	□	□	□	□
What the judge said?	□	□	□	□	□	□

14. Did the jury receive a copy of the transcript of the evidence?
□ Yes □ No

→ (a) Would you have liked a copy of the transcript?.......... □ Yes □ No
(b) Did you ask for a copy?................................ □ Yes □ No

---

→ (c) Did you receive all or only part of the transcript?........ □ All □ Part
(d) Did you ask for the transcript?.......................... □ Yes □ No
(e) In what form was the transcript provided? □ Paper/hard copy of transcript
□ Electronic copy of transcript
(f) How often did you refer to the transcript?

Never 1 2 3 4 5 6 7 Frequently

(g) How strongly do you agree/ disagree with the following statements:

Use of the transcript…	Strongly disagree 1	2	Neither 3	4	Strongly agree 5
i. was helpful	□	□	□	□	□
ii. was distracting	□	□	□	□	□
iii. saved time	□	□	□	□	□

15. Did the jury receive a copy of any expert report(s)?
□ Yes □ No

→ (a) Would you have liked a copy?........................... □ Yes □ No
(b) Did you ask for a copy?................................. □ Yes □ No

→ (c) Did you receive all or only part of the expert report? □ All □ Part
(d) Did you ask for a copy?................................. □ Yes □ No
(e) How often did you refer to the expert report(s)?

Never 1 2 3 4 5 6 7 Frequently

(f) How strongly do you agree/ disagree with the following statements:

Use of the expert report(s)...	Strongly disagree 1	2	3	4	Strongly agree 5
i. was helpful	□	□	□	□	□
ii. was distracting	□	□	□	□	□
iii. saved time	□	□	□	□	□

16. Is there anything the lawyers could have done to make the jury's job easier?
□ No □ Yes

→ In what way?
....
....
....
....

17. To what extent are jurors free to reject the testimony of expert witnesses?

Not at all		Moderately		Very much
1	2	3	4	5
□	□	□	□	□

General Views about Expert Evidence

18. How many hours per week do you watch any or all of the following crime shows:
CSI, CSI: New York, or *CSI: Miami*.............................. ________ (hours per week)
Law & Order.. ________
Criminal Minds... ________
Bones.. ________
NCIS... ________
Other crime shows, please specify: ____________________ ________

19. Out of ten criminal trials, in how many do you expect each of the following?

Testimony by: Number of trials (out of 10)
Forensic scientists (e.g. fingerprints, DNA)....................... ________
Medical doctors.. ________
Accountants.. ________
Psychiatrists/psychologists.................................... ________

20. In court, to what extent do you expect the following witnesses to be male or female?
(Indicate the proportion of experts that you expect to be male or female)

	% male	% female
Forensic scientists (e.g. fingerprints, DNA)	______	______
Medical doctors	______	______
Accountants	______	______
Psychiatrists/psychologists	______	______

21. How much would you expect to be able to trust the following types of evidence?
(Tick the box that corresponds to your views, using the following scale)

	Not at all 1	2	3	4	Very much 5
Forensic scientists (e.g. fingerprints, DNA)	□	□	□	□	□
Medical doctors	□	□	□	□	□
Accountants	□	□	□	□	□
Psychiatrists/psychologists	□	□	□	□	□

Demographic Details

22. What is your gender? .... □ Female □ Male

23. What is your age? .... ______ (in years)

24. What state do you live in? .... □ NSW □ QLD □ VIC

25. Is English your first language? .... □ Yes □ No

26. What country were you born in? .... □ Australia □ Other, specify: ______

27. Have you ever served as a juror before? .... □ Yes □ No

28. What is the highest year that you completed at school? (tick one)
□ Year 9 or lower
□ Year 10
□ Year 11
□ Year 12

29. What is your highest educational qualification, outside of school? (tick one)
□ Trade certificate
□ TAFE course
□ Undergraduate university degree
□ Postgraduate university degree

30. Did you study any science or mathematics subjects in your last two years of high school? □ Yes □ No

31. Did you study any science or mathematics subjects after high school? □ Yes □ No

32. What is your occupation? (Tick one)

- □ Labourer/trade
- □ Professional
- □ Home duties
- □ Unemployed
- □ Other, specify: ____________________
- □ Admin/clerical
- □ Full-time student
- □ Professional in a science field
- □ Retiree/pensioner

Additional Comments

33. Do you have any other comments you would like to make about the expert testimony in this trial?

End of Survey

Thank you for you taking the time to complete this survey.

APPENDIX 2

Juror Interview

Juror Interview

Case name:
Identifying number:
Interview date:
Interviewer's name:

General Views about the Trial

To the best of your recollection....

1. Did you consider this to have been a close case between the prosecution and defence?
   □ No
   □ Yes
   → Why?

2. What were the disputed issues for the jury to decide?

3. Did the expert testimony address this/these disputed issues(s)?
   □ No
   □ I don't know
   □ Yes
   → a) How did the expert testimony address the question(s) in dispute?

General Expert Evidence Questions

4. What is an expert's job in a criminal trial?

5. Did the experts disagree on any issues during this trial?
   □ No
   □ Yes
   → a) What were these?

   b) Was this disagreement important when considering your verdict?

6. Was the expert testimony discussed during deliberations?
   □ No
   □ Yes
   → a) To what extent?

   b) How far into deliberations was the testimony discussed?

   c) For how long was the expert testimony discussed?

7. Was the expert testimony an important issue in the jury's deliberations?
   □ No
   □ Yes

8. Did the judge give you any instructions about expert testimony?
   - □ No
   - □ I don't know
   - □ Yes
     → a) When were these instructions given?

     b) How were they given? (orally/written)

     c) What were these instructions?

     d) Are you able to explain what these instructions meant?

     e) How helpful were these instructions in reaching your verdict?

9. Were there any times when you (or the jury as a whole) would have liked to ask questions about the expert testimony, but did not do so?
   - □ No
   - □ Yes
     → a) Which expert would these questions have been directed to? (all or only some)

     b) What were these questions?

     c) At which point in the trial would you have liked to have been able to ask these questions?

10. Did you receive a copy of the trial transcript?
    - □ Yes →
    - □ No →

    a) Did you receive all of the transcript or only part of it? If you only received part of the transcript, which part(s) did you receive?

    b) In what form did you receive the transcript (electronically or on paper)?

    Was this your preferred form?

    c) How many copies did you receive?

    d) Did you use the transcript in relation to the expert testimony?

    e) How helpful was the transcript for clarifying details regarding the expert testimony?

    f) Did having the transcript increase, decrease, or have no impact upon the length of your deliberations?

    g) Did you ask for a copy of the transcript? If so, in your opinion, was it fair that it was not provided to you?

    h) Do you think it would have been helpful to have had a copy of the transcript during your deliberations? Why/why not?

These questions are about XXXXXX, the expert for the prosecution.

11. What was your impression of this expert? *(in terms of qualifications, content, and demeanour)*

12. What was the expert's role in this case?

13. What did this expert testify about?

14. How well did this expert perform? Did they handle the cross-examination questions well?

15. Which were the most important parts of the testimony provided by this witness?

16. Were there any parts of the expert testimony that you had difficulty understanding?
    □ No
    □ Yes ——➤ If so, what were these?

17. Could this expert have presented his/her evidence in a better way (e.g. visual aids, PowerPoint slides, maps, models, diagrams, photographs, simulations)?
    □ No
    □ Yes ——➤ If so, in what way?

18. If there was no opposing expert to this expert's testimony, did this impact upon your findings in relation to this piece of evidence. Did the lack of opposing expert cause you to make any inferences about the evidence?

19. Overall, what helped you the best to understand this expert's testimony?
    If the juror provides no response, use the following prompts:
    □ The expert's explanations
    □ Your own common sense
    □ Barristers' and/or judge's questions
    □ Prosecutor's and/or defence's closing arguments
    □ Judge's summing up

20. In trying to understand this expert's testimony, would it have been helpful for you to have had access to the internet or relevant books in the jury room?
    □ No
    □ Yes ——➤ What would have been helpful and why?

21. Did you feel that you better understood the expert's testimony and were better able to make a decision once you had discussed the testimony with the other jurors?
    □ No ——➤ If not, why?
    □ Yes ——➤ If so, how?

22. Did the jury receive a copy of this expert's written report during deliberations?
    □ No ——➤ Would you have liked a copy?
    □ Yes ——➤ Was it helpful?

23. Were there any other documents (exhibits, charts, PowerPoint) used by the expert?
    □ No
    □ Yes
    └——➤ a) What were these?

    b) Were they helpful?

These questions are about XXXXXX, the expert for the defence.

24. What was your impression of this expert? *(prompt for qualifications, content and demeanour)*

25. What was the expert's role in this case?

26. What did this expert testify about?

27. How well did this expert perform? Did they handle the cross-examination questions well?

28. Which were the most important parts of the testimony provided by this witness?

29. Were there any parts of the expert testimony that you had difficulty understanding?
    □ No
    □ Yes ——➤ If so, what were these?

30. Could this expert have presented his/her evidence in a better way (e.g. visual aids, PowerPoint slides, maps, models, diagrams, photographs, simulations)?
    □ No
    □ Yes ——➤ If so, in what way?

31. If there was no opposing expert to this expert's testimony, did this impact upon your findings in relation to this piece of evidence. Did the lack of opposing expert cause you to make any inferences about the evidence?

32. Overall, what helped you the best to understand this expert's testimony?
    If the juror provides no response, use the following prompts:
    □ The expert's explanations
    □ Your own common sense
    □ Barristers' and/or judge's questions
    □ Prosecutor's and/or defence's closing arguments
    □ Judge's summing up

33. In trying to understand this expert's testimony, would it have been helpful for you to have had access to the internet or relevant books in the jury room?
    □ No
    □ Yes ——➤ What would have been helpful and why?

34. Did you feel that you better understood the expert's testimony and were better able to make a decision once you had discussed the testimony with the other jurors?
    □ No ——➤ If not, why?
    □ Yes ——➤ If so, how?

35. Did the jury receive a copy of this expert's report?
    □ No ——➤ Would you have liked a copy?
    □ Yes ——➤ Was it helpful?

36. Did the jury receive a copy of this expert's written report during deliberations?
    □ No ——➤ Would you have liked a copy?
    □ Yes ——➤ Was it helpful?

37. Were there any other documents (exhibits, charts, PowerPoint) used by the expert?
    - □ No
    - □ Yes
      → a) What were these?

        b) Were they helpful?

38. Do you have any other comments you would like to make about the expert testimony?

END OF INTERVIEW

Thank you for you taking the time to complete this interview.

APPENDIX 3

Judge Interview

Interview with Judges

These questions are about XXXXXX, the expert called by the prosecution.
Instructions: *Please rate this expert for the following items on the scale provided.*

Dressed formally	1	2	3	4	5	6	7	8	9	10	Dressed informally
This expert was...											
Unfriendly	1	2	3	4	5	6	7	8	9	10	Friendly
Disrespectful	1	2	3	4	5	6	7	8	9	10	Respectful
Unkind	1	2	3	4	5	6	7	8	9	10	Kind
Ill-mannered	1	2	3	4	5	6	7	8	9	10	Well-mannered
Unpleasant	1	2	3	4	5	6	7	8	9	10	Pleasant
Untrustworthy	1	2	3	4	5	6	7	8	9	10	Trustworthy
Untruthful	1	2	3	4	5	6	7	8	9	10	Truthful
Undependable	1	2	3	4	5	6	7	8	9	10	Dependable
Dishonest	1	2	3	4	5	6	7	8	9	10	Honest
Unreliable	1	2	3	4	5	6	7	8	9	10	Reliable
Not confident	1	2	3	4	5	6	7	8	9	10	Confident
Inarticulate	1	2	3	4	5	6	7	8	9	10	Articulate
Tense	1	2	3	4	5	6	7	8	9	10	Relaxed
Shaken	1	2	3	4	5	6	7	8	9	10	Poised
Not self-assured	1	2	3	4	5	6	7	8	9	10	Self-assured
Uninformed	1	2	3	4	5	6	7	8	9	10	Informed
Illogical	1	2	3	4	5	6	7	8	9	10	Logical
Uneducated	1	2	3	4	5	6	7	8	9	10	Educated
Unwise	1	2	3	4	5	6	7	8	9	10	Wise
Unscientific	1	2	3	4	5	6	7	8	9	10	Scientific

These questions are about XXXXXX, the expert called by the defence.
Instructions: *Please rate this expert or the following items on the scale provided.*

Dressed formally	1	2	3	4	5	6	7	8	9	10	Dressed informally
This expert was...											
Unfriendly	1	2	3	4	5	6	7	8	9	10	Friendly
Disrespectful	1	2	3	4	5	6	7	8	9	10	Respectful
Unkind	1	2	3	4	5	6	7	8	9	10	Kind
Ill-mannered	1	2	3	4	5	6	7	8	9	10	Well-mannered
Unpleasant	1	2	3	4	5	6	7	8	9	10	Pleasant
Untrustworthy	1	2	3	4	5	6	7	8	9	10	Trustworthy
Untruthful	1	2	3	4	5	6	7	8	9	10	Truthful
Undependable	1	2	3	4	5	6	7	8	9	10	Dependable

Dishonest	1	2	3	4	5	6	7	8	9	10	Honest
Unreliable	1	2	3	4	5	6	7	8	9	10	Reliable
Not confident	1	2	3	4	5	6	7	8	9	10	Confident
Inarticulate	1	2	3	4	5	6	7	8	9	10	Articulate
Tense	1	2	3	4	5	6	7	8	9	10	Relaxed
Shaken	1	2	3	4	5	6	7	8	9	10	Poised
Not self-assured	1	2	3	4	5	6	7	8	9	10	Self-assured
Uninformed	1	2	3	4	5	6	7	8	9	10	Informed
Illogical	1	2	3	4	5	6	7	8	9	10	Logical
Uneducated	1	2	3	4	5	6	7	8	9	10	Educated
Unwise	1	2	3	4	5	6	7	8	9	10	Wise
Unscientific	1	2	3	4	5	6	7	8	9	10	Scientific

Interview with Judges

Case:
Interview date:
Interviewer's name:
Participant number:

Demographic Details

1. What is your predominant area of judicial practice (e.g. criminal, commercial)?

2. How many years have you served as a judge?

3. Were you a criminal lawyer/barrister previously? If so, for how long?

General Views about the Trial

4. Did you consider this to have been a close case between the prosecution and defence?
   □ No
   □ Yes
   └──► Why?

5. Were there some facts presented during the course of this trial that you think were difficult for jurors to understand?
   □ No
   □ I don't know
   □ Yes
   └──► a) What were they?

6. Were there any legal issues presented during the course of this trial that you think were difficult for jurors to understand?
   □ No
   □ Yes
   └──► a) What were they?

General Views about the Expert Evidence

7. What were the disputed issues for the jury to decide in this trial?

8. Did the expert evidence address these disputed issues?

9. Was there any expert evidence in this trial that was complex for jurors? If so, in what way?

10. Did you take any steps to assist the jury to understand the expert testimony?
    □ No
    □ Yes
    → a) What did you do?
    b) When?

11. Did the experts disagree on any issues(s) during the trial?
    □ No
    □ Yes
    → a) What issues(s) did they disagree on?
    b) Do you think it was hard for the jury to choose between the opinions of these experts?
    □ No
    □ Yes
    → Why? What do you think may have been responsible for the difficulties?

12. Did the jury receive a copy of any expert report(s)?
    □ No
    □ Yes
    (a) Did the jury request a copy of the report? If so, why were they not provided with one?
    (b) Do you think that the jury would be assisted by having read an appropriate written report from the expert prior to hearing the expert evidence?

13. Are there measures that could be taken to assist juries to evaluate expert evidence better?

14. In general, should matters involving complex and conflicting expert evidence be withdrawn from juries and be determined by judges alone or by some other means? Why/why not?

15. Were vior dire procedures used to determine the admissibility of any expert evidence in relation to this case?
    □ No
    □ Yes
    → a) Which expert(s) did this apply to?
    b) Why?

16. Did you use concurrent evidence[1] in this trial?
    □ No → Why not?
    □ Yes
    → a) Was it useful?
    b) Was it an efficient use of court time?

[1] Concurrent evidence (sometimes referred to as hot tubbing) is where multiple experts give their evidence at the same time after having met and agreed to a joint statement identifying the matters where they agree and disagree.

17. In the past five years, have you used concurrent evidence in criminal trials (where appropriate)?
    □ No
    □ Yes ——➤ describe your experience of this

18. What are your views of using concurrent evidence in criminal trials (where appropriate)?

19. In your view, should jurors ask questions of experts?
    □ No
    □ Yes ——➤ How would you facilitate this approach?

20. Do you have any other comments you would like to make about expert evidence in criminal trials generally?

21. In this trial, if you were a defendant, would you prefer to have a judge alone or a jury trial? Why?
    □ Judge alone
    □ Jury trial
    □ No preference

These questions are about XXXXXX, the expert called by the prosecution.

22. What was your impression of this expert? *(prompt for content and demeanour)*

23. What was the expert's role in this case?

24. What did this expert testify about?

25. Did this expert's evidence address any contentious issues? If so, what?

26. How well did this expert perform? Did they handle the cross-examination questions well?

27. Do you think that this expert required further training in their forensic function? Why/why not?
    □ Yes ——↓
    □ No

    In what area(s) does this expert require additional training?

    □ The limits of the forensic expert's role

    □ Knowledge of the law about expert evidence or that relates to their field of expertise

    □ Preparation, content, and layout of written reports

    □ Communication skills in the courtroom

28. Were there any parts of this expert's testimony which you think the jury had difficulty understanding?
    □ Yes ——↓
    □ No

    a) Which parts of their testimony presented difficulty?

b) Did you take any steps to assist jurors to understand this expert's evidence?
□ Yes →
□ No

i. What were these?

ii. Were they effective? If not, why?

29. Do you think the jury might have had difficulty comprehending the judicial instructions in relation to this expert's evidence? If so, what were these difficulties?

30. Did the jury ask any question(s) in relation to this expert?
□ No
□ Yes
→ a) What was the nature of the question(s)?

b) When did the jury ask the question(s)?

c) Which of these questions did you allow? If you (dis)allowed, why?

d) Was it a useful exercise?

31. Did the jury receive a copy of the transcript of this expert's evidence?
□ Yes → Who asked for it? How was it provided? Did you encounter any problem with this?
□ No
→ a) Did you want the jury to have a copy of the trial transcript? Why/why not.

b) Do you think that it would have facilitated juror comprehension of this expert's evidence if the transcript of this expert's evidence was provided to the jury? Why/why not?

32. Did the jury receive a copy of this expert's report?
□ Yes → When? Did you encounter any problem with this?
□ No
→ a) Do you think that it would have facilitated juror comprehension of this expert's evidence if an appropriate report was provided to the jury? Why/why not?

33. Do you have any other comments or concerns about this expert, or any other expert in this case?

These questions are about XXXXXX, the expert called by the defence.

34. What was your impression of this expert? *(prompt for content and demeanour)*

35. What was the expert's role in this case?

36. What did this expert testify about?

37. Did this expert's evidence address any contentious issues? If so, what?

38. How well did this expert perform? Did they handle the cross-examination questions well?

39. Do you think that this expert required further training in their forensic function? Why/why not?
    □ Yes →
    □ No

    In what area(s) does this expert require additional training?

    □ The limits of the forensic expert's role

    □ Knowledge of the law about expert evidence or that relates to their field of expertise

    □ Preparation, content, and layout of written reports

    □ Communication skills in the courtroom

40. Were there any parts of this expert's testimony which you think the jury had difficulty understanding?
    □ Yes →
    □ No

    a) Which parts of their testimony presented difficulty?

    b) Did you take any steps to assist jurors to understand this expert's evidence?
       □ Yes →
       □ No

       i. What were these?

       ii. Were they effective? If not, why?

41. Do you think the jury might have had difficulty comprehending the judicial instructions in relation to this expert's evidence? If so, what were these difficulties?

42. Did the jury ask any question(s) in relation to this expert?
    □ No
    □ Yes
    → a) What was the nature of the question(s)?

    b) When did the jury ask the question(s)?

    c) Which of these questions did you allow? If you (dis)allowed, why?

    d) Was it a useful exercise?

43. Did the jury receive a copy of the transcript of this expert's evidence?
    □ Yes → Who asked for it? How was it provided? Did you encounter any problem with this?
    □ No
    → a) Did you want the jury to have a copy of the trial transcript? Why/why not?

    b) Do you think that it would have facilitated juror comprehension of this expert's evidence if the transcript of this expert's evidence was provided to the jury? Why/why not?

44. Did the jury receive a copy of this expert's report?
    - □ Yes ⟶ When? Did you encounter any problem with this?
    - □ No
      ⟶ a) Do you think that it would have facilitated juror comprehension of this expert's evidence if an appropriate report was provided to the jury? Why/why not?

45. Do you have any other comments or concerns about this expert, or any other expert, in this case?

END OF INTERVIEW

Thank you for you taking the time to complete this interview.

APPENDIX 4

Lawyer Interview

Interview with Lawyers

These questions are about XXXXXX, the expert called by the prosecution.
Instructions: *Please rate this expert for the following items on the scale provided.*

Dressed formally	1	2	3	4	5	6	7	8	9	10	Dressed informally
This expert was...											
Unfriendly	1	2	3	4	5	6	7	8	9	10	Friendly
Disrespectful	1	2	3	4	5	6	7	8	9	10	Respectful
Unkind	1	2	3	4	5	6	7	8	9	10	Kind
Ill-mannered	1	2	3	4	5	6	7	8	9	10	Well-mannered
Unpleasant	1	2	3	4	5	6	7	8	9	10	Pleasant
Untrustworthy	1	2	3	4	5	6	7	8	9	10	Trustworthy
Untruthful	1	2	3	4	5	6	7	8	9	10	Truthful
Undependable	1	2	3	4	5	6	7	8	9	10	Dependable
Dishonest	1	2	3	4	5	6	7	8	9	10	Honest
Unreliable	1	2	3	4	5	6	7	8	9	10	Reliable
Not confident	1	2	3	4	5	6	7	8	9	10	Confident
Inarticulate	1	2	3	4	5	6	7	8	9	10	Articulate
Tense	1	2	3	4	5	6	7	8	9	10	Relaxed
Shaken	1	2	3	4	5	6	7	8	9	10	Poised
Not self-assured	1	2	3	4	5	6	7	8	9	10	Self-assured
Uninformed	1	2	3	4	5	6	7	8	9	10	Informed
Illogical	1	2	3	4	5	6	7	8	9	10	Logical
Uneducated	1	2	3	4	5	6	7	8	9	10	Educated
Unwise	1	2	3	4	5	6	7	8	9	10	Wise
Unscientific	1	2	3	4	5	6	7	8	9	10	Scientific

These questions are about XXXXXX, the expert called by the defence.
Instructions: *Please rate this expert for the following items on the scale provided.*

Dressed formally	1	2	3	4	5	6	7	8	9	10	Dressed informally
This expert was...											
Unfriendly	1	2	3	4	5	6	7	8	9	10	Friendly
Disrespectful	1	2	3	4	5	6	7	8	9	10	Respectful
Unkind	1	2	3	4	5	6	7	8	9	10	Kind
Ill-mannered	1	2	3	4	5	6	7	8	9	10	Well-mannered
Unpleasant	1	2	3	4	5	6	7	8	9	10	Pleasant
Untrustworthy	1	2	3	4	5	6	7	8	9	10	Trustworthy
Untruthful	1	2	3	4	5	6	7	8	9	10	Truthful
Undependable	1	2	3	4	5	6	7	8	9	10	Dependable

Dishonest	1	2	3	4	5	6	7	8	9	10	Honest
Unreliable	1	2	3	4	5	6	7	8	9	10	Reliable
Not confident	1	2	3	4	5	6	7	8	9	10	Confident
Inarticulate	1	2	3	4	5	6	7	8	9	10	Articulate
Tense	1	2	3	4	5	6	7	8	9	10	Relaxed
Shaken	1	2	3	4	5	6	7	8	9	10	Poised
Not self-assured	1	2	3	4	5	6	7	8	9	10	Self-assured
Uninformed	1	2	3	4	5	6	7	8	9	10	Informed
Illogical	1	2	3	4	5	6	7	8	9	10	Logical
Uneducated	1	2	3	4	5	6	7	8	9	10	Educated
Unwise	1	2	3	4	5	6	7	8	9	10	Wise
Unscientific	1	2	3	4	5	6	7	8	9	10	Scientific

Interview with Lawyers

Case:
Interview date:
Interviewer's name:
Participant number:

Demographic Details

1. What is your predominant area of practice?

2. How many years have you been practicing as a lawyer/barrister/prosecutor?

3. If you are a solicitor, do you have specialist accreditation in criminal law?

4. If you are a barrister, are you a Queen's Counsel/Senior Counsel?

General Views about the Trial

5. Did you consider this to be a close case between the prosecution and defence? Why?
   □ Yes
   □ No

6. Were there some facts presented during the course of this trial that you think were difficult for jurors to understand?
   □ Yes →
   □ No
   a) What were they?

7. Were there any legal issues presented during the course of this trial that you think were difficult for jurors to understand?
   □ Yes →
   □ No
   a) What were they?

8. Was the jury given a copy of the trial transcript? Why/why not?

9. What were the disputed issues for the jury to decide in this trial?

10. Did the expert evidence address these disputed issues?

11. Was there any expert evidence in this trial that was complex for jurors? If so, in what way?

12. Did you take any steps to assist the jury to understand the expert testimony?
    - □ No
    - □ Yes
      - → a) What did you do?
      - b) When?

13. Did the experts disagree on any issues(s) during the trial?
    - □ No
    - □ Yes
      - → a) What issues(s) did they disagree on?
      - b) Do you think it was hard for the jury to choose between the opinions of these experts?
        - □ No
        - □ Yes
          - → i. Why? What do you think may have been responsible for the difficulties?

14. Did the jury ask any questions in relation to the expert evidence?
    - □ No
    - □ Yes
      - → a) What was the nature of the questions?
      - b) Was it a useful exercise?

15. Did the jury receive a copy of any expert report(s)?
    - □ No →
    - □ Yes
      - a) Did the jury request a copy of the report? If so, why were they not provided with one?

16. Did you use concurrent evidence[1] in this trial?
    - □ No → Why not?
    - □ Yes
      - → a) Was it useful?
      - b) Was it an efficient use of court time?

17. In the past five years, have you used concurrent evidence in criminal trials (where appropriate)?
    - □ No
    - □ Yes → describe your experience of this

[1] Concurrent evidence (sometimes referred to as hot tubbing) is where multiple experts give their evidence at the same time after having met and agreed to a joint statement identifying the matters where they agree and disagree.

18. What are your views of using concurrent evidence in criminal trials (where appropriate)?

19. In your view, should jurors ask questions of experts?
    - □ No
    - □ Yes → How would you facilitate this approach?

20. In general, should matters involving complex and conflicting expert evidence be withdrawn from juries and be determined by judges alone or by some other means? Why/why not?

21. Do you have any other comments you would like to make about expert evidence in criminal trials generally?

22. In this trial, if you were a defendant, would you prefer to have a judge alone or a jury trial? Why?
    - □ Judge alone
    - □ Jury trial
    - □ No preference

These questions are about XXXXXX, the expert called by the prosecution.

23. If this expert was your witness, describe any preparation time spent with this witness.

24. What was your impression of this expert? *(prompt for content and demeanour)*

25. What was the expert's role in this case?

26. What did this expert testify about?

27. Did this expert's evidence address any contentious issues? If so what?

28. How well did this expert perform? Did they handle the cross-examination questions well?

29. Do you think that this expert required further training in their forensic function? Why/why not?
    - □ Yes ↓
    - □ No

    In what area(s) does this expert require additional training?
    - □ The limits of the forensic expert's role
    - □ Knowledge of the law about expert evidence or that relates to their field of expertise
    - □ Preparation, content, and layout of written reports
    - □ Communication skills in the courtroom

30. Were there any parts of this expert's testimony which you think the jury had difficulty understanding?
    - □ Yes ↓
    - □ No

    a) Which parts of their testimony presented difficulty?

    b) Did you take any steps to assist jurors to understand this expert's evidence?
       - □ Yes ↓
       - □ No

       i. What were these?

       ii. Were they effective? If not, why?

31. Do you think the jury might have had difficulty comprehending the judicial instructions in relation to this expert's evidence? If so, what were these difficulties?

32. Did the jury receive a copy of the transcript of this expert's evidence?
    - □ Yes
    - □ No
      → a) Did you want them to receive a copy?

        b) Do you think that it would have facilitated juror comprehension of this expert's evidence if the transcript of this expert's evidence was provided to the jury? Why/why not?

33. Did the jury receive a copy of this expert's report?
    - □ Yes
    - □ No
      → a) Did you want them to receive a copy?

        b) Do you think that it would have facilitated juror comprehension of this expert's evidence if an appropriate report was provided to the jury? Why/why not?

34. Do you have any other comments or concerns about this expert, or any other expert in this case?

These questions are about XXXXXX, the expert called by the defence.

35. If this expert was your witness, describe any preparation time spent with this witness.

36. What was your impression of this expert? *(prompt for content and demeanour)*

37. What was the expert's role in this case?

38. What did this expert testify about?

39. Did this expert's evidence address any contentious issues? If so what?

40. How well did this expert perform? Did they handle the cross-examination questions well?

41. Do you think that this expert required further training in their forensic function? Why/why not?
    - □ Yes →
    - □ No

      In what area(s) does this expert require additional training?
      - □ The limits of the forensic expert's role
      - □ Knowledge of the law about expert evidence or that relates to their field of expertise
      - □ Preparation, content, and layout of written reports
      - □ Communication skills in the courtroom

42. Were there any parts of this expert's testimony which you think the jury had difficulty understanding?
    - □ Yes
    - □ No

    a) Which parts of their testimony presented difficulty?

    b) Did you take any steps to assist jurors to understand this expert's evidence?
       - □ Yes
       - □ No

       i. What were these?

       ii. Were they effective? If not, why?

43. Do you think the jury might have had difficulty comprehending the judicial instructions in relation to this expert's evidence? If so, what were these difficulties?

44. Did the jury receive a copy of the transcript of this expert's evidence?
    - □ Yes
    - □ No

    a) Did you want them to receive a copy?

    b) Do you think that it would have facilitated juror comprehension of this expert's evidence if the transcript of this expert's evidence was provided to the jury? Why/why not?

45. Did the jury receive a copy of this expert's report?
    - □ Yes
    - □ No

    a) Did you want them to receive a copy?

    b) Do you think that it would have facilitated juror comprehension of this expert's evidence if an appropriate report was provided to the jury? Why/why not?

46. Do you have any other comments or concerns about this expert, or any other expert, in this case?

END OF INTERVIEW

Thank you for you taking the time to complete this interview.

APPENDIX 5

Expert Interview

Interview with Experts

Case Name:

Demographic Details—please complete the following:

1. Gender: □ Male □ Female

2. Age: ____________ (years)

3. What are your educational qualifications? ______________________________

____

____

4. Who is your current employer? ______________________________

5. What is your job title? ______________________________

6. What is your predominant area of practice? ______________________________

7. How long have you worked in this area? ______________________________

8. Approximately how many times per year do you provide expert testimony in court? ______________________________

9. Approximately how many court expert reports per year would you prepare? ______________________________

10. What percentage of your work is:

Criminal trials:		Civil trials:		
For the prosecution	______%	For the plaintiffs	______%	
For the defendants	______%	For the defendants	______%	(Total 100%)

11. Please rate the degree to which you feel that you did the following things when testifying in this case. Use the scale provided.

I feel that I....	Not well 1	2	Moderately well 3	4	Very well 5
remained calm under cross examination	□	□	□	□	□
controlled my emotions when questioned by an aggressive attorney	□	□	□	□	□
maintained a stable tone of voice when speaking	□	□	□	□	□
avoided fidgeting	□	□	□	□	□
maintained a good posture throughout the testimony	□	□	□	□	□
was comfortable on the witness stand	□	□	□	□	□

remained poised when being questioned by an attorney	□	□	□	□	□
maintained eye contact with the jury	□	□	□	□	□
held eye contact with an attorney	□	□	□	□	□
hid my nervousness	□	□	□	□	□
conveyed confidence in my ability	□	□	□	□	□
organized my thoughts	□	□	□	□	□
comfortably admitted when I was uncertain of an answer	□	□	□	□	□
sat up	□	□	□	□	□
leant slightly forward when answering some questions	□	□	□	□	□
provided more than 'yes/no' answers	□	□	□	□	□
acted natural	□	□	□	□	□
was myself when testifying	□	□	□	□	□

Interview with Experts

Case name:
Interview date:
Interviewer's name:
Participant number:

Trial Preparation

12. What was your role as an expert witness in this case?

13. Prior to giving evidence in this trial, did you confer with the solicitors who commissioned your report or the barrister/s who called you?
    □ No → a), b)
    □ Yes → c), d), e)

    a) Did you want to meet with them, prior to giving evidence?

    b) Why did no meeting take place, to your knowledge?

    c) Approximately for how long?

    d) What was the nature of your discussion?

    e) Did this discussion assist you when giving evidence in this trial?

14. Did the lawyers adequately prepare you to give evidence in this case?
    □ No → if not, why not?
    □ Yes

Your Experience During this Trial

15. Do you think that your qualifications were adequately explained to the jury?
    □ No → if not, why not?
    □ Yes

16. Do you think that your experience was adequately explained to the jury?
    □ No → if not, why not?
    □ Yes

17. Were you able to express yourself adequately when the lawyer who called you asked you questions in examination-in-chief?
    □ No ⟶ if not, why not?
    □ Yes

18. Is there a question that the barrister who called you as a witness should have asked you, but didn't?
    □ No
    □ Yes ⟶ what was this question(s)?

19. How did you find testifying in court? What were the positive aspects? What were the negative aspects?

20. Was there anything that could have been done, either before or during your testimony, to enhance your testimony?

21. Do you feel that your opinion was given sufficient value by the court? What is your reason for this view?

22. Were you able to deliver your evidence with intellectual integrity? Why?

23. Did your evidence address any contentious issues? If so what were they?

24. Do you feel that your testimony was delivered in the best way in which to inform the jury? If not, why not?

25. Were there any parts of your testimony that any of the lawyers or judge misunderstood?
    □ No
    □ Yes
    ⟶ a) Who misunderstood?

    b) What did they misunderstand?

    c) When did this misunderstanding occur?

26. Were there any parts of your testimony which you think the jury had difficulty understanding?
    □ Yes ↓
    □ No

    a) Which parts of your testimony presented difficulty?

    b) Did you take any steps to assist jurors to understand your evidence?
       □ Yes ↓
       □ No

       i. What were these (e.g. visual aids)?

       ii. Were they effective? If not, why not?

27. How reasonable is it to expect the jury in this trial to understand the matters you testified about?

28. Did you use visual aids when presenting your evidence to the jury? Why/why not?
    - □ No
    - □ Yes ⟶ what type of visual aids did you use?

29. Did the jury ask questions of you (via the judge) in this trial?
    - □ Yes ⟶ was it a useful exercise?
    - □ No ⟶ how would you have felt if jurors had asked you questions?

30. What has been your general experience with jury questions in past trials?

31. Did the jury receive a copy of your expert report?
    - □ Don't know
    - □ Yes
    - □ No ⟶
      - a) Do you think that it would have facilitated juror comprehension of your evidence if an appropriate report had been provided to the jury? Why/why not?

32. Did you use concurrent evidence[1] in this trial?
    - □ No ⟶ Why not?
    - □ Yes ⟶
      - a) Was it useful?
      - b) Was it an efficient use of court time?

33. In the past five years, have you used concurrent evidence in criminal trials (where appropriate)?
    - □ No
    - □ Yes ⟶ describe your experience of this

34. What are your views of using concurrent evidence in criminal trials (where appropriate)?

35. In this trial, if you were a defendant, would you prefer to have a judge alone or a jury trial? Why?
    - □ Judge alone
    - □ Jury trial
    - □ No preference

Your Opinion of the Opposing Expert

36. Were you given the opportunity to respond adequately to any opposing expert evidence?
    - □ No ⟶ please explain
    - □ Yes
    - □ Not applicable *(I was not present or there was no such opposing expert)*

[1] Concurrent evidence (sometimes referred to as hot tubbing) is where multiple experts give their evidence at the same time after having met and agreed to a joint statement identifying the matters where they agree and disagree.

37. Were there question(s) that the barrister/s who called you should have asked the opposing expert witness, in your view, but didn't?
    - □ Yes ——→ what were the question(s)?
    - □ No
    - □ Not applicable *(I was not present or there was no such opposing expert)*

38. If you heard the opposing expert's testimony:
    a) What was your impression of the opposing expert? *(prompt for content and demeanour)*

    b) What did the opposing expert testify about?

    c) Did this expert's evidence address any contentious issues? If so, what?

    d) How well did this expert perform? Did they handle the cross-examination questions well?

    e) Do you think the opposing expert required further training in their forensic function? Why/why not?
    - □ No
    - □ Yes ——↓

      In what area(s) does the opposing expert require additional training?
      - □ The limits of the forensic expert's role
      - □ Knowledge of the law about expert evidence or that relates to their field of expertise
      - □ Preparation, content, and layout of written reports
      - □ Communication skills in the courtroom

39. Do you have any other comments you would like to make about testifying in this case?

General Views about Expert Evidence in Criminal Jury Trials

40. In general, should matters involving complex and conflicting expert evidence be withdrawn from juries and be determined by judges alone or by some other means? Why/why not?

41. Do you have any other comments you would like to make about expert evidence generally?

END OF INTERVIEW

Thank you for you taking the time to complete this interview.

BIBLIOGRAPHY

Achterstraat, Peter. *Managing Forensic Analysis: Fingerprints and DNA*, (Auditor-General's Report, February 2010), <http://www.audit.nsw.gov.au/ArticleDocuments/142/195_Managing_Forensic_Analysis.pdf.aspx?Embed=Y>.

Aitken, Colin, Paul Roberts, and Graham Jackson. *Fundamentals of Probability and Statistical Evidence in Criminal Proceedings: Practitioner Guide No 1*, (London: Royal Statistical Society's Working Group on Statistics and the Law, 2010).

American Bar Association and Daniel H. Margolis. *Jury Comprehension in Complex Cases: Report of a Special Committee of the ABA Litigation Section*, (Chicago: ABA, 1989).

Arnold, Erik, and Errol Soriano. *The Recent Evolution of Expert Evidence in Selected Common Law Jurisdictions Around the World: A Commissioned Study for the Canadian Institute of Chartered Business Valuators*, (Campbell Valuation Partners Ltd, 23 January 2013).

Bank, Steven C. 'From Mental Health Professional to Expert Witness: Testifying in Court'. *New Directions for Mental Health Services*, no. 69 (spring 1996) 5.

Baum, Frances. 'Researching Public Health: Behind the Qualitative–Quantitative Methodological Debate'. *Social Science and Medicine* 40, no. 4 (February 1995) 459.

Beck, Yoram, and Suzanne Loomer. 'Reforming Expert Evidence'. *National Magazine*, (spring 2015), <http://nationalmagazine.ca/Articles/March-2015-Web/Reforming-expert-evidence.aspx>.

Bentley, David, and Peter Lownds. 'Low Template DNA'. *Archbold Review* 1 (February 2011) 6.

Bentley, David, and Peter Lownds. 'DNA-Analysis of Complex Mixed Profiles: The New Frontier?' *Archbold Review* 8, (September 2012) 5.

Bergin, Patricia. 'The Expert's Lament', (lecture, Land and Environment Court of New South Wales Annual Conference, Sydney, 5 May 2011), <http://www.austlii.edu.au/cgi-bin/sinodisp/au/journals/NSWJSchol/2011/14.html?stem=0&synonyms=0&query=%22concurrent%20evidence%20%22>.

Betts, Sharmila, and Jane Goodman-Delahunty. 'The Case of Kathleen Folbigg: How Did Justice and Medicine Fare?' *Australian Journal of Forensic Sciences* 39, no. 1 (2007) 11.

Binnie, Ian. 'Wrongful Convictions and the Magical Aura of Science in the Courtroom'. *Judicial Review* 10, no. 2 (2011) 141.

Blackwell, Suzanne, and Fred Seymour. 'Expert Evidence and Jurors' Views'. *Psychiatry, Psychology and Law* 22, no. 5 (2015) 673.

Boccaccini, Marcus T., and Stanley L. Brodsky. 'Believability of Expert and Law Witnesses: Implications for Trial Consultation'. *Professional Psychology: Research and Practice* 33, no. 4 (2002) 384.

Bodenhausen, Galen V. 'Stereotypic Biases in Social Decision Making and Memory: Testing Process Models of Stereotype Use'. *Journal of Personality and Social Psychology* 55, no. 5 (November 1988) 726.

Bond, Rod. 'Group Size and Conformity'. *Group Processes and Intergroup Relations* 8, no. 4 (2005) 331.

Bornstein, Brian H., and Edie Greene. 'Jury Decision Making: Implications For and From Psychology'. *Current Directions in Psychological Science* 20, no. 1 (2011) 63.

Breakwell, Glynis M., Jonathan A. Smith, and Daniel B. Wright. *Research Methods in Psychology*, (New York: Sage, 2012).

Brickell, Wendy. 'Is It the CSI Effect or Do We Just Distrust Juries?' *Criminal Justice* 23, no. 2 (summer 2008) 10.

Briody, Michael. 'The Effects of DNA Evidence on Sexual Offence Cases in Court'. *Current Issues in Criminal Justice* 14, no. 2 (2002) 159, <http://www.austlii.edu.au/au/journals/CICrimJust/2002/25.pdf>.

Briody, Michael. 'The Effects of DNA Evidence on Murder Cases in Court'. *Australian and New Zealand Journal of Criminology* 37, no. 2 (August 2004) 231.

British Subject Benchmark Statement: Law: Draft for Consultation (The Quality Assurance Agency for Higher Education, March 2015) <http://www.qaa.ac.uk/en/Publications/Documents/SBS-consultation-Law-15.pdf>.

Brodsky, Stanley. *The Expert Expert Witness: More Maxims and Guidelines for Testifying in Court*, (Washington, DC: American Psychological Association, 1999).

Brodsky, Stanley L. *Coping with Cross-Examination and Other Pathways to Effective Testimony*, (Washington, DC: American Psychological Association, 2004).

Brodsky, Stanley L. *Testifying in Court: Guidelines and Maxims for the Expert Witness*, (Washington, DC: American Psychological Association, 2013).

Brodsky, Stanley L., and others. 'Credibility in the Courtroom: How Likeable Should an Expert Witness Be?' *Journal of the American Academy of Psychiatry and Law* 37, no. 4 (2009) 525.

Brodsky, Stanley, Michael P. Griffin, and Robert J. Cramer. 'The Witness Credibility Scale: An Outcome Measure for Expert Witness Research'. *Behavioral Sciences and the Law* 28, no. 6 (2010) 892.

Brodsky, Stanley, and Tess Neal. 'Preparing and Giving Expert Testimony'. In *Psychologist's Desk Reference*, edited by Gerald Koocher, John Norcross, and Beverly Greene, 3rd edn. (New York: Oxford University Press, 2013).

Brooks, Charles I., Michael A. Church, and Lance Fraser. 'Effects of Duration of Eye Contact on Judgments of Personality Characteristics'. *Journal of Social Psychology* 126, no. 1 (February 1986) 71.

Brownlow, Sheila, Julie A. Rosamond, and Jennifer A. Parker. 'Gender-Linked Linguistic Behavior in Television Interviews'. *Sex Roles* 49, nos 3–4 (2003) 121.

Campbell, Anthony. *The Fingerprint Inquiry*, (Edinburgh: APS Group, 2011), <http://www.webarchive.org.uk/wayback/archive/20150428160103/> <http://www.thefingerprintinquiryscotland.org.uk/inquiry/files/TheFingerprintInquiryReport_Low_res.pdf>.

Canter, David V., and others. 'The Organized/Disorganized Typology of Serial Murder: Myth or Model?' *Psychology, Public Policy and Law* 10, no. 3 (September 2004) 293.

Cashman, Kate, and Terese Henning. 'Lawyers and DNA: Issues in Understanding and Challenging the Evidence'. *Current Issues in Criminal Justice* 24, no. 1 (2012) 69.

Chaiken, Shelly, Akiva Liberman, and Alice H. Eagly. 'Heuristic And Systematic Information Within And Beyond The Persuasion Context'. In *Unintended Thought*, edited by James S. Uleman and John A. Bargh (New York: Guilford Press, 1989).

Chaiken, Shelly, and Yaacov Trope. *Dual Process Theories in Social Psychology* (New York: Guilford Press, 1999).

Champagne, Anthony, Daniel Shuman, and Elizabeth Whitaker. 'Expert Witnesses in the Courts: An Empirical Examination'. *Judicature* 76, no. 1 (1992) 5.

Charman, Steve D. 'The Forensic Confirmation Bias: A Problem of Evidence Integration, Not Just Evidence Evaluation'. *Journal of Applied Research in Memory and Cognition* 2, no. 1 (March 2013) 56.

Cheesman, Elizabeth. 'Hot Tubbing: Concurrent Expert Evidence'. *Bar News* (Summer 2006/7) 54.

Chesterman, Michael, Janet Chan, and Shelley Hampton. *Managing Prejudicial Publicity: An Empirical Study of Criminal Jury Trials in New South Wales*, (Sydney: Law and Justice Foundation of New South Wales, 2001).

Cialdini, Robert. *Influence: The Psychology of Persuasion*, (New York: William Morrow and Company Inc, 2006).

Cialdini, Robert, and Noah Goldstein. 'Social Influence: Compliance and Conformity'. *Annual Review of Psychology* 55, no. 1 (2004) 591.

Cialdini, Robert, and others. 'Managing Social Norms for Persuasive Impact'. *Social Influence* 1, no. 1 (2006) 3.

Clayfield, Matthew. 'Modern Trials Too Difficult for Juries'. *The Australian*, 10 October 2008, <http://www.theaustralian.com.au/archive/news/modern-trials-too-difficult-for-juries/story-e6frg6o6-1111117712224>.

Cohen, Kenneth S. *Expert Witnessing and Scientific Testimony: Surviving in the Courtroom*, (Boca Raton, Florida: CRC Press, 2007).

Colarusso, Calvin A. *The Psychiatric Witness in Court: What Mental Health Professionals Need to Know*, (New York: Rowman & Littlefield, 2014).

Cole, Simon, and Rachel Dioso-Villa. 'Investigating the "CSI Effect": Media and Litigation Crisis in Criminal Law'. *Stanford Law Review* 61, no. 6 (April 2009) 1335.

Committee for the Workshop on the Medicolegal Death Investigation System. *Medicolegal Death Investigation System: Workshop Summary*, (Washington, DC: The National Academies Press, 2003).

Committee on Identifying the Needs of the Forensic Sciences Community, National Research Council. *Strengthening Forensic Science in the United States: A Path Forward*, (Washington, DC: The National Academies Press, 2009).

Commons, Michael L., and others. 'Forensic Experts' Perceptions of Expert Bias'. *International Journal of Psychiatry* 35, nos 5–6 (2012) 362.

Cooper, Joel, Elizabeth A. Bennett, and Holly L. Sukel. 'Complex Scientific Testimony: How Do Jurors Make Decisions?' *Law & Human Behavior* 20, no. 4 (1996) 379.

Cooper, Joel, and Isaac M. Neuhaus. 'The "Hired Gun" Effect: Assessing the Effect of Pay, Frequency of Testifying and Credentials on the Perception of Expert Testimony'. *Law and Human Behavior* 24, no. 2 (2000) 149.

'Cornelius O'Dowd Upon Men and Women, and Other Things in General'. *Blackwood's Edinburgh Magazine* 96, no. 587 (September 1864) 277.

Coroners Court of Queensland. *Practice Direction for the Use of Concurrent Evidence in the Queensland Coronial Jurisdiction*, (2012).

Corti, Louise, and Paul Thompson. 'Secondary Analysis of Archived Data'. In *Qualitative Research Practice*, edited by Clive Seale and Giampietro Gobo (London: Sage, 2004).

County Court of Victoria. *Practice Note: Expert Evidence in Criminal Trials*, (Last updated: 24 June 2014), <https://www.countycourt.vic.gov.au/sites/default/files/forms/Practice%20 Note%20-%20Expert%20Evidence%20in%20Criminal%20Trials_FINAL%20(June%20 2014)_0.pdf>.

Cownie, Fiona, Anthony Bradney, and Mandy Burton. *English Legal System in Context*, (Oxford: Oxford University Press, 2013).

Cramer, Robert J., Stanley L. Brodsky, and Jamie DeCoster. 'Expert Witness Confidence and Juror Personality: Their Impact on Credibility and Persuasion in the Courtroom'. *Journal of the American Academy of Psychiatry and the Law* 37, no. 1 (March 2009) 63.

CrimTrac. *Annual Report: 2013–2014*, (Canberra: Commonwealth of Australia, 2014), <http://www.crimtrac.gov.au/documents/CRIMTRACAnnualReport2013_14.pdf>.

Croke, Antonia, and Louise Mallon. 'Hot-Tub: Lessons from Australia'. *Ashurst: Commercial Litigation Newsletter* (October 2013), <https://www.ashurst.com/publication-item.aspx?id_Content=9604>.

Cromwell, Thomas A. 'The Challenges of Scientific Evidence', (MacFadyen Lecture, 2 March 2011), <http://www.scottishlawreports.org.uk/publications/macfadyen-2011.html>.

Crowley, Michael J., M. Gemma O'Callaghan, and Peter J. Ball. 'The Juridical Impact of Psychological Expert Testimony in a Simulated Child Sexual Abuse Trial'. *Law and Human Behavior* 18, no. 1 (February 1994) 89.

Crown Prosecution Service. *Guidance Booklet for Experts*, (May 2010), www.cps.gov.uk/legal/assets/uploads/files/Guidance_for_Experts_-_2010_edition.pdf.

'"CSI" Earth's No. 1 Show'. *New York Post*, 17 June 2008, <http://nypost.com/2008/06/17/csi-earths-no-1-show/>.

Cunliffe, Emma. *Murder, Medicine and Motherhood*, (London: Bloomsbury, 2011).

Dartnall, Stephanie, and Jane Goodman-Delahunty. 'Enhancing Juror Understanding of Probabilistic DNA Evidence'. *Australian Journal of Forensic Sciences* 38, no. 2 (2006) 85.

Davies, Geoffrey L. 'Recent Australian Developments: A Response to Peter Heerey'. *Civil Justice Quarterly* 23 (October 2004) 396.

Devine, Dennis J., and others. 'Jury Decision Making: 45 Years of Empirical Research on Deliberating Groups'. *Psychology, Public Policy and Law* 7, no. 3 (September 2001) 622.

Devine, Dennis J., and others. 'Deliberation Quality: A Preliminary Examination in Criminal Juries'. *Journal of Empirical Legal Studies* 4, no. 2 (2007) 273.

Devine, Dennis J., and others. 'Strength of Evidence, Extra-evidentiary Influence, and the Liberation Hypothesis: Data from the Field'. *Law and Human Behavior* 33, no. 2 (2009) 136.

Diamond, Shari S., and Jonathan D. Casper. 'Blindfolding the Jury to Verdict Consequences: Damages, Experts, and the Civil Jury'. *Law and Society Review* 26, no. 3 (1992) 513.

Doak, Jonathan, and Claire McGourlay. *Criminal Evidence in Context*, (London: Routledge, 2009).

Downes, Gary. 'Concurrent Expert Evidence in the Administrative Appeals Tribunal: The New South Wales Experience', (lecture, Australasian Conference of Planning and Environment Courts and Tribunals, Hobart, 27 February 2004).

Downes, Gary. 'Ten Years as President', (lecture, 2012 AAT National Conference, Lorne, 20 March 2012), <http://www.aat.gov.au/about-the-aat/engagement/speeches-and-papers/the-honourable-justice-garry-downes-am-former-pre/ten-years-as-president>.

du Sautoy, Marcus. 'Testing Out the Monty Hall Problem'. YouTube, 4 November 2009, <http://www.youtube.com/watch?v=o_djTy3G0pg&feature=related>.

Dummer, Geoffrey W. A., Robert C. Winton, and Michael H. Tooley. *An Elementary Guide to Reliability*, 5th edn. (Oxford: Butterworth–Heinemann, 1997).

Dwyer, Deidre. '(Why) are Civil and Criminal Expert Evidence Different?' *Tulsa Law Review* 43, no. 2 (winter 2007) 381.

Dwyer, Deirdre. *The Judicial Assessment of Expert Evidence*, (Cambridge: Cambridge University Press, 2008).

Edens, John F., and others. '"Hired guns," "Charlatans," and Their "Voodoo Psychobabble": Case Law References to Various Forms of Perceived Bias Among Mental Health Expert Witnesses'. *Psychological Services* 9, no. 3 (August 2012) 259.

Edmond, Gary. 'Constructing Miscarriages of Justice: Misunderstanding Scientific Evidence in High Profile Criminal Appeals'. *Oxford Journal of Legal Studies* 22, no. 1 (2002) 53.

Edmond, Gary. 'Judging Surveys: Experts, Empirical Evidence and Law Reform'. *Federal Law Review* 33, no. 1 (2005) 95.

Edmond, Gary. 'Specialised Knowledge, the Exclusionary Discretions and Reliability: Reassessing Incriminating Expert Opinion Evidence'. *University of New South Wales Law Journal* 31, no. 1 (2008) 1.

Edmond, Gary. 'Actual Innocents? Legal Limitations and their Implications for Forensic Science and Medicine'. *Australian Journal of Forensic Sciences* 43, no. 2 (2011) 177.

Edmond, Gary. 'The Admissibility of Incriminating Expert Evidence in the United States, England and Canada'. *Judicial Officers' Bulletin* 23, no. 8 (2011) 67.

Edmond, Gary. 'Is Reliability Sufficient? The Law Commission and Expert Evidence in International and Interdisciplinary Perspective (Part 1)'. *The International Journal of Evidence and Proof* 16, no. 1 (2012) 30.

Edmond, Gary. '(Ad)Ministering Justice: Expert Evidence and the Professional Responsibilities of Prosecutors'. *University of New South Wales Law Journal* 36, no. 3 (2013) 921.

Edmond, Gary. 'The Admissibility of Forensic Science and Medicine Evidence under the Uniform Evidence Law'. *Criminal Law Journal* 38, no. 3 (2014) 136.

Edmond, Gary. 'The "Science" of Miscarriages of Justice'. *UNSW Law Journal* 37, no. 1 (2014) 376.

Edmond, Gary. 'What Lawyers Should Know About the Forensic Sciences'. *Adelaide Law Review* (2015, forthcoming).

Edmond, Gary, and David Mercer. 'The Politics of Jury Competence'. In *Participation and Technology*, edited by Brian Martin (Wollongong: University of Wollongong, 1998).

Edmond, Gary, Catherine Biber, Richard Kemp, and Glenn Porter. 'Law's Looking Glass: Expert Identification Evidence Derived from Photographic and Video Images'. *Current Issues in Criminal Justice* 20, no. 3 (2009) 337.

Edmond, Gary, and Mehera San Roque. 'The Cool Crucible: Forensic Science and the Frailty of the Criminal Trial'. *Current Issues in Criminal Justice* 24, no. 1 (2012) 51.

Edmond, Gary, and others. 'How to Cross-Examine Forensic Scientists: A Guide for Lawyers'. *Australian Bar Review* 39, no. 2 (2014) 174.

Edmond, Gary, and Mehera San Roque. '*Honeysett v The Queen*: Forensic Science, "Specialist Knowledge" and the Uniform Evidence Act'. *Sydney Law Review* 36, no. 2 (June 2014) 323.

Edwards, Harry. 'Solving the Problems that Plagued the Forensic Science Community'. *Jurimetrics* 50, no. 1 (2009) 5.

Eggleston, Richard. *Evidence, Proof and Probability*, 2nd edn. (London: Weidenfeld and Nicolson, 1983).

Enescu, Raluca, and André Kuhn. 'Serial Effects of Evidence on Legal Decision-Making'. *The European Journal of Psychology Applied to Legal Context* 4, no. 2 (2012) 99.

Englich, Birte, Thomas Mussweiler, and Fritz Strack. 'Playing Dice with Criminal Sentences: The Influence of Irrelevant Anchors on Experts' Judicial Decision Making'. *Personality & Social Psychology Bulletin* 32, no. 2 (February 2006) 188.

Expert Working Group on Human Factors in Latent Print Analysis. *Latent Print Examination and Human Factors: Improving the Practice through a Systems Approach*, (US Department of Commerce, National Institute of Standards and Technology, 2012).

Faigman, David L., and A. J. Bagkioni Jr. 'Bayes' Theorem in the Trial Process: Instructing Jurors on the Value of Statistical Evidence'. *Law and Human Behavior* 12, no. 1 (1988) 1.

Field, Douglas L. *The Expert Expert: The Path to Prosperity and Prominence as an Expert Witness*, (iuniverse, 2013).

Finch, Emily, and Vanessa Munro. 'Lifting the Veil: The Use of Focus Groups and Trial Simulations in Legal Research'. *Journal of Law and Society* 35, special issue: 'Law's Reality: Case Studies in Empirical Research on Law', (June 2008) 30.

Findlay, Mark. 'Juror Comprehension and the Hard Case: Making Forensic Evidence Simpler'. *International Journal of Law, Crime and Justice* 36, no. 1 (2008) 15.

Fisher, Jim. *Forensics Under Fire: Are Bad Science and Duelling Experts Corrupting Criminal Justice?* (New Brunswick, NJ: Rutgers University Press, 2008).

Fisher, Robert. 'The Demeanour Fallacy' (2014) *New Zealand Law Review* 575.

Fiske, Susan T., and Shelley E. Taylor. *Social Cognition: Topics in Social Psychology*, (New York: Random House, 1984).

Forensic Science Regulator. *Codes of Practice and Conduct: For Forensic Science Providers and Practitioners in the Criminal Justice System*, (2014), <https://www.gov.uk/government/uploads/system/uploads/attachment_data/file/351197/The_FSR_Codes_of_Practice_and_Conduct_-_v2_August_2014.pdf>.

Foster, Kenneth R., and Peter W. Huber. *Judging Science: Scientific Knowledge and the Federal Courts*, (Cambridge, Mass: MIT Press, 1999).

Fraser, Jim, John Buckleton, and Peter Gill. 'Review of DNA Reporting Practices by Victoria Police Forensic Services Division'. *Victoria Police News* (April 2010) 3.

Fraud Trials Committee and Eustace W. Roskill. *Frauds Trials Committee Report*, (London: HMSO, 1986).

Freckelton, Ian. *The Trial of the Expert*, (Melbourne: Oxford University Press, 1987).

Freckelton, Ian. 'The Diagnostic Expertise of Psychologists'. *Psychiatry, Psychology and Law* 4, no. 1 (1997) 73.

Freckelton, Ian. 'Wizards in the Crucible: Making the Boffins Accountable'. In *Proceedings of the First World Conference on New Trends in Criminal Investigation and Evidence*, edited by Johannes F. Nijboer and Jan M. Reijntjes (The Hague: Koninklijke Vermande, 1997).

Freckelton, Ian. 'Psychologists' Entitlement to Diagnose'. *Psychiatry, Psychology and Law* 5, no. 1 (1998) 159.

Freckelton, Ian. *Crimes Compensation: Law, Practice and Policy*, (Sydney: LBC Information Services, 2001).

Freckelton, Ian, and Marilyn McMahon. 'Social Science Research and Experimentation in Australian Criminal Proceedings: Prejudicial Pre-trial Publicity and Psychological Research'. *Journal of Law and Medicine* 9 (2002) 347.

Freckelton, Ian. 'Eyewitness Identification Law Reform: The Need for Persistence'. *Journal of Law and Medicine* 20, no. 3 (2013) 503.

Freckelton, Ian. *Scholarly Misconduct: Law, Regulation, and Practice* (Oxford: Oxford University Press, 2016).

Freckelton, Ian, and Hugh Selby. *Expert Evidence: Law, Practice, Procedure and Advocacy*, 6th edn. (Sydney: Thomson Reuters, 2016).

Freckelton, Ian, Prasuna Reddy, and Hugh Selby. *Australian Judicial Perspectives on Expert Evidence: An Empirical Study*, (Melbourne: AIJA, 1999).

Freckelton, Ian, Prasuna Reddy, and Hugh Selby. *Australian Magistrates' Perspectives on Expert Evidence: A Comparative Study*, (Melbourne: AIJA, 2001).

Furnham, Adrian. 'The Robustness of the Recency Effect: Studies Using Legal Evidence'. *The Journal of General Psychology* 113, no. 4 (October 1986) 351.

Garcia-Retamero, Rocio, and Mandeep Dhami. 'On Avoiding Framing Effects in Experienced Decision Makers'. *The Quarterly Journal of Experimental Psychology* 66, no. 4 (April 2013) 829.

Garling, Peter. 'Concurrent Expert Evidence: Reflections and Developments'. *Law Society Journal* 49, no. 10 (2011) 5.

Garling, Peter 'Concurrent Expert Evidence, Reflections and Developments', (lecture, Australian Insurance Law Association Twilight Seminar Series, 17 August 2011).

Garling, Peter. 'Reflections on Concurrent Expert Evidence'. *Bar News* (summer 2011–12) 12.

Gatowski, Sophia I., Shirley A. Dobbin, James T. Richardson, Gerald P. Ginsburg, Mara L. Merlino, and Veronica Dahir. 'Asking the Gatekeepers: A National Survey of Judges on Judging Expert Evidence in a Post-*Daubert* World'. *Law and Human Behavior* 25, no. 5 (2001) 433.

General Medical Council. *Acting as an Expert Witness: Supplementary Guidance*, (July 2008), <http://www.gmc-uk.org/guidance/archive.asp>.

General Medical Council. *Acting as a Witness in Legal Proceedings*, (2013), <http://www.gmc-uk.org/guidance/ethical_guidance/21188.asp>.

Genn, Hazel. *Manchester Concurrent Evidence Pilot: Interim Report*, (January 2012), <http://www.judiciary.gov.uk/wp-content/uploads/JCO/Documents/Reports/concurrent-evidence-interim-report.pdf>.

Gibb, Frances. 'Lord Judge Calls for Jury System that Caters for Computer Generation'. *The Times*, 21 October 2009, <http://www.thetimes.co.uk/tto/law/article2215110.ece>.

Gigerenzer, Gerd. *Gut Feelings: Short Cuts to Better Decision Making*, (London: Penguin Books, 2008).

Gilbert, Daniel T., and Gregory J. Hixon. 'The Trouble of Thinking: Activation and Application of Stereotypic Beliefs'. *Journal of Personality and Social Psychology* 60, no. 4 (April 1991) 509.

Golan, Tal. *Laws of Men and Laws of Nature*, (Cambridge, Mass: Harvard University Press, 2007).

Gold, Alan. *Expert Evidence in Criminal Law: The Scientific Approach*, 2nd edn. (Toronto: Irwin Law, 2009).

Goodman, Jane. 'Jurors' Comprehension and Assessment of Probabilistic Evidence'. *American Journal of Trial Advocacy* 16, no. 2 (winter 1992) 361.

Goodman-Delahunty, Jane. 'Forensic Psychological Expertise in the Wake of Daubert'. *Law and Human Behavior* 21, no. 2 (1997) 121.

Goodman-Delahunty, Jane, Anne Cossins, and Kate O'Brien. 'Enhancing the Credibility of Complainants in Child Sexual Assault Trials: The Effect of Expert Evidence and Judicial Directions'. *Behavioral Sciences & the Law* 28, no. 6 (2010) 769.

Goodman-Delahunty, Jane, Anne Cossins, and Kate O'Brien. 'A Comparison of Expert Evidence and Judicial Directions to Counter Misconceptions in Child Sexual Abuse Trials'. *Australian and New Zealand Journal of Criminology* 44, no. 2 (2011) 196.

Goodman-Delahunty, Jane, Thea Gumbert-Jourjon, and Sandra Hale. 'The Biasing Influence of Linguistic Variations in DNA Profiling Evidence'. *Australian Journal of Forensic Sciences* 46, no. 3 (2014) 348.

Goodman-Delahunty, Jane, and Lindsay Hewson. *Improving Jury Understanding and Use of Expert DNA Evidence: Technical and Background Paper No. 37*, (Australian Institute of Criminology, 2010).

Goodman-Delahunty, Jane, and Lindsay Hewson. 'Enhancing Fairness in DNA Jury Trials'. *Trends & Issues in Crime and Criminal Justice*, no. 392 (March 2010) 1.

Goodman-Delahunty, Jane, and Ben Newell. 'One in How Many Trillion?' *Australasian Science 25*, no. 7 (August 2004) 14.

Goodman-Delahunty, Jane, and Sophie Rabone. 'Multimedia Evidence and the Jury: Applying Principles of Effective Communication', (lecture, 23rd Annual Conference of the Australian Institute of Judicial Administration, Wellington, New Zealand, 2005).

Goodman-Delahunty, Jane, and David Tait. 'DNA and the Changing Face of Justice'. *Australian Journal of Forensic Sciences* 38, no. 2 (2006) 97.

Goodman-Delahunty, Jane, and Hielkje Verbrugge. 'Reality, Fantasy and the Truth about CSI Effects'. *InPsych: The Bulletin of the Australian Psychological Society* 32, no. 4 (2010) 18, <http://www.psychology.org.au/publications/inpsych/2010/august/goodman/>.

Goodman-Delahunty, Jane, and Kosuke Wakabayashi. 'Adversarial Forensic Science Experts: An Empirical Study of Jury Deliberation'. *Current Issues in Criminal Justice* 24, no. 1 (July 2012) 85.

Gornall, Jonathan. 'Was Message of Sudden Infant Death Study Misleading?' *BMJ* 333, no. 7579 (December 2006) 1165.

Goudge, Stephen T. *Inquiry into Pediatric Forensic Pathology in Ontario: Report*, (Ontario Ministry of the Attorney General, 2008). <http://www.attorneygeneral.jus.gov.on.ca/inquiries/goudge/>.

Grant Thornton LLP. *National Litigation Survey Report*, (2015), <http://insights.grantthornton.ca/i/453877-national-litigation-survey-report/2>.

Greaves, Collins. 'The Expert Witness'. In *The Expert Medical Witness*, edited by Rosalind Winfield (Sydney: The Federation Press, 1989).

Gunn, John, and Pamela Taylor. *Forensic Psychiatry: Clinical, Legal and Ethical Issues*, 2nd edn. (London: CRC Press, 2014).

Gutheil, Thomas G. *The Psychiatrist as Expert Witness*, 2nd edn. (Washington, DC: American Psychiatric Publishing, 2009).

Guthrie, Chris, Jeffrey Rachlinski, and Andrew J. Wistrich. 'Inside the Judicial Mind'. *Cornell Law Review* 86, no. 4 (May 2001) 777.

Guthrie, Chris, Jeffrey Rachlinski, and Andrew Wistrich. 'Judging by Heuristic: Cognitive Illusions in Judicial Decision Making'. *Judicature* 86, no. 1 (July–August 2002) 44.

Gwet, Kilem Li. *Handbook of Inter-Rater Reliability*, 3rd edn. (Gaithersburg, Maryland: Advanced Analytics Press, 2012).

Hagan, Kate. '15 Months' Jail a Miscarriage of Justice'. *The Age*, 8 December 2009, p. 1.

Hagen, Margaret A. *Whores of the Court* (New York: Regan Books, 1997).

Hand, Learned. *Historical and Practical Considerations Regarding Expert Testimony*, (Albany: Thomson Gale, 1900).

Hans, Valerie, and others. 'Science in the Jury Box: Jurors' Comprehension of Mitochondrial DNA Evidence'. *Law and Human Behavior* 35, no. 1 (2011) 60.

Health and Safety Executive. 'Expert Evidence'. In *HSE Enforcement Guide (England & Wales)*, (2003), www.hse.gov.uk/enforce/enforcementguide/investigation/expert-intro.htm.

Heerey, Peter. 'Expert Evidence: The Australian Experience'. *Bar Review* 7 (January–February 2002) 166.

Heerey, Peter. 'Recent Australian Developments'. *Civil Justice Quarterly* 23 (October 2004) 386.

Heffernan, Liz. 'Gauging the Reliability of Scientific Evidence in Tort'. *Judicial Studies Institute Journal* 6, no. 1 (2006) 140.

Her Majesty's Inspectorate of Constabulary. *Scottish Criminal Record Office: The Fingerprint Bureau: Primary Inspection 2000*, (2000).

Hodgkinson, Tristram, and Mark James. *Expert Evidence: Law and Practice*, 4th edn. (London: Sweet & Maxwell, 2014).

Hor, Michael. 'When Experts Disagree'. *Singapore Journal of Legal Studies*, no. 1 (2000) 241.

Horan, Jacqueline. 'The Civil Jury System: An Empirical Study'. (PhD dissertation, University of Melbourne, 2006).

Horan, Jacqueline. *Juries in the 21st Century*, (Sydney: The Federation Press, 2012).

Horan, Jacqueline, and Mark Israel. 'Institutional Gate-Keeping and Jury Research'. *Australian and New Zealand Journal of Criminology* (2015, forthcoming).

House of Commons Science and Technology Committee. *Forensic Science on Trial: Seventh Report of Session 2004–05*, (London: The Stationery Office, 2005), <http://www.publications.parliament.uk/pa/cm200405/cmselect/cmsctech/96/96i.pdf>.

Howes, Loene. 'A Step Towards Increased Understanding by Non-Scientists of Expert Reports: Recommendations for Readability'. *Australian Journal of Forensic Sciences* (2015), doi:10.1080/00450618.2015.1004194.

Hughston, Vance, and Tina Jowett. 'In the Native Title "Hot Tub": Expert Conferences and Concurrent Expert Evidence in Native Title'. *Land, Rights, Laws: Issues of Native Title* 6, no. 1 (2014) 1, <http://www.aiatsis.gov.au/_files/ntru/ip_hughstonjowett_web.pdf>.

Imwinkelried, Edward J. 'The Next Step After *Daubert*: Developing a Similarly Epistemological Approach to Ensuring the Reliability of Nonscientific Expert Testimony'. *Cardozo Law Review* 15, no. 6 (April 1994) 2271.

Ingulli, Elaine D. 'Trial by Jury: Reflections on Witness Credibility, Expert Testimony, and Recantation'. *Valparaiso University Law Review* 20 (winter 1986) 145.

Ipp, David. 'Lawyers' Duties to the Court'. *Law Quarterly Review* 114 (January 1998) 63.

Irish Law Reform Commission. *Expert Evidence: Consultation Paper No. 52*, (Dublin: Irish Law Reform Commission, 2008), <http://www.bailii.org/cgi-bin/markup.cgi?doc=/ie/other/IELRC/2008/cp52.html&query=daubert&method=boolean>.

Isenberg, Daniel J. 'Group Polarization: A Critical Review and Meta-Analysis'. *Journal of Personality and Social Psychology* 50, no. 6 (1986) 1141.

Ivković, Sanja Kutnjak, and Valerie P. Hans. 'Jurors' Evaluations of Expert Testimony: Judging the Messenger and the Message'. *Law and Social Inquiry* 28, no. 2 (2003) 441.

Jackson, John, and Sean Doran. *Judge Without Jury: Diplock Trials in the Adversary System*, (Oxford: Clarendon Press, 1995).

Jackson, Rupert. *Review of Civil Litigation Costs: Final Report*, (December 2009), <https://www.judiciary.gov.uk/wp-content/uploads/JCO/Documents/Reports/jackson-final-report-140110.pdf>.

Jonakait, Randolph N. *The American Jury System*, (New Haven: Yale University Press, 2008).

Jones, Carol A. G. *Expert Witnesses*, (Oxford: Oxford University Press, 1994).

Judicial College of Victoria. *Victorian Criminal Proceedings Manual*, (Melbourne: Judicial College of Victoria, 2014), <http://www.judicialcollege.vic.edu.au/eManuals/VCPM/index.htm#27318.htm>.

Juries Commissioner's Office. *2013 Victorian Juror Satisfaction Survey Results*, (2013).

Kagehiro, Dorothy K. 'Jurors Keenly Assess Experts' Credibility'. *The National Law Journal* 24, no. 11 (5 November 2001) B14.

Kaplan, Martin F. 'Discussion Polarization Effects in a Modified Jury Decision Paradigm: Informational Influences'. *Sociometry* 40, no. 3 (1977) 262.

Karson, Michael, and Lavita Nadkarni. *Principles of Forensic Report Writing*, (Washington, DC: American Psychological Association, 2013).

Kaufman, Fred. *Report of the Kaufman Commission on Proceedings Involving Guy Paul Morin*, (Toronto: Ministry of the Attorney General, 1998).

Kaye, David. 'Probability, Individualization, and Uniqueness: What's the Difference?' *Law, Probability & Risk* 8, no. 2 (2009) 85.

Kaye, David H., and Jonathan Koehler. 'Can Jurors Understand Probabilistic Evidence?' *Journal of the Royal Statistical Society: Series A (Statistics in Society)* 154, no. 1 (1991) 75.

Kaye, David H., and others. 'Statistics in the Jury Box: How Jurors Respond to Mitochondrial DNA Match Probabilities'. *Journal of Empirical Legal Studies* 4, no. 4 (2007) 797.

Kennedy, Roger. *Psychotherapists as Expert Witnesses*, (London: Karnac, 2005).

Kim, Young S., Gregg Barak, and Donald E. Shelton. 'Examining the "CSI-Effect" in the Cases of Circumstantial Evidence and Eyewitness Testimony: Multivariate and Path Analyses'. *Journal of Criminal Justice* 37, no. 5 (2009) 452.

Koehler, Jonathan. 'One in Millions, Billions and Trillions: Lessons from *People v Collins* (1968) for *People v Simpson* (1995)'. *Journal of Legal Education* 47, no. 2 (1997) 214.

Koehler, Jonathan J. 'When Are People Persuaded by DNA Match Statistics?' *Law and Human Behavior* 25, no. 5 (2001) 493.

Koehler, Jonathan, Audrey Chia, and Samuel Lindsey. 'The Random Match Probability (RMP) in DNA Evidence: Irrelevant and Prejudicial?' *Jurimetrics Journal* 35, no. 2 (winter 1995) 201.

Kovera, Margaret Bull, Eugene Borgida, April W. Grehsam, Ellen Gray, and Pamela C. Regan. 'Does Expert Psychological Testimony Inform or Influence Juror Decision Making?' *Journal of Applied Psychology* 82, no. 1 (February 1997) 178.

Krauss, Daniel A., and Joel D. Lieberman. *Jury Psychology: Social Aspects of Trial Processes Psychology in the Courtroom*, vol. 1 (Dartmouth: Ashgate, 2012).

Krauss, Daniel A., John G. McCabe, and Joel D. Liberman. 'Dangerously Misunderstood: Representative Jurors' Reactions to Expert Testimony on Future Dangerousness in a Sexually Violent Predator Trial'. *Psychology, Public Policy and Law* 18, no. 1 (February 2012) 18.

Kristjanson, Freya. '"Hot Tubs" and Concurrent Evidence: Improving Administrative Proceedings'. *Canadian Journal of Administrative Law and Practice* 25, no. 1 (March 2012) 79.

Kumar, Miiko. 'Admissibility of Expert Evidence: Proving the Basis for an Expert's Opinion'. *Sydney Law Review* 33, no. 3 (September 2011) 427.

Landsman, Stephan, and Richard Rakos. 'A Preliminary Inquiry into the Effect of Potentially Biasing Information on Judges and Jurors in Civil Litigation'. *Behavioral Sciences & the Law* 12, no. 2 (1994) 113.

Large, Matthew, Olav Nielssen, and Gordon Elliott. 'The Reliability of Evidence about Psychiatric Diagnosis after Serious Crime: Part II. Agreement between Experts and Treating Practitioners'. *Journal of the American Academy of Psychiatry and Law* 38, no. 4 (2010) 524.

Law Commission. *The Admissibility of Expert Evidence in Criminal Proceedings in England and Wales: A New Approach to the Determination of Evidentiary Admissibility—Consultation Paper No. 190*, (London: The Stationery Office, 2009).

Law Commission of England and Wales. *Expert Evidence in Criminal Proceedings in England and Wales: Report No. 325*, (London: The Stationery Office, 2011), <http://www.lawcom.gov.uk/project/expert-evidence-in-criminal-proceedings/#expert-evidence-in-criminal-proceedings>.

Leong, Frederick J. T., and James T. Austin. *Psychology Research Handbook*, (New York: Sage, 2005).

Levesque, Roger J. R. *The Psychology and Law of Criminal Justice Processes*, (New York: Nova Publishers, 2007).

Lieberman, Joel, and others. 'Gold Versus Platinum: Do Jurors Recognise the Superiority and Limitations of DNA Evidence Compared to Other Types of Forensic Evidence?' *Psychology, Public Policy, and Law* 14, no. 1 (2008) 27.

Liptak, Adam. 'Experts Hired to Shed Light Can Leave US Courts in Dark'. *The New York Times*, 11 August 2008, <http://www.nytimes.com/2008/08/12/us/12experts.html?pagewanted=all&_r=0>.

Livingstone, Mia Louise. 'Have We Fired the "Hired Gun"? A Critique of Expert Evidence Reform in Australia and the United Kingdom'. *Journal of Judicial Administration* 18, no. 1 (2008) 39.

Loughnan, Arlie. *Manifest Madness: Mental Incapacity in the Criminal Law*, (Oxford: Oxford University Press, 2012).

Lu, Li, Y. Connie Yuan, and Poppy Lauretta McLeod. 'Twenty-Five Years of Hidden Profiles in Group Decision Making: A Meta-Analysis'. *Personality and Social Psychology Review* 16, no. 1 (February 2012) 54.

Lubet, Stephen, and Elizabeth Boals. *Expert Testimony: A Guide for Expert Witnesses and the Lawyers Who Examine Them*, 3rd edn. (Boulder, Co: Lexis Nexis/NITA, 2014).

Macrae, Neil C., Alan B. Milne, and Galen V. Bodenhausen. 'Stereotypes as Energy-Saving Devices: A Peek Inside the Cognitive Toolbox'. *Journal of Personality and Social Psychology* 66, no. 1 (January 1994) 37.

Madden, Bill, Bill Cockburn, and Tina Cockburn. 'Adapting to Concurrent Expert Evidence in Medical Litigation'. *Journal of Law and Medicine* 22, no. 3 (2015) 610.

Mahoney, Richard, Elisabeth McDonald, Scott Optican, and Yvette Tinsley. *The Evidence Act 2006: Act & Analysis*, 3rd edn. (Wellington: Brookers, 2014).

Malek, Hodge M. *Phipson on Evidence*, 18th edn. (London: Sweet & Maxwell, 2013).

Mann, Michael. 'The "CSI Effect": Better Jurors through Televisions and Science?' *Buffalo Public Internet Law Journal* 24 (2005–6) 211.

Martire, Kristy A., and Richard I. Kemp. 'Can Experts Help Jurors to Evaluate Eyewitness Evidence? A Review of Eyewitness Expert Effects'. *Legal and Criminological Psychology* 16, no. 1 (February 2011) 24.

Matson, Jack V. *Effective Expert Witnessing: Practices for the 21st Century*, (Boca Raton: CRC Press, 2004).

McClellan, Peter. 'Expert Witnesses: The Recent Experience of the Land and Environment Court'. *Judicial Officers Bulletin* 17 (2005) 83.

McClellan, Peter. 'Expert Witnesses: The Experience of the Land & Environment Court of NSW', (lecture, XIX Biennial LawAsia Conference, Gold Coast, 20–24 March 2005).

McClellan, Peter. 'Expert Evidence: Aces Up Your Sleeve?' (lecture, Industrial Relations Commission of New South Wales, 20 October 2006).

McClellan, Peter, 'Who Is Telling the Truth? Psychology, Common Sense and the Law' (lecture, Local Courts of New South Wales Annual Conference, 2 August 2006).

McClellan, Peter. 'Concurrent Expert Evidence', (lecture, Medicine and Law Conference, Law Institute of Victoria, 29 November 2007), <http://www.austlii.edu.au/au/journals/NSWJSchol/2007/15.pdf>.

McClellan, Peter. 'New Method with Experts: Concurrent Evidence'. *Journal of Court Innovation* 3, no. 1 (winter 2010) 259.

McClellan, Peter. 'The Future Role of the Judge: Umpire, Manager, Mediator or Service Provider'. *New South Wales Judicial Scholarship*, no. 44 (2011): <http://www.austlii.edu.au/au/journals/NSWJSchol/2011/44.html>.

McKimmie, Blake M., and others. 'Jurors' Responses to Expert Witness Testimony: The Effects of Gender Stereotypes'. *Group Processes and Intergroup Relations* 7, no. 2 (April 2004) 131.

McKimmie, Blake M., and others. 'It's Not What She Says, It's How She Says It: The Influence of Language Complexity and Cognitive Load on the Persuasiveness of Expert Testimony'. *Psychiatry, Psychology and Law* 20, no. 4 (2013) 578.

McKimmie, Blake M., and others. 'Stereotypical and Counterstereotypical Defendants: Who is He and What was the Case Against Her?' *Psychology, Public Policy and Law* 19 (2013) 343.

McKimmie, Blake M., Emma Antrobus, and Chantelle Baguley. 'Objective and Subjective Comprehension of Jury Instructions in Criminal Trials'. *New Criminal Law Review: An International and Interdisciplinary Journal* 17, no. 2 (spring 2014) 163.

McKimmie, Blake M., Barbara M. Masser, and Renata Bongiorno. 'Looking Shifty But Telling the Truth: The Effect of Witness Demeanour on Mock Jurors' Perceptions'. *Psychiatry, Psychology and Law* 21, no. 2 (2014) 297.

McPherson, Joe W. *Reliability Physics and Engineering: Time-To-Failure Modelling*, (New York: Springer, 2010).

Medical Board of Australia. *Good Medical Practice: A Code of Conduct for Doctors in Australia*, (March 2014), <http://www.medicalboard.gov.au/Codes-Guidelines-Policies/Code-of-conduct.aspx>.

Meintjes-van de Walt, Lirieka. 'Expert Odyssey: Thoughts on the Presentation and Evaluation of Scientific Evidence'. *South African Law Journal* 120 (2003) 352.

Memon, Amina, and Daniel W. Shuman. 'Juror Perception of Experts in Civil Disputes: The Role of Race and Gender'. *Law & Psychology Review* 22 (1998) 179.

Meyer, Carl. *Expert Witnessing: Explaining and Understanding Science*, (London: CRC Press, 1998).

Ministry of Justice. *The Government's Response to the Law Commission's Report: Expert Evidence in Criminal Proceedings in England and Wales*, (Law Com No. 325, 21 November 2013), <https://www.gov.uk/government/uploads/system/uploads/attachment_data/file/260369/govt-resp-experts-evidence.pdf>.

Mivka, Mary. 'An Indelicate Balance: Rule 403 of the Federal Rules of Evidence'. *Evidence* 30, no. 1 (2003) 36.

Mnookin, Jennifer. 'Expert Evidence, Partisanship and Epistemic Competence'. *Brooklyn Law Review* 73, no. 3 (spring 2008) 1009.

Morling, Trevor. *Report of the Royal Commission of Inquiry into the Chamberlain Convictions*, (Canberra, Commonwealth Government Printer, 1987).

Morris, Stuart. 'Getting Real about Expert Evidence', (lecture, National Environment Law Conference, Canberra, 13 July 2005), <http://www.austlii.edu.au/au/journals/VicJSchol/2005/14.pdf>.

Morrison, Carol Myers. 'Can the Jury Trial Survive Google?' *Criminal Justice* 25, no. 4 (2011), <http://www.americanbar.org/content/dam/aba/publications/criminal_justice_magazine/cjw11jurytrial_google.authcheckdam.pdf>.

Mullen, Brian and others. 'Group Cohesiveness and Quality of Decision Making: An Integration of Tests of the Groupthink Hypothesis'. *Small Group Research* 25, no. 2 (1994) 189.

Murphy, Thomas. 'The Admissibility of CCTV Footage in Criminal Proceedings'. *International Journal of Law Computers & Technology* 13, no 3 (1999) 383–404.

Neal, Tess M. S., and Stanley L. Brodsky. 'Expert Witness Credibility as a Function of Eye Contact Behavior and Gender'. *Criminal Justice and Behavior* 35, no. 2 (2008) 1515.

New South Wales Law Reform Commission. *Expert Witnesses: Report No. 109*, (Sydney: New South Wales Law Reform Commission, 2005).

New South Wales Law Reform Commission. *Jury Directions: Report No. 136*, (Sydney: New South Wales Law Reform Commission, 2012).

New Zealand Law Commission. *Evidence: Report No. 55*. vol. 2 (Wellington, NZ: Law Commission, 1999).

Nisbett, Richard, and Timothy Wilson. 'Telling More Than We Can Know: Verbal Reports on Mental Processes'. *Psychological Review* 84, no. 3 (May 1977) 231.

O'Barr, William M. *Linguistic Evidence: Language, Power, and Strategy in the Courtroom*, (New York: Pergamon, 1982).

Odgers, Stephen, and James T. Richardson. 'Keeping Bad Science Out of the Courtroom: Changes in Australian and American Expert Evidence Law'. *University of New South Wales Law Review* 18, no. 1 (1995) 108.

Osborne, Coulter A. *Civil Justice Reform Project: Summary of Findings and Recommendations*, (November 2007), <http://www.attorneygeneral.jus.gov.on.ca/english/about/pubs/cjrp/CJRP-Report_EN.pdf>.

Peckham, Robert F. 'Judicial Response to the Cost of Litigation: Case Management, Two-Stage Discovery Planning and Alternative Dispute Resolution'. *Rutgers Law Review* 37 (winter 1985) 253.

Pennington, Nancy, and Reid Hastie. 'Evidence Evaluation in Complex Decision Making'. *Journal of Personality and Social Psychology* 51, no. 2 (August 1986) 242.

Pennington, Nancy, and Reid Hastie. 'Explaining the Evidence: Tests of the Story Model for Juror Decision Making'. *Journal of Personality and Social Psychology* 62, no. 2 (1992) 189.

Pepper, Rachel. *Expert Evidence in the Land and Environment Court*, (21 January 2013), <http://www.lec.justice.nsw.gov.au/Documents/expert%20evidence%20in%20the%20land%20and%20environment%20court%20v2.pdf>.

Petty, Richard E., and John T. Cacioppo. 'The Elaboration Likelihood Model of Persuasion'. In *Advances in Experimental Social Psychology*, vol. 19, edited by Leonard Berkowitz (New York: Academic Press, 1986).

Phillips, John H. 'Practical Advocacy: The Duty of Counsel'. *Australian Law Journal* 68, no. 11 (1994) 834, <http://www.austlii.edu.au/cgi-bin/LawCite?cit=%281994%29%2068%20Australian%20Law%20Journal%20834>.

Plater, David, and Lucy Line. 'Has the "Silver Thread" of the Criminal Law Lost its Lustre? The Modern Prosecutor as a Minister of Justice'. *University of Tasmania Law Review* 31, no. 2 (2012) 55.

Podlas, Kimberlianne. 'The "CSI Effect": Exposing The Media Myth'. *Fordham Intellectual Property, Media and Entertainment Law Journal* 16 (2006) 429.

Popper, Karl. *The Logic of Scientific Discovery*, (London: Routledge, 1992).

Poynter, Dan. *The Expert Witness Handbook: Tips and Techniques for the Litigation Consultant*, 3rd edn. (Santa Barbara, CA: Para Publishing, 2007).

Public Prosecution Service, *The Path to Justice: Preventing Wrongful Convictions* (autumn 2011), Chap 9: <http://www.ppsc-sppc.gc.ca/eng/pub/ptj-spj/ch9.html>.

Rachlinski, Jeffrey. 'Heuristics and Biases in the Courts: Ignorance or Adaptation?' *Oregon Law Review* 79, no. 1 (spring 2000) 61.

Rachlinski, Jeffrey, and others. 'Does Unconscious Racial Bias Affect Trial Judges?' *Notre Dame Law Review* 84, no. 3 (March 2009) 1195.

Rackemann, Michael E. 'The Management of Experts'. *Journal of Judicial Administration* 21, no. 3 (February 2012) 168.

Rares, Stephen. 'Using the "Hot Tub": How Concurrent Expert Evidence Aids Understanding Issues'. *Federal Judicial Scholarship* (2010) 20.

Rayment, Katherine. 'Faith in DNA: The Vincent Report'. *Journal of Law, Information and Science* 20 (2009–10) 214.

Redmayne, Mike. 'Theorising Jury Reform'. In *The Trial on Trial: Volume 2: Judgment and Calling to Account*, edited by Antony Duff and others (London: Bloomsbury Publishing, 2006).

Redmayne, Mike, Paul Roberts, Colin Aitken, and Graham Jackson. 'Forensic Science in Question'. *Criminal Law Review*, no. 5 (2011) 347.

Rijnbout, Jasmine, and Blake McKimmie. 'Deviance in Organizational Group Decision-Making: The Role of Information Processing, Confidence, and Elaboration'. *Group Processes & Intergroup Relations* 15, no. 6 (2012) 813.

Risinger, D. Michael. 'Navigating Expert Reliability: Are Criminal Standards of Certainty Being Left in the Dock?' *Alberta Law Review* 64, no. 1 (2000) 99.

Rix, Keith. *Expert Psychiatric Evidence*, (London: RC Psych Publications, 2011).

Roberts, Andrew. 'Expert Evidence and Unreliability in the High Court: *Honeysett v The Queen*'. 'Opinions on High' blog, 3 September 2014. <http://blogs.unimelb.edu.au/opinionsonhigh/2014/09/03/roberts-honeysett>.

Roberts, Paul, and Jill Hunter, eds. *Criminal Evidence and Human Rights: Reimagining Common Law Procedural Traditions*, (London: Bloomsbury, 2012).

Roberts, Paul, and Adrian Zuckerman. *Criminal Evidence*, 2nd edn. (Oxford: Oxford University Press, 2010).

Rogers, Richard, and Daniel W. Shuman. *Fundamentals of Forensic Practice: Mental Health and Criminal Law*, (New York: Springer, 2005).

Roskill, Eustace W. L. *Fraud Trials Committee Report*, (London: HMSO, 1986).

Rozenes, Michael. 'The Role of the DPP in the Investigation and Prosecution of Complex Fraud', (lecture, ASC Law Enforcement Conference, Perth, 16 September 1994), <http://www.cdpp.gov.au/news/the-role-of-the-dpp-in-the-investigation-and-prosecution-of-complex-fraud/>.

Ryu, Dongsu. *Improving Reliability and Quality for Product Success*, (Boca Raton, Florida: CRC Press, 2012).

Saks, Michael J. 'The Aftermath of *Daubert*: An Evolving Jurisprudence of Expert Evidence'. *Jurimetrics* 40, no. 2 (winter 2000) 229.

Saks, Michael, and Robert Kidd. 'Human Information Processing and Adjudication: Trial by Heuristics'. *Law and Society* 15, no. 1 (1980–1) 123.

Saks, Michael, and Dawn McQuiston-Surrett. 'The Testimony of Forensic Identification Science: What Expert Witnesses Say and What Factfinders Hear'. *Law and Human Behavior* 33, no. 1 (2009) 436.

Sallavaci, Oriola. *The Impact of Scientific Evidence on the Criminal Trial: The Case of DNA Evidence*, (New York: Routledge, 2014).

Sangha, Bibi, Kent Roach, and Robert Moles. *Forensic Investigations and Miscarriages of Justice: The Rhetoric Meets the Reality*, (Toronto: Irwin Law, 2010).

Schklar, Jason, and Shari Seidman Diamond. 'Juror Reactions to DNA Evidence: Errors and Expectancies'. *Law and Human Behavior* 23, no. 2 (1999) 159.

Schuller, Regina A., Deborah Terry, and Blake M. McKimmie. 'The Impact of an Expert's Gender on Jurors' Decisions'. *Law and Psychology Review* 25 (2001) 59.

Schuller, Regina A., Deborah Terry, and Blake M. McKimmie. 'The Impact of Expert Testimony on Jurors' Decisions: Gender of the Expert and Testimony Complexity'. *Journal of Applied Social Psychology* 35, no. 6 (June 2005) 1266.

Schulz-Hardt, Stefan, and others. 'Biased Information Search in Group Decision Making'. *Journal of Personality and Social Psychology* 78, no. 4 (2000) 655.

Schunk, Dale H., and Judith L. Meece. *Student Perceptions in the Classroom*, (Hillsdale, NJ: Lawrence Erlbaum, 1992).

Schweitzer, N. J., and Michael J. Saks. 'The CSI Effect: Popular Fiction About Forensic Science Affects the Public's Expectations About Real Forensic Science'. *Jurimetrics* 47, no. 3 (2007) 357.

'Scientists "Hot Tubbing" in Rayney Trial Evidence'. *ABC News*, 14 August 2012, <http://www.abc.net.au/news/2012-08-14/research-scientists-give-evidence-at-rayney-trial/4197874>.

Seierstad, Asne. *One of Us: The Story of Anders Breivik and the Massacre in Norway*, (London: Hachette, 2015).

Shannon, Carl. *Royal Commission Report Concerning the Conviction of Edward Charles Splatt*, (Adelaide: Government Printer of South Australia, 1984).

Shelton, Donald E., Young S. Kim, and Gregg Barak. 'A Study of Juror Expectations and Demands Concerning Scientific Evidence: Does the "CSI Effect" Exist?' *Vanderbilt Journal of Entertainment & Technology Law* 9 (winter 2006) 331.

Shelton, Donald E., Young S. Kim, and Gregg Barak. 'An Indirect-Effects Model of Mediated Adjudication: The CSI Myth, the Tech Effect, and Metropolitan Jurors' Expectations for Scientific Evidence'. *Vanderbilt Journal of Entertainment & Technology Law* 12, no. 1 (autumn 2009) 1.

Sherman, Jeffrey W. and others. 'Stereotype Efficiency Reconsidered: Encoding Flexibility under Cognitive Load'. *Journal of Personality and Social Psychology* 75, no. 3 (1998) 589.

Sherman, Jeffrey W., Frederica R. Conrey, and Carla J. Groom. 'Encoding Flexibility Revisited: Evidence for Enhanced Encoding of Stereotype-Inconsistent Information under Cognitive Load'. *Social Cognition* 22, no. 2 (April 2004) 214.

Shuman, Daniel W., Anthony Champagne, and Elizabeth Whitaker. 'Assessing the Believability of Expert Witnesses: Science in the Jurybox'. *Jurimetrics* 37, no. 1 (1996) 23.

Simon, Dan. *In Doubt: The Psychology of the Criminal Justice Process*, (Cambridge, Mass: Harvard University Press, 2012).

Simon, Robert I., and Liza H. Gold. *Textbook of Forensic Psychiatry*, (Washington, DC: American Psychiatric Publishing, 2010).

Slobogin, Christopher. 'The Admissibility of Behavioral Science Information in Criminal Trials: From Primitivism to *Daubert* to Voice'. *Psychology, Public Policy and Law* 5, no. 1 (1999) 100.

Smith, Eliot R., and Jamie DeCoster. 'Dual Process Models in Social and Cognitive Psychology: Conceptual Integration and Underlying Memory Systems'. *Personality & Social Psychology Review* 4, no. 2 (2000) 108.

Smith, Lisa L., and Ray Bull. 'Identifying and Measuring Juror Pretrial Bias for Forensic Evidence: Development and Validation of the Forensic Evidence Evaluation Bias Scale'. *Psychology, Crime and Law* 18, no. 9 (2012) 797.

Smith, Lisa L., and Ray Bull. 'Validation of the Factor Structure and Predictive Validity of the Forensic Evidence Evaluation Bias Scale for Robbery and Sexual Assault Trial Scenarios'. *Psychology, Crime and Law* 20, no. 5 (2014) 450.

Sommers, Samuel, Lindsey Warp, and Corrine Mahoney. 'Cognitive Effects of Racial Diversity: White Individuals' Information Processing in Heterogeneous Groups'. *Journal of Experimental Social Psychology* 44, no. 4 (2008) 1129.

Sonnenstein, David, and Charles Fitzpatrick. 'The Problem of Partisan Experts and the Potential for Reform Through Concurrent Evidence'. *The Review of Litigation* 32, no. 1 (winter 2013) 1.

Stephens, Kerry. *Voir Dire Law: Determining the Admissibility of Disputed Evidence*, (Melbourne: Criminal Law Publications, 1997).

Stern, Leonard D., and others. 'Processing Time and the Recall of Inconsistent and Consistent Behaviors of Individuals and Groups'. *Journal of Personality and Social Psychology* 47, no. 2 (August 1984) 253.

Stone, Vernon A. 'A Primacy Effect in Decision-Making by Jurors'. *The Journal of Communication* 19, no. 3 (September 1969) 239.

Strasburger, Larry H., Thomas Gutheil, and Archie Brodsky. 'On Wearing Two Hats: Role Conflict in Serving as Both Psychotherapist and Expert Witness'. *American Journal of Psychiatry* 154, no. 4 (1997) 449.

Strong, John W. 'Language and Logic in Expert Testimony: Limiting Expert Testimony by Restrictions of Function, Reliability, and Form'. *Oregon Law Review* 71, no. 2 (summer 1992) 349.

Supreme Court of Victoria. *Practice Note No. 2: Expert Evidence in Criminal Trials*, (24 June 2014) <http://assets.justice.vic.gov.au//supreme/resources/49532674-51d5-478a-a5a7-a93a746de768/practice+note+2+of+2014+expert+evidence+in+criminal+trials+25+june+2014.pdf>.

Swenson, Rodney A., David L. Nash, and David C. Roos. 'Source Credibility and Perceived Expertness of Testimony in a Simulated Child-Custody Case'. *Professional Psychology: Research and Practice* 15, no. 6 (December 1984) 891.

Synchronics Group. 'Five Imperatives for Expert Witnesses: Effective Non-Verbal Skills Can Be Learned', <http://www.synchronicsgroup.com/articles/articles_5imperatives_p.htm>.

Szego, Julie. *The Tainted Trial of Farah Jama*, (Cheltenham, Vic: Wild Dingo Press, 2014).

Taylor, Duncan, Jo-Anne Bright, and John Buckleton. 'The Interpretation of Single Source and Mixed DNA Profiles'. *Forensic Science International: Genetics* 7, no. 5 (September 2013) 516.

Thomas, John. 'Expert Evidence: The Future of Forensic Science in Criminal Trials', (2014 Criminal Bar Association Kalisher Lecture, 14 October 2014), <https://www.judiciary.gov.uk/wp-content/uploads/2014/10/kalisher-lecture-expert-evidence-oct-14.pdf>.

Thompson, Bruce. *Reliability: Contemporary Thinking on Reliability Issues*, (New York: Sage, 2002).

Thompson, William, and Edward Schumann. 'Interpretation of Statistical Evidence in Criminal Trials: The Prosecutor's Fallacy and the Defence Attorney's Fallacy'. *Law and Human Behavior* 11, no. 3 (1987) 167.

Tribe, Laurence H. 'Trial by Mathematics: Precision and Ritual in the Legal Process'. *Harvard Law Review* 84, no. 6 (1971) 1329.

Tyler, Tom R. 'Is the CSI Effect Good Science?' *The Yale Law Journal* (February 2006), <http://www.yalelawjournal.org/forum/is-the-csi-effect-good-science>.

Tyler, Tom R. 'Viewing CSI and the Threshold of Guilt: Managing Truth and Justice in Reality and Fiction'. *The Yale Law Journal* 115, no. 5 (2006) 1050.

Valentine, Tim, and Josh P. Davis. *Forensic Facial Identification: Theory and Practice of Identification from Eyewitnesses, Composites and CCTV*, (London: Wiley, 2015).

Victorian Law Reform Commission, *Civil Justice Review: Report* (Melbourne: Victorian Law Reform Commission, 2008).

Victorian Law Reform Commission, *Jury Directions: Final Report* (Melbourne: Victorian Government Printer, 2009).

Vidmar, Neil. 'Expert Evidence, The Adversary System, And The Jury'. *American Journal of Public Health* 95, suppl. 1 (2005) 137.

Vidmar, Neil. 'Lay Decision Making in the Legal Process'. In *The Oxford Handbook of Empirical Legal Research*, edited by Peter Kane and Herbert M. Kritzer (Oxford: Oxford University Press, 2010).

Vidmar, Neil. 'The Psychology of Trial Judging'. *Current Directions in Psychological Science* 20, no. 1 (2011) 58.

Vidmar, Neil, and Shari S. Diamond. 'Juries and Expert Evidence'. *Brooklyn Law Review* 66, no. 4 (2001) 1121.

Vincent, Frank H. R. *Inquiry into the Circumstances that Led to the Conviction of Mr Farah Abdulkadir Jama: Report*, (Victorian Government, 2010), <http://netk.net.au/DNA/Jama.pdf>.

Walker, I. R. *Reliability in Scientific Research: Improving the Dependability of Measurements, Calculations, Equipment, and Software*, (Cambridge: Cambridge University Press, 2011).

Wall, Nicholas. *A Handbook for Expert Witnesses in Children Act Cases*, 2nd edn. (Bristol: Jordans, 2007).

Wallace, Anne. 'Using Video Link to Take Forensic Evidence—Lessons from an Australian Case Study'. *The International Journal of Evidence & Proof* 17, no. 3 (July 2013) 221.

Walsh, Simon. 'Evaluating the Role and Impact of Forensic DNA Profiling on the Criminal Justice System'. (PhD dissertation, University of Technology Sydney, 2009).

Walsh, Simon, and others. 'DNA Profiling and Criminal Justice: A Contribution to a Changing Debate'. *Australian Journal of Forensic Sciences* 36, no. 1 (January–July 2004) 34.

Walton, Douglas. *Appeal to Expert Opinion: Arguments from Authority*, (Pittsburgh: Pennsylvania State Press, 2010).

Ward, Tony. 'Usurping the Role of the Jury? Expert Evidence and Witness Credibility in English Criminal Trials'. *International Journal of Evidence and Proof* 13, no. 2 (2009) 83.

Watkins, Dawn, and Mandy Burton. *Research Methods in Law*, (Oxford: Routledge, 2013).

Waye, Vicki. 'Fact-Finding: Trial by Judge Alone in Serious Criminal Cases'. *Melbourne University Law Review* 27, no. 2 (August 2003) 423.

Wechsler, Hayley J., and others. 'Attorney Beliefs Concerning Scientific Evidence and Expert Witness Credibility'. *International Journal of Law and Psychiatry* (2015).

Weinstein, Ian. 'Don't Believe Everything You Think: Cognitive Bias in Legal Decision Making'. *Clinical Law Review* 9, no. 2 (spring 2003) 783.

Weiser Easteal, Patricia, and Simon Easteal. 'The Forensic Use of DNA Profiling'. *Trends & Issues in Crime and Criminal Justice*, no. 26 (November 1990) 1, <http://aic.gov.au/media_library/publications/tandi_pdf/tandi026.pdf>.

Wheate, Rhonda. 'Jury Comprehension and Use of Forensic Science'. (PhD dissertation, Australian Defence Force Academy, University of New South Wales, 2007).

Wheate, Rhonda. 'The Importance of DNA Evidence to Juries in Criminal Trials'. *International Journal of Evidence & Proof* 14, no. 2 (2010) 129.

White, Jack, Andrew Day, Louisa Hackett, and Thomas J. Dalby, *Writing Reports for Court: An International Guide for Psychologists Who Work in the Criminal Jurisdiction*, 2nd edn. (Brisbane: Australian Academic Press, 2015).

White, Peter. 'Limitations on Verbal Reports of Internal Events: A Refutation of Nisbett and Wilson and of Bem'. *Psychological Review* 87, no. 1 (1980) 105.

Wiener, Michael D., Daniel A. Krauss and Joel D. Liberman. 'Mock Jury Research: Where Do We Go From Here?' *Behavioral Sciences & the Law* 29, no. 3 (May/June 2011) 467.

Wilson, Timothy, and Richard Nisbett. 'The Accuracy of Verbal Reports About the Effects of Stimuli on Evaluations and Behavior'. *Social Psychology* 41, no. 2 (1978) 118.

Wise, Jenny. 'Providing the CSI Treatment: Criminal Justice Practitioners and the CSI Effect'. *Current Issues in Criminal Justice* 21, no. 3 (March 2010) 383, <http://www.austlii.edu.au/au/journals/CICrimJust/2010/3.pdf>.

Wistrich, Andrew J., Chris Guthrie and Jeffrey J. Rachlinski. 'Can Judges Ignore Inadmissible Information? The Difficulty of Deliberately Disregarding'. *University of Pennsylvania Law Review* 153, no. 4 (2005) 1251.

Wood, Lisa C. 'Experts Only: Out of the Hot Tub and into the Joint Conference'. *Anti-Trust* 22, no. 1 (Fall 2007) 89.

Wylie, Ruth. *The Self-Concept: Theory and Research on Selected Topics*, vol. 2, rev. edn. (Lincoln, Neb: University of Nebraska Press, 1979).

Yannoulidis, Stephen. *Mental State Defences in Criminal Law*, (Aldershot: Ashgate, 2012).

Yarnall, Megan A. 'Dueling Scientific Experts: Is Australia's Hot Tub Method a Viable Solution for the American Judiciary?' *Oregon Law Review* 88 (2009) 311.

Young, Neil J. 'Expert Witnesses: On the Stand or in the Hot Tub, How, When and Why', (lecture, Commercial Court CPD Seminar, 27 October 2010).

Young, Warren, Neil Cameron and Yvette Tinsley. *Juries in Criminal Trials Part Two: A Summary of Research Findings: Preliminary Paper 37*, vol. 2 (Wellington: Law Commission, New Zealand, 1999).

INDEX

The manufacturer's authorised representative in the EU for product safety is Oxford University Press España S.A. of El Parque Empresarial San Fernando de Henares, Avenida de Castilla, 2 - 28830 Madrid (www.oup.es/en or product.safety@oup.com). OUP España S.A. also acts as importer into Spain of products made by the manufacturer.
Printed and bound by CPI Group (UK) Ltd, Croydon, CR0 4YY
14/09/2026
02216286-0015